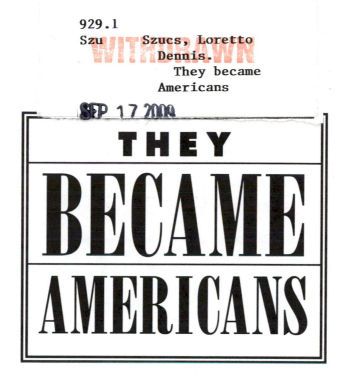

THEY
BECAME
AMERICANS

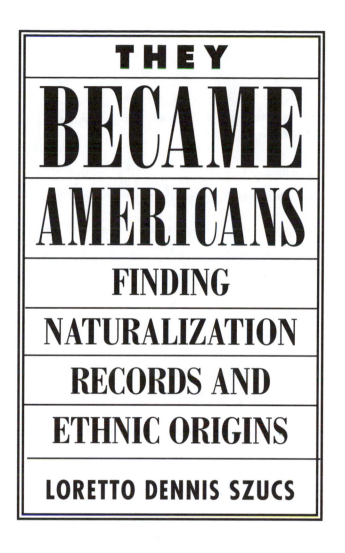

THEY BECAME AMERICANS

FINDING NATURALIZATION RECORDS AND ETHNIC ORIGINS

LORETTO DENNIS SZUCS

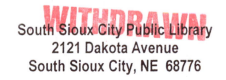

Szucs, Loretto Dennis

They became Americans : finding naturalization records and ethnic origins / by Loretto Dennis Szucs

     p.   cm.

Includes bibliographical references and index

ISBN 0-916489-71-X (soft)

1. Naturalization records—United States—Handbooks, manuals, etc.

2. United States—Genealogy—Handbooks, manuals, etc. I. Title.

CS47.S97   1997   97-4

929'.1'072073–DC21

© 1998 Ancestry Incorporated

P.O. Box 476

Salt Lake City, Utah 84110-0476

First printing 1998

10 9 8 7 6 5 4 3 2 1

Printed in the United States of America

Contents

Acknowledgments

Many generous individuals have provided information, guidance, and support throughout this project. To each of them I owe a great deal.

As with so many of my projects, my good friend and mentor, Sandra Luebking, went out of her way in sharing her time, expertise, and good advice. Marian Smith, historian for the Immigration and Naturalization Service, contributed important information, record samples, and critical suggestions throughout the project. Raymond S. Wright III, Ph.D., AG, and professor at Brigham Young University, also offered invaluable insights and recommendations. Others who read this manuscript and generously offered time and help were Roger Joslyn, CG, FASG; Wendy Elliott, Ph.D.; Gary Mokotoff; Eileen Polakoff; and John Scroggins.

I would also like to thank Kory Meyerink, MLS, AG, for sharing his considerable knowledge as we worked on the "Immigration: Finding Immigrant Origins" chapter of *The Source: A Guidebook of American Genealogy* (rev. ed.). Some of the results of that research are reflected in this volume.

I'm very thankful to my daughters for their hard work and good ideas: Drawing from her extensive experience on the Internet, Juliana Smith generously supplied almost all of the examples in chapter 7, "Naturalization Records Via the Internet." Laura Pfeiffer assisted me throughout the project by organizing great mountains of papers and photographs and by attending to the never-ending details involved in compiling a book. I'm also appreciative of all the encouragement and support of my other two daughters, Diana Sullivan and Patricia Stitz. My husband, Bob, has been very supportive in putting up with work that never ends. I keep telling him life will get back to normal after the next project is finished!

Several individuals took time from their busy schedules at the National Archives in Washington, D.C., and the regions of the National Archives to review and update information about the National Archives' records. They include Rosanne Butler, Connie Potter, and Nancy Malan in Washington; Jim Owens and Helen B. Engle in Waltham (Boston), Massachusetts; Walter Hickey in Pittsfield, Massachusetts; Dr. Robert Morris and John Celardo in New York City; Dr. Robert Plowman and Kellee Green Blake in Philadelphia; Gayle Peters and Mary Ann Hawkins in Atlanta; Peter Bunce, Don Jackanicz, and Scott Forsythe in Chicago; Reed Whitaker and Rose

DeLuca in Kansas City; Kent Carter and Barbara Rust in Fort Worth; Joel Barker and Eileen Bolger in Denver; Phillip Lothyan in Seattle; Waverly Lowell and Daniel Nealand in San Bruno (San Francisco), California; and Diane Nixon and Paul Wormser in Laguna Niguel (Los Angeles), California.

I want to thank Scott Knudsen for capturing the spirit of this book in its cover. Scott skillfully turned various naturalization concepts and a nineteenth-century portrait of Paul F. Pyburn into a beautiful book cover.

Photographs were graciously lent for use in this book by Rev. Charles Banet, Jim Bombach, Kathleen Pryle Dennis, Thomas Fleming, Gary Mokotoff, Dan Pfeiffer, Eileen Polokoff, Ruthellen Riffe, Patricia Stitz, and John P. Sullivan. Nancy Malan's talent shows in the photographs that appear in the chapter on the National Archives.

At Ancestry, several individuals went far beyond the call of duty to help me with this project. Thanks to Matt Grove, Jennifer Utley, Catherine Horman, and especially our general manager, André Brummer, who was extraordinarily supportive of this book from the onset. Thanks are also due to Ancestry's CEO, Dan Taggart, and to Ancestry's president, Paul Allen, for their encouragement and for publishing this work.

The nature of this project, with its widely divergent sources, required the assistance of many people. While every effort was made to be accurate and current with descriptions and addresses, changes and errors are bound to happen. It will be very much appreciated if any inaccuracies are called to the attention of the author by contacting Ancestry, P.O. Box 476, Salt Lake City, UT 84110.

Introduction

SETTING THE SCENE: A NATURALIZATION CEREMONY

Some radiated joy, and some wept openly. Dressed in their finest and representing more than a dozen nations, more than a hundred newly sworn citizens of the United States each took a turn at the podium in the Federal building. Some speaking in heavily accented English, but all with obvious conviction, they told us why they had become Americans that day. Gripping their recently won naturalization certificates, the newest citizens of the United States made it clear that this was a pivotal moment in their lives. "Here in America I am free to do the kind of work I can do best." "In this country my family can own land and a house!" "In America, I am not afraid that the government will come and take my family away in the night!" "My baby will be born in freedom!" One by one, they attested to the enduring power of the American dream, sentiments surely echoed in courts throughout the United States since the first naturalization act in 1790.

It was like a scene from an old patriotic movie, but the intensity of the new citizens' demeanor told us no one was acting. The reasons for their allegiance to the United States were as varied as the many nations they had left behind. But however true their love for and loyalty to their new land seemed to be, it was clear that each had made sacrifices along the way. Some hinted at families left behind. While immigrants might of necessity renounce allegiance to their native countries, could they ever really renounce all the memories and affection they might have had for the places and people of their native lands?

Now, more than ten years after the naturalization ceremony I witnessed, I am still moved by the remembered words and emotions of those new Americans. Since that day, as I have indexed naturalization records, as I have searched for citizenship documents for patrons of the National Archives, as I have researched records in local courts, I realize that every citizenship document represents a person with a story to tell.

While working at the National Archives, I witnessed the great excitement of researchers as they saw for the first time the signature of an ancestor whose decision to become an American had profoundly affected their own lives. More than once, I saw a researcher looking in awe at a naturalization photograph of a parent or a grandparent he or she

★ ★ 1 ★ ★

had never seen before. For some, citizenship papers opened a door to discovering other close relatives who had somehow become "lost" over the years. Words simply can't describe the spiritual quality of a meeting made possible through a simple piece of paper.

Before working on the staff at the National Archives' regional archive in Chicago, I volunteered to index some Detroit naturalizations[1] that were preserved there. It was my first experience with citizenship records. Stuffed in dust-laden cardboard boxes, the files seemed to have been in the most unused corner of the archive for years. The trifolded, yellowing pieces of original American history were brittle and crumbling around the edges. It struck me that the documents were probably the last traces of some peoples' lives. I was looking at records that hadn't seen daylight in perhaps a hundred years or more, and I realized how little I really understood about the process of becoming a naturalized American citizen. For several months I brought my portable typewriter and index cards to

the archive with me, meanwhile reading as much as I could find on naturalization processes and procedures. There wasn't much literature on the subject at the time. The archive's small staff was always helpful and cheerful in retrieving the boxes for my project. It wasn't until I had a job there, however, that I realized these fifty-pound boxes were indeed in the most remote corner at the top of a fourteen-foot shelf. This is why some archivists and court clerks are not very eager to retrieve old records!

Working with the Detroit records taught me a great deal about original records and the perils of any indexing project. It is ever so easy to decipher handwriting incorrectly. Admittedly, I was sometimes unsure of the petitioner's name. When there was some doubt, I created two or more cards, depending on how many ways a name might be interpreted, then cross-indexed them. (I have never trusted an index since that experience.) I also learned how common it was for an alien to begin the citizenship procedure in one place and complete it in another state or county where he or she had taken up residence.

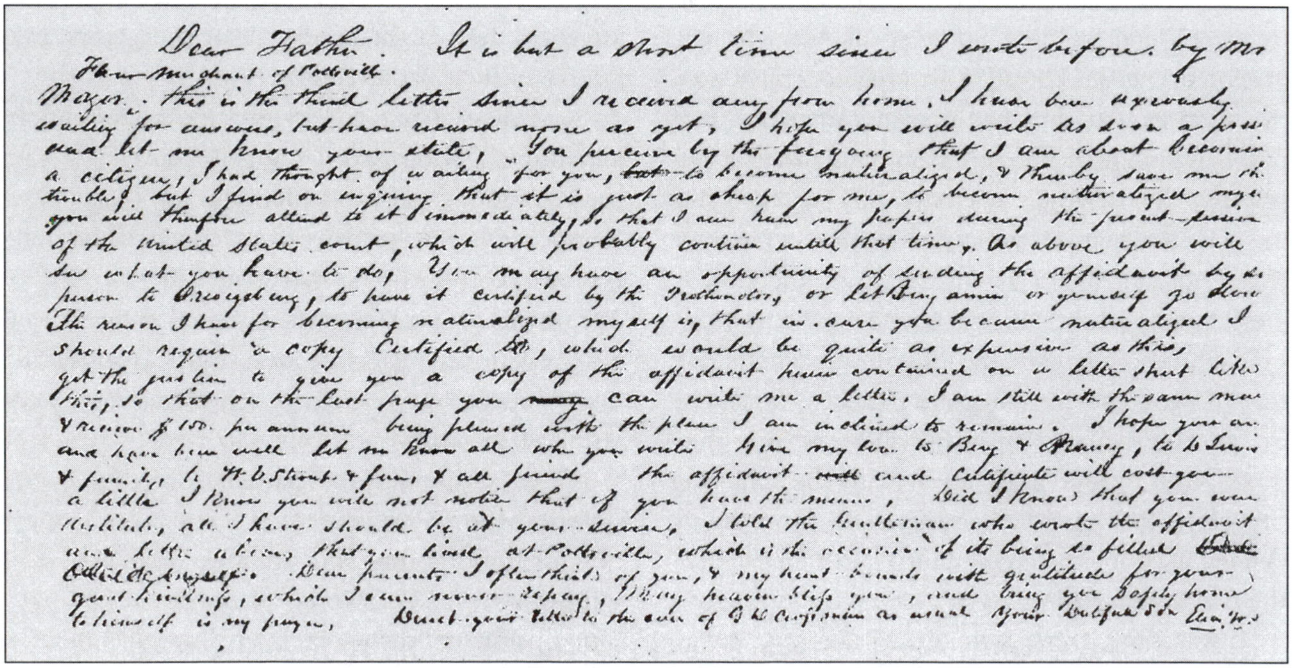

Figure 1. Portion of a letter written by Elias W. Jones to his father in 1844
(tucked into the naturalization file of Elias W. Jones, U.S. District Court,
Eastern District of Michigan, Detroit in the custody of the National Archives–Great Lakes Region).

★   ★   2   ★   ★

And I learned that, before 1922, very few women were naturalized themselves. Women and children derived citizenship from their husbands or fathers. The vast majority of naturalization records before 1906 do not name wives or children who derived citizenship. A remarkable number of our ancestors could not even write their own names; they confirmed their desire to become Americans with their mark: "X." If they couldn't write or spell their own names, why do some of us insist that our family name has never been spelled another way? These and other interesting facts about citizenship are discussed more fully in chapter 2, "Naturalization Court Procedures and Records."

It was in the collection of Detroit naturalizations that I discovered some priceless stories. An example is a letter written by Elias W. Jones of Detroit to his parents in Pennsylvania. The letter, a portion of which is shown here (figure 1), portrays life as it was in 1844. It was filed with final naturalization papers. This insightful document of the past tells of a young man anxiously awaiting a letter from home. He is obviously worried about his parents, and begs to know their "state." He tells his parents that he is "about becoming a citizen," and asks for an affidavit. He assures them: "Did I know that you were ever destitute, all I have should be at your service." Jones's letter, and all the letters and documents in this book, were transcribed exactly as they were found, with no attempt to correct spelling, grammar, or punctuation. Much of their authenticity and charm would be lost if we were to tamper with them.

> Dear Parents I often think of you & my heart bounds with gratitude for your great kindness, which I can never repay, May heaven bless you, and bring you safely home to himself is my prayer.

Whether a document is over a hundred years old with scarcely any visible clues to a personality, or one of recent vintage, rich in biographical detail, it tells us something about its subject and about this country. If you are fortunate enough to find any of your ancestor's naturalization papers, you will be holding a personalized piece of American history.

Some Background on Naturalization Records and the Answers they Hold

Naturalization is the legal procedure by which an alien becomes a citizen of a state or country—the process by which a person acquires nationality after birth. Every nation has different rules that determine citizenship. In the United States, naturalization is a judicial procedure that flows from Congressional legislation. However, from the time the first naturalization act was passed in 1790 until 1906, there were no uniform standards. As a consequence, before September 1906, the various federal, state, county, and local courts generated a wide variety of citizenship records that are stored in sundry courts, archives, warehouses, libraries, and private collections.

Because almost everyone is curious about where their ancestors and relatives came from, as well as if, when, and where they became American citizens, naturalization records are in high demand. The biographical information in citizenship papers assumes importance as a link to the past, and sometimes represents the only way to discover the Old World origins of an individual or a family.

America is a nation of immigrants. Through naturalization records, genealogists, historians, and other scholars trace the stories of individuals and groups. Another value of citizenship papers is that they often fill the gaps where other records are missing. Most states did not require the registration of births and deaths until well after the turn of the twentieth century. Fires, floods, neglect, and other mishaps account for the loss of other records that are regularly used to piece together personal histories. The destruction by fire of the 1890 census makes naturalization records

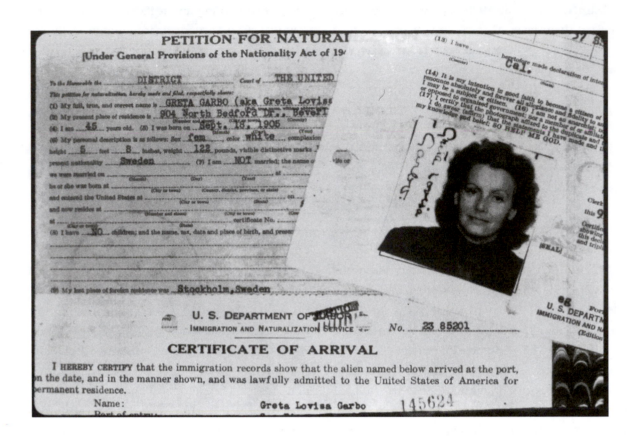

Figure 2. Naturalization records of many Hollywood stars, such as Greta Garbo's proof of citizenship, are found in Record Groups 21, 85, and 200 at the National Archives–Pacific Southwest Region.

a source of unparalleled value for the two-decade gap between the 1880 and 1900 censuses. Attesting to the importance of naturalization documentation is the fact that they are among the most heavily used textual records in the National Archives system. Chapter 6, "Naturalization Records in the National Archives," is dedicated to explaining the citizenship treasures in the National Archives and its regional archives.

As noted earlier, historians are not alone in treasuring the value of these unique documents; individuals and agencies rely on their biographical data to take the place of birth and other records when adequate proof of identity is missing. Social and ethnic historians find that naturalization records are a rich source for analyzing group patterns. In recent years, naturalization indexes have become more widely available in archives, libraries, through microfilm catalogs, and in electronic format, making the documents themselves more accessible.

INFORMATION PROVIDED IN NATURALIZATION DOCUMENTS CREATED AFTER 1906

Sometimes, a naturalization document adds new details about the person who was naturalized, perhaps opening doors to new areas of research. Some petitions for naturalization, particularly those created after 27 September 1906, provide the full name of the applicant, his or her current address, occupation, age, birth date, birthplace, sex, complexion, eye

TRIPLICATE
(To be given to declarant)

No. [illegible]

UNITED STATES OF AMERICA

DECLARATION OF INTENTION
(Invalid for all purposes seven years after the date hereof)

State of New Jersey
County of Bergen
} ss:

In the _____ Common Pleas _____ Court
of _____ Bergen _____ County at Hackensack, NJ

I, _____ Enrico Fermi _____ (Full true name, without abbreviation, and any other name which has been used, must appear here)

now residing at _____ 303 Summit Avenue, Leonia, N.J. _____ (County) _____ (State)

occupation _____ Professor _____, aged _____ 30 _____ years, do declare on oath that my personal description is:

Sex _____ male _____, color _____ white _____, complexion _____ dark light _____, color of eyes _____ gray _____

color of hair _____ dark _____, height _____ 5 _____ feet _____ 9 _____ inches; weight _____ 150 _____ pounds; visible distinctive marks

_____ none _____

race _____ Italian _____; nationality _____ Italy _____

I was born in _____ Rome, Italy _____, on _____ Sept. 29, 1901 _____ (Country) _____ (Year)

I am _____ yes _____ married. The name of my wife or husband is _____ Laura _____

we were married on _____ July 19, 1928 _____ (Year), at _____ Rome, Italy _____ (State or country); she or he was

born at _____ Rome, Italy _____ (State or country), on _____ June 16, 1907 _____ (Day) _____ (Year), entered the United States

at _____ New York, NY _____ (State), on _____ Jan. 2, 1939 _____ (Year), for permanent residence therein, and now

resides at _____ with me _____ (City) _____ (State or country) I have _____ 2 _____ children, and the name, date and place of birth,

and place of residence of each of said children are as follows:

_____ Nella — born Jan. 31, 1931 Giulio — born Feb. 16, 1936 _____
_____ both born Rome, Italy — both reside with me _____

I have _____ not _____ heretofore made a declaration of intention: Number _____, on _____ (Date)

at _____ (City or town) _____ (Name of court)

my last foreign residence was _____ Rome, Italy _____ (City or town) _____ (Country)

I emigrated to the United States of America from _____ Southampton, England _____ (Country)

my lawful entry for permanent residence in the United States was at _____ New York, N.Y. _____ (State)

under the name of _____ Fermi — Enrico _____, on _____ Jan. 2, 1939 _____ (Year)

on the vessel _____ Franconia _____ (If other than by vessel, state manner of arrival)

I will, before being admitted to citizenship, renounce forever all allegiance and fidelity to any foreign prince, potentate, state, or sovereignty, and particularly, by name, to the prince, potentate, state, or sovereignty of which I may be at the time of admission a citizen or subject; I am not an anarchist; I am not a polygamist nor a believer in the practice of polygamy; and it is my intention in good faith to become a citizen of the United States of America and to reside permanently therein; and I certify that the photograph affixed to the duplicate and triplicate hereof is a likeness of me.

I swear (affirm) that the statements I have made and the intentions I have expressed in this declaration of intention subscribed by me are true to the best of my knowledge and belief: So help me God.

_____ Enrico Fermi _____
(Original signature of declarant without abbreviation, also alias, if used)

Subscribed and sworn to before me in the form of oath shown above in the office of the Clerk of said Court, at _____ Hackensack, NJ _____ this _____ 2nd _____ day of _____ December _____, anno Domini, 19__. Certification No. _____ from the Commissioner of Immigration and Naturalization showing the lawful entry of the declarant for permanent residence on the date stated above, has been received by me. The photograph affixed to the duplicate and triplicate hereof is a likeness of the declarant.

[SEAL]

_____ James N. Mercer _____
Clerk of the _____ Common Pleas _____ Court.

By _____ Deputy Clerk.

Form 2202—L-A
U.S. DEPARTMENT OF LABOR
IMMIGRATION AND NATURALIZATION SERVICE

14—2623
U. S. GOVERNMENT PRINTING OFFICE

Nº 187169

Figure 3. In 1939, the well-known physicist Enrico Fermi declared his intention to become a citizen of the United States in Bergen County, New Jersey. Information on Fermi's declaration of intention is typical of that found on naturalization documents of the era.

color, hair color, height, weight, visible distinctive marks, and current and former citizenship. Post-1906 naturalization forms ask for marital status. If married, the applicant was asked the name of the spouse, marriage date, marriage place, birthplace and birth date of spouse, date and place of spouse's entrance to the United States, and current residence of spouse. The form also asked whether or not the spouse was a naturalized citizen and, if the answer was yes, where and when the naturalization took place. The applicant was further asked the number of children born to him or her, the date and place of birth of each, and where and when his or her lawful admission for permanent residence in the United States took place. The signature of the applicant completed the first section of the petition. The sec-

ond part of the petition consisted of the affidavit of witnesses. It included names of witnesses, their addresses, and sworn and signed statements of their knowledge of the applicant. Post-1906 petitions were completed with a signed oath of allegiance.

INFORMATION PROVIDED IN NATURALIZATION DOCUMENTS CREATED BEFORE 1906

Generally speaking, most pre-1906 naturalization papers contain little information of biographical or genealogical value. In the absence of standardized naturalization forms, federal, state, county, and other minor courts of record created their own naturalization documents, which varied greatly in format.

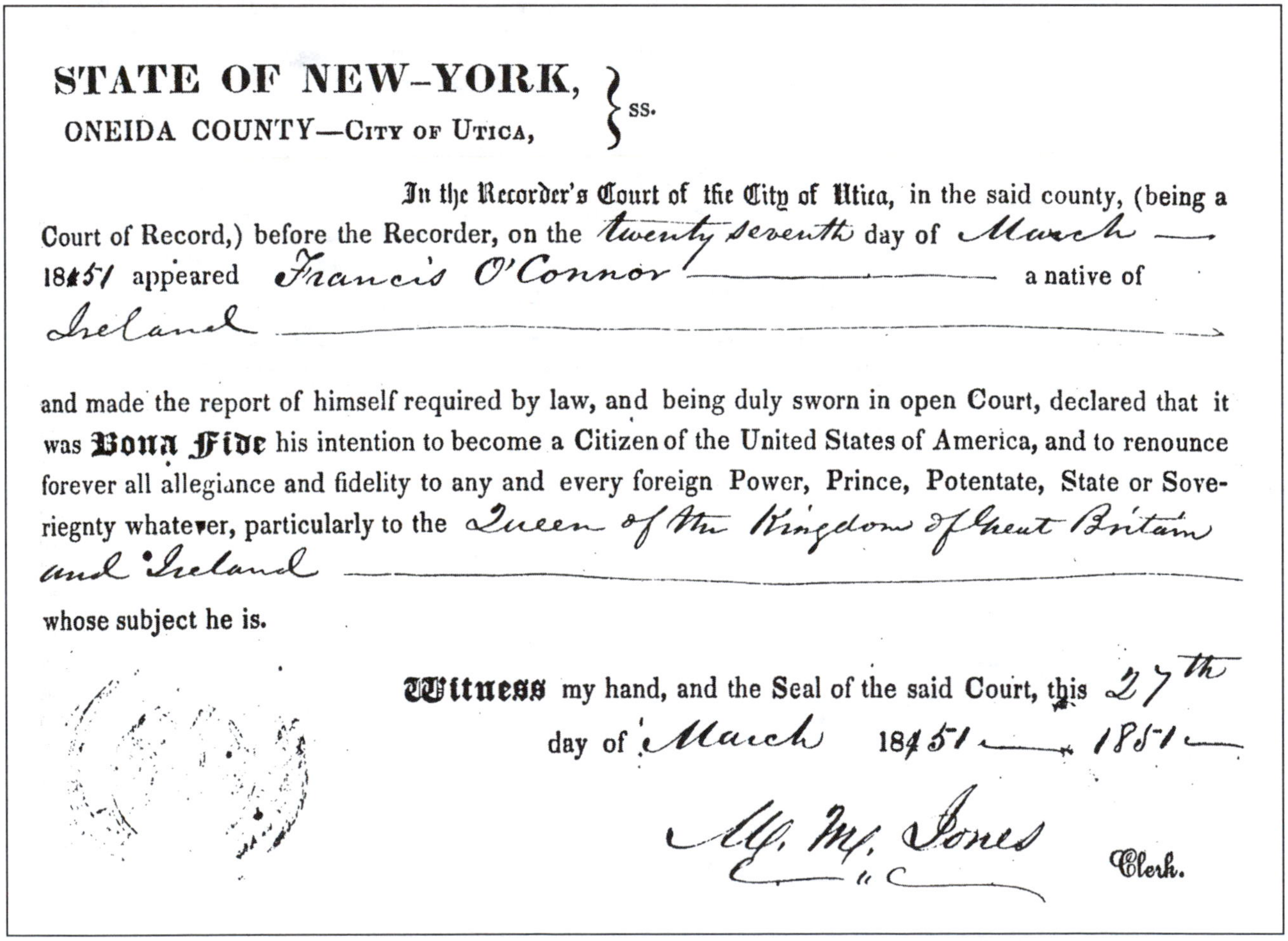

Figure 4. The declaration of intention for Francis O'Connor, filed in Utica, Oneida County, New York, on 27 March 1851, provides little more biographical information than the fact that he was a native of Ireland.

★　　★　　6　　★　　★

In the majority of early cases, only the name of the individual, his or her native country, and the date of the naturalization are given; rarely is the exact town of origin named. There are, however, some wonderful exceptions, so it is usually worth seeking pre-1906 naturalizations. While it is unusual to find such detail, Elias Jones's letter is just one example of the information found in millions of pre-1906 records. No one would ever guess that this letter is part of the 1844 Jones file by casually checking an index or microfilm list.

With careful study of the document itself, and an understanding of what was going on in the times and places immigrants settled, it is often possible to learn a great deal from even sparsely worded documents. Everything gleaned from a naturalization record takes on new meaning if we pause to reflect on what it meant for that individual to become an American in that particular time and place.

Contrasting with the O'Connor document (figure 4) is the declaration of Homer Hays/Homme Heyes (figure 5), from another court but within the same time period. It provides much biographical information.

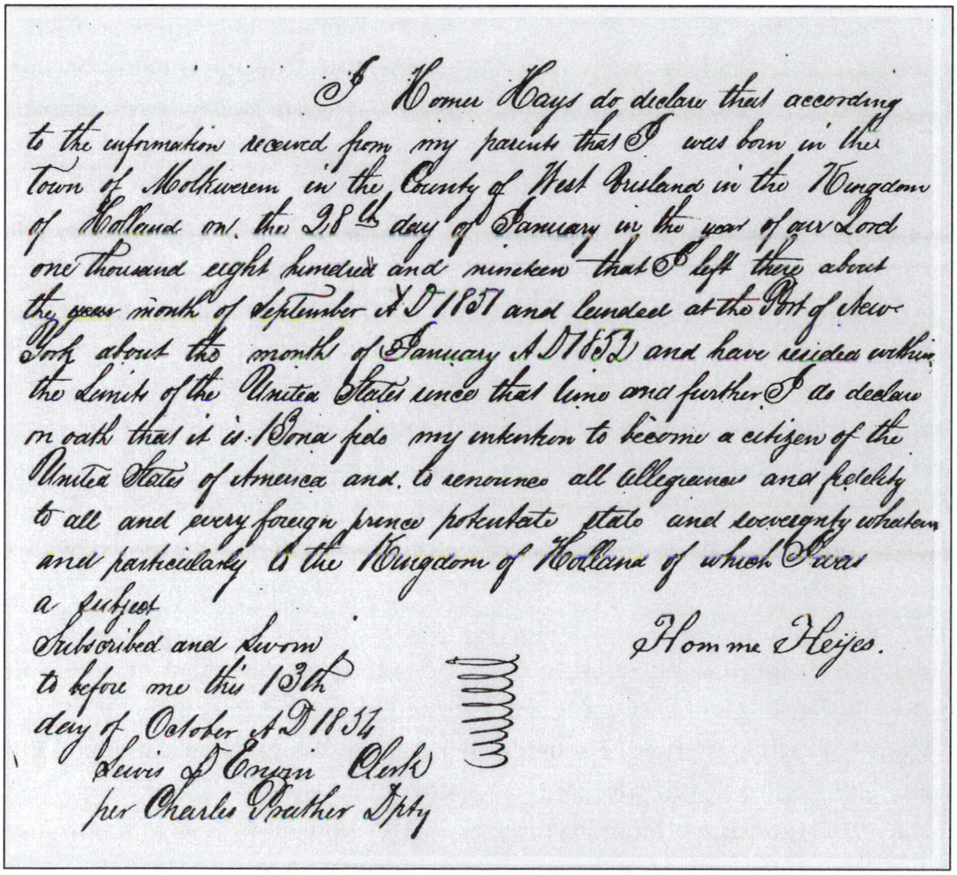

I Homer Hays do declare that according to the information received from my parents that I was born in the town of Molkwerem in the County of West Frisland in the Kingdom of Holland on the 28th day of January in the year of our Lord one thousand eight hundred and nineteen that I left there about the month of September AD 1851

Figure 5. Declaration of intention of Homer Hays. Note that both the given name and the surname of the applicant are spelled differently on the document, and that the name of the court is not even included in the handwritten format. Both of these facts increase the challenge of locating the original document. Linking the names of the clerk and the deputy to an Illinois court operating in 1854 is a potential route to finding this particular citizenship document.

and landed at the Port of New York about the month of January AD 1852 and have resided within the Limits of the United States since that time and further I do declare on oath that it is Bona fide my intention to become a citizen of the United States of America and to renounce all allegiance and fidelity to all and every foreign prince potentate state and sovereignty whatever and particularly to the Kingdom of Holland of which I was a subject

> Homme Heyes
> Subscribed and Sworn
> to before me this 13th day
> of October A D 1854
>
> Lewis D Envin Clerk
> per Charles Prather Dpty

The biggest problem facing anyone looking for a specific naturalization document is that original records have been scattered about over the years. One could give a researcher a list of naturalization records and dates; that might temporarily solve the problem, but it is the equivalent of a fish. I have chosen, therefore, to go beyond the list—teaching the researcher how to fish—to provide a more lasting tool. This volume provides historical context for immigration and naturalization records; gives an explanation of why and how records were created; indicates what the records tell us; discusses whether the records are reliable; and indicates where they are and how they can be found. Personal accounts of immigrants included in the text put things into better perspective. Because naturalization documents are not always available, alternative sources are also explained. This approach provides an intimate look at a wide variety of naturalization records and related materials that focus on foreigners as they became Americans.

While citizenship documents are avidly sought by family historians, both for their sentimental and for their informational value, probably no other records are more difficult to fully understand or locate. Complex and ever-changing naturalization laws and interpretations of laws have resulted in the dissemination of a great deal of incorrect information in this area of research. Unfortunately, many inaccuracies have found their way into print. I hope that this work, based on naturalization laws and presenting documents that were created as a result of the laws, and on firsthand experiences, will guide researchers to naturalization records that are rich in biographical detail.

Once we understand some of the naturalization laws and what was happening behind the scenes, it will be easier to find and make the most of records—or to better understand why records don't exist in the first place. And when a naturalization record isn't available, there is often another record that will provide information on immigrant origins that is as good as, if not better than, naturalization records can provide.

Chapter 1, "The Naturalization Process in the United States," covers the colonial period to the present, explaining the laws, how the laws were carried out, and the resulting records. For example, some aliens who had not completed the naturalization requirements still were able to vote. The chapter discusses these and other citizenship issues and includes an 1868 Chicago newspaper article denouncing "How the Naturalization Business has Been Conducted." Acquainted with some of these hard-to-find contemporary accounts, you will have a better overview of naturalization issues and will be able to better judge evidence in hand. Understanding the times in which our people lived almost always makes a search more productive and enjoyable.

This book also describes little-known aspects of naturalization records like the naturalization stub books, kept by some courts, that can divulge as much as any other citizenship document; the records of thousands of American-born women who lost their American citizenship because they married foreigners; and the fact that thousands of aliens who served in the Civil War and other military engagements were able to expedite the naturalization process. During the course of American history, many courthouses have suffered floods and fires that destroyed naturalization records. As explained in this text, recreated court records sometimes contain better information than the original records. Chapter 1 explains the records, how and why they were created, and how they can be used effectively.

SEEING IS BELIEVING

In my estimation, there is no better way to understand the naturalization process than to actually see and study the records that were produced. With that in mind, this volume offers a large variety of examples of naturalization papers and indexes. Copies of other old records, such as census records, birth and death records, city directories, passenger lists, military pension papers, draft cards, and voter registrations, that may help locate citizenship records are also included because of their value in placing a person in time and place. Once you know where and when a person lived, it is easier to discover his or her citizenship status.

Some documents reproduced here are difficult to read in their original form. Difficult-to-read handwriting presents one of the more challenging aspects of research in original records. We may have to work hard at deciphering some old handwriting styles, but often the effort is well worth it. Elias Jones's words, tightly squeezed onto his naturalization paper, may cause eyestrain, but who could possibly explain better the why and how of naturalization as he experienced it? His full mes-

---

THE GOAL OF THIS WORK

Give a man a fish
and you will feed
him for a day.
Teach him to fish
and feed him
for a lifetime

—Lao Tzu

---

sage, which was hidden away for more than 150 years in his naturalization file, is reproduced in this book, as are other insightful letters from Joseph Terdina, written from Austria in 1909; Jeremiah Curtin, written while he was aboard the ship bringing him to America; and Raffalle Campobasso's hard luck story, written from Italy somewhere around 1900. Nicholas Simon's petition for naturalization in 1939 (figure 6) provokes the question of what his fate might have been had he remained in his native Germany. Clues to if, how, where, and when a person may have become naturalized are provided in the text and illustrations. Each chapter begins with a chapter table of contents to provide an at-a-glance reference to facilitate use of the section.

HOW THIS BOOK WILL HELP YOU

Over the years, a number of books have been published on the subject of naturalization records. While each is helpful in its own way, none has accomplished exactly what this work attempts to do:

- To provide an accurate, readable, and interesting historical framework for the citizenship process
- To suggest ways of finding naturalization records
- To expose the weaknesses and strengths of records
- To point to a great array of alternative sources for finding immigrant origins in case naturalization records are not to be found
- To help you enjoy these rich sources of Americana

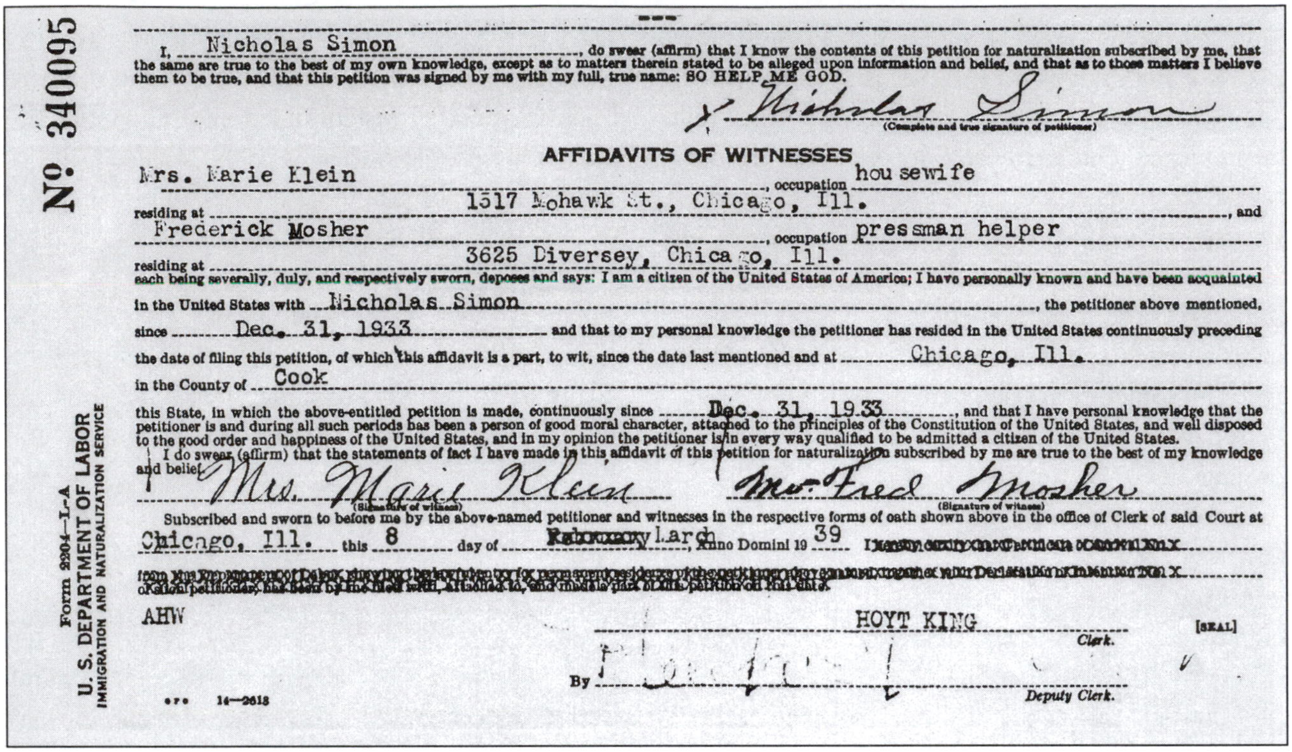

Figure 6. Affidavits of witnesses, a portion of Nicholas Simon's petition for naturalization. Names of witnesses on naturalization documents often yield important clues for furthering research.

When I first dreamed of writing this book, I thought it should be the ultimate inventory of naturalization records, together with all the addresses where those records can be found. Currently, most books on the subject are lists of records, locations of the records, with date spans as best as can be determined by the compiler at the time of publication. However, unless the compiler has direct access to every court, every archive, every library, and every historical agency that ever collected naturalization records, the compilation can't be complete, and it is unlikely that information gathered in such an ambitious project could be entirely accurate.

Most courts accumulate a tremendous volume of paper as populations grow and case files add up. When space runs out in a courthouse, older records that are no longer needed on a day-to-day basis are moved to other storage locations. Courts regularly ship all or parts of a naturalization collection to a warehouse or archive and keep the index to those particular records for their own reference. Occasionally, the reverse is true; an archive will have an index to records that are retained by a court. Archives and historical agencies regularly acquire new records, and retention schedules change. Microfilming, indexing, and conversion of records to electronic format will continue for years to come. Lists of microfilmed records rarely reflect all of the extant records in a given place. Having worked with microfilming teams, I know that for every record that is filmed, there are probably at least three more that are left unfilmed because of the associated cost and time constraints of microfilming vast volumes of records. The status of record collections and the microfilming of them is always in flux.

Those of us who have attempted to compile information from every state, every county, every archive, every library, and every other hiding place of a particular kind of record know that it is an impossible job. Surveys never do the job adequately. Naturalization records are particularly hard to track because collections are frequently splintered. Detroit, Wayne County, Michigan, is a typical example. There is no comprehensive index to all naturalizations filed in the Detroit area. Wayne County Court naturalization records were transferred from that court to the Michigan State Archives; the naturalization records of the Recorder's Court of Detroit were transferred from that court to the Burton Historical Collection in the Detroit Public Library; the National Archives' Great Lakes Region in Chicago had custody of the records filed at the U.S. District Court from 1837 to 1959 and at the old U.S. Circuit Court in Detroit from 1837 to 1903. The Great Lakes Region has a surname index for the U.S. District and Circuit Court records only for the years 1837 to 1903. There is no index at Chicago for the 1904-to-1959 portion of the record group. The Great Lakes Region also has custody of the U.S. District Court 1904-to-1959 naturalizations for Detroit. These records are arranged strictly by petition number (not alphabetically by name or chronologically by naturalization date). The court itself retained the only index for the post-1903 records. The U.S. District Court in Detroit retains the more recent records concerning naturalization.

To be most successful in finding answers to immigrant questions, we need to be aware of all our options for finding records. The catalog approach usually overlooks the most fascinating and rare citizenship-related documents. Often, the records overlooked on the lists are the ones that can reveal the most about people. Vast quantities of records exist, but they are scattered far and wide. Without a full understanding of the citizenship process and of record-keeping systems, it is easy to miss many of these wonderful story-telling documents.

Many of the records covered here are not mentioned in current naturalization publications simply because the records have not been indexed or microfilmed or are not included in standard collec-

tion descriptions routinely handed out to researchers. Unfortunately, some researchers look at such lists of naturalizations and assume that they are all-inclusive. As many of the examples here show, most lists are far from complete.

The only state-by-state list of naturalizations in this book is that in chapter 6, "Naturalization Records in the National Archives." The reason for this exception is that, once federal records are retired to the National Archives system, they are not likely to be moved. If records are moved within the National Archives, they are generally easy to track.

WHEN NATURALIZATION RECORDS CAN'T BE FOUND

Unfortunately, there will be some cases where naturalization documentation cannot be found simply because an immigrant did not become naturalized. Historically, the number of non-naturalized aliens in the United States has been surprisingly large. Tabulations of the 1890 through 1930 censuses indicate that 25.7 percent of the foreign-born population was naturalized or had filed only declarations of intention.[2] As John Newman points out in *American Naturalization Processes and Procedures 1790–1985*, "Many aliens lived their lives as positive contributors to their community and new nation without formally acquiring citizenship."[3] He further notes that the constitutions of some states allowed aliens who had filed only declarations of intention to vote, and, except for certain periods when full citizenship was required, to own land.

Another important point made by Newman is the fact that many individuals believed themselves to be citizens by derivation from parent or spouse. There are thousands of documented cases regarding individuals who lived for many years under the false assumption that they were U.S. citizens, only to be shocked to learn that they had to go through the entire naturalization procedure to gain rights they believed they already had.

The example shown here is that of Alfred John Moorshead (figure 7), who filed a petition for naturalization in the U.S. District Court for the Northern District of Illinois, Eastern Division, Chicago. The petitioner states that "sometime before arriving at the age of 21 my father, William Thomas Moorshead, (now deceased) advised me that he had been naturalized as a citizen and that therefore I was a citizen." Moorshead continued: "About July 1, 1919, I saw an article in the paper which raised a doubt in my mind as to my citizenship, and I have no means of knowing where my father was naturalized." Meanwhile, the petitioner adds that "I have voted; signed incorporation papers in the State of Illinois, which requires citizenship, and have served on juries."

FINDING ETHNIC ORIGINS WITHOUT NATURALIZATION RECORDS

If you believe the statistics which tell us that only about one-quarter of the foreign-born were ever naturalized, you will immediately understand that other ways to find that distant city or little town where your personal history began have to be found. Because naturalization records are not available for everyone, a number of alternative sources presented in this book should help you to find your ethnic origins.

Chapter 2, "How to Find Naturalization Records and Ethnic Origins," is an overview of twenty-six sources and strategies to help you find ethnic origins. Rarely will one record or one approach provide the full story of the immigrant experience. Used in conjunction with each other, the array of records can provide a virtual biography of an individual or family and their American experience.

THE IMMIGRATION AND NATURALIZATION SERVICE

Chapter 5 describes millions of files of immigrants that are available through the Immigration and Naturalization Service (INS). Did you realize that an alien who, for one reason or another, did not become an American citizen may have left a record with more details than any naturalization record? Such rare finds can get right to the heart of an immigrant ancestor's personality. This books includes examples of all of these unique papers and tells you where they were found.

KEEPING UP WITH THE EVER-CHANGING STATUS OF NATURALIZATION COLLECTIONS

One of the most dramatic advances in immigration research has come about because of the explosion of information and services available on the Internet. The World Wide Web pages of the INS, the National Archives, most state archives, and many historical and genealogical organizations provide firsthand, up-to-date information on immigration and naturalization record collections. Some home pages actually provide searchable databases! Ancestry's Web site (http://www.ancestry.com) can connect you to these and hundreds of other collections that are of value to genealogists and historians. In a matter of minutes and at virtually no cost, you can be informed of the current status of almost any information you will need in your research. Chapter 7, "Naturalization Records and the Internet," will put you in touch with some exciting new opportunities.

More than twenty-five years of experience of researching hundreds of family histories, editing genealogical publications, and helping patrons at the National Archives has taught me (1) that the best answers to ethnic identity do not always come from naturalization documents or other immigration sources, and (2) that those who do not search "the real records" miss very important clues and much of the joy of discovery. Providing a list is like providing a fish. But show the researcher why and how records were created, where they will be found, and how to use them most effectively, and the net gain will be far greater.

U. S. DEPARTMENT OF LABOR
NATURALIZATION SERVICE

AFFIDAVIT OF PETITIONER.

THIS FORM TO BE USED IN EVERY CASE WHERE A PETITION FOR NATURALIZATION IS FILED UNDER THE SUBDIVISION, SECTION 4, ACT OF JUNE 29, 1906, AS AMENDED BY THE ACT OF MAY 9 1918 (PUBLIC No 144). It is required by section 4 of the act of 1906, which provides, in part, that "The petition shall set forth * * * every fact material to his naturalization and required to be proved upon the final hearing of his application."

Three copies should be made, one attached to the original petition by the clerk of court, and the other two copies forwarded to the Bureau of Naturalization for record purposes.

In the U. S. District Court of for the Northern District of Illinois, Eastern Division, Chicago.

In the matter of the Petition of

ALFRED JOHN MOORSHEAD

To be admitted a citizen of the United States. | Petition No. ....

The petitioner above named, being first duly sworn, on oath deposes and says:

FIRST.—That on Sept 12, 1919, I filed a petition for naturalization in the court named above, and submit this affidavit, under the terms of section 4 of the naturalization act of 1906, to be filed with and made a part of said petition.

SECOND.—On the date indicated immediately below I was informed by the following-named person or persons that I was a citizen of the United States.

Sometime before arriving at the age of 21 my father, William Thomas
(Date as near as known.)

Moorshead, (now deceased) advised me that he had been naturalized as a citizen
(Here state the name or names of affiant's informants, their occupation at the time such information was given, address at that time, and present address, if known.)

and that therefore I was a citizen.

(If the affiant knew he was not a citizen, but believed he could become such without a compliance with the general requirements of the naturalization laws, he should state the steps he thought it necessary to take, and the reason for his impression.)

THIRD.—I continued to believe as above indicated until the date shown below when I became apprised under the following circumstances that my impression was erroneous.

About July 1, 1919, I saw an article in the paper which raised a doubt
(Date.)

in my mind as to my citizenship, and I have no means of knowing where my father was naturalized.

FOURTH.—I have exercised the following rights and duties of a citizen of the United States:

I voted; signed incorporation papers in the State of Illinois, which requires citizenship, and have served on juries.
(This statement should include dates and all pertinent facts. (If the affiant has held public office, served on jury, voted, or proved up on public land, all the particulars should be set forth.)

Alfred John Moorshead
(Original signature of affiant.)

Subscribed and sworn to before me this ~~8th~~ 12 day of September, 1919

[SEAL]

J. V. Bees
Clerk of Court.

14—6

Figure 7. Affidavit of petitioner, Alfred John Moorshead.
The original document is located at the National Archives–Great Lakes Region, Chicago.

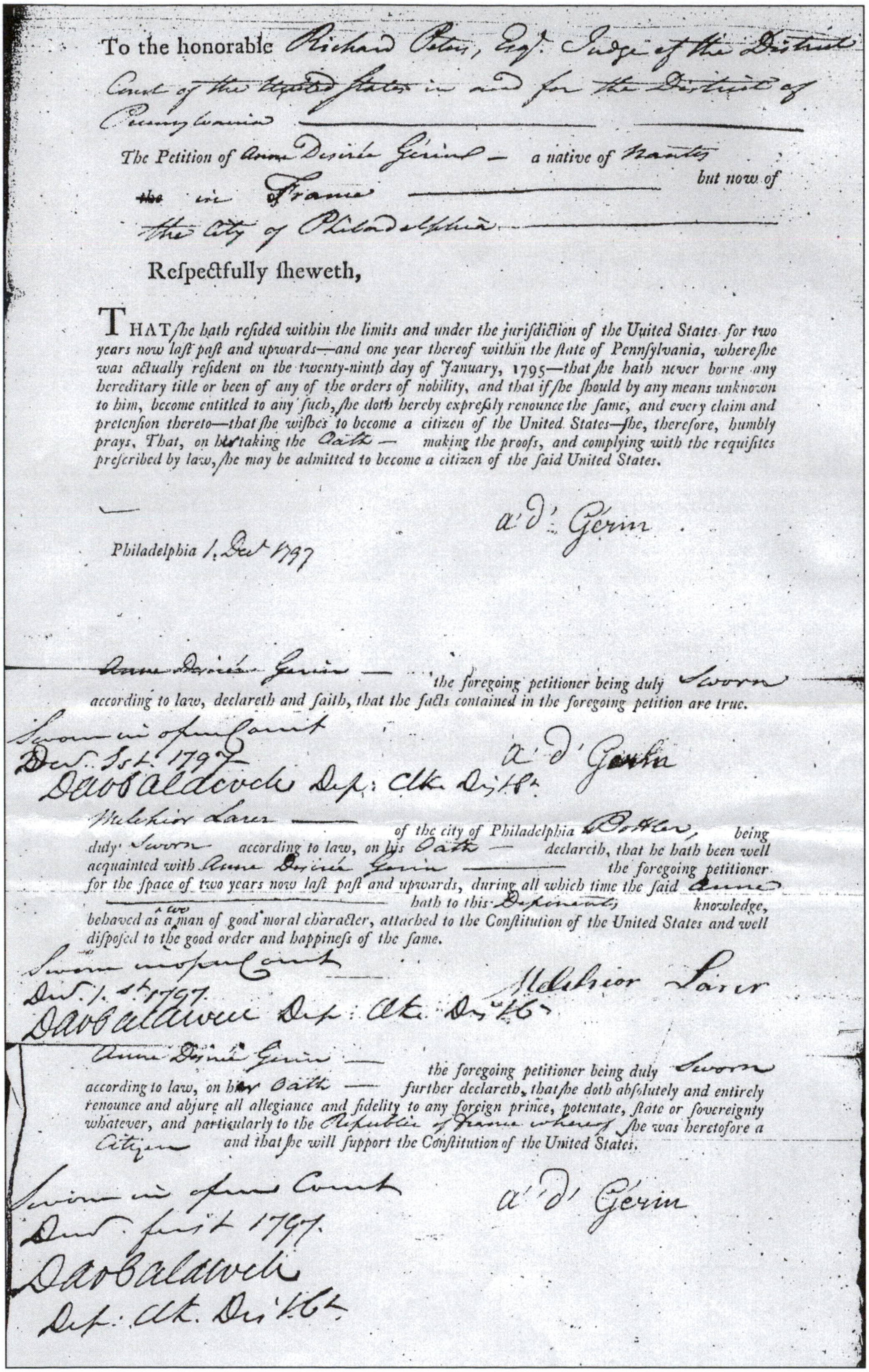

To the honorable Richard Peters, Esqr. Judge of the District Court of the United States in and for the District of Pennsylvania

The Petition of Anne Desirée Gérin — a native of Nantes in France but now of the City of Philadelphia

Respectfully sheweth,

THAT she hath resided within the limits and under the jurisdiction of the United States for two years now last past and upwards—and one year thereof within the state of Pennsylvania, where she was actually resident on the twenty-ninth day of January, 1795—that she hath never borne any hereditary title or been of any of the orders of nobility, and that if she should by any means unknown to him, become entitled to any such, she doth hereby expressly renounce the same, and every claim and pretension thereto—that she wishes to become a citizen of the United States—she, therefore, humbly prays, That, on her taking the Oath — making the proofs, and complying with the requisites prescribed by law, she may be admitted to become a citizen of the said United States.

A. D. Gérin

Philadelphia 1. Decr 1797

Anne Desirée Gérin — the foregoing petitioner being duly Sworn according to law, declareth and saith, that the facts contained in the foregoing petition are true.

Sworn in open Court Decr. 1st. 1797
David Caldwell Dep: Clk. Distt.

A. D. Gérin

Melchior Larer — of the city of Philadelphia Potter, being duly Sworn according to law, on his Oath — declareth, that he hath been well acquainted with Anne Desirée Gérin — the foregoing petitioner for the space of two years now last past and upwards, during all which time the said Anne — hath to this Deponent's knowledge, behaved as a woman of good moral character, attached to the Constitution of the United States and well disposed to the good order and happiness of the same.

Sworn in open Court Decr. 1st 1797
David Caldwell Dep: Clk. Distt.

Melchior Larer

Anne Desirée Gérin — the foregoing petitioner being duly Sworn according to law, on her Oath — further declareth, that she doth absolutely and entirely renounce and abjure all allegiance and fidelity to any foreign prince, potentate, state or sovereignty whatever, and particularly to the Republic of France whereof she was heretofore a Citizen and that she will support the Constitution of the United States.

Sworn in open Court Decr. first 1797.
David Caldwell
Dep: Clk. Distt.

A. D. Gérin

Figure 8. Naturalization certificate of Anne Desirée Gérin, 1797.

NOTES

1. Loretto Dennis Szucs. *Index to Naturalizations in the United States Circuit and District Courts, Eastern District, Michigan*. Midlothian, Ill.: the compiler, 1976. Subsequently published in a series in the *Detroit Society for Genealogical Research Magazine* (1982–85).

2. John J. Newman. *American Naturalization Processes and Procedures 1790–1985*. Indianapolis: Indiana Historical Society, 1985, 1.

3. Ibid.

SEARCHING FOR AN IMMIGRANT'S ORIGINS:
QUICK REFERENCE

- To begin the search for an immigrant's origins, learn as much as you can about that person, including full name, approximate birth date, native country, approximately when that person came to the United States, and where that person lived after his or her arrival in the United States.

- Since 1790, naturalizations in the United States have been performed according to federal law.

- Before 1906, any federal, state, or local court of record (a court having a seal or that kept records) could naturalize aliens.

- Aliens intending to be naturalized citizens first filed a declaration of intention to become a citizen.

- Declarations of intention are instruments by which applicants for U.S. citizenship renounced allegiance to foreign sovereignties and declared their intentions to become U.S. citizens.

- A declaration of intention usually preceded proof of residence or a petition to become a citizen by two or more years.

- In most years, a declaration of intention was not required if the person had been honorably discharged from the U.S. military or had entered the country when a minor (under the age of twenty-one).

- After five years (except for a brief period when the laws changed) in the United States, an alien could petition a court to be naturalized.

- Naturalization petitions are instruments by which those who had declared their intention to become a U.S. citizen and who had met the residence requirements made formal application for U.S. citizenship.

- Many aliens waited more than the required five years to become naturalized.

- Many aliens who filed declarations of intention never completed the process by petitioning for naturalization.

- Naturalization depositions are formal statements in support of an applicant's petition by witnesses designated by the applicant.

- Certificates or records of naturalization and oaths of allegiance are documents which granted citizenship to petitioners.

- Courts held hearings on the petition of an alien and took testimony from witnesses to determine whether the alien met residence and character requirements.

- When the petition was accepted, the alien took the oath of allegiance and the court recorded the final naturalization order or certificate.

- Before 1906, the final order was usually recorded in the court's minute or order book, and the court usually issued the new citizen a certificate of naturalization.

- Before 1906, naturalization forms (records) varied significantly from state to state, county to county, and year to year.

- Between 1855 and 1922, an alien woman became a citizen automatically if she married an American citizen.

- A woman could derive citizenship from her naturalized father or her husband (derivative citizenship).

- Relatively few single women became naturalized citizens before 1922, and married women could not be naturalized on their own unless they were widowed or divorced.

- Non-native minor children became American citizens when their parents were naturalized.

- Former slaves were made citizens by the ratification of the Fourteenth Amendment to the U.S. Constitution in 1868.

- American Indians were made citizens by federal laws passed in 1887 and 1924.

- Aliens from China, Japan, and other East and South Asian countries were barred from becoming citizens from 1882 to 1943.

- Expedited naturalization proceedings were available to aliens who were U.S. Army veterans from 1862; U.S. Navy veterans from 1894; and wartime enlisted servicemen and women from 1918.

- Under the 1906 Basic Naturalization Act, naturalization forms were standardized and the U.S. Bureau of Immigration and Naturalization, later the Immigration and Naturalization Service (INS), examined petitions for naturalization.

- After 1906, the standardized naturalization records contain more biographical information then previously.

- The INS has duplicate naturalization records for individuals who were naturalized after 1906.

- Women twenty-one years of age or over were entitled to citizenship in 1922, and derivative citizenship was discontinued.

Colonial New York.

Chapter One Highlights

- *Colonial America and British law*
- *Oaths of allegiance*
- *Continental Congress*
- *Revolutionary War*
- *First naturalization act: 1790*
- *1798 legislation*
- *1802 act*
- *Citizenship by group*
- *Mass immigration, 1819–1860*
- *The foreign vote*

- *Women and children*
- *1922 act*
- *Minors*
- *Land ownership and citizenship*
- *Immigration and Naturalization Service*
- *Post-1906 naturalization records*
- *A sense of history and immigration routes*
- *Military service*
- *African Americans and Native Americans*
- *The Great Depression*
- *World War II and alien registration*

The Naturalization Process in the United States: Historical Background

COLONIAL AMERICA AND BRITISH LAW

The naturalization process in what is now the United States has been an important issue since the seventeenth century. American colonists, subject to the British crown, considered themselves only "inhabitants" of the colonies. Persons born within royal dominions were subjects of the king and therefore assumed protection of the laws of Great Britain. Thus, colonial naturalization policies modeled those of England.

According to English law, aliens could acquire citizenship either by letters of denization or by naturalization through an act of parliament. Denization, though not requiring an oath of loyalty, allowed the transfer of properties and real estate to heirs. Aliens who wished to qualify for public office, to vote, to own a ship, and, in most cases, to own land, had to become naturalized British citizens. Only through parliamentary action could an alien obtain full citizenship status. Colonial laws were designed to attract immigrants by making citizenship and land available.

Regulation of naturalization policies in the colonies before the American Revolution came under the jurisdiction of the British government and the individual colonies. Granting of citizenship was a function of the "state" and not the "nation." An Englishman residing in an American colony was entitled to become a citizen not only of that colony, but also of any other colony to which he might move. Aliens, however, were obliged to observe the citizenship regulations of the colony in which they resided and did not always have the freedom to carry citizenship rights from one colony to another. Naturalization policies allowed individual colonies to embrace newcomers deemed worthy of citizenship and to disallow anyone who posed a threat to their religious, political, or ethnic control.

Laws designed to limit citizenship and its accompanying privileges were passed by the British Parliament and the individual colonies. Yet, "neither royal charters, nor parliamentary statutes, nor common law principles explicitly conferred upon colonial authorities the right to adopt aliens as subjects." However, charters such as that of the Virginia Company (1612) allowed admission of "any Person or Persons, as well as Strangers and Aliens . . . being in Amity with us, as any our natural Liege Subjects born in any of our Realms and Dominions."[1]

Becoming a naturalized citizen was not a concern of the first Europeans on American shores. What could properly be called "citizenship documentation" for this period may be sparse, but there are some very important alternative sources. One exceptional compiled source, praised for its documentation, is Henry Z Jones's *The Palatine Families of New York: A Study of the German Immigrants who Arrived in Colonial New York in 1710*, 2 vols. (Universal City, Calif.: the author, 1985). In this work, which is based on original records from New York and Germany, Jones identifies all of the immigrants who arrived in this first of major German groups to come to America, their families in New York, their towns of origin, and relatives in Germany.

Robert Charles Anderson's *The Great Migration Begins: Immigrants to New England 1620–1633* (Boston: New England Historic Genealogical Society, 1995) is the most comprehensive collection. This three-volume genealogical work discusses some nine hundred heads of household who settled in all of New England. In compiling the work, Anderson explored every available source, both compiled and original, in all of the early towns, as well as the colonial records.

Jones's and Anderson's works, along with thousands of others, are more fully described in *Printed Sources*, edited by Kory M. Meyerink (Salt Lake City: Ancestry, 1998).

OATHS OF ALLEGIANCE

The *oath of allegiance* was a renunciation of claims to the throne of England by "pretenders" and a denial of the right of the pope to outlaw a Protestant monarch. Most citizenship records of the American colonial period consist only of lists of oaths of allegiance signed by individuals as they disembarked from immigrant ships. Most surviving colonial records are preserved in the states in which they were created; they are usually available in published form. State historical societies and archives are generally the places to begin searching for these early records. Probably the best known of these early records are three passenger lists compiled for Pennsylvania German immigrants in Ralph B. Strassburger and William John Hinke's *Pennsylvania German Pioneers: A Publication of Original Lists of Arrivals in the Port of Philadelphia from 1727 to 1808*, 3 vols. (Norristown: Pennsylvania German Society, 1934): (1) the captains' lists made on board the ships from their manifests; (2) lists of oaths of allegiance to the king of Great Britain, signed by all male immigrants over the age of sixteen who were well enough to march in procession to a magistrate (these two lists were submitted to the Pennsylvania government on large, loose sheets of paper, not all of which have survived); and (3) lists of signers of the oath of fidelity and abjuration (figure 1-1). Males over sixteen who were well enough to walk to the courthouse also signed these renunciations in a series of bound ledger volumes. They have survived intact; however, Strassburger and Hinke estimate that only two out of five passengers signed these lists.

In 1740, Parliament enacted new laws that allowed the colonies to naturalize aliens without having to obtain a special act in London. However, these laws failed to end disputes over the jurisdiction and authority of colonial governments that overrode English law with their own acts. In 1773, the crown disallowed naturalization acts from Pennsylvania and New Jersey and, through an order-in-council, instructed colonial governors to cease assenting to such statutes. This strict policy prompted the charge in the Declaration of Independence that George III had endeavored to limit

> Citizenship records created before the first naturalization act of 1790 are rare. Most of those that survived are preserved in the states in which they were created, and most surviving collections have been published.

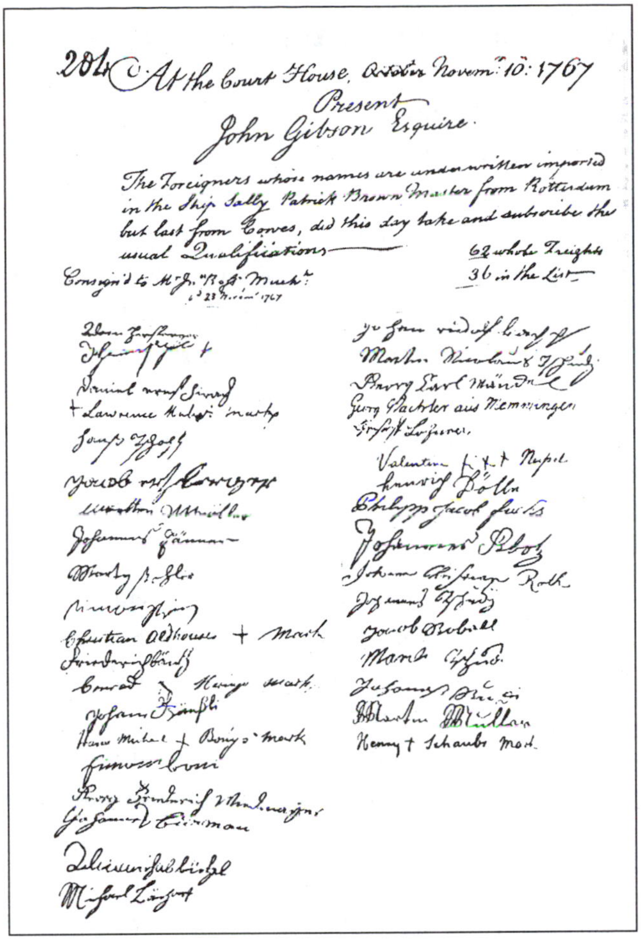
284 At the Court House, October Novem.r 10: 1767
Present
John Gibson Esquire.

The Foreigners whose names are underwritten imported in the Ship Sally Patrick Brown Master from Rotterdam but last from Cowes, did this day take and subscribe the usual Qualifications

62 whole Freights
36 in the List

Consign'd to M.r Jn.o Rob.t Mueh.t
23 Novem.r 1767

Figure 1-1. From Ralph B. Strassburger with William J. Hinke, Pennsylvania German Pioneers, *3 vols. (Norristown: Pennsylvania German Society, 1934), vol. 2, page 829.*

the population growth of the colonies by "obstructing the laws for the naturalization of foreigners."

Continental Congress

The Continental Congress resolved on 6 June 1776, "that all persons abiding within any of the United Colonies and deriving protection from the laws of the same owe allegiance to the said laws, and are members of such colony."[2] No oath was required from members of the Continental Congress nor from soldiers enlisting in the Continental army. Those enlisting during the revolution were sworn to be true to the United States of America and to serve them honestly and faithfully. Congress later required an oath for all officers in Continental service and for all holding civil office from Congress.

Revolutionary War

During the revolutionary war, American colonists continually tried to lure foreigners in the British army (many of them were Hessians) away from the British with offers of land and citizenship. In August 1776, Congress adopted a report designed to encourage the Hessians and other foreigners to quit the British service by extending protection to all those who would settle among them, regardless of nationality and religion, and to give them civil and religious freedom. It was resolved that each defector from the British army should be given fifty acres of land. Later the same month, on 27 August 1776, it was determined that lands given should be proportionate to the rank held by foreign officers leaving the British service to become citizens of "these states."[3]

As the American colonies became independent states, residents who were British citizens had to choose between American or British citizenship. If they chose to remain British, they became alien enemies in the place of their residence and were forced to move. Individuals who remained were and continued to be American citizens, even though they might find themselves in territory occupied by the British. "He that owed primary allegiance to Great Britain now owed primary alle-

> The federal government and the states began keeping records, including naturalization documentation, in 1790.

giance to the United States, but it was no treason to adhere to the king's government."[4]

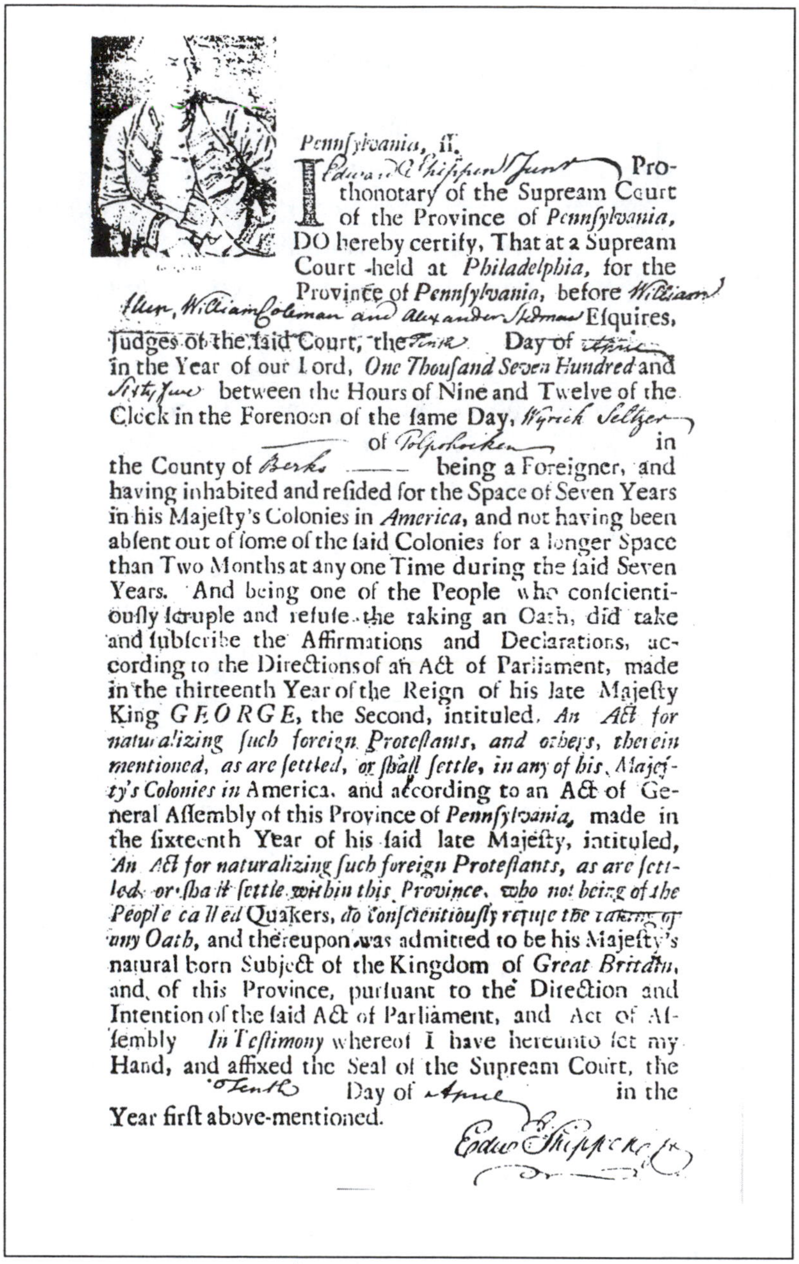

Pennſylvania, ſſ.

I Edward Shippen Junr Prothonotary of the Supream Court of the Province of *Pennſylvania,* DO hereby certify, That at a Supream Court held at *Philadelphia,* for the Province of *Pennſylvania,* before William Allen, William Coleman and Alexander Stedman Eſquires, Judges of the ſaid Court, the Tenth Day of April in the Year of our Lord, *One Thouſand Seven Hundred* and Sixty five between the Hours of Nine and Twelve of the Clock in the Forenoon of the ſame Day, Wyrick Seltzer of Tolpohocken in the County of Berks being a Foreigner, and having inhabited and reſided for the Space of Seven Years in his Majeſty's Colonies in *America,* and not having been abſent out of ſome of the ſaid Colonies for a longer Space than Two Months at any one Time during the ſaid Seven Years. And being one of the People who conſcientiouſly ſcruple and refuſe the taking an Oath, did take and ſubſcribe the Affirmations and Declarations, according to the Directions of an Act of Parliament, made in the thirteenth Year of the Reign of his late Majeſty King *GEORGE,* the Second, intituled, *An Act for naturalizing ſuch foreign Proteſtants, and others, therein mentioned, as are ſettled, or ſhall ſettle, in any of his Majeſty's Colonies in* America, and according to an Act of General Aſſembly of this Province of *Pennſylvania,* made in the ſixteenth Year of his ſaid late Majeſty, intituled, *An Act for naturalizing ſuch foreign Proteſtants, as are ſettled, or ſhall ſettle within this Province, who not being of the People called* Quakers, *do conſcientiouſly refuſe the taking of any Oath,* and thereupon was admitted to be his Majeſty's natural born Subject of the Kingdom of *Great Britain,* and of this Province, purſuant to the Direction and Intention of the ſaid Act of Parliament, and Act of Aſſembly *In Teſtimony* whereof I have hereunto ſet my Hand, and affixed the Seal of the Supream Court, the Tenth Day of April in the Year firſt above-mentioned.

Edw. Shippen Jr.

Figure 1-2. Certificate of Naturalization of Wyrick Seltzer, 10 April 1765, Pennsylvania Supreme Court, from Earl W. Ibach's Hub of the Tulpehocken *(Womelsdorf, Pa.: the author, 1975), page 52. (Used by permission.)*

THE FIRST NATURALIZATION ACT

Passed by Congress on 26 March 1790, the first naturalization act (1 Stat. 103) provided that any free white person over the age of twenty-one who had resided for at least two years in the United States might be granted citizenship on application to any common law court in any state where he or she had resided for at least one year. The process required an applicant to visit any common law court of record, prove to the satisfaction of the court that he or she was of good moral character, and take an oath of allegiance to the United States Constitution. A judge then ruled on the applicant's petition, and citizenship was granted to those who satisfied the court. Married women and children under the age of twenty-one derived citizenship from their husbands and fathers, respectively. Children of unsuccessful applicants could apply for citizenship in their own right when they reached the age of twenty-one.

The Constitution of the United State gives Congress the power to establish a uniform rule of naturalization. Since 1790, the naturalization process has been controlled exclusively by the federal government and administered by the various state and local courts.

During the next five years, Americans became increasingly uncomfortable with the liberal policy toward immigrants. Refugees fleeing the upheavals of the French Revolution for American shores heightened fears of an immigrant takeover. Connecti-

Lancaster County ss May 30th 1778

I Do hereby certify that Christopher Kelly hath voluntarily taken and subscribed the Oath Affirmation of Allegiance and Fidelity, as directed by an Act of General Assembly of Pennsylvania, passed the 13th Day of June, A. D. 1777.

Witness my Hand and Seal, the 30th Day of May A. D. 1778 (Seal) Jacob Cook

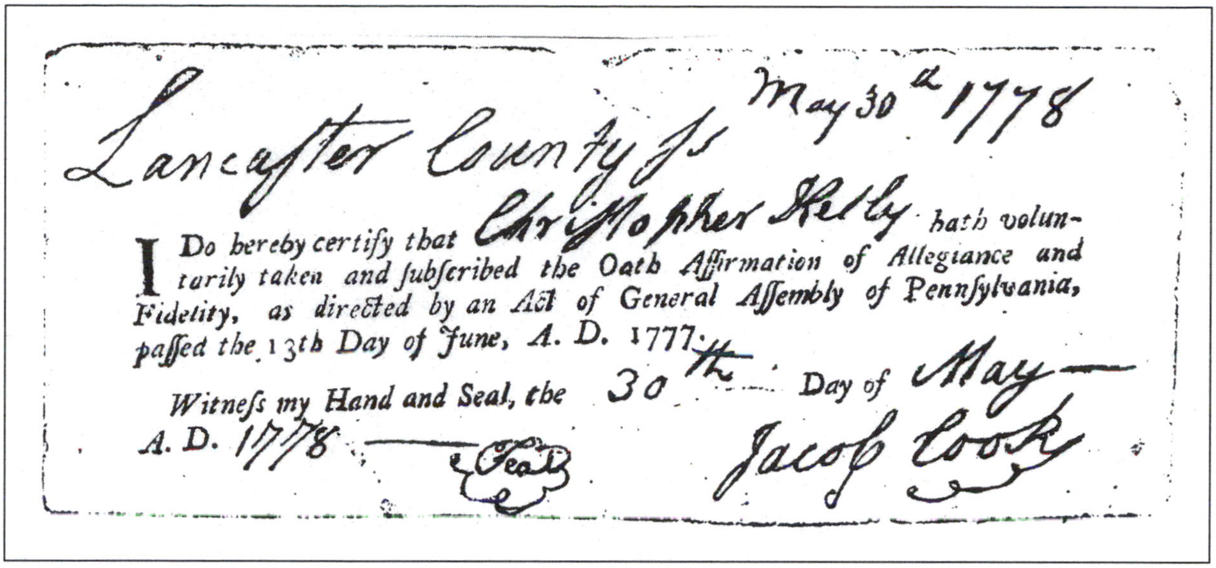

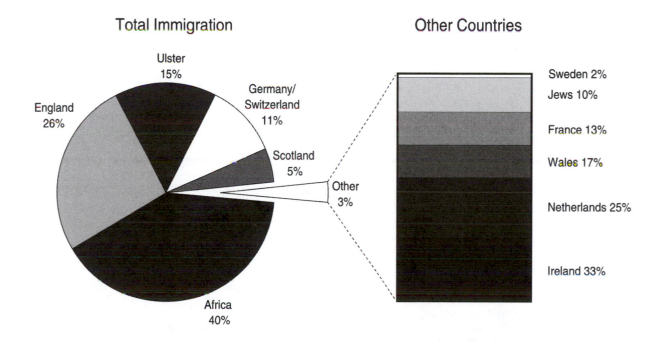

Figure 1-3. "Oath Affirmation of Allegiance and Fidelity, as directed by an Act of General Assembly of Pennsylvania, passed the 13th day of June, A.D. 1777." The original document was donated to the National Society, Daughters of the American Revolution. If you were indexing this naturalization, how would you spell Christopher's last name?

Total Immigration
Ulster 15%
Germany/ Switzerland 11%
Scotland 5%
Other 3%
Africa 40%
England 26%
Other Countries
Sweden 2%
Jews 10%
France 13%
Wales 17%
Netherlands 25%
Ireland 33%

Figure 1-4. Total immigration to the United States to 1790.

cut Federalist Oliver Wolcott wrote in 1794, "there is much to be apprehended from the great numbers of violent men who emigrate to this country from every part of Europe." In the following year a New York Republican, William Vans Murray, was probably expressing the sentiments of his neighbors when he complained that newcomers "coming from a quarter of the world so full of disorder and corruption...might contaminate the purity and simplicity of the American character."[5]

On 29 January 1795, Congress repealed the 1790 act and passed a more stringent law (1 Stat. 414) titled "an act to establish an uniform rule of naturalization; and to repeal the act heretofore passed upon that subject." Except for a brief period (1798 to 1802), the law established the eligibility and proce-

dural requirements that have since been the foundation of U. S. naturalization policy and legislation. Conditions of naturalization under the new law were the following:

- Free white aliens were required to declare in court their intention to become citizens of the United States and to renounce any allegiance to a foreign prince, potentate, state, or sovereignty.

- The period of residence required for citizenship was increased from two to five years, including one year in the state or territory in which the court was held and to which application was made.

- Aliens who had "borne any hereditary title, or

Table 1-1. Top U.S. Ancestry Groups in 1790 and 1990

1790 U.S. Ancestry
(Based on Evaluated 1790 Census Figures)

1990 U.S. Ancestry
(1990 U.S. Census)

Ancestry Group	Number (1790 Estimate)	Percentage of Total	Ancestry Group	Number	Percentage of Total
English	1,900,000	47.5	German	57,981,710	23.3
African	750,000	19.0	Irish	38,735,539	15.6
Scotch-Irish	320,000	8.0	English	32,651,788	13.1
German	280,000	7.0	African American	23,777,098	9.6
Irish	200,000	5.0	Hispanic*	17,418,496	7.0
Scottish	160,000	4.0	Italian	14,664,550	5.9
Welsh	120,000	3.0	Franco-American*	13,176,333	5.3
Dutch	100,000	2.5	Polish	9,366,106	3.8
French	80,000	2.0	Native American	8,708,220	3.5
Native American	50,000	1.0	Dutch	6,227,089	2.5
Spanish	20,000	0.5	Scotch-Irish	5,617,773	2.3
Swedish and other	20,000	0.5	Scottish	5,393,581	2.2
			Swedish	4,680,863	1.9
			Norwegian	3,869,395	1.6
			Russian	2,952,987	1.2
Total U.S. population	4,000,000	100	Total U.S. population	248,708,823	100

* Hispanic comprises Spanish, Mexicans, and other Latin Americans of Spanish ancestry;
Franco-American comprises French (except Basque), French Canadian, and Acadian/Cajun.

been of any of the orders of nobility" were required to renounce that status.

- The naturalization procedure was changed from a one-step to a two-step process, requiring the alien to first file a *declaration of intention*, sometimes referred to as the *first paper*, at least three years before entering a *petition for admission to citizenship* (also known as the *second* or *final paper*). These actions would be taken before the supreme, superior, district, or circuit court of any state or territory, or before a circuit or district court of the United States. As with the 1790 act, citizenship was automatically granted to the wives and minor children of those naturalized.

1798 LEGISLATION

From 1798 to 1800, during a wave of xenophobia that accompanied an undeclared war with France, Federalist leaders pushed through Congress four alien and sedition acts curbing freedom of speech and of the press and curtailing the rights of foreigners in the United States. The Alien Act, approved on 25 June 1798 (1 Stat. 570), was the first national attempt to regulate immigration. In particular, the naturalization law "was designed to keep 'hordes of wild Irishmen' away from the polls for as long as possible."[6]

The 1798 legislation required:

- The filing of a declaration of intention at least five years before admission to citizenship.
- Residence of fourteen years in the United States, and residence of five years in the state or territory where the court was held.
- A law that allowed the president to deport any alien he judged dangerous to the United States. It ended in 1800 after its two-year term because of political abuse, but shows that immigration policy has been a political

issue since the nation's founding.

- The clerk of each court to forward copies of declarations of intention, a report of registry (some courts combined the declaration of intention and the registry), and a report of naturalization proceedings to the U.S. secretary of state.

Condemned for its severity, the 1798 law was replaced with a new naturalization law in 1802 (2 Stat. 153) that basically reasserted the provisions of the 1795 act.

The act of 1802 specified that free white aliens might be admitted to citizenship provided they:

- Declared their intention to become citizens before a competent state, territorial, or federal court at least three years before admission to citizenship.
- Took an oath of allegiance to the United States.
- Had resided at least five years in the United States and at least one year within the state or territory where the court was held.
- Renounced allegiance to any foreign prince, potentate, state, or sovereignty.
- Satisfied the court that they were of good moral character and were attached to the principles of the Constitution.

The act also specified that children of naturalized citizens were considered to be citizens.

The 1802 act was the last major change in naturalization laws until 1906. During the intervening 104 years a number of minor revisions were made, including a reduction in the waiting period between filing the declaration of intention and the naturalization from three to two years, and the requirement that petitioners attest that they were not anarchists. Most of the changes merely altered or clarified details of evidence and certification without changing the basic nature of the admission procedure.

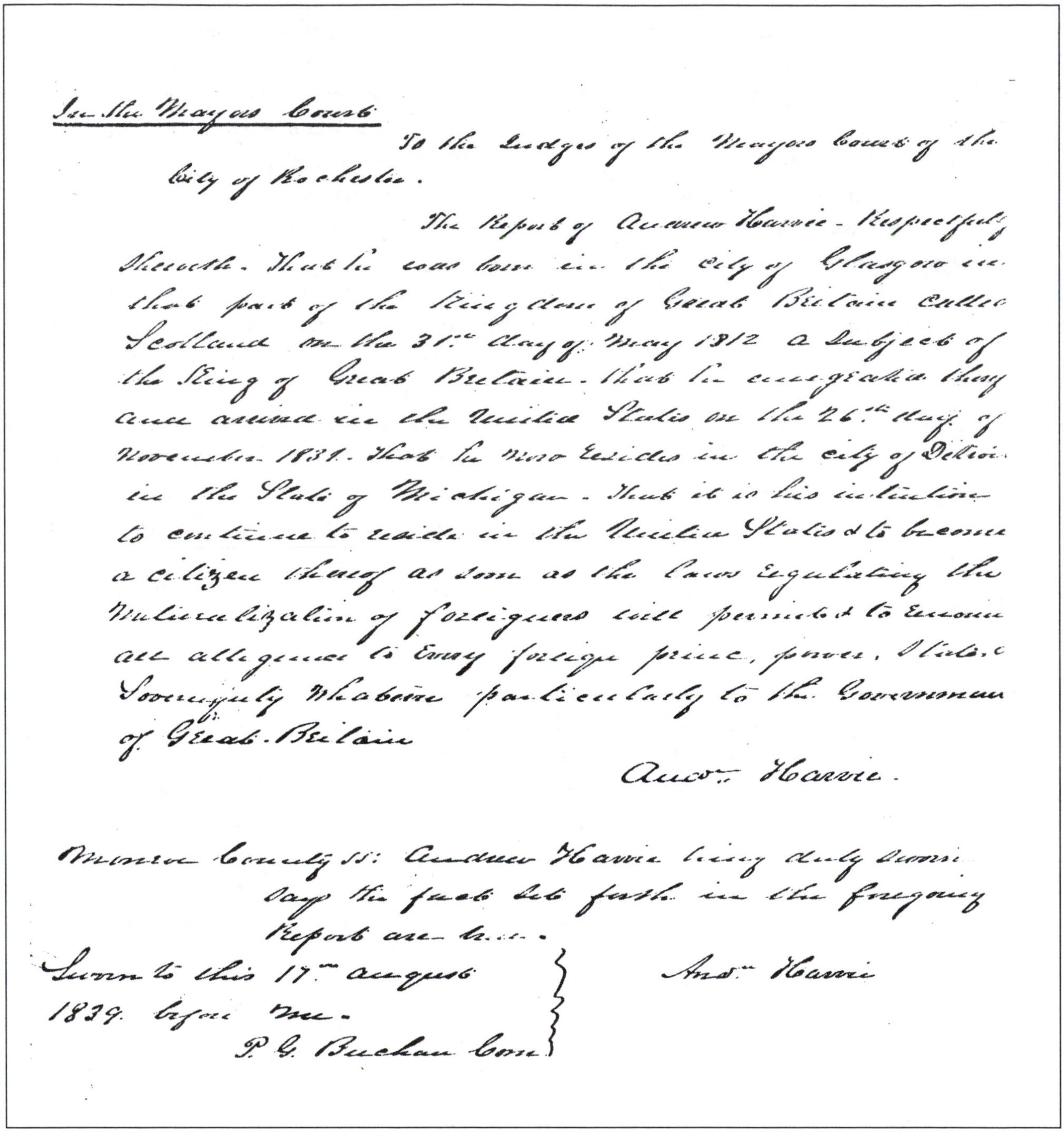

Figure 1-5. Handwritten oath of Andrew Harris.
Difficult-to-read handwriting and faded ink on old documents such as this one complicate searches for naturalization papers.
Is the applicant's name Harvie or Harris?
If any other words on this paper were transcribed incorrectly, it might be of little consequence;
however, if the indexer of these naturalization papers incorrectly interpreted the key identifier—the surname—
it is doubtful that anyone searching for Andrew will ever find this fascinating document.
Consider the fact that indexes to court records are usually compiled by individuals long after the records were created. Addition-
ally, the index may have been created by someone with limited interest, time, or interpretive skills.

Transcription of Andrew Harris's oath
(see figure 1-5):

In the Mayors Court
To the Judges of the Mayors Court of the City of
Rochester.

The Report of Andrew Harris—Respectfully
Showeth—That he was born in the city of Glasgow in that part of the Kingdom of Great Britain called Scotland on the 31st day of May 1812 a subject of the King of Great Britain that he emigrated thereof and arrived in the United States on the 26th day of November 1837. That he now resides in the city of Detroit in the State of Michigan—That it is his intention to continue to reside in the United States & to become a citizen thereof as soon as the laws legalizing the naturalization of foreigners will permit & to

renounce all allegiance to every foreign prince, power, State, & Sovereignty Whatsoever particularly to the Government of Great Britain

Andw. Harvie

Monroe County ss: Andrew Harris being duly sworn says the facts set forth in the foregoing Report are true.

Sworn to this 17th August
Andw. Harris
1839 before me—
P.G. Buchan Com.

CITIZENSHIP BY GROUP

As the United States acquired territory by treaty and purchase, it also acquired jurisdiction over people living on that land. Those living in territories

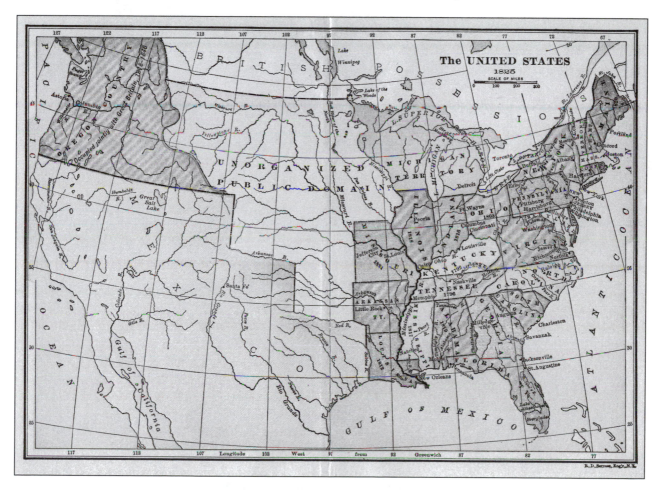

Figure 1-6. The United States in 1825.

Figure 1-7. Ship crowded with passengers.

acquired through these treaties were usually awarded citizenship en masse. Acquisitions included Louisiana (1803), Florida—including Mississippi and Alabama—(1819), and Alaska (1867). By joint resolution of Congress, Texas residents were granted citizenship in 1845. By acts of Congress, citizenship was conferred upon residents of Hawaii in 1900, of Puerto Rico in 1917, and of the Virgin Islands in 1927.

The United States has always agreed to validate property titles of persons who become citizens because they lived on newly acquired territories. To validate the title, however, a private land claim had to be filed. These claims can be very valuable. The cur-

rent landowner had to document claim to the title. If the grant was originally given to a father or grandfather, the claimant also had to prove descent. Some of these land claims contain four to seven generations of genealogical proof in the form of family Bible pages, original land transactions, genealogy charts, and affidavits and testimonies of neighbors and relatives.

MASS IMMIGRATION, 1819 TO 1860

The extraordinary flood of immigration in the early part of the nineteenth century was one of the great wonders of the time. The 1819 Steerage Acts regarding travel on sailing ships were the first means that the fed-

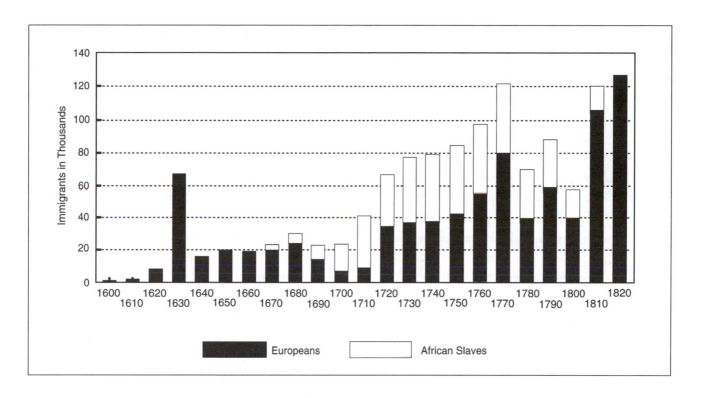

Figure 1-8. Pre-1820 immigration to the United States.

eral government had to monitor the incoming flow of humanity. Between 1820 and 1840, immigrants from Germany, Ireland, and the United Kingdom, spurred by war, unemployment, and famine, comprised 70 percent of the total. Between 1841 and 1860, more than 87 percent of immigrants coming to American shores came from these three countries. Motivation came from both sides of the Atlantic. The lure of fertile, attainable American land was great; Ireland's crop failures of 1846 and 1847, Germany's economic crises of the 1840s, political revolutions across Europe in 1848, and the industrialization of Europe motivated millions to leave their homelands. Largely because of the industrialization, masses of unskilled laborers accounted for the largest number of workers coming into America.[7]

THE FOREIGN VOTE

Politicians were quick to recognize the collective voting strength of naturalized citizens. Political parties went to great lengths to court immigrants from the moment they arrived on American soil. In New York City, newcomers were met at the boat. A "naturalization bureau" was set up to advise and assist aliens in filling out naturalization papers. "It was common knowledge that many of these adopted citizens voted before they had fulfilled the federal residence requirement of five years. Wittingly or unwittingly, the foreigners contributed to the notoriously unscrupulous tactics of political parties in New York City. Democrats and Whigs, and later Republicans perpetrated election frauds."[8] An 1845 congressional committee investigating naturalization frauds reported that "in New York, New Orleans, and Philadelphia it was a common practice on the eve of elections for immigrants, many of them not yet qualified by residence, to be naturalized in droves at the instigation of the political machines."[9]

The following article, which appeared in the *Chicago Tribune*, 19 April 1868 (page 1), was reproduced in the *Chicago Genealogist* 18 (Winter 1987): 39–54.

**List of New Voters Manufactured by
O'Hara's Special Deputies the Past Week
Also the Names of the Persons
Who Acted as "Sponsors"
The Duty of the Republicans
in the Premises
How the Naturalization Business
has Been Conducted**

The first column of the following list of names represents persons to whom Dan O'Hara's special deputies have issued naturalization papers during the past week, on the first application, and before declaring intentions. Each of these names is supposed to represent a man who emigrated to the United States while yet under eighteen years of age, and who has resided in this country five years, and in Illinois one year, and is now over twenty-one years of age. Each name in the second column represents a man who swore that the name opposite his is that of a man who, of his personal knowledge, bears a good moral character, has resided in the United States five years, and in Illinois one year, and came to this country under eighteen years of age. From what has already been found out, it is safe to say that not more than half, perhaps two-thirds, of the entire list are not entitled to naturalization; hundreds of them have not been in the United States five years, and other hundreds came into this country after they were eighteen years of age. Many of these men are from thirty to fifty years of age, and others of them are not yet twenty-one. Some came to the United States last year, and a few left Cork this spring.

Take the whole lot together, it is doubtful whether one-third of them have been lawfully naturalized. Let every citizen scan the list carefully, and if he recognizes any names whom he knows came to the United States when over eighteen years, or have not been five years in the country, or are now under 21-years, he is earnestly requested by the Republican Central Committee to report the facts forthwith to the Republican Headquarters at No. 161 Washington St., where

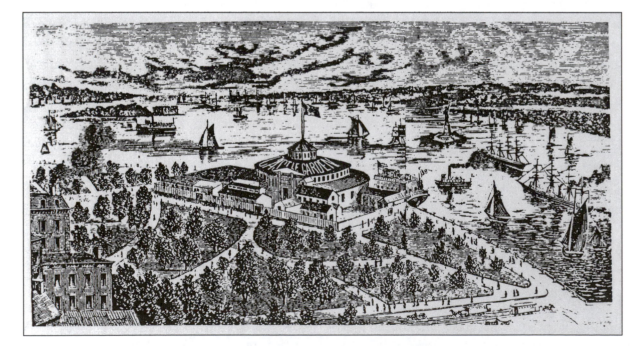

*Figure 1-9. In 1855, Castle Garden, the predecessor of Ellis Island,
became the official receiving station for immigrants entering the Port of New York.*

steps will be taken at once to protect the polls against such spurious voters. Those who have fraudulently taken naturalization papers, or have falsely vouched them, are liable to be sent to the Penitentiary. The members of the Grant club have already "spotted" over 300 bogus voters, and Monday's investigations will probably double the number. Several of the rascals have already been arrested and jugged, and the jail yearns for more of them. It is the firm determination of the Republican Executive Committee to protect the purity of the ballot box at all hazards. This scoundrelism that has been carried on by the Copperheads in the naturalization business can only be broken by defeating their candidates and electing Colonel R.W. Smith, Judge, and Charles Loding, Clerk of the Recorder's Court. But examine the subjoined lists carefully and stick a pin wherever you find suspicious names.

There is little doubt that naturalization fraud has been a continuing problem in the United States. The above article was submitted to the *Chicago Genealogist* by Suzanne Furgal, together with the list of "suspicious names." The intention here is not to reproduce the names (they can be found in the original source and in the *Chicago Genealogist*) but to encourage the researcher to consider the circumstances and the political climate of that time period before drawing conclusions about an individual's citizenship status. While there may have been an element of truth in the article, Irish-Americans enjoyed little respect at the time, and it is clear that the Republican newspaper had strong political motives in printing the names.

Women and Children

An act of 10 February 1855 granted citizenship to alien wives of citizens if they "might lawfully be naturalized under the existing laws" (10 Stat. 604). Prior to 1922, women and children automatically became U.S. citizens when their husbands or fathers did.

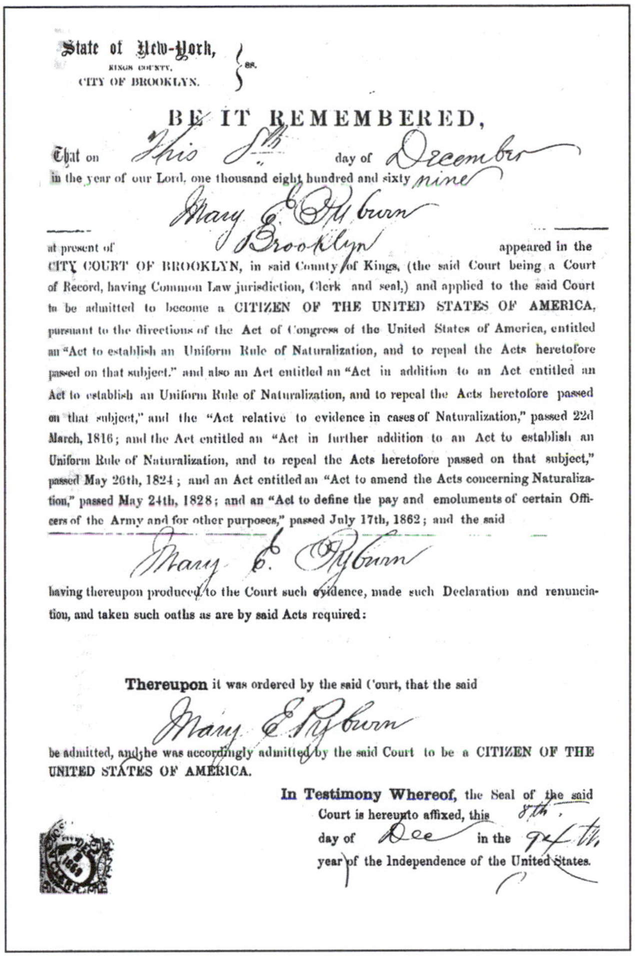

State of New-York, }
KINGS COUNTY, } ss.
CITY OF BROOKLYN. }

BE IT REMEMBERED,

That on This 8th day of December in the year of our Lord, one thousand eight hundred and sixty nine

Mary E. Pyburn

at present of Brooklyn appeared in the CITY COURT OF BROOKLYN, in said County of Kings, (the said Court being a Court of Record, having Common Law jurisdiction, Clerk and seal,) and applied to the said Court to be admitted to become a CITIZEN OF THE UNITED STATES OF AMERICA, pursuant to the directions of the Act of Congress of the United States of America, entitled an "Act to establish an Uniform Rule of Naturalization, and to repeal the Acts heretofore passed on that subject," and also an Act entitled an "Act in addition to an Act entitled an Act to establish an Uniform Rule of Naturalization, and to repeal the Acts heretofore passed on that subject," and the "Act relative to evidence in cases of Naturalization," passed 22d March, 1816; and the Act entitled an "Act in further addition to an Act to establish an Uniform Rule of Naturalization, and to repeal the Acts heretofore passed on that subject," passed May 26th, 1824; and an Act entitled an "Act to amend the Acts concerning Naturalization," passed May 24th, 1828; and an "Act to define the pay and emoluments of certain Officers of the Army and for other purposes," passed July 17th, 1862; and the said

Mary E. Pyburn

having thereupon produced to the Court such evidence, made such Declaration and renunciation, and taken such oaths as are by said Acts required:

Thereupon it was ordered by the said Court, that the said

Mary E. Pyburn

be admitted, and she was accordingly admitted by the said Court to be a CITIZEN OF THE UNITED STATES OF AMERICA.

In Testimony Whereof, the Seal of the said Court is hereunto affixed, this 8th day of Dec in the 94th year of the Independence of the United States.

Figure 1-10. Brooklyn citizenship document for Mary E. Pyburn.
Before 1922, the vast majority of alien women derived citizenship from husbands or fathers who were already American citizens or as they became citizens. However, the example of Mary E. Pyburn, naturalized in a Brooklyn, New York, court in 1869, points to the possibility of exceptions to the rule. Indexes to naturalizations should be searched for all family names.

Unfortunately, there was rarely any mention of marital status on pre-1906 naturalization documents, so early naturalization records are not good sources for obtaining names and biographical details for spouses and children. While it was definitely the exception rather than the rule, some women, especially single adults, found it necessary or desirable to independently take the steps to become naturalized citizens (figure 1-11). The names of individuals given

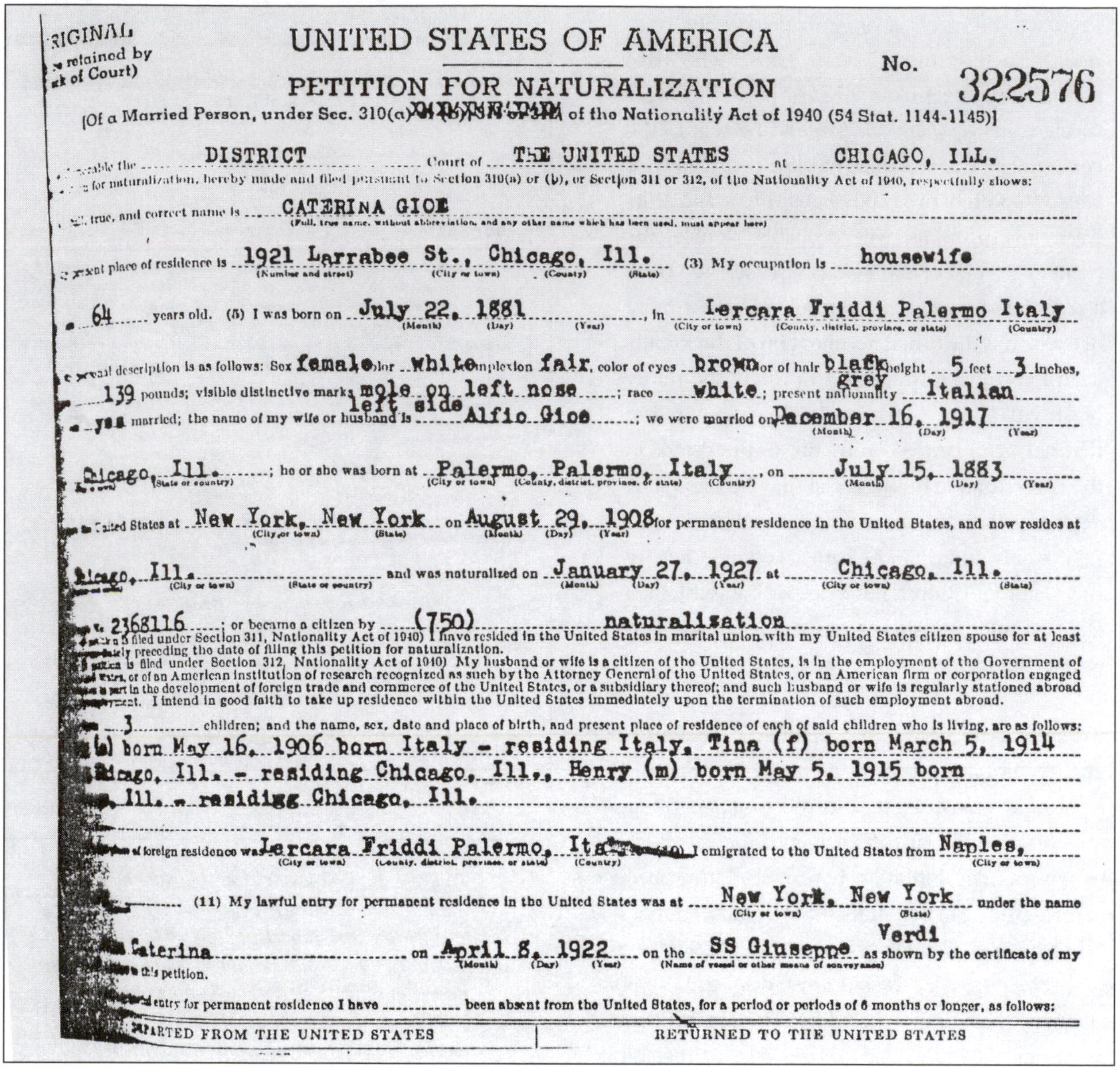

Figure 1-11. The petition of Caterina Gioe provides biographical information for her husband and her children, as well as for her.

citizenship by legislative act were often omitted from the record, and the group was sometimes referred to as a whole.

After 1906, it became mandatory to provide the name, age, and birth date of a spouse along with the marriage date and place and the names, ages, and birthplaces of minor children.

Widows sometimes assumed the responsibility of becoming naturalized upon the death of their husbands. An act of 26 March 1804 allowed widows and children of deceased applicants who had filed a declaration of intention, but who died before the naturalization process could be completed, to become citizens by taking the prescribed oath. Documents filed in the federal courts in the Eastern District of Michigan in 1872 provide interesting testimony (see figure 1-12):

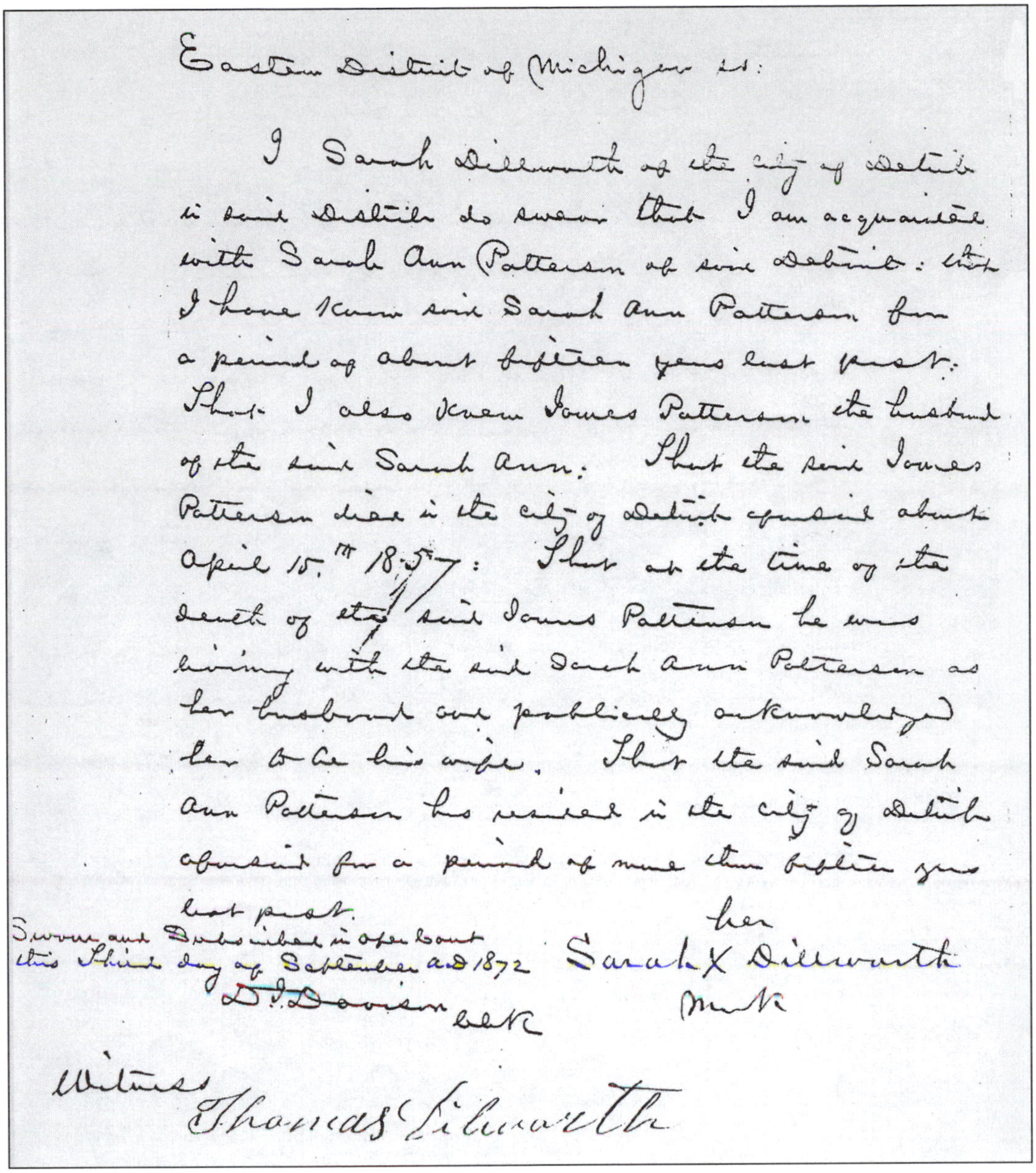
Eastern District of Michigan ss:

I Sarah Dillworth of the city of Detroit in said District do swear that I am acquainted with Sarah Ann Patterson of said District: that I have known said Sarah Ann Patterson for a period of about fifteen years last past: That I also knew James Patterson the husband of the said Sarah Ann: That the said James Patterson died in the city of Detroit aforesaid about April 15th 1857: That at the time of the death of the said James Patterson he was living with the said Sarah Ann Patterson as her husband and publicly acknowledged her to be his wife. That the said Sarah Ann Patterson has resided in the city of Detroit aforesaid for a period of more than fifteen years last past.

Sworn and subscribed in open Court this Third day of September AD 1872
D. I. Davison Clerk

her
Sarah X Dillworth
mark

Witness Thomas Dillworth

Figure 1-12. Handwritten oath of Sarah Dillworth. From Sarah Ann Patterson's file (no. 1735), District Court of the Unites States, Detroit Michigan, now at the National Archives–Great Lakes Region, Chicago.

I Sarah Dillworth of the city of Detroit in said District do swear that I am acquainted with Sarah Ann Patterson of said District: that I have known said Sarah Ann Patterson for a period of about fifteen years last past; That I also knew James Patterson the husband of said Sarah Ann: That the said James Patterson died in the city of Detroit aforesaid about April 15th 1857. That at the time of the death of said James Patterson he was living with the said Sarah Ann Patterson as her husband and publicly acknowledged her to be his wife. That the said Sarah Ann Patterson has resided in the city of Detroit aforesaid for a period of more than fifteen years last past.

Sworn and subscribed in open Court in this Third day of September AD 1872

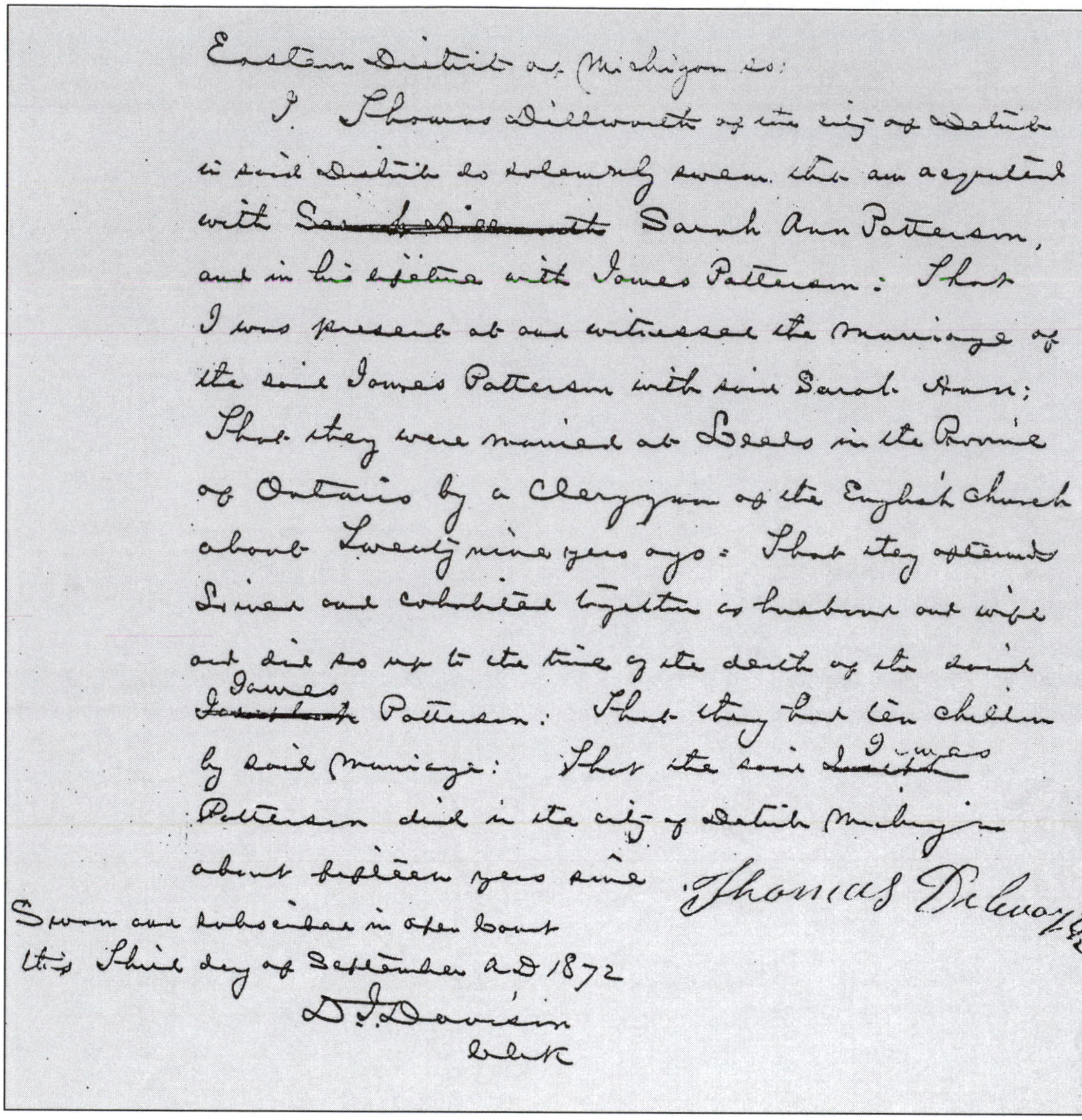

Eastern District of Michigan ss:
I Thomas Dilworth of the city of Detroit
in said District do solemnly swear that am acquainted
with Sarah Ann Patterson,
and in his lifetime with James Patterson: That
I was present at and witnessed the marriage of
the said James Patterson with said Sarah Ann;
That they were married at Leeds in the Province
of Ontario by a Clergyman of the English church
about twenty nine years ago: That they afterwards
lived and cohabited together as husband and wife
and did so up to the time of the death of the said
James Patterson: That they had ten children
by said marriage: That the said James
Patterson died in the city of Detroit Michigan
about fifteen years since Thomas Dilworth
Sworn and subscribed in open Court
this Third day of September AD 1872
D J Davison
Clerk

Figure 1-13. Handwritten affidavit of Thomas Dilworth. From Sarah Ann Patterson's file (no. 1735), District Court of the Unites States, Detroit Michigan, now at the National Archives–Great Lakes Region, Chicago.

An accompanying document in Sarah Ann Patterson's naturalization file is the affidavit (see figure 1-13):

> I Thomas Dilworth of the city of Detroit in said District do solemnly swear that am acquainted with Sarah Ann Patterson, and in his lifetime with James Patterson: That I was present at and witnessed the marriage of the said James Patterson with said Sarah Ann; That they were married at Leeds in the Province of Ontario by a clergyman of the English church about twenty nine years ago: That they afterwards lived and cohabited together as husband and wife and did so up to the time of the death of said James Patterson: That they had ten children by said marriage; That the said James Patterson died in the city of Detroit Michigan about fifteen years since. Thomas Dilworth
>
> Sworn and subscribed in open Court
> this Third day of September AD 1872

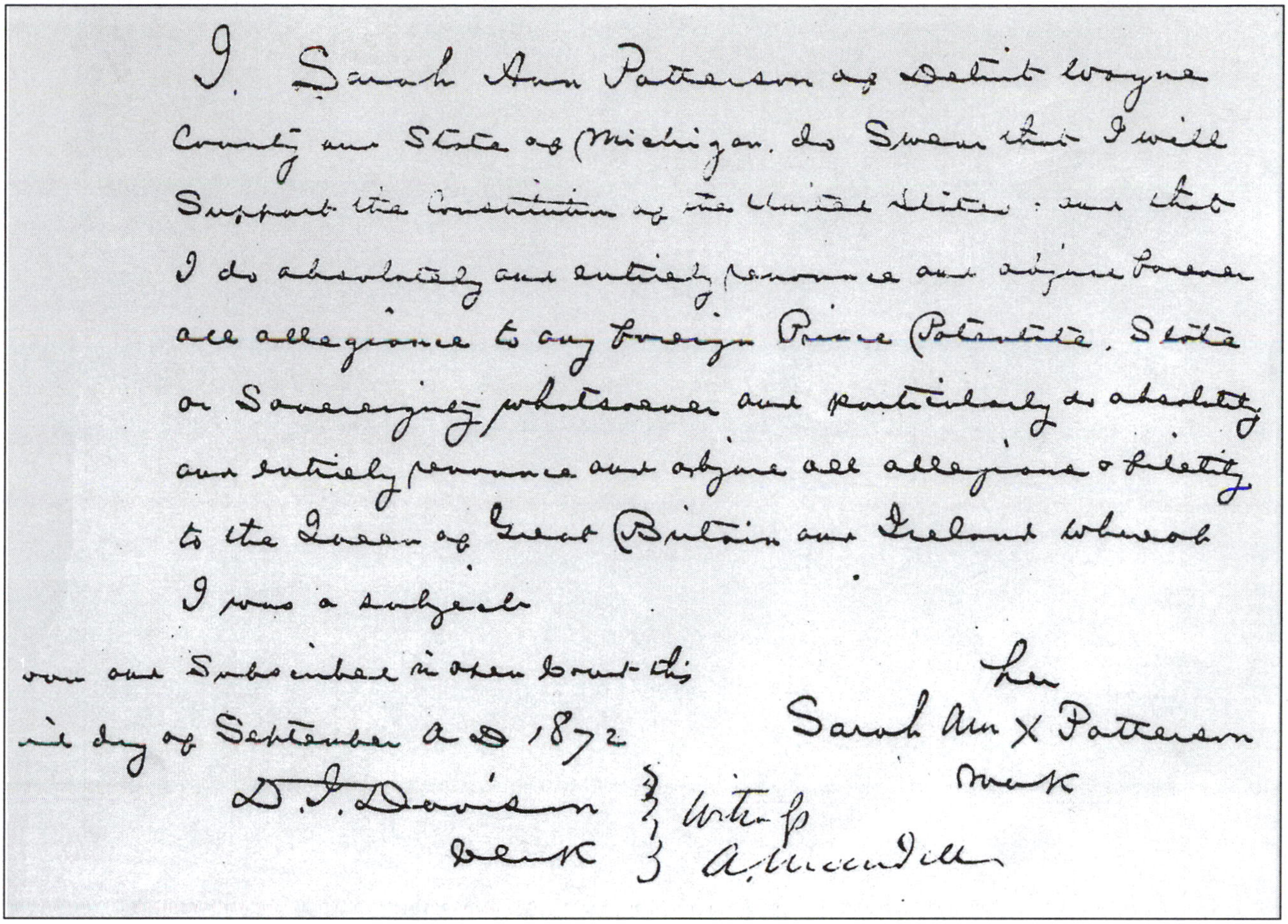

[Figure: Handwritten oath of Sarah Ann Patterson]

Figure 1-14. Handwritten oath of Sarah Ann Patterson. From Sarah Ann Patterson's file (no. 1735),
District Court of the Unites States, Detroit Michigan, now at the National Archives–Great Lakes Region, Chicago.

The fourth and last document in the file was a sworn and signed (with her mark) oath (see figure 1-14):

> I, Sarah Ann Patterson of Detroit Wayne County and State of Michigan, do swear that I will support the Constitution of the United States and that I do absolutely and entirely renounce and abjure forever all allegiance to any foreign Prince Potentate, State or Sovereignty whatsoever and positively & absolutely and entirely renounce and abjure all allegiance & fidelity to the Queen of Great Britain and Ireland whereof I was a subject.

1922 ACT

An act of 22 September 1922 (42 Stat. 1021) had significant effects on the status of women. By this act a woman could not become a citizen by virtue of her marriage to a citizen, but, if eligible, she might be naturalized by compliance with the naturalization laws. No declaration of intention was required. Moreover, the act specifically provided that "any woman citizen who marries an alien ineligible to citizenship shall cease to be a citizen" (section 3). Further, no woman whose husband was not eligible to become a citizen was to be naturalized during the marriage (section 5). Figure 1-11 is an example from the thousands of documents created when American-born women

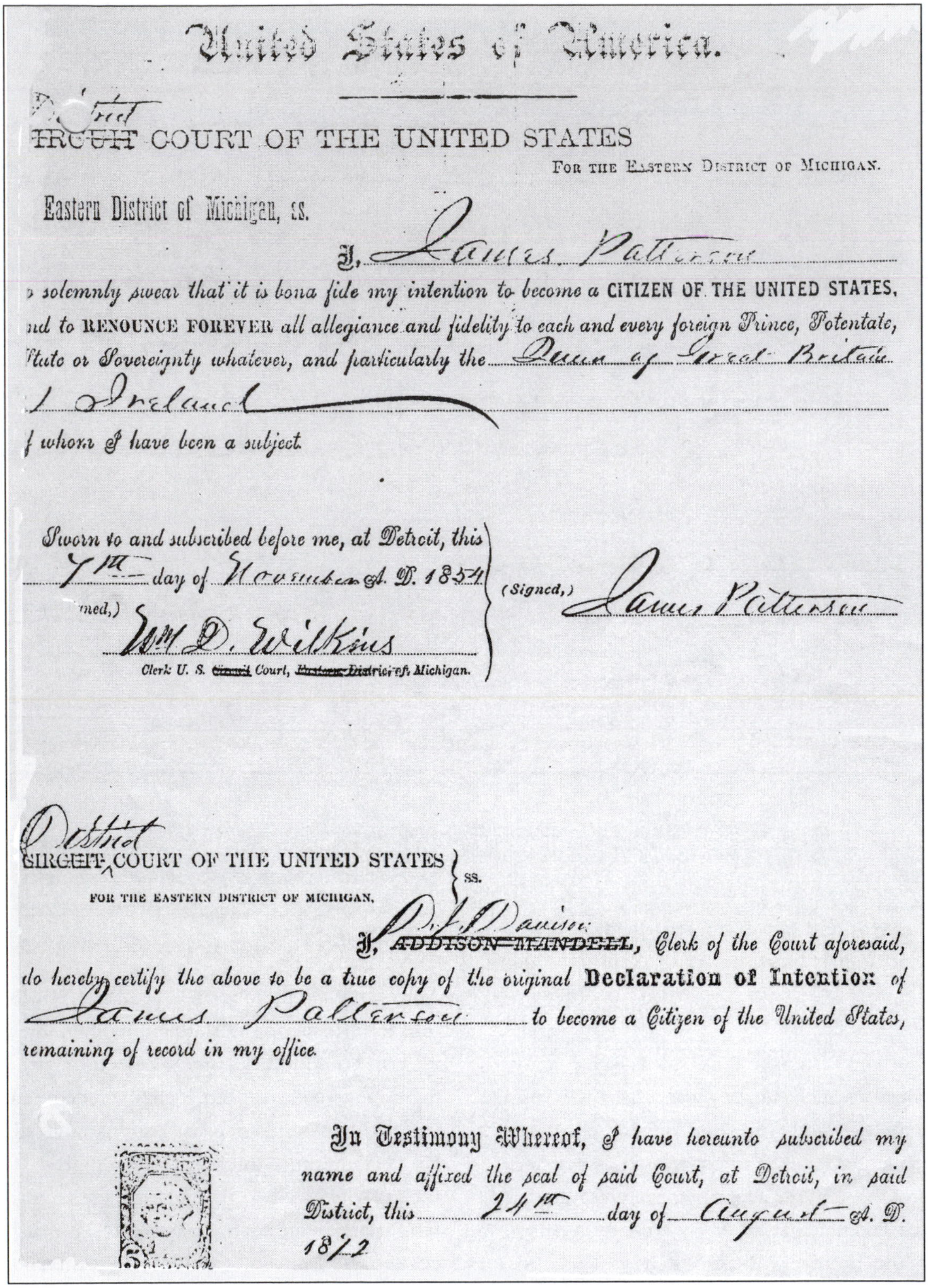

United States of America.

~~CIRCUIT~~ District COURT OF THE UNITED STATES
FOR THE EASTERN DISTRICT OF MICHIGAN.

Eastern District of Michigan, ss.

I, James Patterson

[d]o solemnly swear that it is bona fide my intention to become a CITIZEN OF THE UNITED STATES, [a]nd to RENOUNCE FOREVER all allegiance and fidelity to each and every foreign Prince, Potentate, [S]tate or Sovereignty whatever, and particularly the Queen of Great Britain [&] Ireland [o]f whom I have been a subject.

Sworn to and subscribed before me, at Detroit, this 7th day of November A. D. 1854

[(Sig]ned,) Wm D. Wilkins
Clerk U. S. ~~Circuit~~ Court, ~~Eastern District~~ of Michigan.

(Signed,) James Patterson

~~CIRCUIT~~ District COURT OF THE UNITED STATES
FOR THE EASTERN DISTRICT OF MICHIGAN, ss.

I, ~~ADDISON MANDELL~~ D. J. Davison, Clerk of the Court aforesaid, do hereby certify the above to be a true copy of the original Declaration of Intention of James Patterson to become a Citizen of the United States, remaining of record in my office.

In Testimony Whereof, I have hereunto subscribed my name and affixed the seal of said Court, at Detroit, in said District, this 24th day of August A. D. 1872

Figure 1-15. Declaration of intention of James Patterson, 1854. From Sarah Ann Patterson's file (no. 1735), District Court of the Unites States, Detroit Michigan, now at the National Archives—Great Lakes Region, Chicago.

who had lost their citizenship because of marriage to a foreigner sought to reclaim their citizenship. An act of 3 March 1931 repealed section 5 of the 1922 law, and section 3 was amended so that citizenship was not lost by a woman solely through marriage (46 Stat. 1511).

"Independent Citizenship for Married Women" was a key issue at the first convention of the National League of Women Voters held in 1920. The league issued the following statement:

> Believing that American born women resident in the United States should not forfeit their citizenship by marriage with aliens, and that alien women should not acquire citizenship by marriage with Americans but rather by meeting the same requirements as those provided for the naturalization of alien men, we urge federal legislation insuring to women of the United States the same independent status for citizenship as that which now obtains for men.[10]

MINORS

An act of 26 May 1824 allowed minor aliens who had lived in the United States for three years before age twenty-one, and for two years after to apply for naturalization without a previous declaration of intention. Minors, however, were required to file a declaration at the time of their admission and to comply with other aspects of the law. A law of 24 February 1911 excused the requirement for a minor filing a declaration of intention.

LAND OWNERSHIP AND CITIZENSHIP

The promise of land ownership in the United States has always been a lure for immigrants. During the early years of U.S. history, individual states had their own requirements regarding land purchases. Some states required aliens to make a declaration of intention before they could buy land. In some cases, an oath to that effect was recorded in the court in the county where the land being purchased was located.

The Homestead Act of 20 May 1862 provided a special incentive for foreigners to obtain citizenship; it specified that only U.S. citizens, or immigrants who had filed a declaration of intention to become a citizen, were eligible to own land. Those filing claims took an oath that they were over the age of twenty-one or were married and the head of a family. Also included in the process was a sworn statement as to citizenship and, if naturalized, where and when the naturalization took place. The citizenship information in homestead files makes these an especially important source to investigate. Homesteading acts and records are discussed in detail in *Land and Property Research in the United States* by E. Wade Hone (Salt Lake City: Ancestry, 1997).

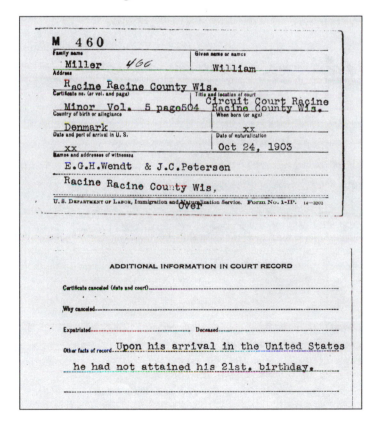

Figure 1-16. Soundex index card for William Miller, who "had not attained his 21st birthday" upon his arrival in the United States.

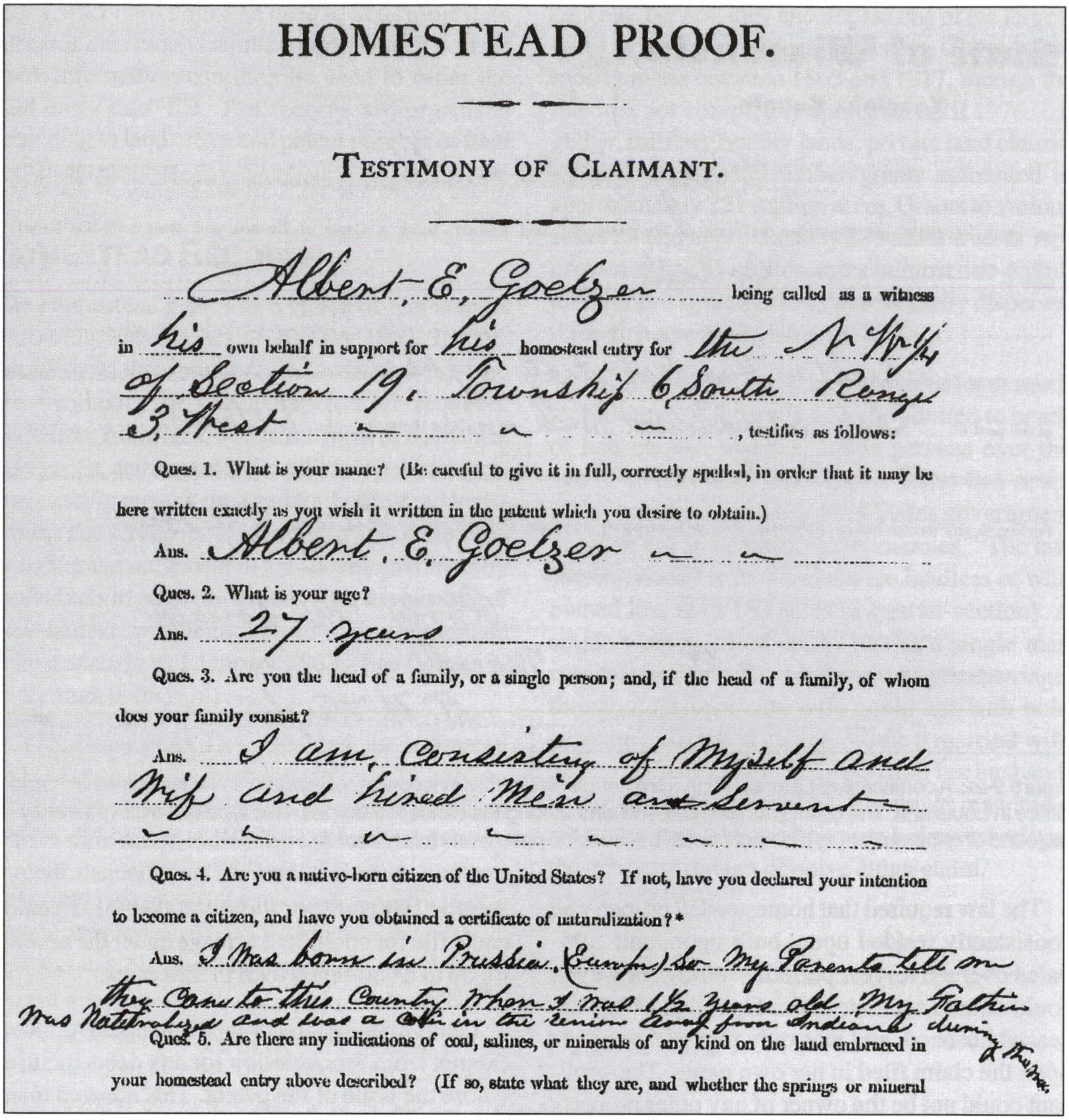

HOMESTEAD PROOF.

TESTIMONY OF CLAIMANT.

Albert, E, Goetzer .... being called as a witness in _his_ own behalf in support for _his_ homestead entry for _the N W ¼ of Section 19, Township 6 South Range 3 West_ ...., testifies as follows:

Ques. 1. What is your name? (Be careful to give it in full, correctly spelled, in order that it may be here written exactly as you wish it written in the patent which you desire to obtain.)

Ans. _Albert, E, Goetzer_

Ques. 2. What is your age?

Ans. _27 years_

Ques. 3. Are you the head of a family, or a single person; and, if the head of a family, of whom does your family consist?

Ans. _I am, Consisting of Myself and Wif and hired Men and Servent_

Ques. 4. Are you a native-born citizen of the United States? If not, have you declared your intention to become a citizen, and have you obtained a certificate of naturalization? *

Ans. _I was born in Prussia (Europe) So My Parents tell me they Came to this Country when I was 1½ years old My Father was Naturalized and was a Coln in the union troop from Indiana during the_

Ques. 5. Are there any indications of coal, salines, or minerals of any kind on the land embraced in your homestead entry above described? (If so, state what they are, and whether the springs or mineral

Figure 1-17. Homestead proof. The proof was among many papers ordinarily found in a land-entry case file for a homestead. This one states: "I was born in Prussia (Europe), so my parents tell me they came to this country when I was 1 1/2 years old. My father was naturalized and was a Coln. in the Union Army and from Indiana during the war." (Used by permission. Courtesy of E. Wade Hone.)

IMMIGRATION AND NATURALIZATION SERVICE

Between 1882 and 1891 the secretary of the treasury had general supervision over immigration. The office of superintendent of immigration of the Department of the Treasury was established by an act of 3 March 1891. The office was designated a bureau in 1895 with responsibility for administering the alien contract labor laws. In 1900 administration of the Chinese exclusion laws was added, and in 1903 the bureau became part of the Department of Commerce and Labor. Functions relating to naturalization were assigned in 1906, and the bureau's name was changed to the Bureau of Immigration and Naturalization. It was transferred to the Department of Labor by an act of 4 March 1913 as the Bureau of Immigration and the Bureau of Naturalization. Executive Order 6166 of 10 June 1933 reunited those bureaus to form the Immigration and Naturalization Service (INS), which was transferred in 1940 to the Department of Justice. Chapter 5 in this volume describes the Immigration and Naturalization Service more fully.

Before 27 September 1906, naturalization records were maintained by the creating courts. In the vast majority of cases, the court recorded an individual's declaration of intention only once. However, if the applicant did not complete the citizenship process in the court in which the declaration of intention was filed, the applicant had to offer proof to the second court that the first step had been completed. For this reason, it is not uncommon to find a declaration of intention for a person that was filed in one court attached or filed with that individual's petition or "final papers" in another state or county or another court within the same county.

POST-1906 NATURALIZATION RECORDS

By the beginning of the twentieth century, the steadily increasing number of immigrants entering the United States prompted significant procedural changes, shifting the responsibility away from county clerks, who had previously administered most citizenship records. The creation of the Bureau of Immigration and Naturalization under the act of 29 June 1906 (32 Stat. 596 sec. 3) provided the first uniform rule for the naturalization of aliens throughout the United States.

After September 1906, courts were ordered to use standard naturalization forms prescribed by the Bureau of Immigration and Naturalization. The new forms included a declaration of intention to become a citizen, a petition for naturalization, and a certificate of naturalization. The new citizenship papers were expanded to include each applicant's age, occupation, personal description, date and place of birth, citizenship, present and last foreign addresses, ports of embarkation and entry, name of vessel or other means of conveyance, and date of arrival in the United States; also required were spouse's and children's full names with their respective dates and places of birth, and residence at the date of the document.

After 1906, duplicate copies of declarations and petitions were forwarded to the Bureau of Naturalization in Washington, D.C. A third copy of the declaration was given to the declarant. The naturalizing court issued original certificates of naturalization to new citizens and forwarded duplicate certificates to the Immigration and Naturalization Service in Washington, D.C. By law, the naturalizing courts had to number and file original declarations, petitions, and naturalization certificate stubs or the equivalent of a naturalization certificate stub.

A SENSE OF HISTORY AND IMMIGRATION ROUTES

A sense of history is important to successful research in immigration records. Group migration patterns frequently provide invaluable clues. Because the greatest number of European immigrants entered the United States through eastern port cities, most searches (at

TRIPLICATE

No. 78582

UNITED STATES OF AMERICA

DECLARATION OF INTENTION

(Invalid for all purposes seven years after the date hereof)

United States of America |
Northern District Of Illinois | ss:

In the _____ District _____ Court
of _____ the United States at Chicago, Ill.

I, THORWALD DOSSING
now residing at 5160 Montorse Avenue,
(Number and street) (City or town) (County) (State)
occupation Laborer, aged 32 years, do declare on oath that my personal description is:
Sex Male, color white, complexion fair, color of eyes blue
color of hair blonde, height 5 feet 11 inches; weight 135 pounds; visible distinctive marks
one
race Scandanavian; nationality Danish
I was born in Serup, Denmark on November 15, 1897
(City or town) (Country) (Month) (Day) (Year)
I am not married. The name of my wife or husband is _____
we were married on _____, at _____; she or he was
(Month) (Day) (Year) (City or town) (State or country)
born at _____, on _____, entered the United States
(City or town) (State or country) (Month) (Day) (Year)
at _____ on _____, for permanent residence therein, and now
(City or town) (State) (Month) (Day) (Year)
resides at _____ I have no children, and the name, date and place of birth,
(City or town) (State or country)
and place of residence of each of said children are as follows: _____

I have not heretofore made a declaration of intention: Number _____, on _____
(Date)
at _____
(City or town) (State) (Name of court)
my last foreign residence was Winnipeg, Canada
I emigrated to the United States of America from Winnpeg, Candad
(City or town) (Country)
my lawful entry for permanent residence in the United States was at Noyes, Minnesota
(City or town) (State)
under the name of Thorvald N. Dossing on April 22, 1927
(Month) (Day) (Year)
on the vessel XXXX C. N. RR.
(If other than by vessel, state manner of arrival)

I will, before being admitted to citizenship, renounce forever all allegiance and fidelity to any foreign prince, potentate, state, or sovereignty, and particularly, by name, to the prince, potentate, state, or sovereignty of which I may be at the time of admission a citizen or subject; I am not an anarchist; I am not a polygamist nor a believer in the practice of polygamy; and it is my intention in good faith to become a citizen of the United States of America and to reside permanently therein; and I certify that the photograph affixed to the duplicate and triplicate hereof is a likeness of me: So HELP ME GOD.

Thorwald N. Dossing.
(Original signature of declarant without abbreviation, also alias, if used)

Subscribed and sworn to before me in the office of the Clerk of said Court, at Chicago, Illinois this 9th day of June anno Domini 19 30 Certification No. 11-22477 from the Commissioner of Naturalization showing the lawful entry of the declarant for permanent residence on the date stated above, has been received by me. The photograph affixed to the duplicate and triplicate hereof is a likeness of the declarant.

CHARLES M. BATES,

_____
Clerk of the U. S. DISTRICT Court.

By _____, Deputy Clerk.

14—2623 U. S. GOVERNMENT PRINTING OFFICE 1947

[SEAL]

Form 2202–L–A.
U. S. DEPARTMENT OF LABOR
NATURALIZATION SERVICE

Figure 1-18. Declaration of intention of Thorwald N. Dossing.

(9) My lawful admission for permanent residence in the United States was at ...Sault Ste. Marie, Mich............... under the nam __Samuel Ichiye Hayakawa_____ on _____March 5, 1937_____ on the _____Foot via ice____

(10) Since my lawful admission for permanent residence I have not been absent from the United States, for a period or periods of 6 months or longer, except as foll

DEPARTED FROM THE UNITED STATES			RETURNED TO THE UNITED STATES		
PORT	DATE (Month, day, year)	VESSEL OR OTHER MEANS OF CONVEYANCE	PORT	DATE (Month, day, year)	VESSEL OR OTHER ME. OF CONVEYANCE

(11) It is my intention in good faith to become a citizen of the United States and to renounce absolutely and entirely all allegiance and fidelity to any foreign p potentate, state, or sovereignty of whom or which at this time I am a subject or citizen. (12) It is my intention to reside permanently in the United States. (am not and have not been for a period of at least 10 years immediately preceding the date of this petition a member of or affiliated with any organization prosc by the Immigration and Nationality Act or any section, subsidiary, branch affiliate or subdivision thereof nor have I during such period engaged in or performe of the acts or activities prohibited by that act. (14) I am able to read, write and speak the English language (unless exempted therefrom). (15) I am, and been during all the periods required by law, a person of good moral character, attached to the principles of the Constitution of the United States and well dis to the good order and happiness of the United States. I am willing, if required by law, to bear arms on behalf of the United States, or to perform noncom service in the Armed Forces of the United States, or to perform work of national importance under civilian direction (unless exempted therefrom). (16) I resided continuously in the United States of America for the term of 5 years at least immediately preceding the date of this petition, to wit, since __March 5, 1937__ and continuously in the State in which this petition is made for the term of 6 months at least immediately preceding the date of this pe to wit, since ____September 1939____; and during the past 5 years I have been physically present in the United States for at least or of that period. (17) I have ____not____ heretofore made petition for naturalization: No. _____ on _____ at _____ in the _____ Court, and such petitio denied by that Court for the following reasons and causes, to wit: _____

(18) Attached hereto and made a part of this, my petition for naturalization, are the affidavits of at least two verifying witnesses required by law.

(19) Wherefore I, your petitioner for naturalization, pray that I may be admitted a citizen of the United States of America, and that my name be chan _____NONE_____ I, aforesaid petitioner, do swear (affirm) that I know t tents of this petition for naturalization subscribed by me, and that the same are true to the best of my knowledge and belief, and that this petition is signed by n my full, true name: SO HELP ME GOD.

ALIEN REGISTRATION NO. A-1 389 775

Samuel Ichiye Hayakawa

Figure 1-19. Portion of the late Senator Samuel Hayakawa's petition for naturalization.

least for the first naturalization papers) begin in or around a port of entry. Because ship passenger fares to Canada were sometimes half the price of those to the United States, Europeans often found the northern route to be the only one they could afford. A surprisingly large number of European emigrants went to Canada and stayed—sometimes for a generation or more—before immigrating into the United States. Thorwald Dossing, like so many others who came through Canada, states in his declaration of intention that he entered the United States on a train; consequently, he will not be found on a passenger list for a U.S. port of entry (figure 1-18). A portion of the late Senator Samuel Ichiya Hayakawa's petition for naturalization shows that he lawfully entered the United

States at Sault Ste. Marie, Mich. on foot, "via ice," on 5 March 1937 (figure 1-19).

The declaration of intention and petition for naturalization for Joe Polich (figures 1-20 and 1-21) are typical of forms used after 1906. Even at first glance, naturalization papers tend to reveal a great deal about an individual.

While the post-1906 documents generally contain much biographical data, as with any other source of information, there may be inaccuracies and inconsistencies. Consider the documents shown here for Joe Polich. In Joe's declaration of intention, signed 24 May 1915, he claimed to have been born on the "1st day of April, anno Domini 1894" in Hieljin, Austria, but his petition for naturalization, dated 1 June 1922, shows

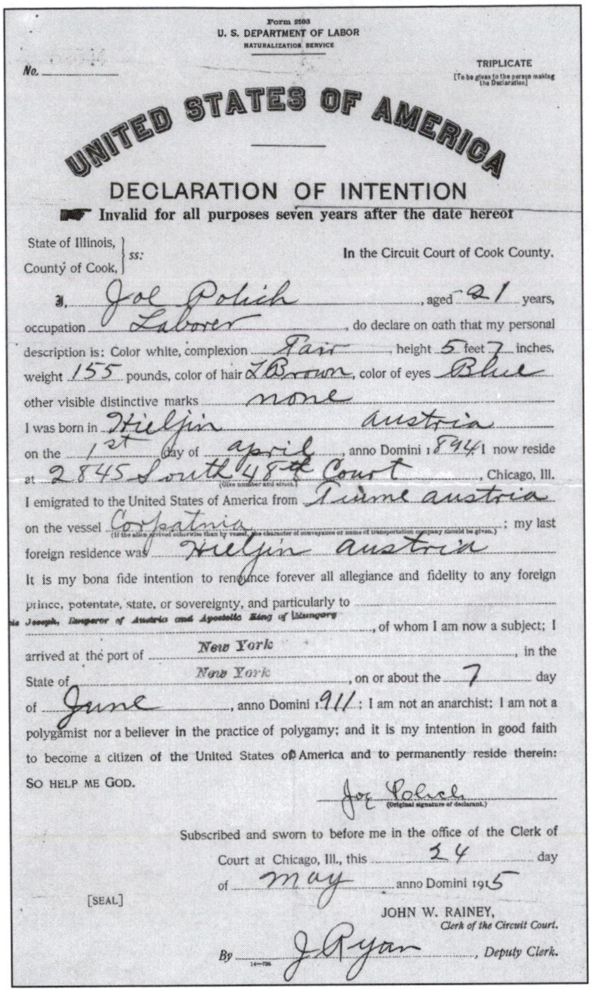

Figure 1-20. Declaration of intention of Joe Polich.

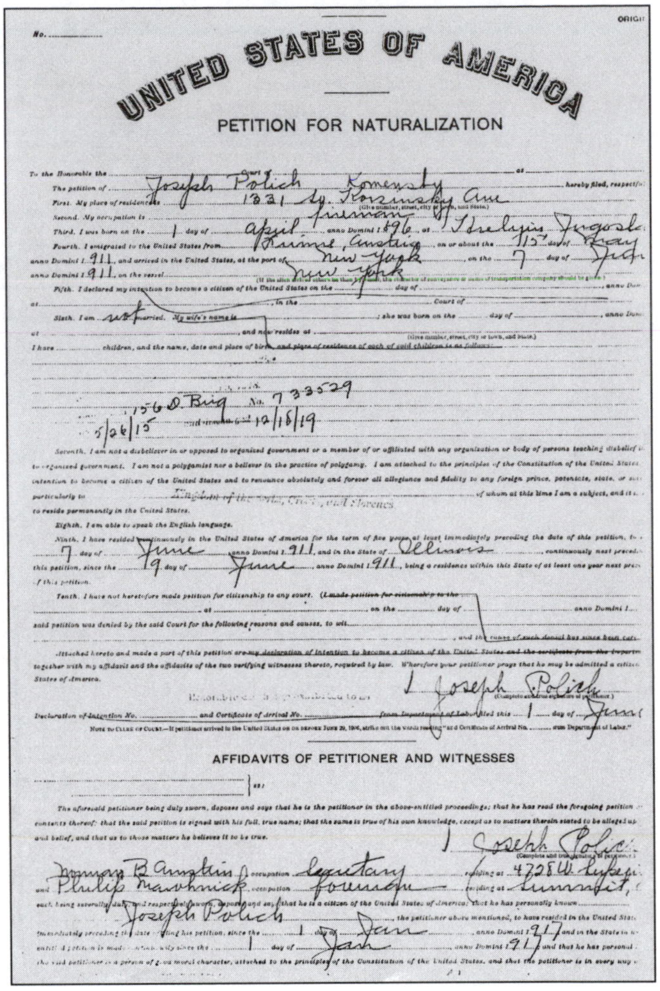

Figure 1-21. Petition for naturalization of Joe Polich.

his birth date as 1 April 1896 at Hrelyus, Jugoslavia. We can imagine that boundary changes resulting from World War I might account for the different birthplace, but what would account for the discrepancy in the year of birth? Was it a slip of memory over the years? (In earlier times and in different cultures, people tended to be less conscious of birth dates than we are today.) Is it a clerical error? Is it possible that Joe Polich wanted to appear a little older when he first applied so that he could get on with the naturalization process? Most citizenship papers present consistent information that will solve mysteries; others, like these, create new mysteries. While the stamp on Joe's petition is so light that it is impossible to read it all, the words "enlisted in 156 D Brig on 5/26/15,

and discharged 12/18/19" open up an entirely new area of potential research in military records.

MILITARY SERVICE

Aliens who served in the U.S. military and received honorable discharge were given special consideration. An act of 17 July 1862 (12 Stat. 597) stated that:

Any alien, of the age of twenty-one years and upwards, who has enlisted, or may enlist in the armies of the United States, either the regular or the volunteer forces, and has been, or may be hereafter, honorably discharged, shall be admitted to become a citizen of the United States, upon his petition, without any previous declaration of intention to become such; and he shall not be required to prove more than one year's residence.

Designed to encourage aliens to enlist during the Civil War, this legislation applied to later wars as well. Many individuals have misunderstood this law and reported it to mean that those serving in the military gained automatic citizenship. It should be emphasized that this was not the case; with the length of residency shortened and the declaration of intention waived, the process of naturalization was expedited. Instead of naturalization "first papers," some courts may have filed military discharges for some individuals. Frequently, military papers were filed independently, making it necessary to consult a separate military index. Military naturalization records were, however, included in the Work Projects Administration (WPA)-created indexes described later. It should be noted that, when the WPA indexes were microfilmed, the reverse sides of normally blank index cards were sometimes missed. An index card for William C. Wilson (figure 1-22) illustrates the importance of a thorough search.

An act of 26 July 1894 (28 Stat. 124) extended naturalization privileges to those who had "served five consecutive years in the United States Navy or one enlistment in the United States Marine Corps" so long as they had received an "honorable discharge."

Another modification regarding the naturalization of soldiers, sailors, and veterans came about because of World War I. An act of 9 May 1918 (40 Stat. 542) consolidated military naturalization laws and stated that: "Any alien serving in the military or naval service of the United States during the time this country is engaged in the present war may file his petition for naturalization without making the preliminary declaration of intention and without proof of the required five years residence within the United States." The act provided for immediate naturalization of alien soldiers, waiving the required declaration of intention or first papers, the certificate of arrival, and proof of residence entirely. Members of the armed forces were naturalized at military posts and nearby courts instead of at their legal residences.

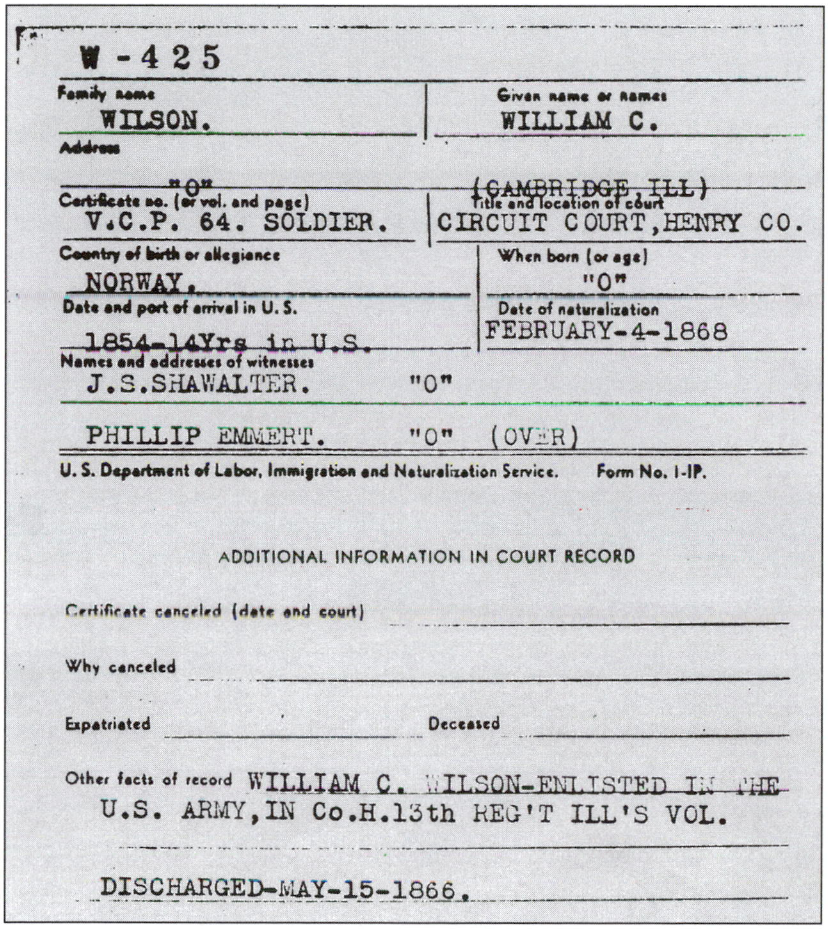
W-425

Family name: WILSON.
Given name or names: WILLIAM C.
Address: "O" (CAMBRIDGE, ILL)
Certificate no. (or vol. and page): V.C.P. 64. SOLDIER.
Title and location of court: CIRCUIT COURT, HENRY CO.
Country of birth or allegiance: NORWAY.
When born (or age): "O"
Date and port of arrival in U. S.: 1854-14Yrs in U.S.
Date of naturalization: FEBRUARY-4-1868
Names and addresses of witnesses: J.S.SHAWALTER. "O"
PHILLIP EMMERT. "O" (OVER)

U. S. Department of Labor, Immigration and Naturalization Service. Form No. 1-IP.

ADDITIONAL INFORMATION IN COURT RECORD

Certificate canceled (date and court)
Why canceled
Expatriated
Deceased
Other facts of record: WILLIAM C. WILSON-ENLISTED IN THE U.S. ARMY, IN Co.H.13th REG'T ILL'S VOL.
DISCHARGED-MAY-15-1866.

Figure 1-22. Naturalization index card for William C. Wilson. (The original card is at the National Archives—Great Lakes Region, Chicago.)

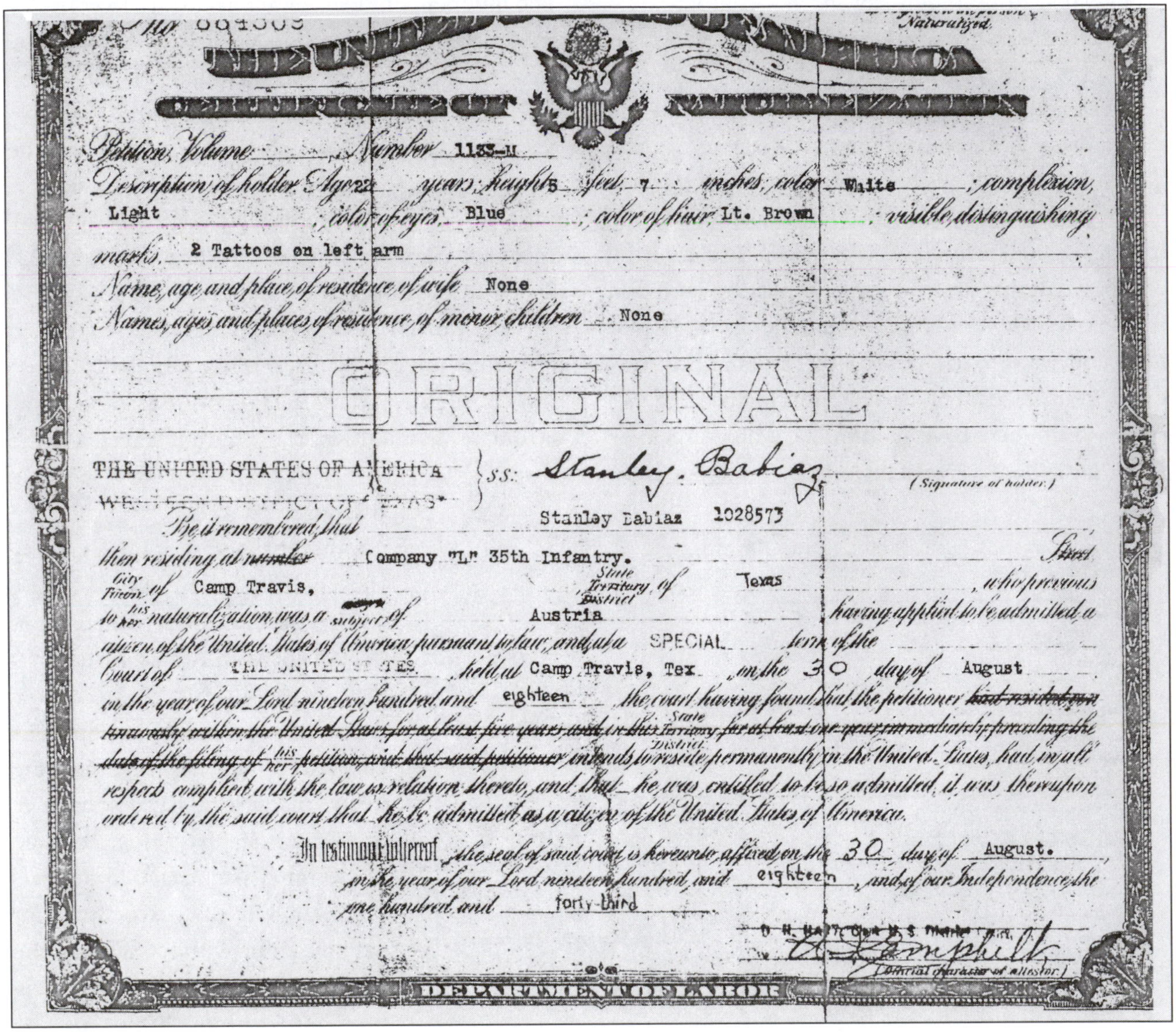

Naturalized

CERTIFICATE OF NATURALIZATION

Petition, Volume ______ Number 1133-M

Description of holder: Age 22 years; height 5 feet, 7 inches; color White; complexion, Light; color of eyes, Blue; color of hair, Lt. Brown; visible distinguishing marks, 2 Tattoos on left arm

Name, age, and place of residence of wife None

Names, ages, and places of residence of minor children None

ORIGINAL

THE UNITED STATES OF AMERICA } ss. Stanley Babiaz (Signature of holder.)

~~WESTERN DISTRICT OF TEXAS~~

Be it remembered, that Stanley Babiaz 1028573

then residing at ~~number~~ Company "L" 35th Infantry. ~~Street~~

City/Town of Camp Travis, State/Territory/District of Texas, who previous to his naturalization was a subject of Austria having applied to be admitted a citizen of the United States of America pursuant to law, and at a SPECIAL term of the Court of THE UNITED STATES held at Camp Travis, Tex. on the 30 day of August in the year of our Lord nineteen hundred and eighteen the court having found that the petitioner ~~had resided continuously within the United States for at least five years, and in this State/Territory/District for at least one year immediately preceding the date of the filing of his petition, and that said petitioner~~ intends to reside permanently in the United States, had in all respects complied with the law in relation thereto, and that he was entitled to be so admitted, it was thereupon ordered by the said court that he be admitted as a citizen of the United States of America.

In testimony whereof the seal of said court is hereunto affixed on the 30 day of August. in the year of our Lord nineteen hundred and eighteen, and of our Independence the one hundred and forty third

(Official character of attestor.)

DEPARTMENT OF LABOR

Figure 1-23. Certificate of naturalization of Stanley Babiaz, who served in Company L, Thirty-fifth Infantry. A search for his naturalization records in his hometown was unsuccessful because he was naturalized in Texas, where he was stationed in the Army in 1918.

African Americans and Native Americans

A law approved on 14 July 1870 opened the naturalization process to persons of African nativity or descent (16 Stat. 256). In the early years, American Indians were admitted to citizenship through treaty provisions and under special statutes. Before 1924, the most important law relating to Indian citizenship was the Allotment Act of 8 February 1887 (24 Stat. 387). This statute conferred citizenship on (1) every Indian born in the United States to whom allotments were made by this act or any law or treaty and (2) every Indian born in the United States who had voluntarily taken up within its limits a residence that was "separate and apart from any tribe of Indians" and had "adopted the habits of civilized life." By an act of 9 August 1888, every Native American woman who was a member of a tribe and married to a U.S. citizen was declared to be a citizen (25 Stat. 392). An act of 2 June 1924 provided that all Indians born in the United States were to be citizens (43 Stat. 253).

"The INS and the Singular Status of North American Indians," by Marian L. Smith, in *American Indian Culture and Research Journal* 21 (1): 135–54 (1997), is an in-depth study of the question of Indian citizenship.

THE GREAT DEPRESSION

The number of aliens going to court to become American citizens has fluctuated over time. Various historical events have driven the numbers upward or downward. For example, "naturalizations increased during the Great Depression. Immigrants mainly had economic reason to naturalize in these years, as citizens were hired first in a country where jobs were

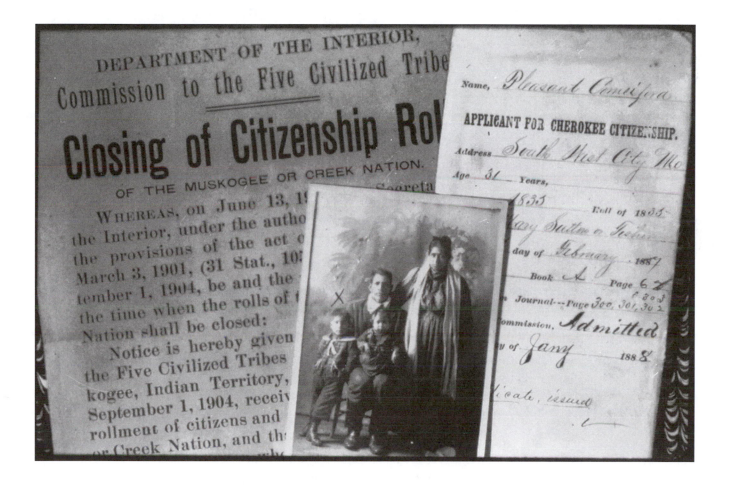

Figure 1-24. Closing of citizenship rolls. Not to be confused with American citizenship papers are citizenship rolls of the Five Civilized Tribes, among the papers of the Bureau of Indian Affairs (now in the regional system of the National Archives).

John Menkalski.

Julia Cukras Menkalski.

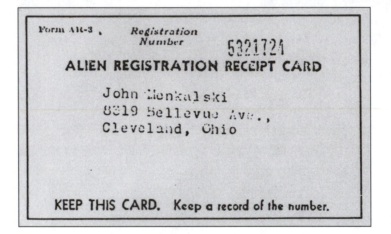

Figure 1-25. John Menkalski's alien registration card.

scarce. Also benefits from many social programs created by the New Deal went only to citizens."[11]

WORLD WAR II AND ALIEN REGISTRATION

Since 1845 there have been many attempts to create or require a record of aliens within the United States. A 1906 law mandated the beginning of such a registry. But not until the Alien Registration Act of 1940 was passed as a war measure did a registry formally come into existence. The new law caused incoming immigrants and all aliens in the United States to be fingerprinted and to register annually with the INS.

As John Newman notes, "Many aliens lived their lives as positive contributors to their community and new nation without formally acquiring citizenship."[12] John Menkalski was just one of millions of aliens who, for one reason or another, were never formally naturalized. His alien registration card is shown in figure 1-25. His wife, Julia Cukras Menkalski, died in 1911—before married women could be naturalized in their own right.

NOTES

1. Green, Linda R. "Citizenship and Naturalization in Colonial America." *Illinois State Genealogical Society Quarterly* 24 (3): 152-58 (Fall 1992).

2. Franklin, Frank George. *The Legislative History of Naturalization in the United States*. New York: Arno Press and the New York Times, 1969, 2.

3. Ibid., 5.

4. Ibid.

5. Jones, Maldwyn Allen. *American Immigration*. Chicago: University of Chicago Press, 1960, 82.

6. Divine, Robert A., et al. *America Past and Present*. Glenview, Ill.: Scott, Foresman and Co., 1984, 202.

7. U.S. Department of Justice, Department of Immigration and Naturalization Service. *An Immigrant Nation: United States Regulation of Immigration, 1798-1991*. Washington, D.C., 1981, 4.

8. Ernst, Robert. *Immigrant Life in New York City 1825-1863*. Syracuse, N.Y.: Syracuse University Press, 1994, 162.

9. Jones, 154.

10. Cetina, Judith G. "A Study of American Naturalization Laws Affecting Women." *Journal of the Cuyahoga County Archives* 1 (1981): 11.

11. U.S. Department of Justice, 12.

12. John J. Newman. *American Naturalization Processes and Procedures 1790-1985*. Indianapolis: Indiana Historical Society, 1985, 1.

BIBLIOGRAPHY

Cetina, Judith G. "A Study of American Naturalization Laws Affecting Women." *Journal of the Cuyahoga County Archives* 1 (1981): 11-23.

Hone, E. Wade, with Heritage Consulting and Services. *Land and Property Research in the United States*. Salt Lake City: Ancestry, 1997.

Hutchinson, E. P. Legislative *History of American Immigration Policy 1798-1965*. Philadelphia: University of Pennsylvania Press, 1981-.

Strassburger, Ralph B., and William John Hinke. *Pennsylvania German Pioneers: A Publication of Original Lists of Arrivals in the Port of Philadelphia from 1727 to 1808*. 3 vols. Norristown: Pennsylvania German Society, 1934.

Home sources, such as photographs, often divulge clues to family members, relationships, and ethnic origins. Shown is the family of Aloysius and Amelia Maday.

Chapter Two Highlights

- *Home sources*
- *When there are no home sources*
- *Finding long-lost cousins*
- *Outside sources*
- *Census records*
- *City directories*
- *Vital records: births, marriages, deaths*
- *Cemetery records*
- *Ecclesiastical records*
- *Local histories*
- *Ethnic histories*
- *Newspapers*
- *Obituaries*

- *Military records*
- *Social Security records*
- *Homestead records*
- *Voter registration records*
- *Passports*
- *Naturalization and other court records*
- *Passenger lists*
- *Genealogical and historical organizations*
- *Periodical Source Index (PERSI)*
- *Archives*
- *Libraries*
- *The Family History Library*
- *Research approaches*

How to Find Immigration and Naturalization Information

MILLIONS OF IMMIGRANTS FROM ALL OVER THE WORLD have brought unique customs and great diversity to the United States. Immigrants' experiences were not isolated. Groups were forced to leave by religious oppression, famine, agricultural and industrial revolution, the threat of conscription, and war. Other groups were lured by the American dream—the idea of commoners being able to own their own land. Certain principles of research may be applied to almost any country, but there comes a time in every investigation when the specific history and customs of the place from which an ancestor emigrated need to be understood to some degree.

From the documented and well-studied experiences and patterns of national groups, we can begin to understand the motives and individual histories of our own ancestors as they molded their destinies by leaving behind all that they had known. With an understanding of the customs and rules of the times in which our ancestors traveled, we can know what kinds of records may have been created. Some of these record sources are unique to particular groups and might be the sole means of discovering the specific origins of certain ancestors. However, any search for documents pertaining to our ancestors should begin in our own homes.

HOME SOURCES

When was the last time you searched through old family papers, scrapbooks, photo albums, a family Bible, or that old box in the attic or basement that hasn't been opened in years? The best place to begin searching for a family member's citizenship papers is in your own home. Set aside some time to pore over any documents that may give clues about all the places where and when your family lived. Knowing where an immigrant lived is a key to discovering the whereabouts of his or her naturalization documents.

The certificate of naturalization for Fabian Holler (figure 2-1) tells us that he was living at 4168 Helen Street in Detroit when he was naturalized in 1924. While the certificate provides a generous amount of biographical detail, even more information about Fabian Holler could be discovered by researching the rest of his file, which should be in the records of the United States District Court, Eastern District of Michigan, Southern Division, at Detroit (now preserved at the National Archives–Great Lakes Region in Chicago).

Surprising clues may survive in the form of family stories and in letters, diaries, journals, religious

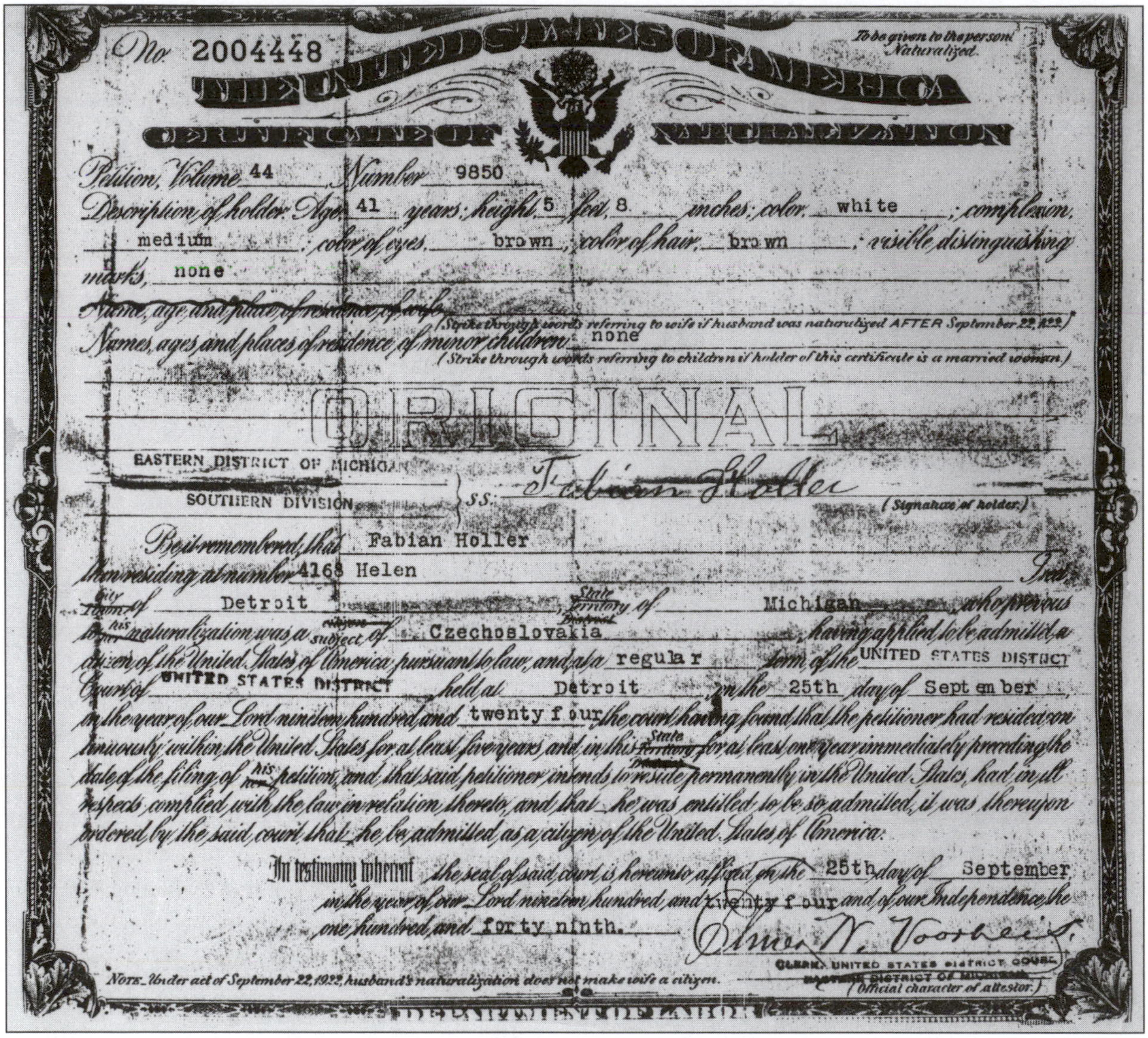

No 2004448

To be given to the person Naturalized.

THE UNITED STATES OF AMERICA

CERTIFICATE OF NATURALIZATION

Petition, Volume 44 Number 9850

Description of holder: Age 41 years; height 5 feet, 8 inches; color white; complexion medium; color of eyes brown; color of hair brown; visible distinguishing marks none

~~Name, age and place of residence of wife~~

(Strike through words referring to wife if husband was naturalized AFTER September 22, 1922.)

Names, ages and places of residence of minor children none

(Strike through words referring to children if holder of this certificate is a married woman.)

ORIGINAL

EASTERN DISTRICT OF MICHIGAN
SOUTHERN DIVISION } ss: Fabian Holler

(Signature of holder.)

Be it remembered, that Fabian Holler then residing at number 4168 Helen Street, City of Detroit, State of Michigan, who previous to his naturalization was a subject of Czechoslovakia, having applied to be admitted a citizen of the United States of America pursuant to law, and at a regular term of the UNITED STATES DISTRICT Court of UNITED STATES DISTRICT held at Detroit on the 25th day of September in the year of our Lord nineteen hundred and twenty four, the court having found that the petitioner had resided continuously within the United States for at least five years and in this State for at least one year immediately preceding the date of the filing of his petition, and that said petitioner intends to reside permanently in the United States, had in all respects complied with the law in relation thereto, and that he was entitled to be so admitted, it was thereupon ordered by the said court that he be admitted as a citizen of the United States of America.

In testimony whereof the seal of said court is hereunto affixed on the 25th day of September in the year of our Lord nineteen hundred and twenty four and of our Independence the one hundred and forty ninth.

Elmer W. Voorheis

CLERK, UNITED STATES DISTRICT COURT, EASTERN DISTRICT OF MICHIGAN

(Official character of attestor.)

Note. Under act of September 22, 1922, husband's naturalization does not make wife a citizen.

Figure 2-1. Certificate of naturalization for Fabian Holler of Detroit. He was naturalized in 1924.

records, postcards, photographs, scrapbooks, and mementos that have been saved over the years. One researcher, for example, was able to discover the area in Germany from which her family had emigrated because of a photograph in which her grandmother appeared in a lace cap. As she learned from reading about the country, that particular lace was a distinctive part of the costume worn in a specific region of Germany. An African American was able to determine the tribe from which his family had come through oral tradition and the distinctive pattern in a cloth that had been handed down in the family. A watchmaker's descendant learned the town of the family's origin when she investigated the origin of the timepiece she had inherited. Songs, dances, food, recipes, costumes, memorabilia, and other distinctive items can provide important clues for finding ethnic origins.

While family traditions tend to become exaggerated—especially those regarding an immigrant's importance in the old country—they usually contain usable facts that will serve to begin research. However, these clues may be meaningless unless you have an understanding of the customs, geography, and history of the ethnic group. Linked with a basic knowledge of the immigrant's homeland—including the leading industry of the native district, common occupations, names of nearby towns, rivers, mountains, and other features of the area—a family story, tradition, or heirloom can provide the breakthrough that will identify an immigrant's exact origins.

Even if you find no naturalization documents or other clues to origins, a search through the attic may bring something better still. A few years ago, a friend found a forgotten tin box in a closet in the house where her father had once lived. Among the items in the box was this insightful letter written by her father, Jeremiah Curtin, as he came across the ocean on a ship from Ireland in 1924.

Dear Mother,

Just a few lines to let you know that I am getting through just fine. I know that you long to get a letter. Well Mother, please do not be troubled. I got through the inspection just fine. I did not go through the baths. I got a letter of recommendation from Murphy himself, and another lad by the name of Sweeney. Jeremiah Sweeney's first cousin, he is. I came out better than him himself. Poor fellow had to go through the baths and they gave him trouble at every turn. But keep it dark because he is a very nice fellow. I think I am at home here on the ship for a while. We are having a swell time. But I saw the fires on the hill. I could not go down until we went out of sight. I felt very lonesome as I was passing the cape. Most everyone was sick on Sunday. The weather was very bad for two days. This is Thursday. It is a fine day. We are having great sport. We were dancing last night until 1 o'clock. We had another examination yesterday and we will have still another before we can go ashore. I got through fine, Mother. There are some of the boys and girls who must go through the baths on board the ship. Well, Mother, it's a fine thing to be clean! But you did cut the

money a little short for me. I was charged 14 shillings at Murphy's boarding house. But Murphy did a good turn for me with the letter, you know. They say you must show your landing money, and if I am asked to show my 5 pounds, I don't know what I will do because I'm far from it. Well, I know you did not have it or you would have seen me through. And I won't forget you. It's about time for me to help you now. Mother, don't be lonesome and tell father not to be lonesome because I will be home after 7 years. Tell father that I won't forget him. It was very hard to see him crying. Well, Mother, I will write again when I land. So I must now finish.

From your fond son, Jeremiah

Jeremiah had to squeeze his thoughts onto both sides of a single sheet of paper. In order to get all he had to say into such a small space, he wrote around the edges and even used the space he had left open for the greeting. The letter speaks well for itself, but there are a few things unsaid that we must understand to fully appreciate Jeremiah's experience. The "examination" he refers to was one of the humiliating examinations steerage passengers had to endure for the sake of the health and welfare of all the passengers. Many immigrants left home in a perfectly clean state, only to be infected in the boarding houses where they stayed before sailing. If lice or infections were found by inspectors, special medicated baths were ordered, to the great shame of the afflicted. Jeremiah also mentions the "fires on the hill." When ships left Queenstown in County Cork, the last part of Ireland to be seen was Clear Island. Customarily, when an Islander emigrated, bonfires were lit on all the hills as a sign of farewell.

WHEN THERE ARE NO HOME SOURCES

If your own home is devoid of any kind of handed-down information or memorabilia, as mine was

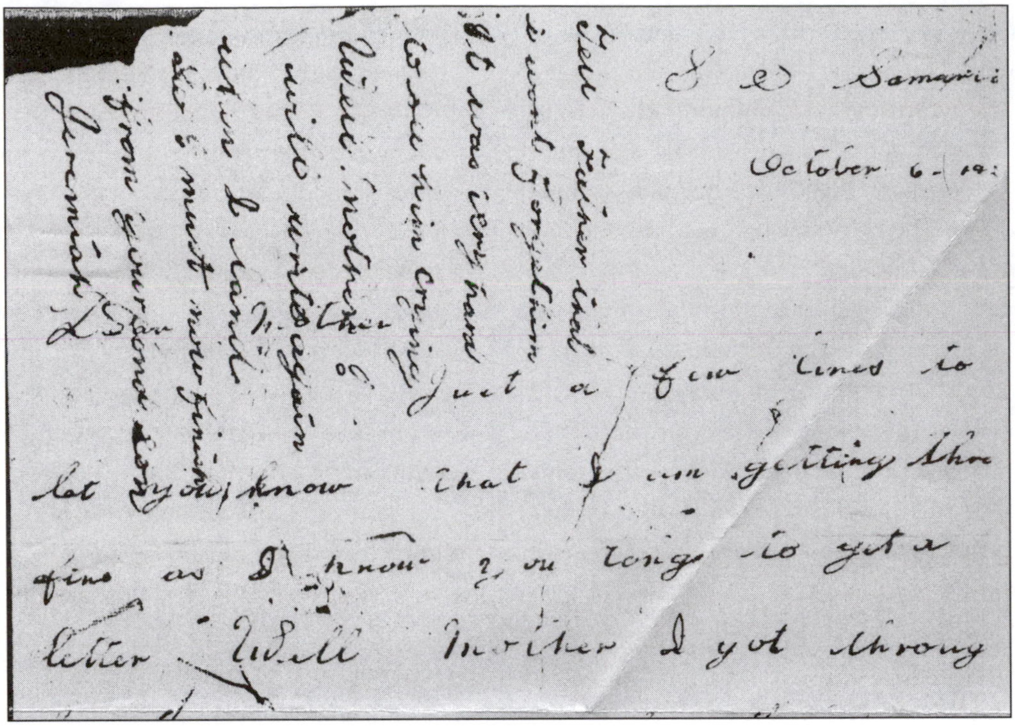

Figure 2-2. A portion of Jeremiah Curtin's letter. (Letter reproduced courtesy of Gerry Curtin Ganley.)

when I began investigating my family history, it's time to call relatives who might be able to tell you all you need to know about the family. Older relatives are likely to remember some of the things you will need to begin your search. If you don't already know, ask for grandparents' or great-grandparents' names, about when they were born and grew up, when and where they were married, who their children were, occupations, religious affiliation, and what their foreign origins were—the exact names of the towns from which they emigrated, if possible. Gather as much information from home and those around you as you can.

For most of us, however, the search for citizenship papers will involve a lot more work than searching at home. You may not have inherited all the family information and will have to carry out your search in distant places. *Naturalization records are notoriously hard to find*, mainly because old records are generally moved from the courts that originally issued them. But, by using your

best detective skills and following a logical progression, the hunt for naturalization papers can be quite fruitful and extremely interesting.

FINDING LONG-LOST COUSINS

An experience in my family illustrates the benefits of finding unknown or unfamiliar cousins. The name of the town in Poland which my mother-in-law's father had left more than ninety years ago was somehow forgotten over time. Shortly before she died, my American-born mother-in-law got in touch with a long-lost cousin (who is now, unfortunately, lost to the family again). The cousin had shared some funeral photographs with her that my husband, in turn, inherited. The inscriptions on the backs of the photographs (figures 2-3 and 2-4) could be the key to tracking the family origins in Poland.

If you do not know your ancestor's family origins and have not come up with naturalization certificates or solid clues to their whereabouts in your

Figure 2-3. The casket of Josephine Borucki, 23 June 1948.

Figure 2-4. Family by the casket of Josephine Borucki, 23 June 1948, at the cemetery in Wyszkowce, Poland.

own home, what are the chances that some close or distant cousin might have the information or documents? Someone else in the family might have naturalization certificates which they would allow you to copy—but only if you make your interest known. The way families are scattered all over the world these days, it may be that you, like so many others, have lost touch with (or never knew) the person who holds such family treasures, including naturalization papers. If an individual was naturalized, the certificate would probably have been highly prized. If any family document was likely to have been kept from one generation to the next, it will be that cherished proof of U.S. citizenship.

If you have lost contact with someone in the family who is likely to have a naturalization record, there are effective means for finding them. The most necessary pieces of information are the name of the relative who may be in possession of the papers and where that person lives. By using an online (Internet) directory search, such as Switchboard (http://www.Switchboard.com), you can look up anyone with a listed telephone number in the United States. If you don't have Internet capability, most public libraries have telephone directories on CD-ROM and will assist you in conducting a directory search online. More fascinating potential for the Internet is discussed in chapter 7.

Directories have research potential that stretches far beyond naturalization searches. For example, I had wanted to find my deceased cousin's sons for twenty years. Because she and her family lived on the East Coast, far from where I grew up in Texas, I lost all contact with her children when she died at a young age. I didn't know her sons' names and wasn't sure where they lived. However, I had inherited a wonderful collection of letters that my uncle (my cousin's father) had written to my mother when he was serving in France during World War I. He died after the war as a result of wounds received in the war, and I thought these grandsons would probably love to have these letters from a grandfather they had never known. I learned my cousin's married name from an aunt who passed away shortly after I became interested in my family's history. I could only hope that her children had remained in New Jersey, where she lived just before her death, or in New York, where most of our family had lived for generations.

I was able to get a telephone listing for the surname for the two states from Switchboard's site on the World Wide Web. The timing was just right, and it seemed like one of those things that was meant to be: the first person I called gave me the information I needed. My cousin's husband had recently died; however, his widow (his second wife) was able to put me in touch with my cousin's children. My

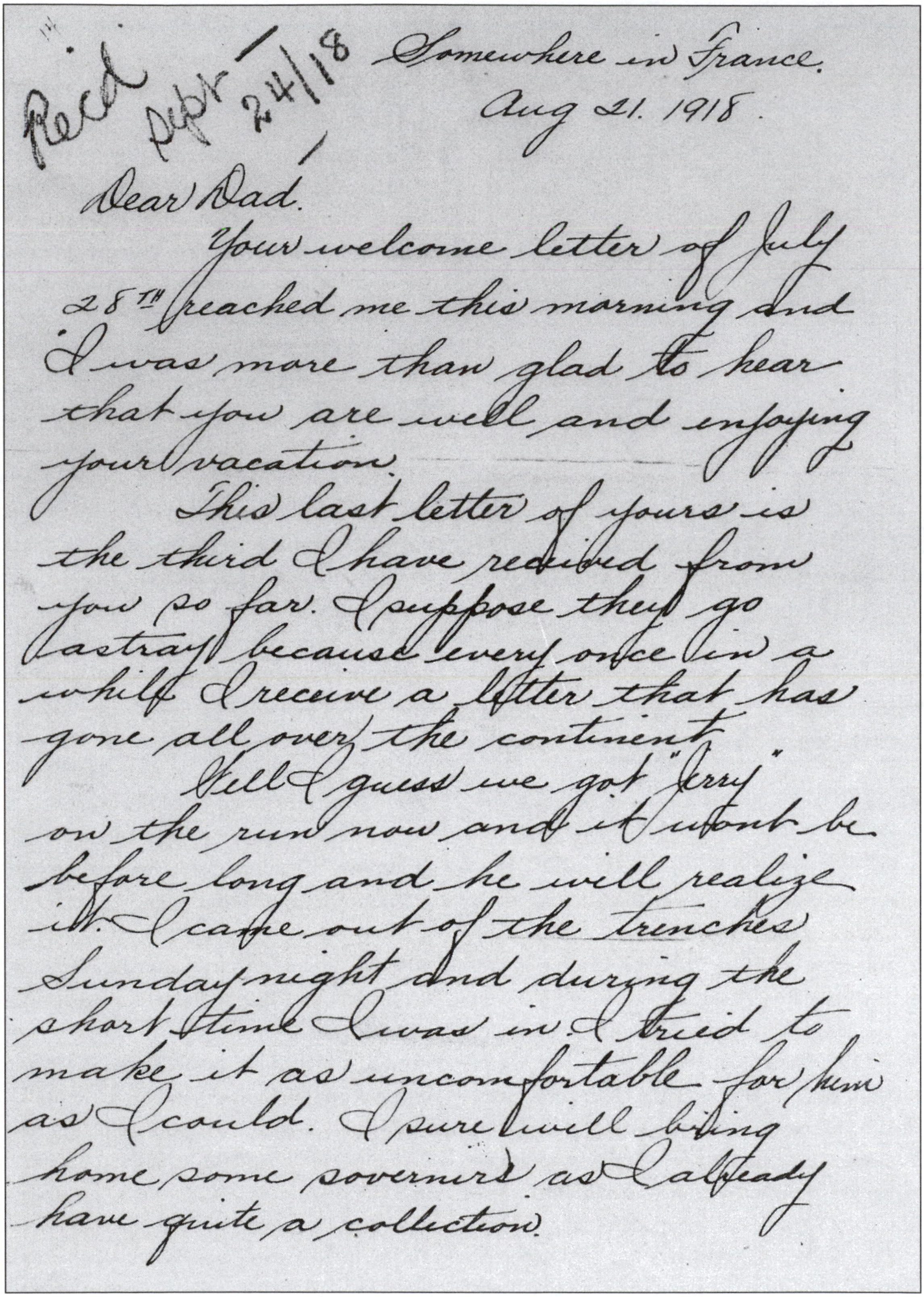

Recd
Sept
24/18

Somewhere in France.
Aug 21. 1918.

Dear Dad.

Your welcome letter of July 28th reached me this morning and I was more than glad to hear that you are well and enjoying your vacation.

This last letter of yours is the third I have received from you so far. I suppose they go astray because every once in a while I receive a letter that has gone all over the continent.

Well I guess we got "Jerry" on the run now and it wont be before long and he will realize it. I came out of the trenches Sunday night and during the short time I was in I tried to make it as uncomfortable for him as I could. I sure will bring home some sovenirs as I already have quite a collection.

Figure 2-5. Letter sent by Edwin Dyer from France.

cousin's son—the one whose name I had just received ten minutes before—called me. He said he had been thinking that he would like to know more about his family and now was absolutely stunned to learn that he had family on his mother's side. He told me it was as though "ghosts had been swirling" around since his father's death just a month before. He had always thought his mother's father was an only child, as his mother was, because he had never heard about her far-away relatives.

A few weeks after speaking with my cousin over the telephone, I was unexpectedly sent to New York on a business trip. It was sheer pleasure to see my cousin's joy as I handed over those eighty-year-old letters. He thanked me by saying, "you have given me a grandfather. Where before I had nothing but one grainy photograph, a steel box with his initials engraved, and my imagination, I will now have his words, second only to our acts of love and kindness in what we can leave the world." Now he is intensely interested in the family's history, and I am thrilled to have found this new cousin. Meeting this young man and giving him those pieces of his past would probably never have happened were it not for the fact that, through the Internet, I was able to quickly and easily find the needed telephone number.

Explore your own family tree. Maybe one of *your* long-lost cousins has citizenship documentation, or other clues that will lead you to naturalization papers and to the family stories, records, and photographs you'd love to see.

OUTSIDE SOURCES

Once you have explored all the family sources, hopefully you will have found names, dates, and places to begin the search for your family's origins. Where you continue your search for naturalization papers will depend on how much you have already learned about the individual you are researching. If you have in hand the certificate conferred by the court on the day the naturalization took place, for example, your search for further documentation may not be difficult at all; simply note the name of the court that awarded citizenship, then contact that court or the archive where records are stored for that particular court.

There are many wonderful and fascinating avenues to be explored in the process of your search. Information found in libraries and archives, federal and state census records, old city directories, cemetery records, vital records, court records, newspapers, religious records, land records, military records, Social Security records, ship passenger lists, genealogical society files, occupational records, and in some less-than-obvious places may come together to form a unique family portrait. Any or all of these sources combined may lead to the citizenship information you are looking for.

CENSUS RECORDS

Since 1790, the federal government has taken a census every ten years. Census records from 1790 to 1920 (with the exception of the 1890 census, which was almost completely destroyed by fire) are available on microfilm at the National Archives and throughout its regional system, at many libraries with genealogical collections, and in the Family History Library and its system of family history centers. Access to collections in archives and libraries is discussed later.

Because almost all state records are indexed for almost all years, a census is a logical starting point for determining family origins. Statewide census indexes enable a researcher to pinpoint where individuals were living in the years when the census was taken. Judging from ages and birthplaces, it is usually possible to estimate the date of arrival in the United States, even in earlier censuses. Census records from as early as 1850 indicate state or country of birth for individuals and possible dates of immigration. Later census records provide more specific information on individuals as well as their parents. U.S. Federal census records are widely available on microfilm in many large libraries and archives

While U.S. census records rarely indicate the town, city, or foreign province of an individual's birth, significant immigration facts can be gleaned from the federal census enumerations, especially in later years. From 1850 to 1870, every person's country or state of birth was shown. Censuses from 1880 to 1920 asked for the birthplaces of each person's parents as well. (Because the *country* of birth was asked for on the census, responses such as Hannover, Baden, or Cassel invariably refer to the German states, not the cities of the same names.)

The 1850 through the 1920 census schedules are especially good starting points for tracking families. The 1900 census was the first to indicate how long immigrants had been in the United States and whether they had been naturalized. The 1910 census asked for the year of immigration and citizenship status, as well as the language spoken. 1900 through 1920 census schedules identified citizenship status with the following: *a* for alien; *pa* for individuals who had applied but not completed the naturalization process; and *na* for naturalized.

The 1920 census asked for the year of immigration; whether naturalized; if so, the year of naturalization; whether the person was able to speak English; and many more questions that have significance for family historians, such as place of birth and mother tongue (not only for the individual but for that person's mother and father as well). Due to boundary changes in Europe resulting from World War I, enumerators of the 1920 census were instructed to spell out the name of the city, state, province, or region of respondents who declared that they or their parents had been born in Germany, Austria-Hungary, Russia, or Turkey. Interpretation of the birthplace varied from one enumerator to another. Some failed to identify specific birthplaces within those named countries; others provided an exact birthplace in countries not designated in the instructions.[1]

If you are unable to find your own ancestor's country of origin in census records, the discovery of another relative's origins or those of others of the same surname may prove helpful. Because there are many printed index books and Soundex microfilms (see chapter 4) available, it may prove useful to survey

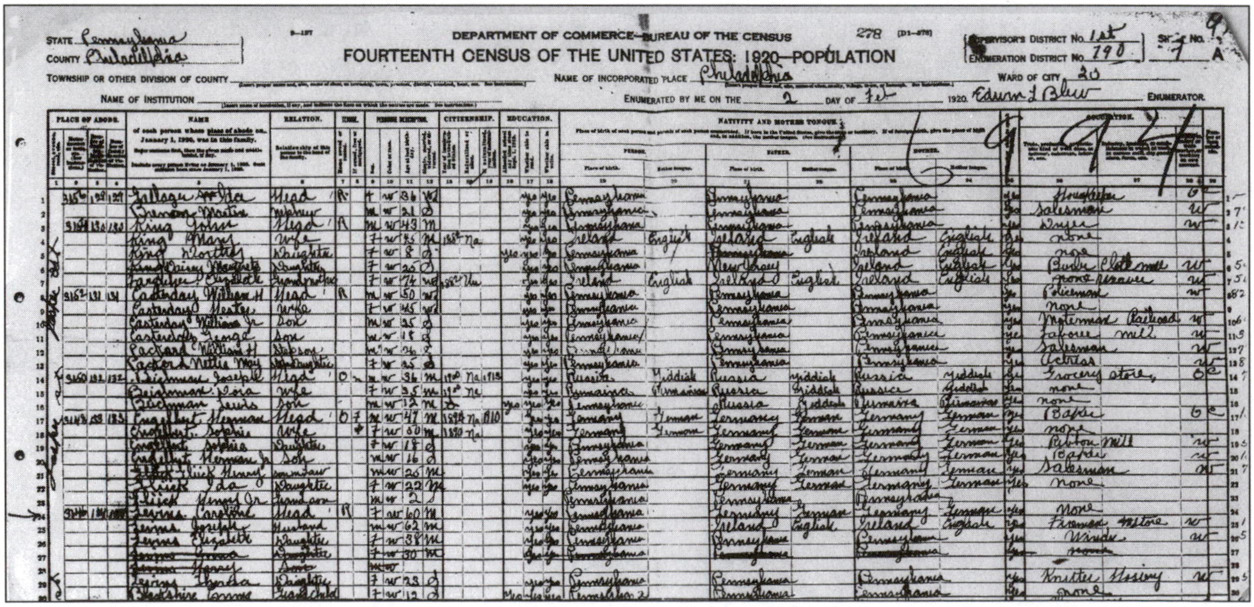
DEPARTMENT OF COMMERCE—BUREAU OF THE CENSUS
FOURTEENTH CENSUS OF THE UNITED STATES: 1920—POPULATION

Figure 2-6. A portion of a page from the 1920 Census of the United States showing residents on Lake Street in Philadelphia.

Figure 2-7. Census records are a good starting point for beginning immigration research.

the occurrence of a given surname in a statewide index. Frequently, individuals of the same family settled in close proximity. Concentrations of an unusual surname can provide a starting place to search for additional information.

State censuses can also be useful in tracking family origins. In addition to the standard questions asked by federal censuses, the 1925 Iowa State Census, for example, asked for the names of parents, mother's maiden name, nativity of parents, place of parents' marriage, military service, occupation, and religion. Chapter 5, "Research in Census Records," in *The Source: A Guidebook of American Genealogy* (Salt Lake City: Ancestry, 1997), pages 134–135, has a more thorough description of state and federal census records.

While census records are extremely useful in immigration research, the information provided in them is not entirely reliable. An individual might not have remembered his or her age exactly. Sometimes, immigrants, fearing a strange new government, did not answer questions honestly—especially those that related to citizenship status. Sometimes immigrants could not remember accurately the date of their arrival in the U.S. or the date of their naturalization; however, when they did and they were recorded correctly, these dates will facilitate naturalization and passenger list searches.

CITY DIRECTORIES

City directories are among the best sources for tracking an immigrant through the years. Immigrants typically settled in cities, especially on the East Coast, until they could find better opportunities in rural areas. City directories generally provide the names, occupations, and addresses of working adults in any given household; they are an important means of tracking individuals from one year to another. While some directories of residents date back to a city's earliest days, no directory is all-inclusive. Unfortunately, foreigners, especially those who did not speak English, were the most frequently excluded or overlooked. Some groups, such as the Poles in Chicago, independently published city or community directories in their own language to compensate. Ethnic and local historical societies have frequently microfilmed or reprinted these special directories. The example of an old Brooklyn, New York, directory (figure 2-8) is typical of the format used in American city directories throughout the nineteenth century.

While city directories seldom, if ever, name the town or country from which the immigrant came, they can provide other important information. For example, from a directory you might learn when the immigrant arrived (within a year or two). Carefully tracking the addresses of others with the same surname may reveal the whereabouts of previously unknown relatives. The Family History Library and many large public libraries have good collections of old city directories.

Vital Records: Births, Marriages, Deaths

The amount of information provided in vital records varies from one county to another and from year to year. As a rule, vital records are limited in their usefulness as clues to immigrant origins; in most instances, records of births, marriages, and deaths provide only the country of birth and not the hoped-for native town. Still, it is always worth seeking out every vital record available for every member of the family.

First look for records related to the immigrant's death; these may give his or her date and place of birth or the names of parents, relatives, or friends. Death records can also provide important clues regarding religion, naturalization, length of residence, date of arrival, and property in the old country.

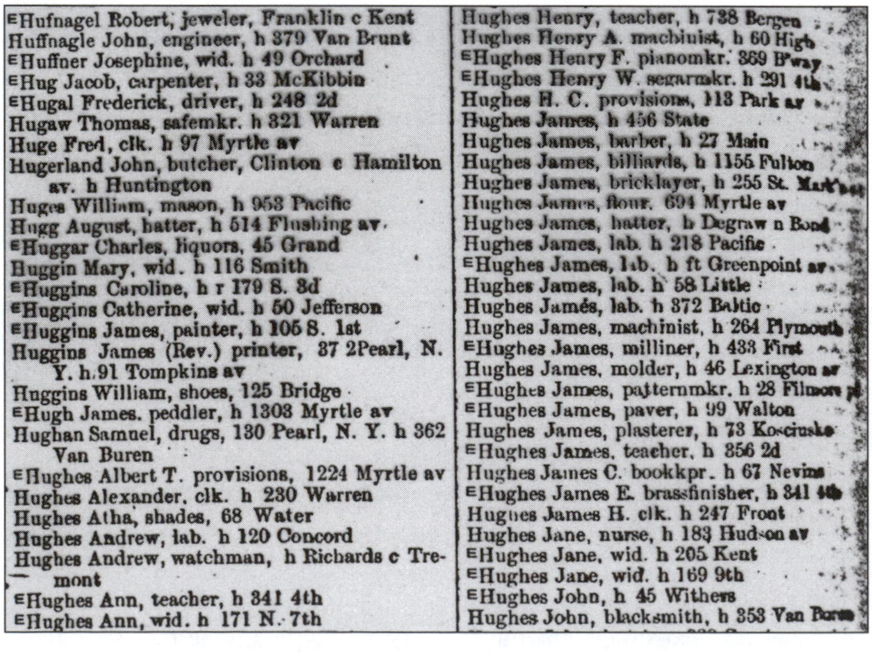
ᴱHufnagel Robert, jeweler, Franklin c Kent
Huffnagle John, engineer, h 379 Van Brunt
ᴱHuffner Josephine, wid. h 49 Orchard
ᴱHug Jacob, carpenter, h 33 McKibbin
ᴱHugal Frederick, driver, h 248 2d
Hugaw Thomas, safemkr. h 321 Warren
Huge Fred, clk. h 97 Myrtle av
Hugerland John, butcher, Clinton c Hamilton av. h Huntington
Huges William, mason, h 953 Pacific
Hugg August, batter, h 514 Flushing av.
ᴱHuggar Charles, liquors, 45 Grand
Huggin Mary, wid. h 116 Smith
ᴱHuggins Caroline, h r 179 S. 3d
ᴱHuggins Catherine, wid. h 50 Jefferson
ᴱHuggins James, painter, h 106 S. 1st
Huggins James (Rev.) printer, 37 2Pearl, N. Y. h 91 Tompkins av
Huggins William, shoes, 125 Bridge
ᴱHugh James. peddler, h 1303 Myrtle av
Hughan Samuel, drugs, 130 Pearl, N. Y. h 362 Van Buren
ᴱHughes Albert T. provisions, 1224 Myrtle av
Hughes Alexander. clk. h 230 Warren
Hughes Atha, shades, 68 Water
Hughes Andrew, lab. h 120 Concord
Hughes Andrew, watchman, h Richards c Tremont
ᴱHughes Ann, teacher, h 341 4th
ᴱHughes Ann, wid. h 171 N. 7th
Hughes Henry, teacher, h 738 Bergen
Hughes Henry A. machinist, h 60 High
ᴱHughes Henry F. pianomkr. 369 B'way
ᴱHughes Henry W. segarmkr. h 291 4th
Hughes H. C. provisions, 113 Park av
Hughes James, h 456 State
Hughes James, barber, h 27 Main
Hughes James, billiards, h 1155 Fulton
Hughes James, bricklayer, h 255 St. Mark's av
Hughes James, flour, 694 Myrtle av
Hughes James, hatter, h Degraw n Bond
Hughes James, lab. h 218 Pacific
ᴱHughes James, lab. h ft Greenpoint av
Hughes James, lab. h 58 Little
Hughes James, lab. h 372 Baltic
Hughes James, machinist, h 264 Plymouth
ᴱHughes James, milliner, h 433 First
Hughes James, molder, h 46 Lexington av
ᴱHughes James, patternmkr. h 28 Filmore pl
ᴱHughes James, paver, h 99 Walton
Hughes James, plasterer, h 73 Kosciusko
ᴱHughes James, teacher, h 356 2d
Hughes James C. bookkpr. h 67 Nevins
ᴱHughes James E. brassfinisher, h 341 4th
Hughes James H. clk. h 247 Front
Hughes Jane, nurse, h 183 Hudson av
ᴱHughes Jane, wid. h 205 Kent
ᴱHughes Jane, wid. h 169 9th
ᴱHughes John, h 45 Withers
Hughes John, blacksmith, h 353 Van Buren

Figure 2-8. City directory for Brooklyn, New York, 1872.

Figure 2-9. Cornelius and Catherine Murphy Fleming (ca. 1880),
whose families emigrated from Ireland to Canada and then to the United States.
Great numbers of Europeans entered North America through Canadian ports because
ship fares to Canada were cheaper than fares to American ports.

After death records, seek out records of other vital events, such as the immigrant's marriage and children's births. Vital record entries for marriages and births of the immigrant's children kept by civil authorities can provide important clues. Generally, records of later periods contain more information than earlier ones. While indication of birthplace is rare, it does appear occasionally and it is important to locate every possible record, even when the likelihood of finding immigration information is slight.

As in every other aspect of genealogical research, the records of siblings, aunts and uncles, and even distant relatives can be very important. For example, the children of one Irish family who decided to trace their ancestry documented events and activities of their father's, grandfather's, and great-grandfather's lives back to the immigrant's arrival in the United States in 1836. To their great disappointment, other than the census and death records noting Ireland as the birthplace, nothing in any of the records provided clues to specific origins in Ireland. At the suggestion of a professional researcher, the family began to collect information on all the other children of the immigrant, their common ancestor. Fortunately, on the death certificate of the eighth of the immigrant's twelve children, specific information appeared. The father's birthplace was listed as Wexford and the mother's as Queenstown. Had the research not been extended to include the great-uncles and great-aunts, it is doubtful that the project could have progressed.

CEMETERY RECORDS

Cemetery records are important sources for immigrant research. Sometimes the only recording of an original name or exact birthplace is on a tombstone or in a sexton's records. For example, one family historian had reached a dead end in researching the name Doner in New York. After many attempts to locate

*Figure 2-10. A family at a Jewish cemetery
in Long Island, New York.
(Photo reproduced courtesy of Eileen Polakoff.)*

*Figure 2-11. A monument in
St. Casimir Cemetery, Chicago.
Cemetery monuments sometimes indicate ethnic origins.*

*Figure 2-12. A monument in a cemetery
in Las Cruces, New Mexico.
(Photo reproduced courtesy of James Otto Bombach.)*

cemetery records, the historian discovered that the original cemetery deed had been recorded under the name Dooner. Alerted to the original spelling, the researcher was able to determine when family members changed the name spelling and to continue researching the original spelling in older records.

Often, children and other relatives of immigrants honored a deceased ancestor by noting a person's birthplace on his or her tombstone. Ethnic cemeteries, ethnic sections of larger cemeteries, and family burial plots of immigrants can be outstanding sources for determining ethnic origins. Whenever possible, visit cemeteries personally to inspect and photograph monuments.

ECCLESIASTICAL RECORDS

Associating with local religious congregations helped to alleviate "culture shock" for immigrants. The church was a haven that offered services in a familiar tongue, and its officials and other members were often known to the immigrant. The formality of christening a child born en route to America or solemnizing a marriage that began as a shipboard romance provided a ritual sanction for the move. In some denominations, letters of recommendation for church membership were surrendered shortly after arrival. Few loose documents kept by individual immigrants have survived, but some religious denominations kept records of recommendations and removals.

Whenever possible, study immigrant church registers; patterns sometimes emerge that will identify the foreign emigration point for an entire group. For example, while looking for an immigrant in Catholic church records in a small Indiana town, a genealogist searched baptism and marriage entries in several ledgers. The native towns for many of those receiving the sacraments were noted in the church registers, as were the native towns of the witnesses and sponsors. Unfortunately, there was no such notation identifying the birthplace of the subject of interest.

Figure 2-13. A monument in a cemetery in Lansing, Illinois, indicating that the deceased were born in the Netherlands.

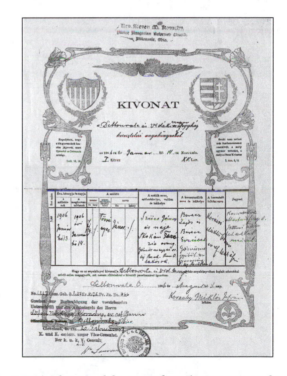

Figure 2-14. A baptismal document from the Hungarian reformed church in Dillonvale, Ohio, showing Hungarian origins.

Figure 2-15. Muriel Dyer at her Irish first communion, Brooklyn, New York, 1910.

The astute family historian did not give up, however. Knowing that sponsors and witnesses are frequently close relatives and friends, he noted the names of all the towns mentioned in the registers during the time the family resided in the parish. Next, he found a detailed map of the area near a recognizable city mentioned in the church register. Some towns were not on the map, but most were, though their names had been misspelled in the registers. This study revealed that a large number of towns cited were within a thirty-mile radius of the central city on the detailed map. Once the Indiana genealogist focused on a specific area in Germany, another genealogist specializing in German research was able to find emigration records for the family of interest.

LOCAL HISTORIES

Despite their tendency to focus on society's most prominent citizens, state and local histories,

Figure 2-16. Class at the Holy Innocents School, Brooklyn, New York, 1917.

biographies, and biographical encyclopedias can be useful for finding some immigrants' origins. State, county, and local histories were especially popular during the late nineteenth century and the first twenty or thirty years of the twentieth century. Many were produced on a subscription basis, and biographical sketches of the subscribers formed a substantial part of each history. Centennial publications of various institutions, organizations, churches, cities, and towns were frequently financed and formatted in a similar manner. If the subject of a biographical sketch was an immigrant, his or her exact birthplace might be noted. Even the foreign birthplace of the subject's parents might be mentioned in a published history. If an immigrant or his parents did not make it into the pages of a biographical work, the accomplishments of a sibling or one or more descendants might appear somewhere in print.

Local histories often mention less prominent immigrants along with the prominent. Common folk became especially important if they were among an area's original settlers. Immigrants often considered it a mark of success to be included in the typical local histories of the nineteenth century, even if they had to pay to be included. If an immigrant was willing to spend the necessary money, the publisher would include him, no matter how obscure he was. Often, the names of immigrants are included in lists of early settlers as members of a founding church, as original town settlers, landholders, school teachers, or in cemetery records. Bibliographies of local histories and biographical sources are available for most counties, states, and provinces (in Canada) where immigrants settled.

Published histories of towns, counties, or regions in which an immigrant ancestor lived are often key to identifying his or her national and ethnic origin. Histories of a locality's churches, schools, or businesses may also mention the immigrant. If an ancestor is included with the area's founding families or was a prominent citizen, a local history may include

Figure 2-17. Mokotoff father and son.
(Photo reproduced courtesy of Gary Mokotoff.)

an account of his or her life. Examples from A. T. Andreas's *History of Cook County, Illinois* (Chicago: A. T. Andreas, Publisher, 1884), pages 444–45, follow.

WILLIAM F. FOSTER, farmer, P.O. Evanston, was born in the county of Cavan, Ireland, September 12, 1799. He came to Auburn, N.Y., in 1811, and lived there for five or six years; then went to Onondaga County and worked in salt mines for twenty-eight years; then went to Canton, Ohio, and in 1839 came to Chicago. In 1840 he came to Gross Point (now Evanston), and worked at the trade as cooper, in 1848 coming to his present home on Ridge Avenue. He went to California in 1850, and returned in 1852, and has since lived at his present home. He was married to Miss Mary Sammons, of Johnstown, N.Y., in April, 1820. She died April 18, 1876, leaving six children— Martha A. (Now Mrs. James Dennis, of Glen Cove), Jeannette (Mrs. George Kearney, now deceased), Helen (now Mrs. J. C. Garland of Missouri), Mary, (now Mrs. S.V. Kline, deceased of Evanston), John J., and William (deceased). The father of Mrs. Foster, Jacob, and his brother Frederick, were the first men shot in the Revolutionary War at Johnstown, and were kept prisoners for one year.

MAX HAHN, Township Supervisor, was born in Bavaria, Germany, December 18, 1834. He learned the trade of shoemaking from his father. In 1857 he came to Evanston and carried on that business for fifteen years, for two years of the time having two stores, one of which he sold out to J.C. Fusey. He closed out his business and since 1876 has been Township Supervisor. Since June 3, 1882, he has been connected with Chicago Post-Office. He was married to Miss Anna Schneider, of New Trier Township, Cook County, February 1, 1864.

JOHN HARGREAVES, cabinet-maker, was born in Cheshire, England, October 3, 1835, and learned his trade in Macclesfield, England. He came to Evanston in 1873, and first worked for George Iredale up to 1879, since which time he has carried on his own business. He was married to Miss Martha Hall, of Cheshire, England, December 25, 1853. They have six children— Luther J., Richard T., Alfred W., Harriet A., George A. and Francis G.

ETHNIC HISTORIES

Some of the best sources of information about a given group or individual originate in the ethnic community itself. Immigrant groups clung together to sustain their memories and culture, and to maintain a sense of connectedness with the old country. Every

Figure 2-18. Wood engraving of Dr. William Bradshaw Egan, born in Lake Killarney, County Kerry, Ireland, 28 September 1808. From History of Cook County, Illinois, by A. T. Andreas (Chicago: A. T. Andreas, Publisher, 1884).

ethnic organization in the United States has played a role in preserving and perpetuating group identity and national pride. Hundreds of ethnic organizations have flourished and published periodicals, newspapers, and historical and biographical albums—frequently in their native tongues. Histories produced by ethnic presses may focus on national, state, or local history. A typical volume reviews the history of the group from its earliest involvement in American history, extols the group's contributions to the development of the United States, and pays tribute to members of the ethnic group who had become prominent for one reason or another. Biographical sketches in these volumes tend to describe members only in the most glowing terms, but frequently the degree of detail is very useful. Many a genealogical breakthrough can be attributed to an ethnic biographical sketch. Examples of ethnic histories include Martin Ulvestad's *Nordmaendene I Amerika* [Norwegians in America], 2 vols. (Minneapolis: History Book Company's Forlag, 1907–10), Rose Rosicky's *A History of Czechs (Bohemians) in Nebraska* (Omaha: Czech Historical Society of Nebraska, 1929); *The Story of the Irish in Boston together with Biographical Sketches of Representative Men and Noted Women*, ed. and comp. by James Bernard Cullen (Boston: James B. Cullen & Co., 1889), and *Poles of Chicago, 1837–1937: A History of One Century of Polish Contribution to the City of Chicago,* *Illinois* (Chicago: Polish Pageant, 1937).

The following extraction is a typical example of a biographical sketch found in Charles Ffrench's *Biographical History of the American Irish in Chicago* (Chicago: American Biographical Publishing, 1897). While the subject of the sketch was born in Chicago, his father's and mother's Irish origins are correctly identified. Interestingly, the introductory paragraph was replicated in similar publications by the same company for attorneys in other cities. The flattering and frequently used introductions were very effective marketing tools for biographical publishers wishing to sell subscriptions.

Figure 2-19. Biographical sketches from Giovanni E. Schiavo's The Italians in Chicago: A Study in Americanization *(New York: Arno Press, 1975).*

Francis T. Murphy

This great Western metropolis contains a great many able men who have made the law the profession of their lives. That all should be equally successful in such a career, would be an impossibility; the prizes in life's battle are few and far between, and the fortunate must be gifted with qualifications of a diverse character, exceptional legal ability, good judgement, ready perception, and also personal charm of manner or power of intellect sufficient to dominate and control their fellow men. Among the representative lawyers of the west, there are but a few who possess these necessary characteristics in a higher degree than the subject of the present sketch, the big, genial-natured, open-hearted young lawyer, Francis T. Murphy.

He was born in this city where he was destined to make himself so well known, January 25th, 1863, his father, Thomas Murphy being a native of County Meath, Ireland and his mother from West Meath. It is from his father unquestionably that Francis T. inherits his perseverance and energy, for Thomas Murphy left the dear old land as a mere boy of twelve, traveled all alone to the far country beyond the seas, where he possessed neither kith nor kin, friend nor acquaintance, and when the big ocean journey was finished, set off once more across the continent to Chicago, determined to seek a living and possible fortune in the boundless West. In this city he fought his way, married, and in 1894 died at the comparatively premature age of fifty-seven.

Mr. Murphy was married April 11th, 1893, in Chicago, to Mary V. Halpin, the daughter of one of Chicago's best known citizens. A man of intensely social nature, the chief delight of Frank Murphy—as he is generally known—is to be surrounded with his friends and to dispense the historical hospitality. For fast horses he admits a decided partiality, and is fortunate in the possession of several that can show a good pace.

NEWSPAPERS

Newspapers provide a variety of immigration information. Search the local newspapers where the immigrant settled as well as the ethnic newspapers in the immigrant's language or for his or her cultural group. In addition to obituaries (described below), newspapers from the immigrant's lifetime may also give the following kinds of information to help find an immigrant's place of origin:

- Lists of passengers or new arrivals
- Immigrants treated in a local hospital
- Lists of immigrants who came as indentured servants or apprentices
- Queries about missing relatives or friends
- Marriage announcements
- Notices of probates of estates

Many immigrants had relatives and friends who preceded them to America, and frequently the late-comers tried to locate their compatriots with newspaper advertisements. Approximately ten German-language newspapers served German immigrants around Philadelphia by 1776, in addition to the English-language newspapers. Examples of extracts of inquiries and advertisements include Anita L. Eyster's "Notices by German and Swiss Settlers Seeking Information of Members of their Families, Kindred, and Friends Inserted Between 1742–1761 in *Pennsylvania Berichte* and 1762–1779 in the *Pennsylvania Staatsbote*," *Pennsylvania German Folklore Society* 3 (1938): 32–41; and Edward Hocker, *Genealogical Data Relating to the German Settlers of Pennsylvania from Advertisements in German Newspapers Published in Philadelphia and Germantown, 1743–1800* (Baltimore: Genealogical Publishing Co., 1981).

*Figure 2-20. American obituaries, in English and foreign-language newspapers,
can be good sources for learning ethnic origins.*

Many Irish who settled in Boston used the newspapers to seek friends and relatives who had arrived earlier. Often, their queries indicated what part of Ireland the person they were seeking had come from. Abstracts of thousands of notices from 1831 to 1856 have been gathered by Ruth-Ann Harris and Donald M. Jacobs in *The Search for Missing Friends: Irish Immigrant Advertisements Placed in the Boston Pilot* (Boston: New England Historic Genealogical Society, 1989–93).

Ethnic newspapers can be particularly helpful. According to Lubomyr R. and Anna T. Wynar, *Encyclopedic Directory of Ethnic Newspapers and Periodicals in the United States*, 2d ed. (Littleton, Colo.: Libraries Unlimited, 1976), "The major function of

the ethnic press lies in its role as the principal agent by which the identity, cohesiveness, and structure of an ethnic community are preserved and perpetuated." Unusual or special events in the lives of working-class immigrants that routinely went unnoticed by major daily newspapers often warranted lengthy articles in ethnic and religious newspapers. Birth, marriage, anniversary, and death notices and articles in ethnic newspapers can be invaluable sources for discovering immigrant origins. Even the mention of a professional promotion, a trip to visit family in the native country, or that an individual was running for public office, may provide personal details not found elsewhere.

OBITUARIES

Obituaries are excellent sources for biographical information about immigrants. In addition to the name and death date of the immigrant, surviving family members, church affiliation, spouses, parents, occupations, burial places, and, most importantly, the native town in the old country may be noted. For many an immigrant, an obituary may have been the only biographical sketch ever written for him or her.

Research on Carl Schultz, a Mecklenburg immigrant to Wisconsin, was stymied because of his common name and the lack of good biographical information. His obituary, while not providing the town of origin, gave the year of immigration, which made it possible to identify him in the Hamburg passenger lists, where his native town was indicated.

Obituaries were usually published in local and church newspapers. Some also appear in church, professional, company, and school periodicals. Although brief death notices appeared in the earliest newspapers, traditional obituaries are most common after the mid-1800s. You are most likely to find obituaries of immigrants who lived in rural areas rather than in large cities.

Search smaller, local newspapers that focused on community news, such as weekly newspapers. Many such newspapers are available on microfilm; public libraries can usually obtain copies via interlibrary loan. Local historical societies and libraries in the town where a newspaper was published may also have copies. Many North American newspapers are listed in *Newspapers in Microform: United States,* 2 vols. (Washington, D.C.: Library of Congress, 1984).

MILITARY RECORDS

Military records are among the most important and most extensive U.S. records of genealogical value. Because the military needed to fully identify the soldiers who fought and the veterans who received pensions, birth information is common in military records. Immigrants were often ready recruits for the military—especially those who had few relatives in America. Many were willing to fight for their adopted country (including, paradoxically,

*Figure 2-21. A Union soldier assists a wounded comrade.
(Photo reproduced courtesy of the National Archives.)*

VOLUNTEER SERVICE.
(Civil War or War with Spain.)

John Fortenbacher

Co A , 45 Reg't N.Y. Inf

age 20 , height 5 feet, 4 inches,

complexion fair ,

eyes blue , hair dark ,

place of birth Elchersheim Baden

occupation barber ;

was enrolled Sept 1 , 1862,

and m/out July 6 , 1865.

as of Co A 5th N Y

Inf to which transfd

June 65

From _____ , 18 , to m/out, 18 ,

he held the rank of Pvt

and the rolls on file for that period show him

present except as follows: —

No record of deser-

tion or absence

without leave,

Figure 2-22. Part of a volunteer service file for Spanish-American War veteran John Fortenbacher, Co. A, Forty-fifth Regiment, New York Infantry, age twenty. It indicates that he was born in Elchersheim, Baden (Germany).

Form 1 1928 REGISTRATION CARD No. 139

1 Name in full Luigi Capriotti Age, in yrs. 28
2 Home address 208 Howland ave Kenosha Wis
3 Date of birth October 2 1888
4 Are you (1) a natu.-born citizen, (2) a naturalized citizen, (3) an alien, (4) or have you declared your intention (specify which)? Declarant
5 Where were you born? Comunanza Ascolipiceno Italy
6 If not a citizen, of what country are you a citizen or subject? Italy
7 What is your present trade, occupation, or office? labour
8 By whom employed? Simmons Mfg Co. Where employed? Kenosha Wis.
9 Have you a father, mother, wife, child under 12, or a sister or brother under 12, solely dependent on you for support (specify which)? Step mother
10 Married or single (which)? Single Race (specify which) Caucasian
11 What military service have you had? Rank Private , branch Infantry years one year , Nation or State Italy
12 Do you claim exemption from draft (specify grounds)? Step mother support

I affirm that I have verified above answers and that they are true.

Luigi Capriotti

Figure 2-23. World War I draft card for Luigi Capriotti indicating his birthplace in Italy.

Figure 2-24. Edwin Dyer, World War I.

those who had left their native countries to avoid military service). As with most other genealogical records, the more recent records include more information than do earlier records. Indeed, records of revolutionary war service seldom identify the birthplace of the soldier, let alone his native origins. By the time of the Civil War, however, enlistment records usually indicated at least the country where an immigrant was born, and sometimes the town. Although immigration decreased during the Civil War, a surprisingly large number of immigrants who

Figure 2-25. Edward Pfeiffer, U.S. Navy, and memorabilia. (Reproduced courtesy of Dan Pfeiffer.)

arrived in the early years of the war enlisted in the army. To receive a Civil War pension, veterans did not have to provide proof of birth; however, the veteran's birthplace was often included on pension application forms.

By the end of the nineteenth century, military enlistment records almost invariably indicated the town of birth. Most significant military records created during the twentieth century will aid researchers seeking the native towns of immigrants born after 1875. World War I draft records documented virtually every adult male between the ages of eighteen and forty-five in the years 1918 to 1920. World War II draft records have recently become available for some states, and they are found in some regions of the National Archives. World War II draft records would include virtually any male immigrant born between 1875 and 1900, whether he had been naturalized or not. James C. Neagles thoroughly describes military records in *U.S. Military Records: A Guide to Federal and State Sources, Colonial America to the Present* (Salt Lake City: Ancestry, 1994).

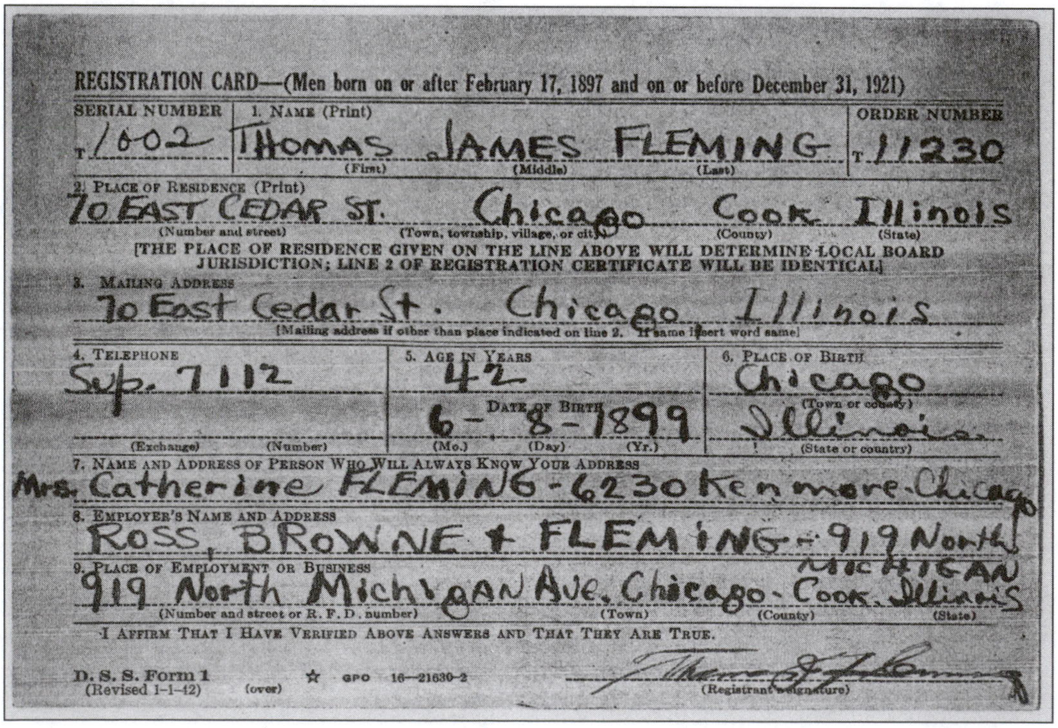

Figure 2-26. World War II draft card for Thomas Fleming.

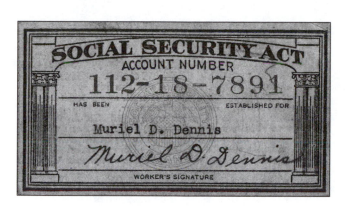

Figure 2-27. Social Security card of Muriel Dennis.

SOCIAL SECURITY RECORDS

Beginning in the 1930s, the federal government made Social Security benefits available for an increasingly large number of U.S. citizens. To apply for these benefits, the individual had to file an application for a Social Security number. This application, called an SS no. 5 form, required a specific statement about the person's date and place (town) of birth. By the 1940s, many citizens had obtained Social Security numbers; among them were many of the immigrants born in the last third of the nineteenth century. The Social Security Death Benefit Database is available to search at http://www.ancestry.com at no charge.

HOMESTEAD RECORDS

Homestead records can also offer valuable clues. Much of the great prairie land of the United States and Canada was settled by immigrants. Immigrants were required to have at least filed a declaration of intent to be naturalized before applying for homestead land, and the application often called for spe-

cific birth information. Indeed, the immigrant ancestor may have had any number of dealings with the federal government, even including federal court cases. Any such records will be important in documenting the immigrant's life; if the records date from after the Civil War (1865), they very likely will provide significant information about the immigrant's foreign origins. See more on homestead records in chapter 1. Homestead records are among the many land records that are well described by Wade Hone in *Land and Property Research in the United States* (Salt Lake City: Ancestry, 1997).

VOTER REGISTRATION RECORDS

Voter registrations, while not available for every city or county in the United States, can be valuable sources of immigration information. Typically, the registrations are kept with the county records (usually in list form) and provide the full name, address, birth date, birthplace, and, for naturalized citizens, the naturalization court and date of naturalization (figure 2-29). Many lists note the number of years the voter had been a resident of the state and county.

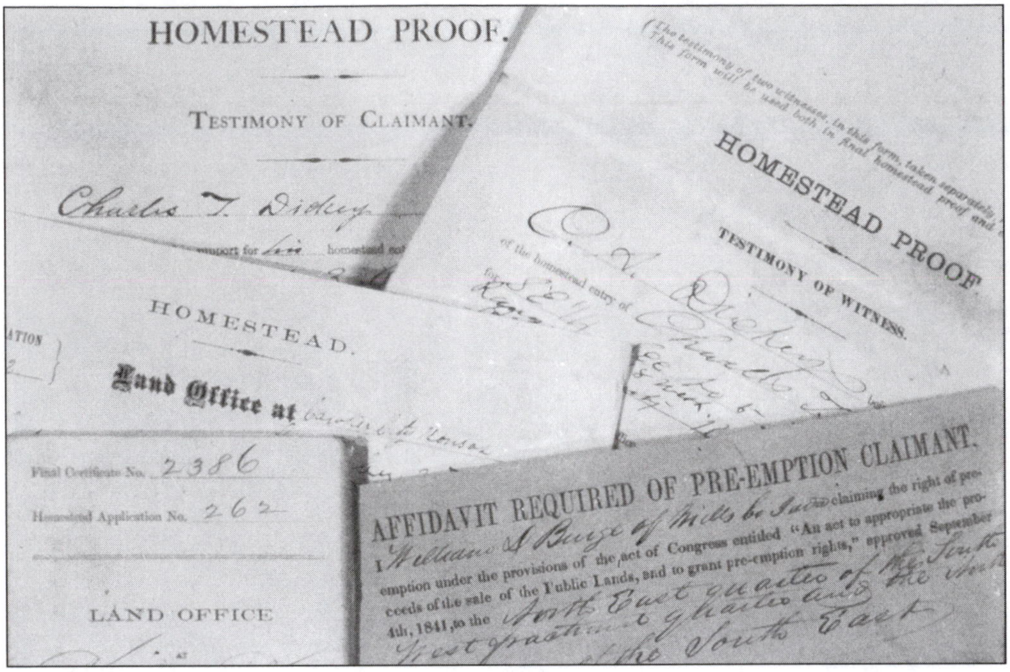

Figure 2-28. Citizenship status and naturalization papers are often included in homestead files.

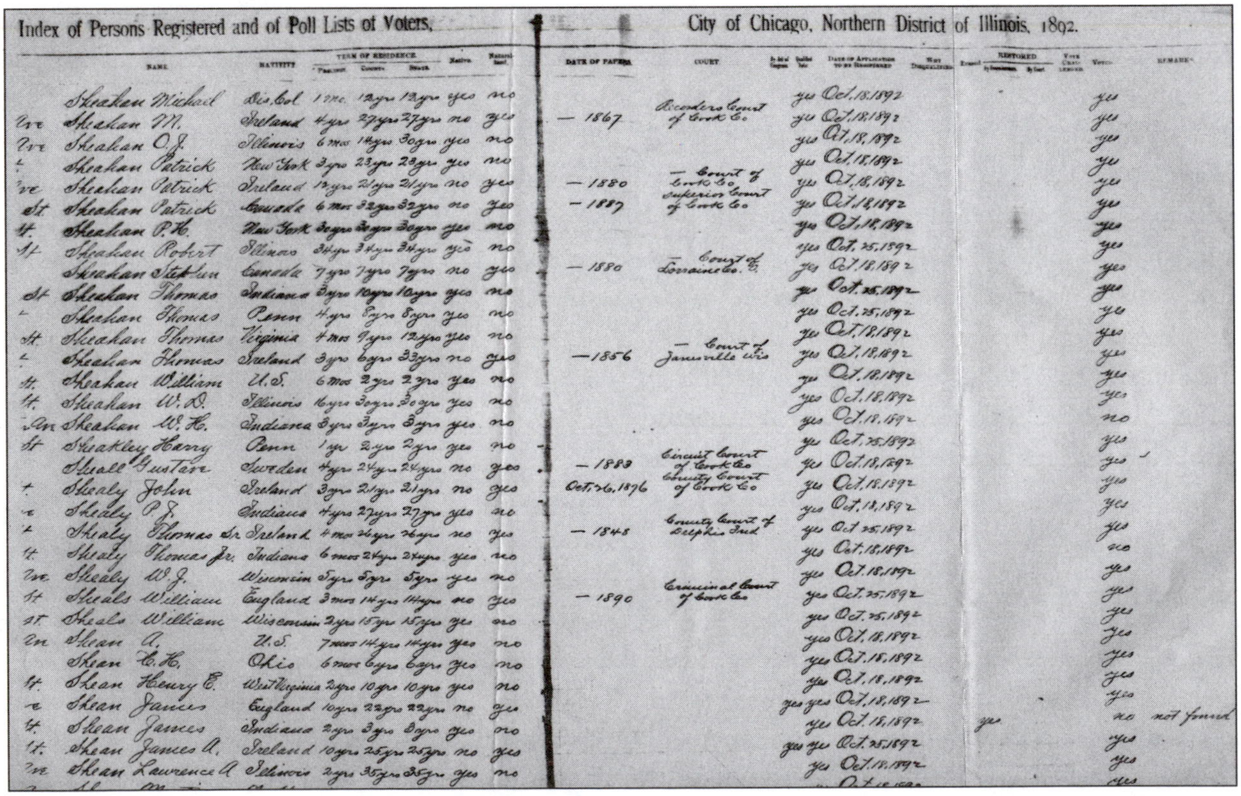

Figure 2-29. Voter registration index.

PASSPORTS

Some immigrants applied for U.S. passports to go back to their native countries to visit relatives. These records usually indicate the person's birthplace or the destination for the visit, which is likely to have been near the native town.

More than 2,150 microfilm rolls of U.S. passport records from the National Archives and Department of State have been released for research. These records from the U.S. Passport Office are travel documents "attesting to the citizenship and identity of the bearer." People from all walks of life used passports. The first extant passport given to an individual is dated July 1796. Passports became more popular in the late 1840s but, until the outbreak of World War I in 1914, American citizens were generally permitted to travel abroad without passports. Naturally, the requirement to carry a passport caused a significant increase in the numbers issued. By 1930, the U.S. government had issued more than 2.5 million passports.

To receive a U.S. passport, a person had to submit proof of U.S. citizenship, usually in the form of a letter, affidavits of witnesses, or certificates from clerks or notaries. By 1888 there were separate application forms for native citizens, naturalized citizens, and derivative citizens (those who derived their citizenship from the citizenship of others). Passport applications often include information regarding an applicant's family status, date and place of birth, residence, naturalization (if foreign born), and other biographical information. Twentieth-century applications often include marriage and family information as well as dates, places, and names of ships used for travel.

The microfilmed passport records, registers, and indexes are available from the earliest dates to around 1925. They are arranged in several sets, and each passport application series is arranged chronologically. A number is assigned to most applications. For some years there are registers but no actual applications. You must use the registers and indexes to determine an application's date (and number, where applicable) in order to locate a particular application. Applications for 1925 and later are in the custody of the Passport Office, Department of State, 1425 K Street N.W., Washington, DC 20520. Microfilm copies are available from the Family History Library of The Church of Jesus Christ of Latter-day Saints (LDS church) and through its many family history centers.

NATURALIZATION AND OTHER COURT RECORDS

Before 1906, an alien could be naturalized in any court of record. In most cases it is best to begin the search for naturalization documents in courts in the county were the immigrant is known to have resided. Many immigrants, anxious to become citizens, began the citizenship process by taking out *first papers* in the county where they first arrived in the United States. One might have started the process somewhere on the East Coast, for example, and then completed the requirements in the county or state when final residency was established somewhere else. Chapter 4 provides an extensive description of naturalization processes and records in the courts.

Other court records can be very useful in reconstructing family history; many can also provide clues to immigrant origins. Probate, guardianship, divorce, name changes, and adoption files are just a few of the potentially rich information sources to be found in American courts. Chapter 7, "Research in Court Records," by Arlene H. Eakle, Ph.D., in *The Source: A Guidebook of American History*, edited by Loretto Dennis Szucs and Sandra Hargreaves Luebking, rev. ed. (Salt Lake City: Ancestry, 1997), provides a great deal of information on court records and how to use them effectively.

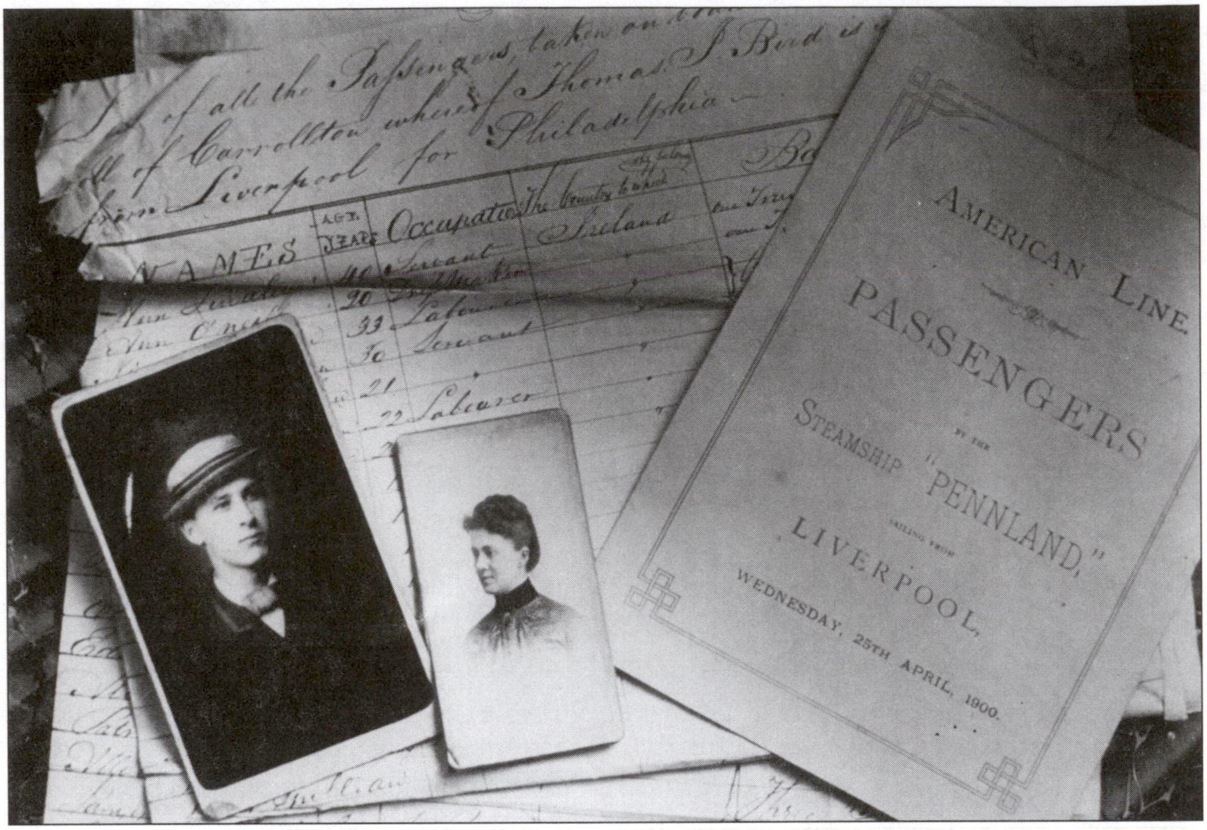

Figure 2-30. Most of the available passenger arrival lists have been microfilmed and may be viewed at the National Archives, family history centers of The Church of Jesus Christ of Latter-day Saints (LDS church), and some libraries.

SHIP PASSENGER ARRIVAL LISTS

Passenger arrival lists can be among the most interesting sources for documenting an ancestor's immigration. Unfortunately, however, lists were not kept for every ship, some lists have been lost, and many are not indexed. The content of passenger lists changed significantly over the years, and information is sparse on earlier lists: only the immigrant's name, age, and country of origin or the ship's last port of call were typically required. Passenger lists created before the 1890s rarely indicate the immigrant's town of origin. The format of lists in the 1890s gradually evolved to include more detailed information, including the place of origin. Some include sex, age, occupation, and place of residence when the ticket was purchased. On some lists, the

passengers are grouped into family units; on others they are listed by tickets. On some they are arranged in alphabetical order; on others they are arranged in the order in which the passengers boarded the ship. The name of the ship's master and dates of departure and arrival will be found on some. Later lists, like those for Hamburg, give date and place of birth, date and parish of confirmation, marital status, and state or city of destination

The vast majority of immigration records are the passenger arrival lists kept by the U.S. Federal government (after 1820) or by other authorities (cities, states, port officials, and shipping lines). However, there are several other significant record sources for immigrants. They exist in published or manuscript form and include naturalization records, records of border crossings, passports, records of immigrant societies, alien registration, consular records, and others.

While at least some passenger lists have been indexed for virtually every U.S. port, a large number remain unindexed. And, as is true of all indexes, those that do exist contain errors—especially errors of omission (indexers sometimes inadvertently skip individuals on passenger lists). And individuals who departed from a country illegally may not have been recorded at all. Children who emigrated with their parents were often not included on early lists. Even if you find the name you are looking for in the index, in many cases it will be impossible to confirm with a great degree of certainty that it actually refers to the person whom you are researching. Illegible handwriting on passenger lists, combined with misspelled names, incorrect ages, and only a vague reference to a country or region of origin, give passenger lists the distinction of being the most difficult-to-use immigration sources. Furthermore, you may not know if the immigrant traveled alone, or with other family members or friends. In other words, how will you know if John Miller, age twenty-three, laborer, is the person you are seeking if there are several others of the same name and similar description?

As with other government documents, passenger lists were not intended to be genealogical documents; rather they were a means of monitoring immigrant arrivals. Historically, up to seven different passenger lists were created—perhaps more for some groups of passengers. These include lists made and filed with (1) the port of embarkation, (2) ports of call along the route, (3) the port of arrival, (4) newspapers at the port of departure, (5) newspapers at cities of arrival, (6) a copy kept with or as part of the ship's manifest (figure 2-31), and (7) notations of passengers in the ship's log. In addition, some travelers recorded information about their fellow passengers in diaries, journals, and letters. If the group was chartered by a government agency, a specific church, or an emigrant aid society, a list may have been kept with the official archives of the project. If the ship was quarantined for disease, a copy of the list was attached to medical reports. Germans arriving in Pennsylvania from 1727 to

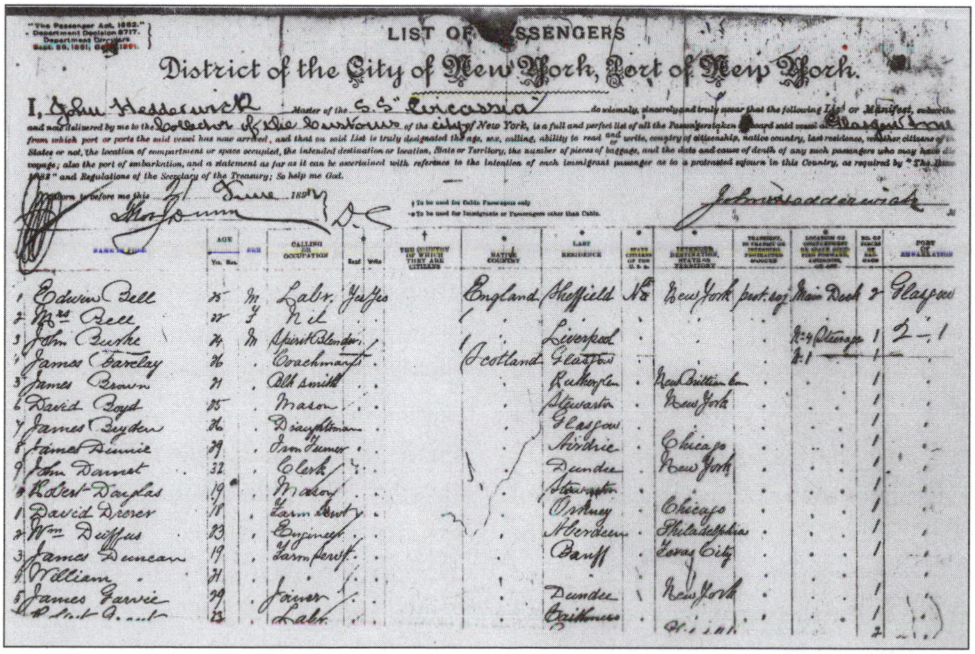
LIST OF PASSENGERS

District of the City of New York, Port of New York.

I, John Hesserwick, Master of the S.S. Circassia ...

Name in Full	Age	Sex	Calling or Occupation	Native Country	Last Residence	Intended Destination
1 Edwin Bell	25	M	Labr.	England	Sheffield	New York
2 Mrs Bell	27	F	Nil			
3 John Burke	24	M	Spirit Blender		Liverpool	
4 James Barclay	26		Coachman	Scotland	Glasgow	
5 James Brown	21		Blk smith		Rutherglen	New Brittain
6 David Boyd	25		Mason		Stewarton	New York
7 James Bryden	26		Draughtsman		Glasgow	
8 James Binnie	29		Iron Turner		Airdrie	Chicago
9 John Dannet	32		Clerk		Dundee	New York
10 Robert Douglas	19		Mason		Stewarton	
1 David Drever	18		Farm Servt		Orkney	Chicago
2 Wm Duffus	23		Engineer		Aberdeen	Philadelphia
3 James Duncan	19		Farm Servt		Banff	Jersey City
4 William	21					
5 James Garvie	29		Joiner		Dundee	New York
6 Robert Grant	23		Labr.		Caithness	

Figure 2-31. Microfilm copies of passenger lists may be searched at selected archives and libraries.

Figure 2-32. The Port of New York was by far the most-used port of entry to the United States. Ellis Island served from 1892 to 1954.

1808 were required to take an oath of allegiance and an oath of abjuration when they landed in Philadelphia. All able-bodied heads of families were taken immediately before a magistrate when they arrived.

Some of these passenger lists are official lists that were required by law; others were private recordings. For family historians, the fact that multiple copies were sometimes made improves the chances that at least one survived for most immigrants. The main problem is in finding the lists.

Official U.S. government passenger lists are available from 1820 through 1945 for most of the ports in the United States that have customs houses.

Those available in the National Archives on microfilm are tabulated in *Immigration and Passenger Arrivals: A Select Catalog of National Archives Microfilm Publications*, rev. ed. (Washington, D.C.: National Archives Trust Fund, 1991). They are divided into customs passenger lists (original lists, copies, or abstracts) and immigration passenger lists (State Department transcripts, lists) with pertinent indexes. Microfilm publication call numbers are given where appropriate. Copies are also available for searching at the Family History Library and its family history centers located throughout the United States. Selected passenger lists are available at some public libraries. The Allen County Public

Library in Fort Wayne, Indiana, for example, has a large collection of passenger list microfilms.

No official records exist until those of the late nineteenth century for persons entering the United States through Canada or Mexico (see "Border Crossings," below). Lists for the Pacific Coast ports are in the possession of the Customs Service in those ports or have been transferred to National Archives regional centers on the West Coast. The National Archives has recently microfilmed available records for these ports. There are a few passenger lists for San Francisco at the National Archives-Pacific Sierra Region, in San Bruno, California. Other official lists were destroyed by fire in 1851 and 1940. Reconstructed lists are indexed in P. William Filby with Mary K. Meyer, *Passenger and Immigration Lists Index* (Detroit: Gale Research Co., 1981–).

Figure 2-33. A passenger on the Ward Line, ca. 1920.

In addition to the passenger lists kept by state and federal governments, there are some city lists. The Baltimore City Passenger Lists, 1833 to 1866, have a Soundex index. The originals are in the Baltimore City archive, and the Family History Library has microfilm copies that can be borrowed from its family history centers.

For pre-1820 official lists, researchers must rely on surviving ship cargo manifests. Many colonial and U.S. ports kept copies of manifests filed as a requirement of clearance. Extant manifests have been scattered among archives, museums, and other historical agencies, but most have been published and are indexed in *Passenger and Immigration Lists Index*.

Passenger lists created after 1820 are usually separate documents if the ship was a passenger liner. If the ship was a cargo vessel which also carried passengers, passengers were listed on the ship's manifest with the master, crew, and cargo. Some people were actually shipped by the pound as if they were trunks of books or bales of wool. Before 1820, most immigrants were not declared as passengers, and many were landed in harbors where customs houses had not been established. Masters who landed passengers without permission, however, could be forced to return them or give security to customs officials by bond to cover costs of removal for illegal entry. Some ports required the payment of a head tax and issued certificates or permits to land. When the federal government began to regulate immigration in 1820, each ship was required by law to submit an official list of passengers carried. Masters who failed to comply could be fined and denied port clearance.

Federal control brought about the creation of three types of passenger arrival records: *customs passenger lists, immigration passenger lists,* and *customs lists of aliens*. All of them are available for searching, with some restrictions. A thorough discussion of the nature and history of U.S. passenger lists is Michael Tepper's *American Passenger Arrival Records* (Baltimore: Genealogical Publishing Co., 1988). A succinct guide to using those lists and the available indexes is John P. Colletta's *They Came in Ships: A Guide to Finding Your Immigrant Ancestor's Arrival Record*, rev. ed. (Salt Lake City: Ancestry, 1993).

PUBLISHED PASSENGER LISTS AND INDEXES

One of the most significant developments in genealogy in the past fifteen years is the publication of indexes to immigration lists. The largest project is the *Passenger and Immigration Lists Index* (cited above), which contains more than 2 million entries for immigrants from the British Isles and Europe. In this source, all names in each list are indexed: where maiden names are found, the women are indexed under both their married and maiden names; if a man has two or more given names, he is listed under each of his given names in the source. By contrast, Ralph B. Strassburger and William John Hinke's *Pennsylvania German Pioneers: A Publication of Original Lists of Arrivals in the Port of Philadelphia from 1727 to 1808* (Norristown: Pennsylvania German Society, 1934) includes Johannes Andreas Hoffman from three different lists. All three lists, however, are indexed under Johannes Andreas only. Thus, if you were looking for Andreas Hoffman, you would find only two entries in the index, when there are actually three. In Filby's *Passenger and Immigration Lists Index*, however, he is indexed under both Johannes and Andreas, thus making him retrievable from the Strassburger and Hinke compilation as well. In Filby's index, each immigrant is identified by name (spelled as it appeared in the source), age (if given), place of arrival, year of arrival, source code, and page number. All persons traveling together are listed with the head of the household as a group and cross-referenced to all family members who immigrated together.

The *Passenger and Immigration Lists Index* covers only lists that have been printed. It does not include entries from the original passenger arrival records. As these materials are published, however, they will be indexed in future *Index* volumes. The list of sources appears in two forms: a short title with key and a full bibliographic entry. It is easy to photocopy the short title list on four pages and keep it with your research notes.

An important aid to the series is P. William Filby, comp., *Passenger and Immigration Lists Bibliography, 1538–1900,* 2nd ed. (Detroit: Gale Research Co., 1988). This bibliography updates Harold Lancour's original *Bibliography of Passenger Lists* (New York: New York Public Library, 1937), rev. and enl. by Richard Wolfe (New York: New York Public Library, 1963) and expands it from 262 titles to more than 2,550. Each source listed is cited in full with a descriptive annotation of contents, coverage, and related immigration lists. For the sources that have been reprinted, the facts of publication for the reprint are given. This bibliography will continue to expand as Filby adds new sources to the index. It is the "master list" from which sources to be included in the *Passenger and Immigration Index* are selected. By 1994, more than 2,200 of the sources had been indexed. Each annual index adds approximately one hundred sources to the total number indexed each year. However, sources continue to be published, so there is no apparent end to this indexing project.

Of the original 262 lists described in Lancour's bibliography drawn from printed sources, 30 percent are emigrant lists recorded at the port of embarkation, 8 percent are passenger lists recorded at the port of arrival, 4 percent are ships' lists, and approximately 15 percent are compiled works on settlers in specific localities drawn from church records, convict and pauper lists, naturalizations, customs lists, legal papers and petitions, county histories, oaths of allegiance, and other records. Filby's bibliography continues this broad coverage.

COLONIAL LISTS

Before 1820, the American colonies made virtually no effort to require lists of immigrants arriving in what is now the United States. Indeed, before the revolutionary war (1775 to 1783), there was no federal government to make such a request. Therefore, control of immigration was left to the original colonies. Inasmuch as they were *British* colonies, and nearly eighty percent of the white immigrants before 1790 came from British countries, there was no need to record these arrivals. According to Michael Tepper, even for ships carrying the original colonists—first purchasers, first planters, etc.—there are few actual lists of passengers.

In light of this situation, it is fortunate that any colonial immigrants were recorded. In fact, a large majority of immigrant families have been documented, but, as Tepper points out when discussing the original settlers, they "are largely recorded—where they are recorded at all—in ancillary records and documents." Use of such "ancillary records," including lists of departure from British countries, is a boon to colonial immigration studies. They allow identification of at least some members of an immigrant's family (usually the head) for upwards of seventy to eighty percent of the colonial white immigrants. The vast majority of these records have been published over the past few decades, with the happy result that virtually all of them are indexed in Filby's *Passenger and Immigration Lists Index*.

Because of the great interest in, and availability of, the colonial Pennsylvania lists, some discussion is warranted here. Beginning in 1727, Pennsylvania required that non-British immigrants (essentially Germans) be identified. Three passenger lists were compiled for these Pennsylvania German immigrants: (1) the captain's lists made on board the ship by the ship's mate from the manifest; (2) lists of oaths of allegiance to the king of Great Britain that were signed by all male immigrants over age sixteen who were well enough to march in procession to a magistrate (the captain's lists and the oaths of allegiance were submitted to the Pennsylvania government on large, loose sheets of paper; not all of them have survived); and (3) lists of signers of the oath of fidelity and abjuration. This oath was a renunciation of claims to the throne of England by "pretenders" and a denial of the right of the pope to outlaw a Protestant monarch. Those males over age sixteen who were well enough to walk to the courthouse also signed these renunciations in a series of bound ledger volumes that have survived intact. The editors of *Pennsylvania German Pioneers*, Strassburger and Hinke, estimated that only two out of five passengers are recorded on the signed lists.

The original order of the names on the lists is important. The first signatures are often those of the leaders, for the Palatines (immigrants from the Rhine River Valley of Germany—the Palatinate) came in groups. The names themselves are significant, for they may represent a whole church group or a group of related families. For these reasons, copy the whole passenger list where the ancestor appears and study the names carefully. The lists serve as a check to identify the correct ancestor in church registers, census lists, news announcements, and other records. The spelling of names on the captains' lists is often inaccurate and different from the way the names appear on the other two.

U.S. CUSTOMS PASSENGER LISTS (1820 TO 1905)

Custom passenger lists were filed by the ship masters with the collector of customs in each port. The original lists were prepared in duplicate on board ship and signed by the master of the vessel (under oath) and the customs authority. One copy was filed with the collector of customs; the other copy was returned to the master to be kept with the ships' papers. On the list, the master was also required to record births and deaths during the voyage. Under a British/American law of 1855, copies of the passenger lists for British ships were also given to the British consuls in the American port.

Original lists are extant for seven U.S. ports only. Copies or abstracts of the original lists were made by the collectors of customs and sent quarterly to the secretary of state. In them, the information was usually abbreviated, and copying errors were undoubtedly made. Transcriptions were also made for 1819 to 1832 lists from the copies sent to the Department of State. These are arranged by name of district or port, name of vessel, and name of passenger. The transcripts are third-generation copies and, as such, contain many errors.

Customs officials were also responsible to see that each ship entering and leaving port was licensed and registered. They also recorded ships' manifests listing crew, passengers, and cargo; ships' logs with statements on the conditions of the passengers and births, marriages, and deaths at sea; payroll accounts with signatures for seamen; ships' accounts for provisions advanced to emigrants; and miscellaneous documents that related to the ship itself. These documents, sometimes called *shipping records* (or *customs records*) can be found in the possession of the shipping company, the customs house, or in local archives or the National Archives.

IMMIGRATION PASSENGER LISTS (1883 TO 1945)

As a result of an act of 1882 (22 Stat. 214), immigrants arriving in the United States were to be recorded by federal immigration officials. The resulting lists date from 1891 for most ports and from 1883 for the port of Philadelphia. The National Archives has microfilmed these lists, which contain the following information: name of master, name of vessel, ports of arrival and embarkation, date of arrival, and, for each passenger, name, place of birth, last legal residence, age, occupation, sex, and remarks.

With the introduction of standard federal forms in 1893, passenger list information was changed to include the name of the shipmaster, name of vessel, ports of arrival and embarkation, date of arrival, and the following information for each passenger: full name; age; sex; marital status; occupation; nationality; last residence; final destination; whether in the United States before and, if so, when and where; whether going to join a relative and, if so, the relative's name, address, and relationship to the passen-

ger. Other revisions of the format included race (1903); personal description and birthplace (1906); and name and address of the nearest relative in the immigrant's home country (1907). It should be noted that these lists include not only names of immigrants but also of visitors and Americans returning from abroad. Passenger lists are arranged by port and thereunder by date. Records of a few ports have been indexed, some for limited years.

BORDER CROSSINGS

The National Archives of the United States has several collections of arrival indexes and manifests for persons crossing the border between the United States and Canada. Most of these are listed as records of the St. Albans District, but they are not limited to those who actually came through St. Albans. Rather, the district encompassed most of the U.S.-Canadian border. The records begin in 1895 and cover arrivals as late as 1954. The microfilmed collections, most of which are also available through the Family History Library and its centers, include the following.

St. Albans District Manifest Records of Aliens Arriving from Foreign Contiguous Territory. These 1,169 rolls of microfilm include Soundex cards and original manifests giving detailed information pertaining to border crossings. All crossings (from Maine to Washington) are included between 1895 and 1915. Beginning in 1915, the records are limited to border crossing in the New York-Vermont region; however, this includes major eastern Canadian seaports where U.S. officials processed ship passengers bound for the United States. This collection includes:

Soundex Index to Canadian Border Entries Through the St. Albans, Vermont District, 1895-1924. These four hundred rolls of index cards give complete geographic coverage to 1915. Some of these index cards are the actual records of crossing; in those cases there is no original manifest.

Soundex Index to Entries into the St. Albans, Vermont District Through Canadian Pacific and Atlantic Ports, 1924-1952. The ninety-eight rolls of index cards in this set pertain to border crossing in the New York-Vermont area.

Manifests of Passengers Arriving in the St. Albans, Vermont District Through Canadian Pacific and Atlantic Ports, 1895-1954. These 640 rolls are the ship lists of arrivals indexed by the above Soundex cards.

Manifests of Passengers Arriving in the St. Albans, Vermont District Through Canadian Pacific Ports, 1929-1949. These twenty-five rolls of microfilm supplement the above passenger lists.

Alphabetical Index to Canadian Border Entries Through Small Ports in Vermont, 1895-1924. These six rolls of microfilm are of card indexes of arrivals at small ports in Vermont. Each port is arranged alphabetically. This is especially useful for identifying Canadians who settled in New England.

Detroit District Manifest Records of Aliens Arriving from Foreign Contiguous Territory. This collection includes 117 rolls of microfilm of the original card manifests, arranged alphabetically, for persons entering the United States through Detroit, and some other Michigan ports from 1906 to 1954. An additional twenty-three rolls include passenger and alien crew lists of vessels arriving at Detroit, 1946 to 1957.

Recently, the National Archives has begun microfilming border crossings for later years in western Canada and for arrivals across the Mexican border. Information on these records is sketchy but will undoubtedly be described in genealogical periodicals as the records become available.

INDEXED PORTS

Indexes for the Port of New York are available only for the years 1820 to 1846, 1897 to 1902, 1902 to 1943, and 1944 to 1948. While far from complete, a monumental effort is under way to index ship passenger lists for the Port of New York for the years between 1846 and 1897. The significant interest and advances in computer technology should make this long-awaited project a reality.

In addition to the above-mentioned indexes for the Port of New York, the following major ports have been indexed:

- Baltimore: 1820 to 1897, 1897 to 1952
- Boston: 1848 to 1891, 1902 to 1906, 1906 to 1920, and 1899 to 1940
- New Orleans: 1853 to 1899, 1900 to 1952
- Philadelphia: 1800 to 1906, 1883 to 1948

WHEN PASSENGER LISTS ARE NOT INDEXED

As noted in the very detailed description of passenger lists in *Guide to Genealogical Research in the National Archives,* rev. ed. (Washington, D.C.: National Archives Trust Fund Board, 1991), page 41, the lists were "written by many different hands over many years and conditions of their preservation before they were placed in the National Archives were not ideal." Many lists are difficult to read; some brittle pages have broken away, and smeared ink has blurred words beyond recognition. Unless an immigrant's name can be found in an index, or unless the exact date and port of arrival are known, searching through voluminous and hard-to-read passenger lists can be exhausting and futile work. After microfilming the records, the National Archives transferred them to the Balch Institute at Temple University in Philadelphia, so originals are no longer available for inspection.

For the Port of New York, there are some potentially helpful finding aids. On twenty-seven rolls of

National Archives microfilm is *Registers of Vessels Arriving at the Port of New York from Foreign Ports, 1789–1919*. The volumes, most of which identify ships by name, country of origin, type of rig, date of entry, master's name, and last port of embarkation, are arranged in the order of the ships' arrival; some portions are arranged alphabetically by vessel as well. If a researcher can eliminate some vessels because of port of embarkation or date, the search may be more manageable. More readily available to most is Bradley W. Steuart's *Passenger Ships Arriving in New York Harbor (1820–1850)* (Bountiful, Utah: Precision Indexing, 1991). The latter covers unindexed peak immigration years. A volume that has been in use for years is *The Morton Allan Directory of European Passenger Steamship Arrivals* (Immigrant Information Bureau, 1931). The *Morton Allan Directory* includes information on vessels arriving at New York (1890 to 1930) and at Baltimore, Boston, and Philadelphia (1904 to 1926).

GENEALOGICAL AND HISTORICAL ORGANIZATIONS

Many historical, lineage, genealogical, fraternal, and ethnic societies have records concerning immigrants; they should be approached early in most searches. Such societies often collect records, such as family and local histories, oral histories, church records, newspapers, cemetery collections, passenger lists, manuscripts, organization membership applications, early settler indexes, military records, directories, and other records which may help with your search. Genealogical and historical societies exist for almost every geographic locality. Historical societies for most ethnic and religious groups also exist—for example, the American Historical Society of Germans from Russia. Also search for pioneer or old settler societies. Contact societies to learn about their services and hours. They are usually very cooperative and can help locate good local researchers.

The publications of genealogical and historical societies are especially rich and unique sources of local information. Some genealogical societies, libraries, and archives maintain surname registries that have proved useful in linking individuals with similar research interests. These organizations tend to focus on the ethnic groups prominent in their respective areas, and this focus will be reflected in their publications. Newsletters and quarterlies published by societies can be especially rich sources of information on immigrant groups. There are also single-ethnic genealogical and historical societies that have been organized for the purpose of promoting study and preservation of specific national and religious groups. *The Ancestry Family Historian's Address Book* (Salt Lake City: Ancestry, 1997) is a listing of names and addresses of genealogical societies and other important places you may need for immigration and naturalization research. It includes Internet addresses, which are not found in most address books published for the genealogical market.

Genealogical, lineage society, religious, and historical periodicals are most helpful when you know the area in which an immigrant settled and his or her ethnic group. Genealogical and historical societies usually publish periodicals about the people in the geographic area or ethnic group they cover. Family organizations often publish newsletters with immigrant information. Periodicals often reprint a wide variety of material, including abstracts from original sources that discuss immigrants. Periodicals may include:

- Passenger list abstracts
- Naturalization list abstracts
- Sketches about early pioneers
- Ethnic group background information
- Genealogical sketches
- Pedigrees and ahnentafels

PERIODICAL SOURCE INDEX

The *Periodical Source Index (PERSI)* is a comprehensive subject index to genealogy and local history periodicals written in English and French-Canadian since 1800. It is produced by the Allen County Public Library in Fort Wayne, Indiana. (It includes literature dating from the 1700s, though the literature dating from before 1800 is less complete.)

PERSI is a work in progress which has more than 1 million citations that index nearly four thousand genealogical and historical publications. Articles are indexed according to locality, family (surname), and/or research methodology. When you find an appropriate citation in *PERSI*, you will be able to follow a link from the citation to information on the publisher of the article. *PERSI* is available through Ancestry's Web site on the Internet (http://www.ancestry.com), and it has been published by Ancestry on CD-ROM.

ARCHIVES

Without a doubt, the largest collection of federal naturalization records that are of interest to family historians is held by the various regional archives of the National Archives. Because of the volume and complexity of naturalization records held by the National Archives, an entire chapter of this book is dedicated to that subject (see chapter 5).

Many state archives and historical societies preserve and make available older naturalization records. For example, the New Jersey State Archives has New Jersey naturalization records for the colonial period and for part of the nineteenth century; most of them are indexed. *Guide to Family History Sources in the New Jersey State Archives*, 2nd ed. (Trenton: Division of Archives and Records Management, New Jersey Department of State, 1990) lists the following holdings:

Chancery Court declarations and naturalizations, 1832–62
Supreme Court naturalizations: bound volumes, 1851–73
Numbered files, 1761, 1790–1860

Index to Supreme Court minutes, 1681–1837
Petitions to the legislature for naturalization, 1749–1810

The *Guide to Family History Sources in the New Jersey State Archives* also notes that "Most naturalization records from the 1800s to the present are filed at each county clerk's office. As mentioned in the previous section, the State Archives has microfilm copies of most of these records, up to 1906." Many other state archives and historical societies have published guides to their collections. For addresses, see appendix B.

LIBRARIES

Given the enormous volume of naturalization records that exist, only a relatively small number of them have been indexed—and even fewer original documents appear in published form. However, because it is usually easiest to begin a naturalization search in a well-indexed publication, library collections should not be overlooked. Large libraries with genealogical collections and genealogical society libraries often provide the best starting places. Published naturalizations and their related indexes are described in chapter 4.

Libraries, archives, and historical societies in the area where an immigrant settled may have collected previous research about local people. For example, local genealogy collections, vertical files, scrapbooks, school records, newspapers, obituaries, and histories of organizations, towns, and counties are sources that may reveal something about an immigrant's origins.

Large public libraries and libraries with special genealogical collections (possibly one near your home) are among the best places to begin research after personal sources have been exhausted. Among the largest and best-known genealogical collections in the United States are the Family History Library (discussed below), the Library of Congress, Allen

County Public Library (Fort Wayne, Indiana), the New York Public Library, the New England Historic Genealogical Society Library, the State Historical Society of Wisconsin Library, and the Dallas Public Library. Addresses of these and other libraries and archives are in appendix B . If you write before visiting, you may be able to obtain a guide to a library's collections, usually free or for a small fee. (Be sure to call before visiting to be certain the library is open and that you can obtain access to the material you need. Many libraries close collections while they remodel, and some are closed on certain days of the week and for local holidays.) For an in-depth study of library materials and how to use them most effectively, see Kory Meyerink, ed., *Printed Sources* (Salt Lake City: Ancestry, 1998).

THE FAMILY HISTORY LIBRARY

The Family History Library of the LDS church is the largest library in the world specializing in genealogical and family history material. The scope of the library's collections and easy access provided by its thousands of branch libraries (family history centers) makes it useful for every family historian. Its history dates back to 1894, when the Genealogical Society of Utah was founded to gather and preserve the various records that help people trace their ancestry. Shortly after its founding, the society opened a library that later became the Family History Library. In 1938, the society began preserving records on microfilm. Birth, marriage, death, probate, immigration, military, and many other records in more than fifty countries have been (and continue to be) microfilmed. Among them are millions of naturalization records. Through this activity, as well as a carefully planned purchasing program, the Family History Library has acquired the world's largest collection of genealogical information.

Since 1944, the library (as well as the Genealogical Society of Utah) has been wholly owned and operated by the LDS church. All persons, regardless of religion, are welcome to visit the library and use its collections and services at no charge. In 1964, a system of branch libraries, now called family history centers, was established to give more people wider access to the library's resources.

The heart of the library's collection includes approximately 2 million rolls of microfilmed records and more than 500,000 microfiche. The collection includes records kept by individuals, as well as by governments, churches of many denominations, and other organizations. The library's substantial collection of records for many areas of the world dates from around 1550 to around 1920. To honor "rights of privacy" regulations, the library has few records of living persons.

The Family History Library currently supports more than 2,500 family history centers throughout the world. As branches of the Family History Library, they can provide access to almost all of the microfilm and microfiche maintained at the main library. Because of the LDS church's interest in genealogical research, these centers have been provided to give church members and the entire public use of the library's resources without having to travel to Salt Lake City.

Family history centers have been established in most LDS stake center buildings. (A stake is a group of six to twelve "wards," or congregations.) Through them, microfilm and microfiche copies of the records at the Family History Library in Salt Lake City can be borrowed for a small handling fee. The books at the main library, which mostly comprise printed family histories, do not circulate, but more than half of them are available on microfilm.

Family history centers are found throughout the United States and in dozens of foreign countries, generally near large population centers. Usually these centers are equipped with microfilm and microfiche reading machines, computers with the *FamilySearch* program, a copy of the *Family History Library Catalog*, and other major genealogical sources, such as the *International Genealogical Index*.

The Family History Library and the family history centers have millions of names of individuals that will be found in naturalization indexes and other immigration topics. To locate a family history center near you, contact a local congregation of The Church of Jesus Christ of Latter-day Saints (see the white pages of a telephone directory) or a local genealogical society. In addition, a list of family history centers in your state can be obtained from the Family History Library, 35 North West Temple Street, Salt Lake City, UT 84150 (telephone: 801-240-2331). Many of the naturalization records that are available from the Family History Library are listed with microfilm roll numbers in *Guide to Naturalization Records of the United States* by Christina K. Schaefer (Baltimore: Genealogical Publishing Co., 1997)

Research Approaches

In their eagerness to learn which town or city was home to their ancestors, researchers frequently spend time and energy looking in the wrong places—or in the wrong sequence. For example, as novices, many are tempted to begin immigrant research with a search of ship passenger lists.

Most researchers have a strong desire to find detailed documentation of the ship on which an ancestor came to America. Such a passage, after all, is a seminal event in the history of any family. From a passenger list, we hope to learn exactly where an immigrant ancestor came from, how old he or she was at the time, what occupation he or she claimed, the ports of departure and arrival, and anything possible about the journey. But getting answers to these questions depends on when and where an ancestor arrived in the United States. Until the 1880s, a typical passenger list gave only the name, age, sex, occupation, country of origin, and destination of the passenger. The native town was seldom named.

Is the port of the ancestor's arrival known with certainty? Are passenger arrival lists indexed for the port of entry and for the right time period? If there is an index for the port, will the person of interest appear in the index, or can he or she be identified in the long list of frequently misspelled names? If the surname is a common one, how will the person be distinguished from others of the same name? While many individuals traveled in groups, making them easier to find, a larger number came to the United States on their own. Unless you are fairly certain of the date and port of arrival, or unless you can quickly and surely identify the immigrant by name, age, occupation, or traveling companions, it may be better to postpone a passenger list search until you've investigated other sources.

Because there is no single source that always indicates place of origin, it is crucial to thoroughly search all available original records; this increases your chances of finding the place of origin. You may learn additional identifying facts about the immigrant, and you can develop a fuller biography and better family group records for the immigrant. Checking a variety of resources will often turn up circumstantial evidence, such as the date of arrival, which will help you search for a native town.

Among local records, first seek records related to the immigrant's death. These include church records, vital records, obituaries, cemetery records, and probate records. They may give the immigrant's date and place of birth, or the names of parents and other relatives or friends. They can also provide important clues about religion, naturalization, length of residence, arrival, and property in the old country.

After death records, seek the records of other vital events, such as the immigrant's marriage and the births of children. Vital record entries for marriages and births were kept by both church and civil authorities. Other local original records include a wide variety of record types. Use census records, court records, and land and property records to establish where an immigrant settled, his or her occupation, neighbors, and other information.

By studying a combination of the records explained in this book, it is usually possible to estimate an immigrant's year of arrival in the United States. Even when an immigrant's census or naturalization records do not provide a specific arrival date, noting the dates and places of birth of the immigrant's children in census records or tracking urban dwellers in city directories may help determine the immigration date. Look for clues to these dates in places where the individual or family first settled and in land purchases.

NOTE

1. Szucs, Loretto Dennis, and Sandra Hargreaves Luebking. *The Source: A Guidebook of American Genealogy.* Rev. ed. Salt Lake City: Ancestry, 1997, 117–18.

BIBLIOGRAPHY

Andreas, A. T. *History of Cook County, Illinois.* Chicago: A. T. Andreas Publisher, 1884.

Cullen, James Bernard, ed. *The Story of the Irish in Boston Together With Biographical Sketches of Representative Men and Noted Women.* Boston: James B. Cullen & Company, 1889.

Hone, E. Wade, and Heritage Consulting and Services. *Land and Property Research in the United States.* Salt Lake City: Ancestry, 1997.

Lainhart, Ann S. *State Census Records.* Baltimore: Genealogical Publishing Co., 1992.

Morawski, Henry. *Poles of Chicago 1837–1937: A History of One Century of Polish Contribution to the City of Chicago, Illinois.* Chicago: Polish Pageant, 1937.

New Jersey Department of State, Division of Archives and Records Management. *Guide to Family History Sources in the New Jersey State Archives.* 2nd ed. Trenton, N.J., 1990.

Rosicky, Rose. *A History of Czechs (Bohemians) in Nebraska.* Omaha: Czech Historical Society of Nebraska, 1929.

Schaefer, Christina K. *Guide to Naturalization Records of the United States.* Baltimore: Genealogical Publishing Co., 1997.

Smith, Juliana Szucs. *The Ancestry Family Historian's Address Book: A Comprehensive List of Local, State, and Federal Agencies and Institutions and Ethnic and Genealogical Organizations.* Salt Lake City: Ancestry, 1998.

Szucs, Loretto Dennis, and Sandra Hargreaves Luebking. *The Source: A Guidebook of American Genealogy.* Rev. ed. Salt Lake City: Ancestry, 1997.

Ulvestad, Martin. *Nordmaendene I Amerika* [Norwegians in America], 2 vols. Minneapolis: History Book Company's Forlag, 1907–10.

*The Jasper County, Indiana, courthouse has records
for that county dating back to 1865.*

Chapter Three Highlights

- *Court records*
- *Local court records*
- *Federal court records*
- *The naturalization process*
  - *Declaration of intention (first papers)*
  - *Petition (second, or final, papers)*
  - *Naturalization oaths*
  - *Certificate of naturalization*
  - *Certificates of arrival*

- *Finding naturalization records by following emigration patterns*
- *Court boundaries and jurisdictions*
- *Re-recorded court records*
- *Indexes*
- *Unexpected treasures*
- *When information sources don't match*
- *Tips on accessing court records*
- *The Family History Library and its family history centers*

CHAPTER THREE

Naturalization Courts and Processes

COURT RECORDS

Court records are the essence of history. Millions of court documents attest to the building of the United States and to the everyday affairs of common individuals. Court records represent American life—the customs, attitudes, and social structures; the interrelationships between private and public sectors; the struggles and frustrations of individuals and groups. Perhaps more than any other single record category, court records mirror America.

For a nation of immigrants fascinated by its ethnic past, American courts offer a wealth of detailed records. Among court records, naturalization documents are some of the most frequently used by family historians.

The power of naturalization is vested exclusively in Congress by the Constitution. Since 1790, Congress has implemented laws requiring naturalization to occur in a court of record. The courts have had a variety of names which differ from one state to another, such as supreme, circuit, district, common pleas, chancery, probate, superior, and equity. Many naturalization documents are shown in this chapter because there is no better way to illustrate the diversity of forms that were used. The documents speak for themselves.

LOCAL COURT RECORDS

Aliens hoping to become American citizens were required to go to a court and fill out the necessary forms. Before 1906, an alien could be naturalized in any court of record. In most cases, it is best to begin a search for naturalization documents in courts in the county where an immigrant is known to have resided. After the mandatory residence period (which was, with a few exceptions, five years), an alien was required to bring two witnesses and present himself in court to fill out a petition for citizenship, take an oath of allegiance, and prove that the residency requirements were satisfied. Anxious to become citizens, many immigrants began the citizenship process by taking out first papers in the county where they first arrived in the United States, then completed the requirements in the county in which they lived when the time requirement was met. For example, John Kopp took out his first papers in Philadelphia (figure 3-1) and completed the citizenship process in Detroit. The declaration and final papers are filed together in the National Archives–Great Lakes Region in Chicago, along with millions of other federal records from six Midwestern states. Whether affidavits and final oaths were recorded on separate forms depended on the court

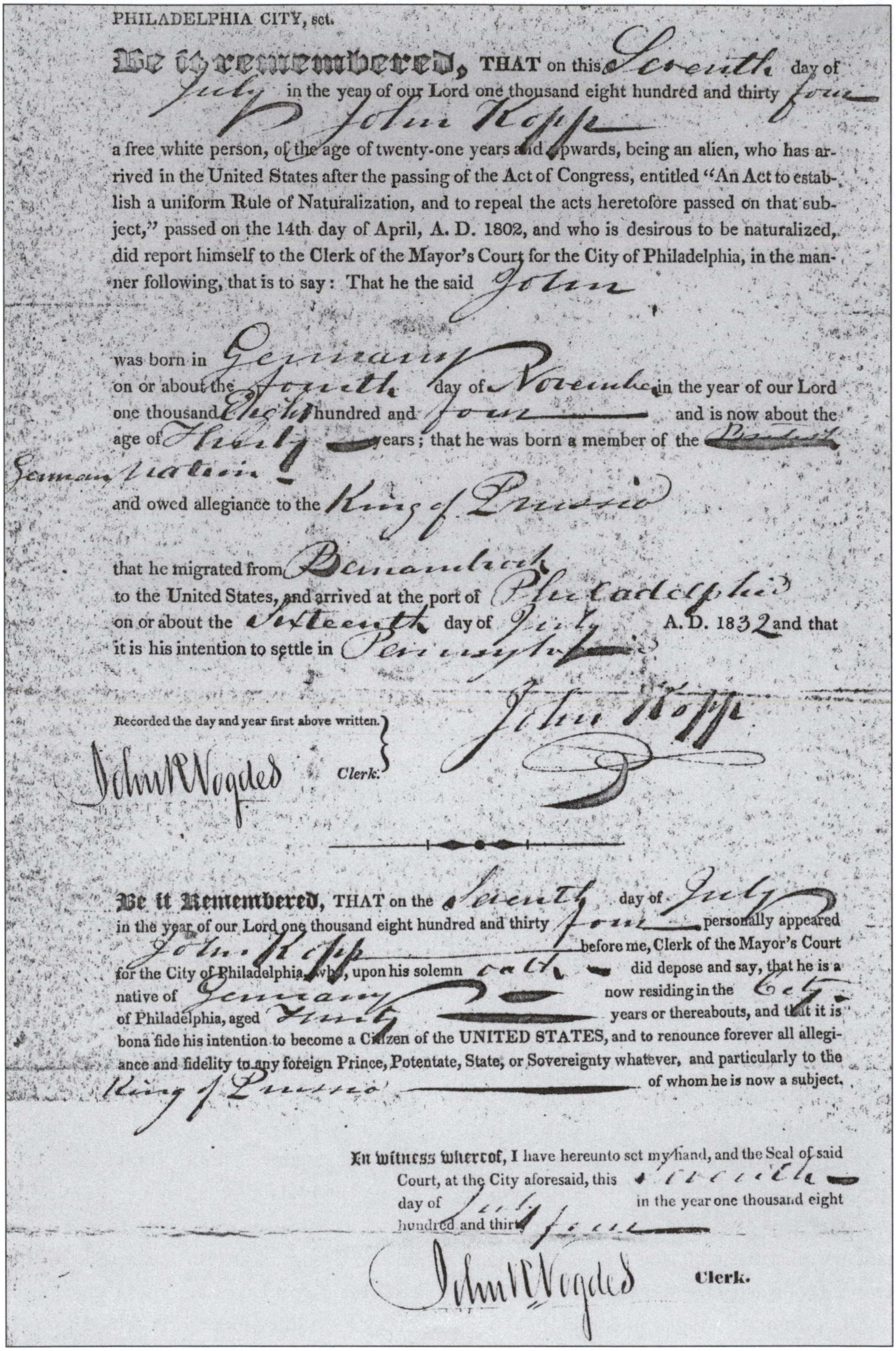

PHILADELPHIA CITY, sct.

Be it remembered, THAT on this Seventh day of July in the year of our Lord one thousand eight hundred and thirty four John Kopp a free white person, of the age of twenty-one years and upwards, being an alien, who has arrived in the United States after the passing of the Act of Congress, entitled "An Act to establish a uniform Rule of Naturalization, and to repeal the acts heretofore passed on that subject," passed on the 14th day of April, A. D. 1802, and who is desirous to be naturalized, did report himself to the Clerk of the Mayor's Court for the City of Philadelphia, in the manner following, that is to say: That he the said John

was born in Germany on or about the fourth day of November in the year of our Lord one thousand Eight hundred and four and is now about the age of Thirty years; that he was born a member of the German nation

and owed allegiance to the King of Prussia

that he migrated from Bernambruck to the United States, and arrived at the port of Philadelphia on or about the Sixteenth day of July A. D. 1832 and that it is his intention to settle in Pennsylvania

John Kopp

Recorded the day and year first above written.
John R Vogdes Clerk.

Be it Remembered, THAT on the Seventh day of July in the year of our Lord one thousand eight hundred and thirty four personally appeared John Kopp before me, Clerk of the Mayor's Court for the City of Philadelphia, who, upon his solemn oath did depose and say, that he is a native of Germany now residing in the City of Philadelphia, aged Thirty years or thereabouts, and that it is bona fide his intention to become a Citizen of the UNITED STATES, and to renounce forever all allegiance and fidelity to any foreign Prince, Potentate, State, or Sovereignty whatever, and particularly to the King of Prussia of whom he is now a subject.

In witness whereof, I have hereunto set my hand, and the Seal of said Court, at the City aforesaid, this Seventh day of July in the year one thousand eight hundred and thirty four

John R Vogdes Clerk.

Figure 3-1. Declaration of intention of John Kopp from the Philadelphia Mayor's Court, 1834.

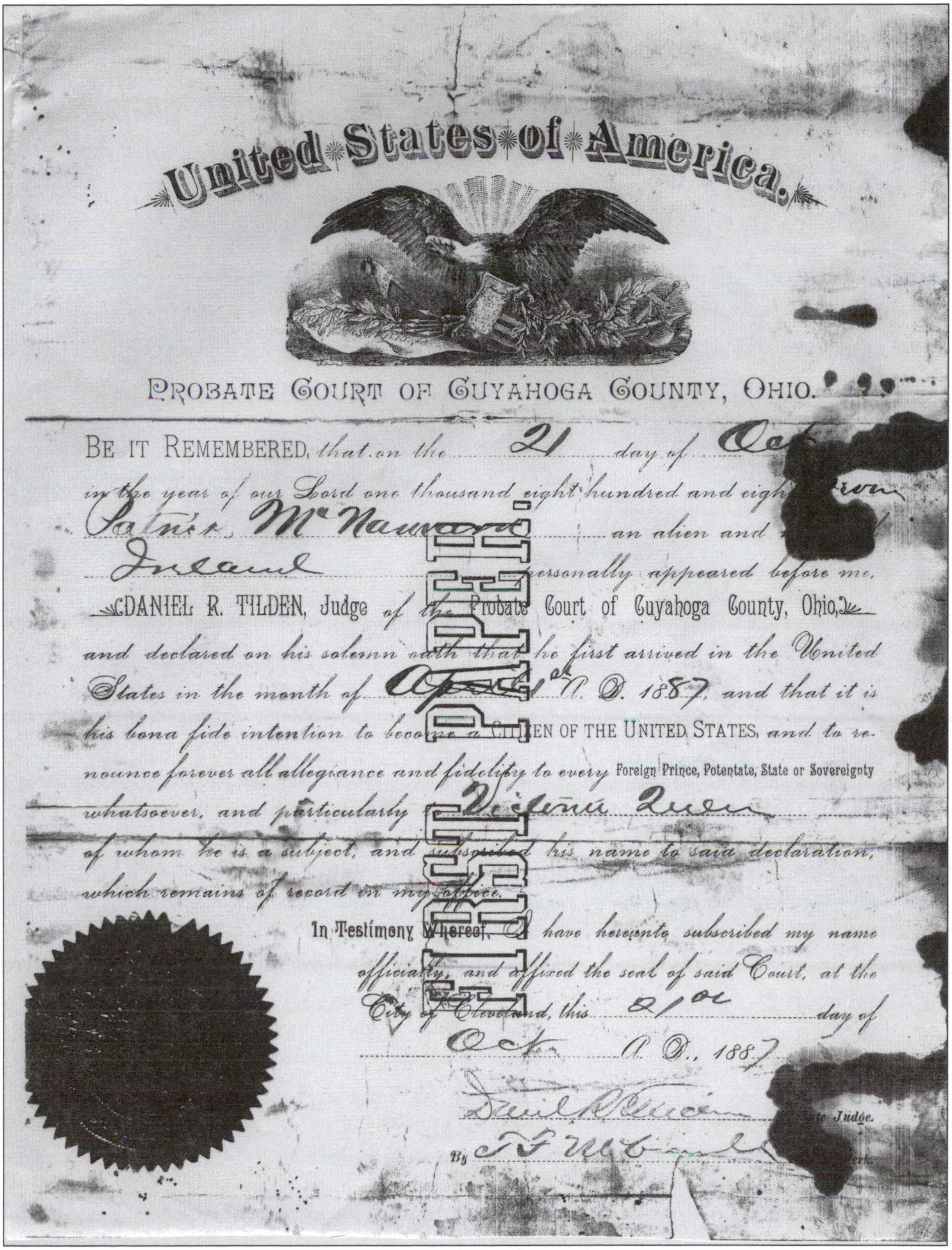

United States of America.

PROBATE COURT OF CUYAHOGA COUNTY, OHIO.

BE IT REMEMBERED, that on the 21 day of Oct in the year of our Lord one thousand eight hundred and eighty seven Patrick McNamara an alien and [illegible] Ireland personally appeared before me, DANIEL R. TILDEN, Judge of the Probate Court of Cuyahoga County, Ohio, and declared on his solemn oath that he first arrived in the United States in the month of April A. D. 1887, and that it is his bona fide intention to become a CITIZEN OF THE UNITED STATES, and to renounce forever all allegiance and fidelity to every Foreign Prince, Potentate, State or Sovereignty whatsoever, and particularly Victoria Queen of whom he is a subject, and subscribed his name to said declaration, which remains of record in my office.

FIRST PAPER.

In Testimony Whereof, I have hereunto subscribed my name officially, and affixed the seal of said Court, at the City of Cleveland, this 21st day of Oct A. D., 1887

Daniel R. Tilden [illegible] Judge.

By T F McBride [illegible] Clerk.

Figure 3-2. First paper (declaration of intention) of Patrick McNamara, Cuyahoga County (Cleveland), Ohio.

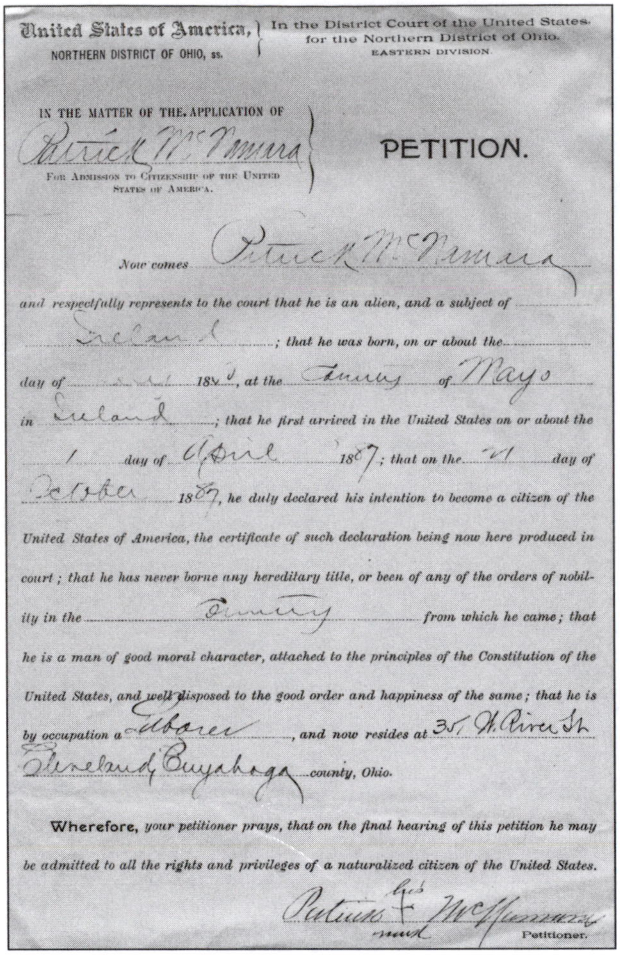

United States of America, NORTHERN DISTRICT OF OHIO, ss. } In the District Court of the United States for the Northern District of Ohio. EASTERN DIVISION.

IN THE MATTER OF THE APPLICATION OF Patrick McNamara FOR ADMISSION TO CITIZENSHIP OF THE UNITED STATES OF AMERICA. } PETITION.

Now comes Patrick McNamara *and respectfully represents to the court that he is an alien, and a subject of* Ireland *; that he was born, on or about the* ... *day of* ... *18*... *, at the* County *of* Mayo *in* Ireland *; that he first arrived in the United States on or about the* 1 *day of* April *18*87 *; that on the* ... *day of* October *18*89 *, he duly declared his intention to become a citizen of the United States of America, the certificate of such declaration being now here produced in court; that he has never borne any hereditary title, or been of any of the orders of nobility in the* County *from which he came; that he is a man of good moral character, attached to the principles of the Constitution of the United States, and well disposed to the good order and happiness of the same; that he is by occupation a* Laborer *, and now resides at* 35 W. River St. Cleveland, Cuyahoga *county, Ohio.*

Wherefore, *your petitioner prays, that on the final hearing of this petition he may be admitted to all the rights and privileges of a naturalized citizen of the United States.*

Patrick his mark McNamara, Petitioner.

Figure 3-3. Petition of Patrick McNamara, Cuyahoga County (Cleveland), Ohio.

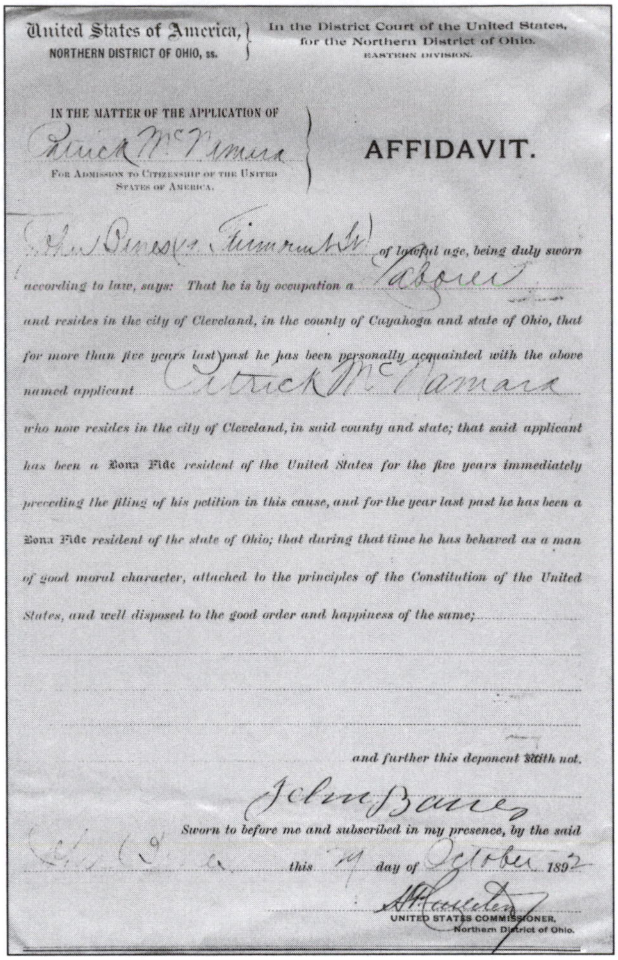

United States of America, NORTHERN DISTRICT OF OHIO, ss. } In the District Court of the United States for the Northern District of Ohio. EASTERN DIVISION.

IN THE MATTER OF THE APPLICATION OF Patrick McNamara FOR ADMISSION TO CITIZENSHIP OF THE UNITED STATES OF AMERICA. } AFFIDAVIT.

... *of lawful age, being duly sworn according to law, says: That he is by occupation a* Laborer *and resides in the city of Cleveland, in the county of Cuyahoga and state of Ohio, that for more than five years last past he has been personally acquainted with the above named applicant* Patrick McNamara *who now resides in the city of Cleveland, in said county and state; that said applicant has been a Bona Fide resident of the United States for the five years immediately preceding the filing of his petition in this cause, and for the year last past he has been a Bona Fide resident of the state of Ohio; that during that time he has behaved as a man of good moral character, attached to the principles of the Constitution of the United States, and well disposed to the good order and happiness of the same;*

and further this deponent saith not.

John Barnes

Sworn to before me and subscribed in my presence, by the said ... *this* ... *day of* October *189*2

UNITED STATES COMMISSIONER, Northern District of Ohio.

Figure 3-4. Affidavit of a witness on behalf of Patrick McNamara, Cuyahoga County (Cleveland), Ohio.

and the year. When they exist as separate papers, they are usually filed with the final papers, as in the case of Patrick McNamara, who was naturalized in the Cuyahoga County Court (Cleveland), Ohio. See figures 3-2, 3-3, 3-4, and 3-5.

Federal Court Records

From 1790 until very recently, any individual could be naturalized in a federal court, although most people went to local courts. After 1906, the vast majority of naturalizations took place in federal courts, although some local courts continued to naturalize long after that date (see figure 3-6).

Records of naturalization proceedings in federal courts are usually among the records kept in the district in which such proceedings took place. Some federal court naturalization records are still in the custody of the court; others have been transferred to the National Archives in Washington, D.C., or to other locations in the National Archives regional system.

Understanding the establishment and evolution of the federal court system is important for effective use of U.S. District Court naturalization records. The Judiciary Act of 24 September 1789 established a national judiciary system separate and distinct from those of the states. The act, while providing for a Supreme Court, also established a system of circuit and district courts and allowed for the transition

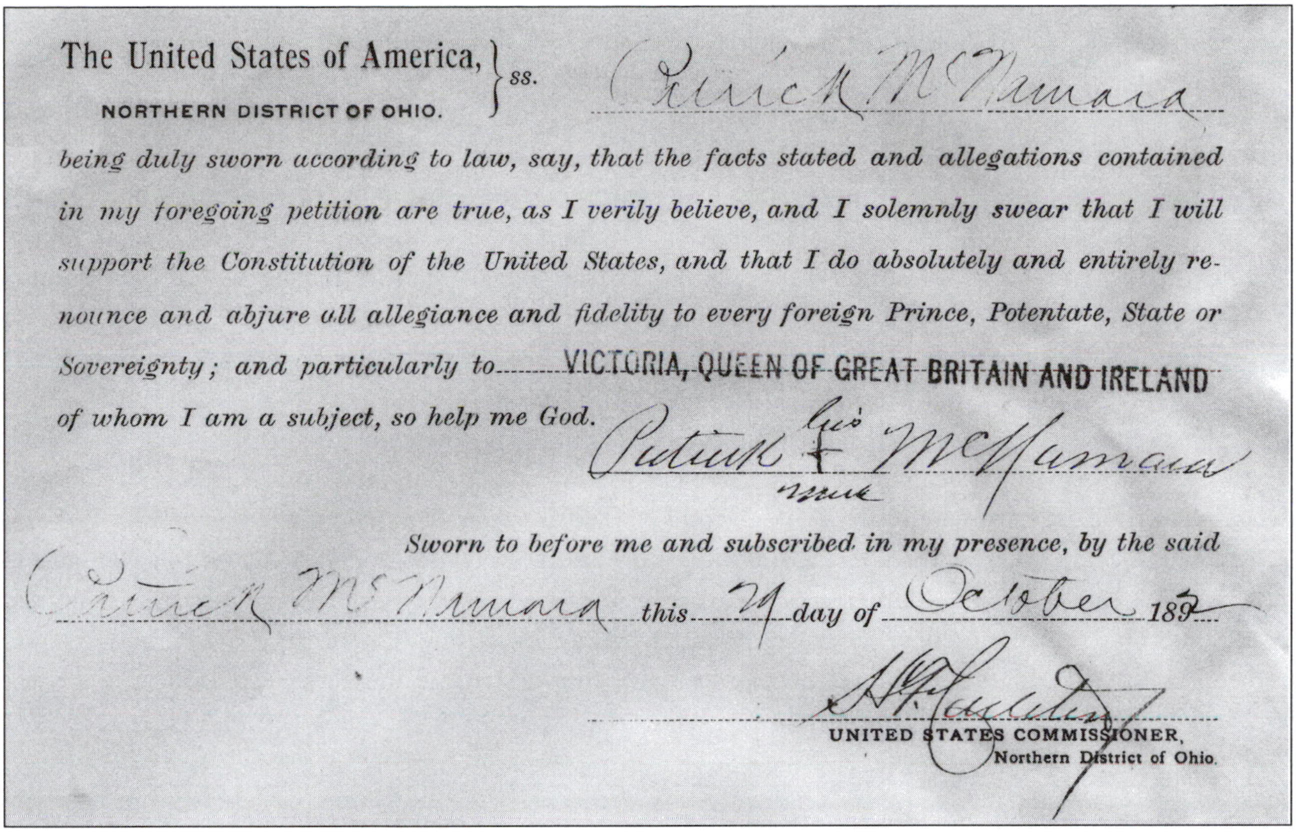
The United States of America, } ss. Patrick McNamara
NORTHERN DISTRICT OF OHIO.

being duly sworn according to law, say, that the facts stated and allegations contained in my foregoing petition are true, as I verily believe, and I solemnly swear that I will support the Constitution of the United States, and that I do absolutely and entirely renounce and abjure all allegiance and fidelity to every foreign Prince, Potentate, State or Sovereignty; and particularly to VICTORIA, QUEEN OF GREAT BRITAIN AND IRELAND *of whom I am a subject, so help me God.*

Patrick his X mark McNamara

Sworn to before me and subscribed in my presence, by the said Patrick McNamara *this* 29 *day of* October *189*

UNITED STATES COMMISSIONER,
Northern District of Ohio.

Figure 3-5. Final oath of Patrick McNamara, Cuyahoga County (Cleveland), Ohio.

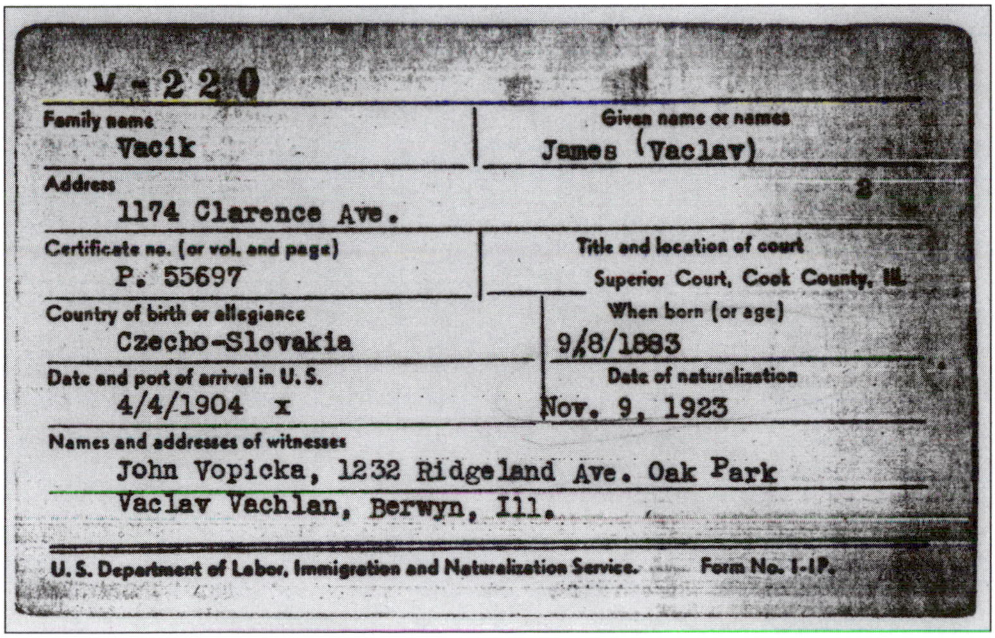
V-220

Family name	Given name or names
Vacik	James (Vaclav)

Address
1174 Clarence Ave. 2

Certificate no. (or vol. and page)	Title and location of court
P. 55697	Superior Court, Cook County, Ill.

Country of birth or allegiance	When born (or age)
Czecho-Slovakia	9/8/1883

Date and port of arrival in U.S.	Date of naturalization
4/4/1904 x	Nov. 9, 1923

Names and addresses of witnesses
John Vopicka, 1232 Ridgeland Ave. Oak Park
Vaclav Vachlan, Berwyn, Ill.

U.S. Department of Labor, Immigration and Naturalization Service. Form No. I-IP.

Figure 3-6: The Soundex index card for James (Vaclav) Vacik, who was naturalized in the Superior Court of Cook County, Illinois, 9 November 1923.

within newly admitted states of the territorial courts into the federal system.

Initially, three circuit courts were created by the 1789 act. These were designated the Southern, Middle, and Eastern circuits. Their jurisdiction extended to all matters that could be tried under federal statutes. In 1802, realignment resulted in six circuits embracing all the states then in the Union, with the exception of Kentucky, Tennessee, Ohio, and Maine (Maine at that time was still a part of Massachusetts). Each of these circuits was designated by number. In 1807, Congress created the Seventh Circuit, to consist of the states of Tennessee, Kentucky, and Ohio. In 1820 Maine was admitted to the Union and added to the First Circuit. No other changes were made until 1837, when nine new states were admitted to the Union. Congress then created two new

circuits, the Eighth and Ninth, and all twenty-six states were assigned to circuits.

In 1842, Alabama and Louisiana were detached from the Ninth Circuit and designated as the Fifth Circuit. The states that comprised the former Fifth Circuit were assigned either to the Fourth or the Sixth circuits. During the Civil War, circuit court operations in the Southern states were suspended, and Confederate courts conducted the business of the judiciary.

By 1862, the states admitted to the Union since 1842 had been assigned to enlarged circuits, and circuit court jurisdiction of the district courts in Texas, Florida, Wisconsin, Minnesota, Iowa, and Kansas was abolished. There were now ten circuits, with the area comprising California, Nevada, and Oregon being designated the Tenth Circuit. The next year,

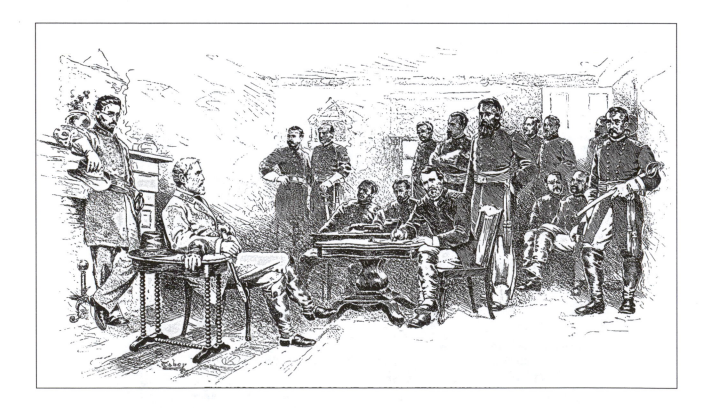

Figure 3-7. An awareness of historical events is critical to naturalization and ethnic research. During the Civil War, circuit court operations in the Southern states were suspended, and Confederate courts conducted the business of the judiciary.

Indiana was detached from the Seventh Circuit and assigned to the Eighth Circuit.

By an act of 23 July 1866, the Tenth Circuit was abolished and all the states were divided among the nine circuits. From 1866 to 1929, new states were assigned to either the Eighth or Ninth circuits. In 1929 a Tenth Circuit was recreated from the Eighth Circuit. Since that time, the District of Columbia has been recognized as constituting an Eleventh Circuit.

Until 1869, the circuit court was held by a justice of the U.S. Supreme Court and the district court judge. In that year, the office of circuit judge was created to relieve the Supreme Court justices of circuit duty. The appointed circuit judges were often required to travel over several states.

The act of 2 March 1892 transferred the appellate jurisdiction of the circuit courts to the newly created Circuit Courts of Appeal. The circuit courts were left with rather limited powers, and their work often overlapped that of the district courts. The Judiciary Act of 1911 abolished the circuit courts. Their records and remaining jurisdiction were transferred to the district courts.

In addition to circuit courts, the Judiciary Act of 1789 created district courts in each state. District courts had limited jurisdiction from 1789 to 1866, except in those states that were not included in a circuit. In the few states where only one federal court (known as the district court) existed, the district court exercised complete federal jurisdiction.

Initially, each district or circuit court served an entire state; but as the volume of litigation increased and a growing population expanded, Congress authorized two or more courts for a state. An act of 29 April 1802 was the first such authorization. This act divided North Carolina into three districts and Tennessee into two districts for the purpose of holding district court. Other such sectioning followed, with Florida being divided into four districts in 1862.

In 1838, some districts were organized into divisions. The first was New York, when the state's Northern District was grouped by counties into the Northern, Eastern, and Western divisions of the Northern District. These divisions were later abolished, and this pattern was not used again until after 1859, when Iowa was separated into divisions. However, since that time, the procedure has been commonplace, although not all states have been partitioned. Divisions have been known by the name of the city in which the court for that division is held, although some are named for points of the compass. In only two states, Kansas and Minnesota, have the divisions been numbered.

Territorial district courts were generally established by the organic act which created the territory. They had jurisdiction over federal, civil, criminal, and bankruptcy actions as well as civil and criminal jurisdiction (similar to state courts). Records created by a territorial or provisional court acting in its capacity as a federal court often became the property of the federal district court. As each territory achieved statehood, federal districts and federal courts were established by the admitting statute. Further changes in organization were determined by individual acts; thus, courts came to vary from state to state.

Chapter 6, "Naturalization Records in the National Archives," provides information on naturalization records that have been transferred from the old U.S. Circuit and the U.S. district courts.

THE NATURALIZATION PROCESS

Aliens interested in becoming citizens of the United States generally took the following steps.

Declaration of Intention (First Papers): Usually, the *declaration of intention*, or *first papers*, was the first step in the naturalization process. Normally, the first papers were completed soon after arrival in the United States, depending on the laws in effect at the time (See appendix A, "Major Settlements, Immigration, and Naturalization: A Chronology.") Certain groups, such as women and children, were exempt in early years. After 1862, those who were honorably discharged from U.S. military service were excused from this initial procedure. Until 1906, the content of forms for declaration of intention varied dramatically from one county to another and from one court to another. A large percentage of the first papers created before 1906 contain very little biographical information. Declarations of intention produced after 15 September 1906 generally contain the following information: name, address, occupation, birthplace, nationality, country from which emigrated, birth date or age, personal description, date of intention, marital status, last foreign residence, port of entry, name of ship, date of entry, and date of document. Declarations of intention, affidavits, petitions, and oaths of allegiance were generally filed together in the court

in which the final steps to citizenship were taken.

A number of declarations of intention are shown below to demonstrate the variety of information they contain. The first two samples are from New York. It is interesting that the earlier declaration of intention (1847), from Rochester, Monroe County (figure 3-8), provides more biographical information about William Patterson than the Brooklyn, Kings County, declaration of Thomas Griffith (figure 3-9), sworn to in 1868, provides about Griffith. The former document tells us that William Patterson was of the "City of Rochester," "but late of the Township of Cringleford England." Patterson

declares, upon oath in open Court, that he was born in the Township of Cringleford England a

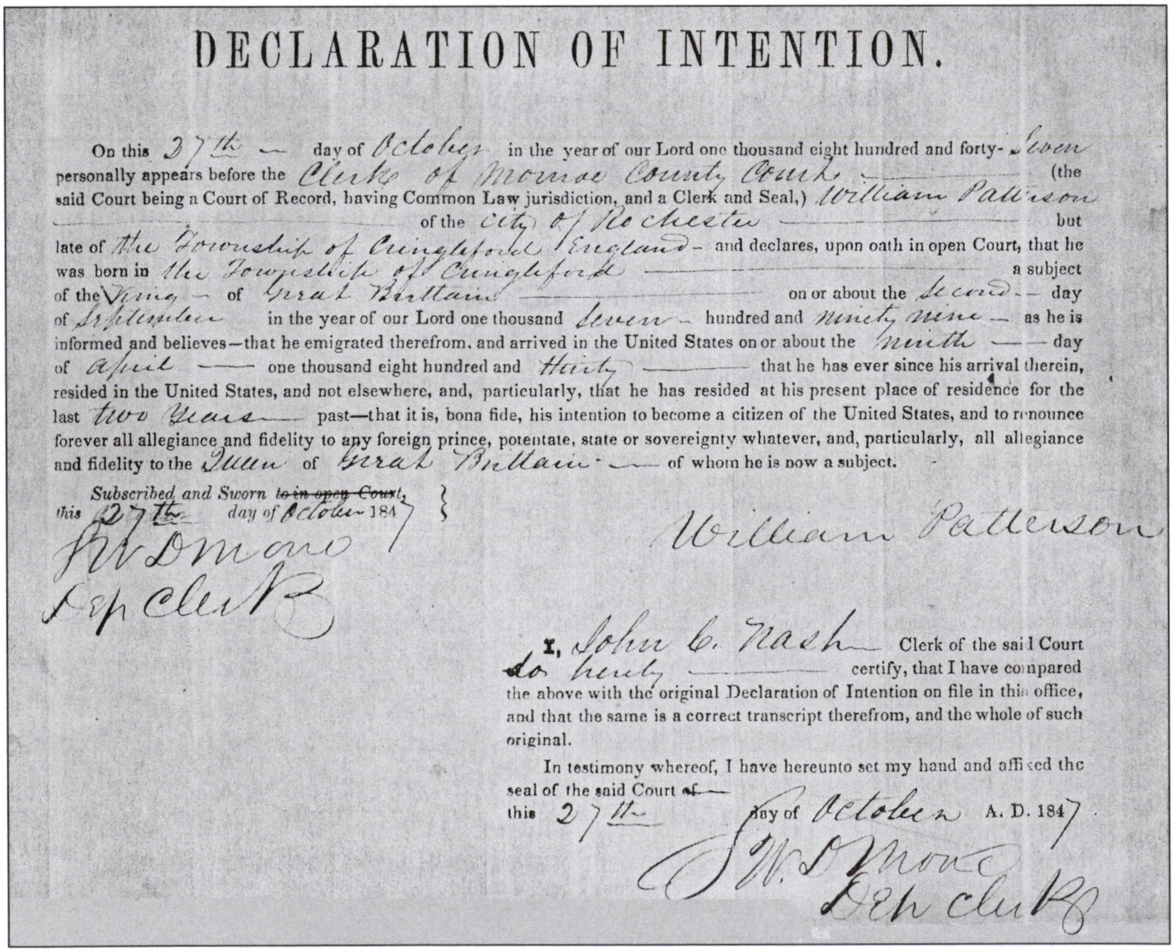

Figure 3-8. 1847 declaration of intention of William Patterson of Rochester, New York.

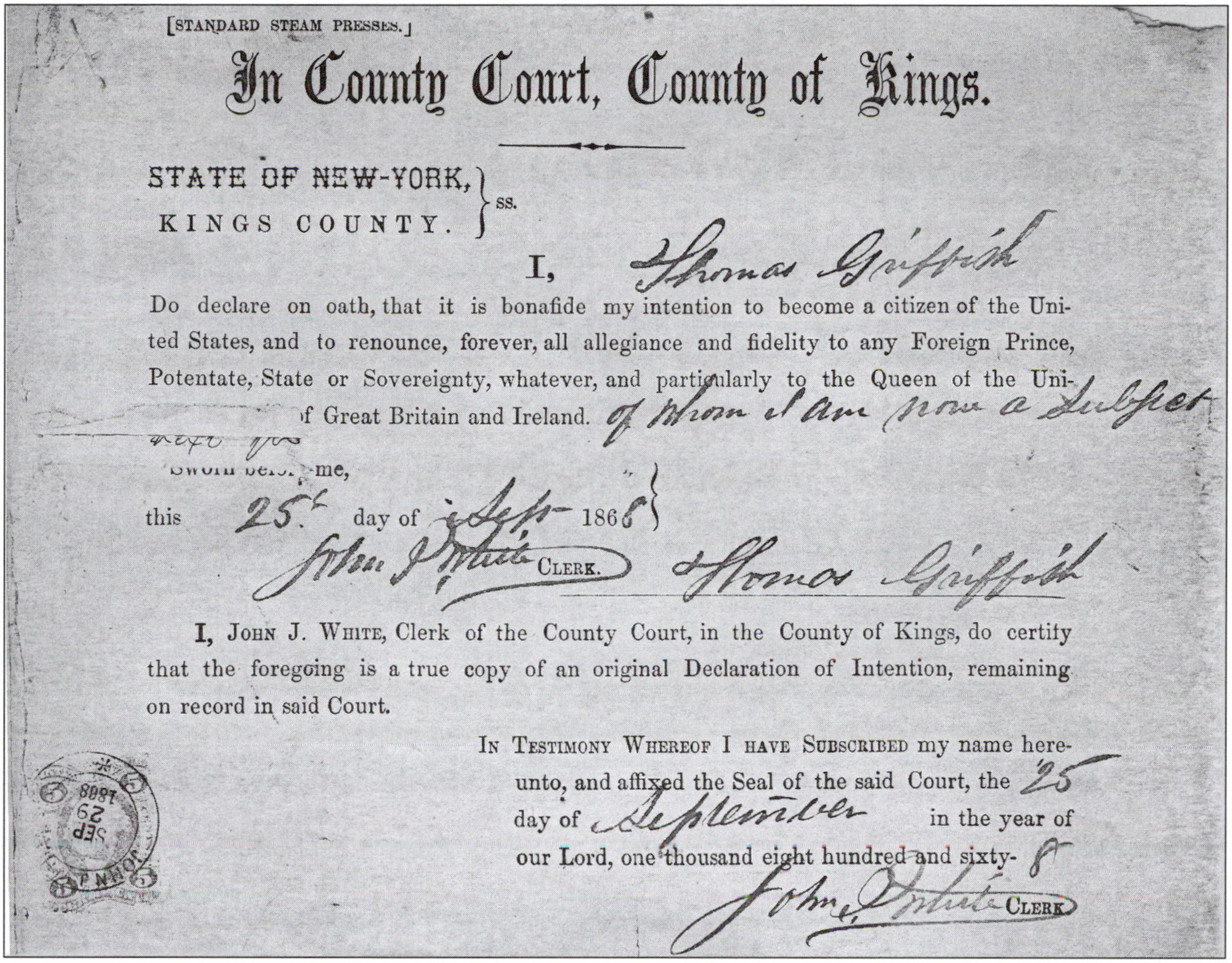

[STANDARD STEAM PRESSES.]

In County Court, County of Kings.

STATE OF NEW-YORK, }
KINGS COUNTY. } SS.

I, Thomas Griffith

Do declare on oath, that it is bonafide my intention to become a citizen of the United States, and to renounce, forever, all allegiance and fidelity to any Foreign Prince, Potentate, State or Sovereignty, whatever, and particularly to the Queen of the United [Kingdom o]f Great Britain and Ireland. of whom I am now a Subject

Sworn before me,
this 25th day of Sept 1868

John J White CLERK. Thomas Griffith

I, JOHN J. WHITE, Clerk of the County Court, in the County of Kings, do certify that the foregoing is a true copy of an original Declaration of Intention, remaining on record in said Court.

IN TESTIMONY WHEREOF I HAVE SUBSCRIBED my name hereunto, and affixed the Seal of the said Court, the 25 day of September in the year of our Lord, one thousand eight hundred and sixty-8

John J White CLERK.

Figure 3-9. 1868 declaration of intention of Thomas Griffith, sworn to in Kings County, New York.

subject of the King of Great Brittain [*sic*] or about the Second day of September in the year of our Lord one thousand Seven hundred and ninety nine as he is of April one thousand eight hundred and thirty that he has ever since his arrival therein, resided in the United States, and not elsewhere, and, particularly, that he has resided at his present place of residence for the last two years past—that it is, bonafide, his intention to become a citizen of the United States, and to renounce forever all allegiance and fidelity to any foreign prince, potentate, state or sovereignty whatsoever, and, particularly, all allegiance and fidelity to the Queen of Great Brittain of whom he is now a subject.

The declaration from Brooklyn, New York, dated and signed by Thomas Griffith, simply tells the reader that Thomas declared his intention and renounced his allegiance to the queen of Great Britain and Ireland and that he did so in Kings County Court on 25 September 1868.

Michael Tobin, a native of Ireland, went to Carroll County Court "at a County Court of the third Judicial District of the State of Maryland, began and held at the Court House in the town of Westmin-

Figure 3-10. Because so many pre-1906 naturalizations do not provide
any evidence of towns of origin, other sources must be consulted.
A photograph in an old family album provided the Irish origins of the Pryle family of County Donegal.
A postcard in the same album showed the church that the family attended.

DUN LEWY R.C. CHURCH AND ERRIGAL MOUNTAIN, CO. DONEGAL.

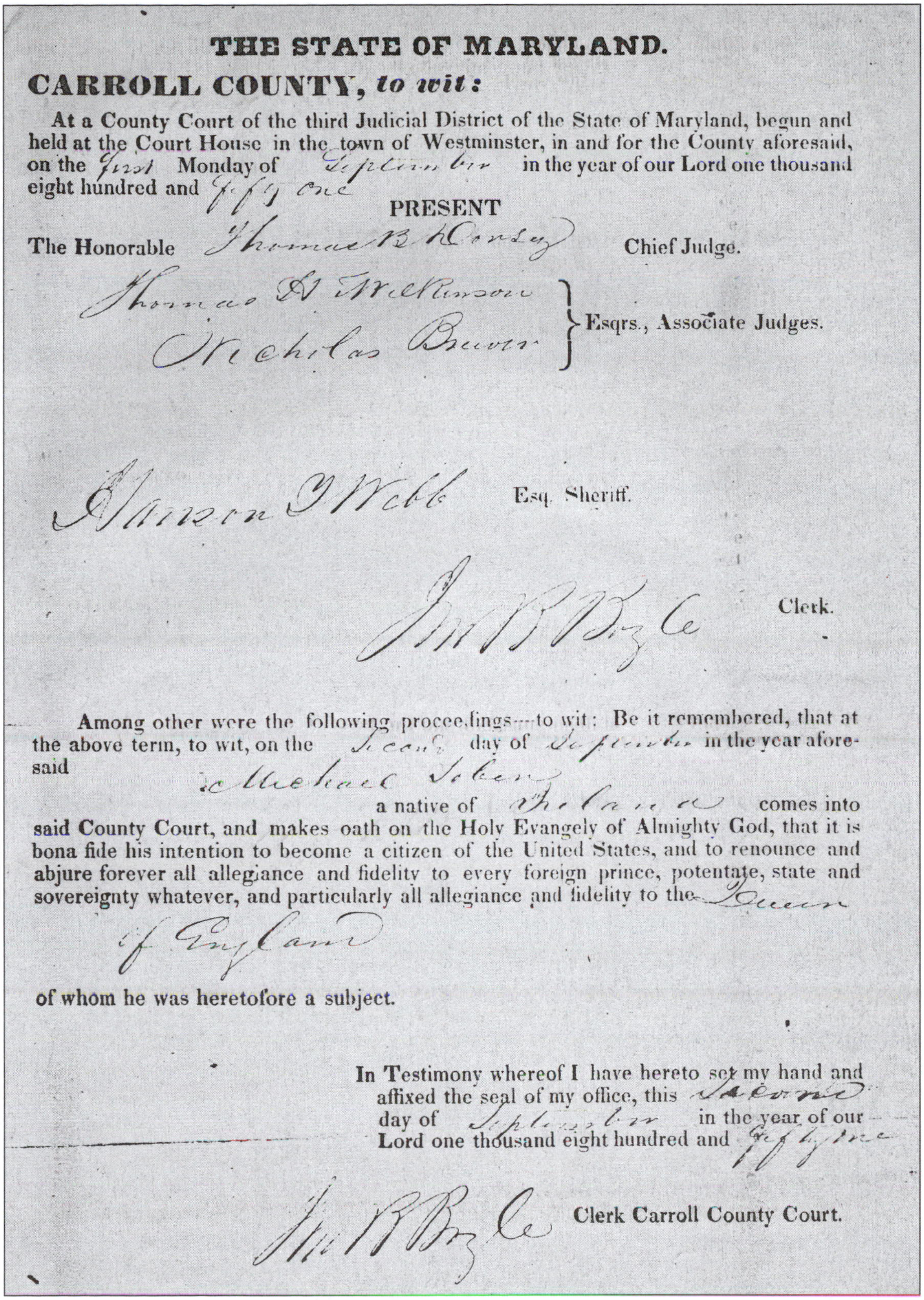

THE STATE OF MARYLAND.

CARROLL COUNTY, *to wit:*

At a County Court of the third Judicial District of the State of Maryland, begun and held at the Court House in the town of Westminster, in and for the County aforesaid, on the *First* Monday of *September* in the year of our Lord one thousand eight hundred and *fifty one*

PRESENT

The Honorable *Thomas B. Dorsey*   Chief Judge.

Thomas H. Wilkinson
Nicholas Brewer   } Esqrs., Associate Judges.

Hanson J. Webb   Esq. Sheriff.

Jno. B. Boyle   Clerk.

Among other were the following proceedings—to wit: Be it remembered, that at the above term, to wit, on the *Second* day of *September* in the year aforesaid *Michael Tobin* a native of *Ireland* comes into said County Court, and makes oath on the Holy Evangely of Almighty God, that it is bona fide his intention to become a citizen of the United States, and to renounce and abjure forever all allegiance and fidelity to every foreign prince, potentate, state and sovereignty whatever, and particularly all allegiance and fidelity to the *Queen of England* of whom he was heretofore a subject.

In Testimony whereof I have hereto set my hand and affixed the seal of my office, this *Second* day of *September* in the year of our Lord one thousand eight hundred and *fifty one*

Jno. B. Boyle   Clerk Carroll County Court.

Figure 3-11. 1851 declaration of Michael Tobin, from Carroll County, Maryland.

*Figure 3-12. When naturalization papers do not yield biographical information,
it often pays to search for immigration documents of other relatives who may have immigrated later
or completed naturalization requirements in a court that required more specific information.
(Photos reproduced courtesy of Kathleen Pryle Dennis.)*

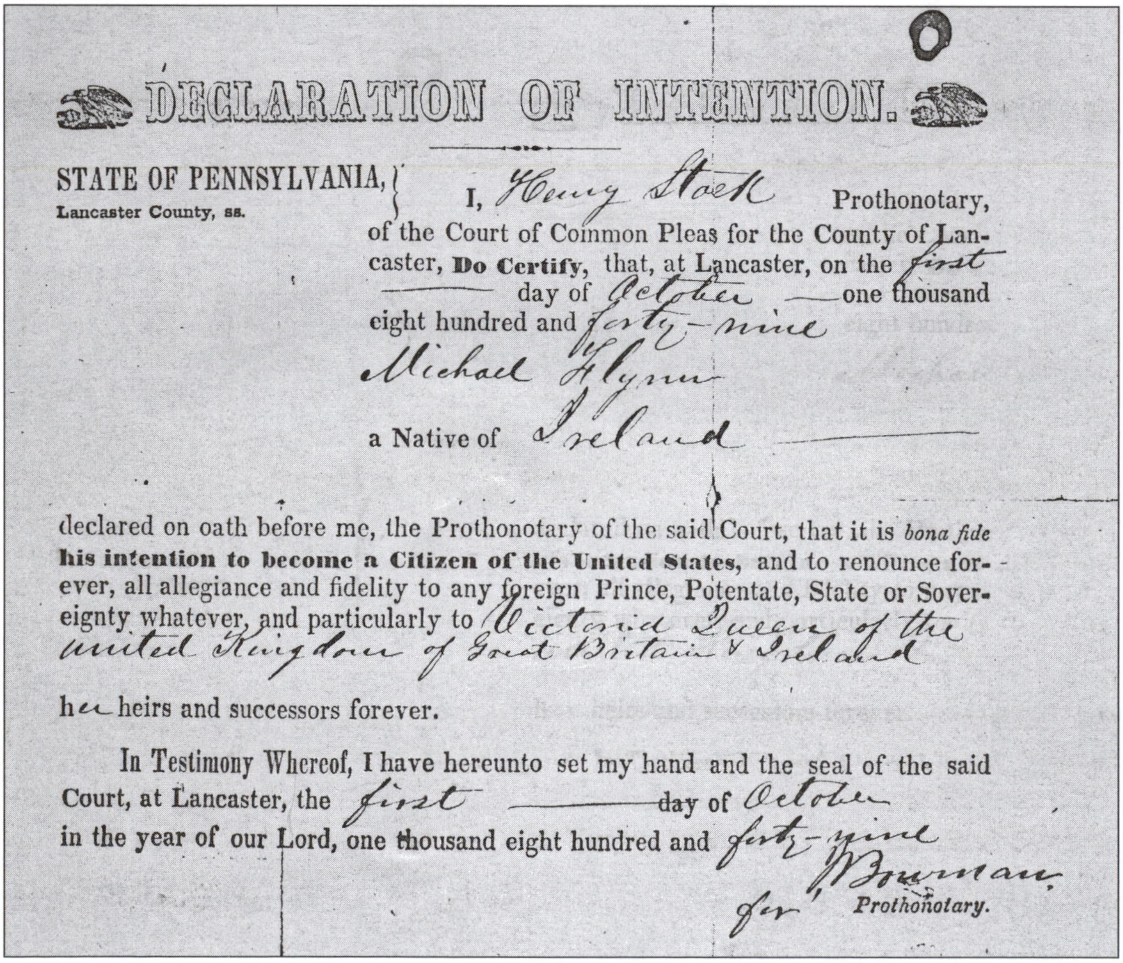

DECLARATION OF INTENTION.

STATE OF PENNSYLVANIA,
Lancaster County, ss.

I, *Henry Stoek* Prothonotary,
of the Court of Common Pleas for the County of Lancaster, **Do Certify**, that, at Lancaster, on the *first* day of *October* one thousand eight hundred and *forty-nine*

Michael Flynn

a Native of *Ireland*

declared on oath before me, the Prothonotary of the said Court, that it is *bona fide*
his intention to become a Citizen of the United States, and to renounce forever, all allegiance and fidelity to any foreign Prince, Potentate, State or Sovereignty whatever, and particularly to *Victoria Queen of the united Kingdom of Great Britain & Ireland*

h*er* heirs and successors forever.

In Testimony Whereof, I have hereunto set my hand and the seal of the said
Court, at Lancaster, the *first* day of *October*
in the year of our Lord, one thousand eight hundred and *forty-nine*

Bowman
for Prothonotary.

Figure 3-13. 1849 declaration of intention of Michael Flynn of Lancaster County, Pennsylvania.

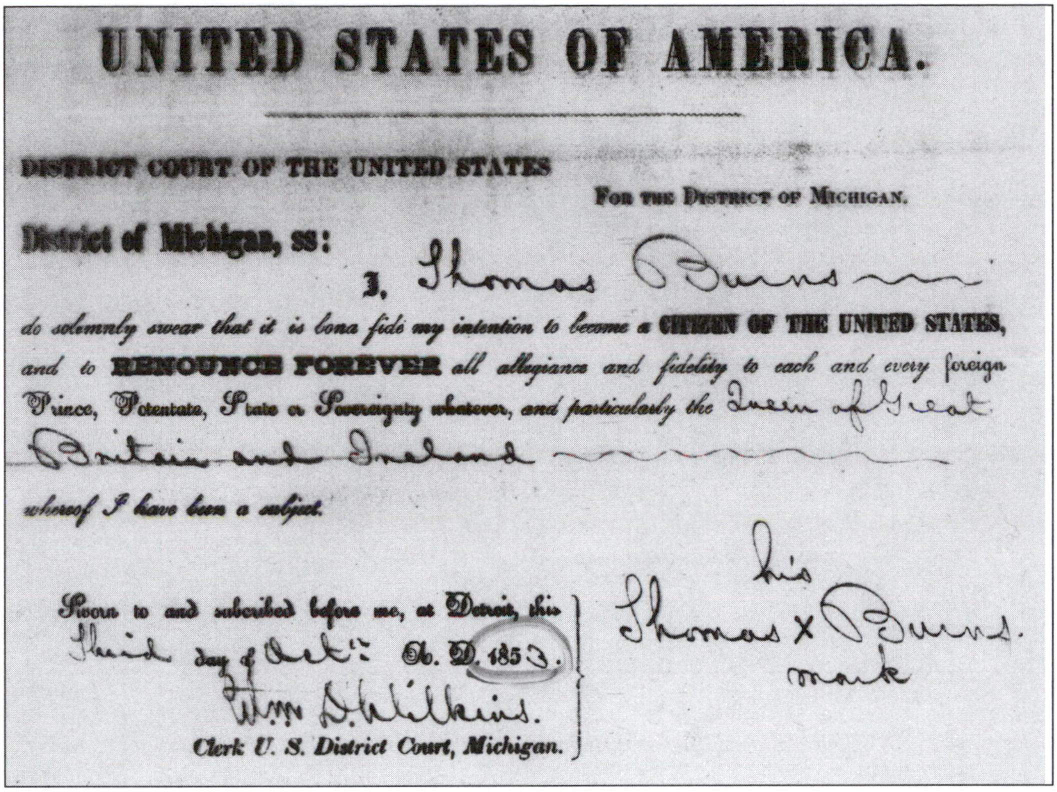

Figure 3-14. 1853 declaration of Thomas Burns in U.S. District Court, Detroit.

ster, in and for the County aforesaid, on the first Monday of September in the year of our Lord one thousand eight hundred and fifty one." There Michael "comes into said County Court, and makes oath on the Holy Evangely of Almighty God, that it is his bonafide intention to become a citizen of the United States...." (see figure 3-11).

Except for his declaration's slightly more decorative appearance, anyone looking for information on Michael Flynn would get little more satisfaction than from the declaration of intention described immediately before. In Lancaster County, Pennsylvania, Michael Flynn, a native of Ireland, renounced forever his allegiance to "Victoria, queen of the United Kingdom and of Great Britain & Ireland on the first day of October, in the year of our Lord, one thousand eight hundred and forty-nine" (figure 3-13). Here, at least, the search is narrowed down to Ireland.

Many of these documents fail to state the specific nativity of the declarant, making us guess which of the British isles or colonies it could have been. Such is the case with Thomas Burns, who went before the U.S. District Court for the District of Michigan on 3 October 1853. The document does not indicate, precisely, where in the British Isles he came from. Another disappointment for some will be the lack of a signature. Thomas Burns, like so many others of his era, could only express his desire to become a citizen by marking the declaration with his sign, "X" (figure 3-14).

Some naturalization papers answer questions for researchers; others present more questions than they answer. Lawrence Heffernan is not a name most people would identify as Irish, but the so-named person claimed to be a native of Ireland. The Court of Common Pleas of Franklin County, Ohio, did not provide anything more specific about his birthplace on the 1838 form (figure 3-15). If Lawrence completed the naturalization process by going to a court whose forms required

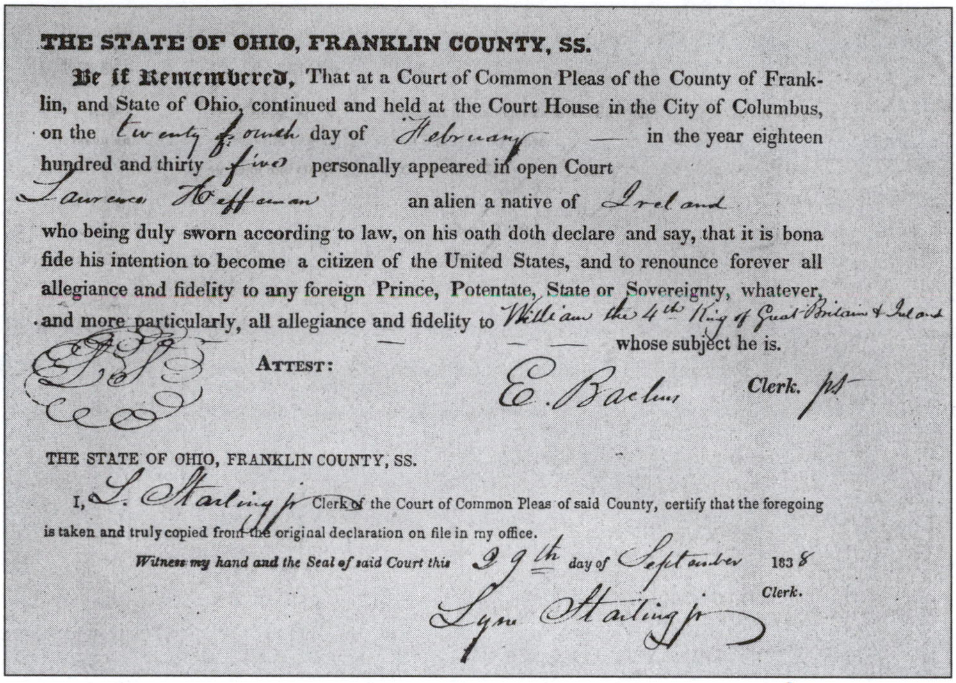

Figure 3-15. *1838 declaration of Lawrence Heffernan, Court of Common Pleas, Franklin County, Ohio.*

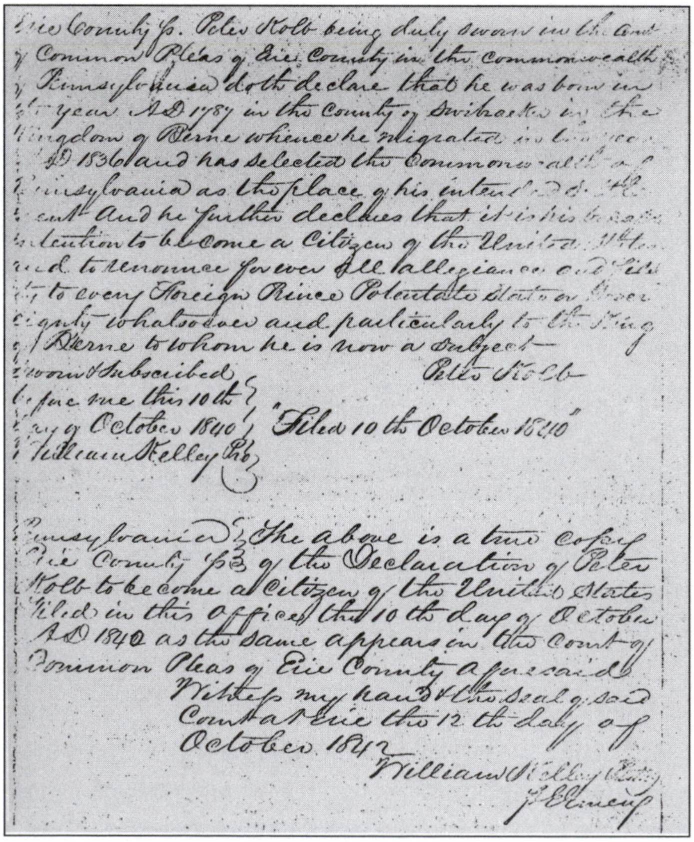

Figure 3-16. *1840 declaration of Peter Kolb.*

more information, the mystery of Heffernan's actual birthplace might be solved.

The most difficult declarations of intention to work with are those that were not of the fill-in-the-blank kind but were completely handwritten. Collections of handwritten manuscripts are often the last to be indexed because deciphering and extracting names from them is so time consuming. Peter Kolb appeared in an Erie County, Pennsylvania, court on 10 October 1840 to declare his intention; his declaration is worth reading. It says that he was "born in the year AD 1787 in the County of Swibacker in the Kingdom of Berne whence he migrated in the year AD 1836 and has selected the Commonwealth of Pennsylvania as the place of his intended settlement" (figure 3-16).

Not only did naturalization forms vary from one country to another, but the courts, for various reasons, often changed their forms from year to year. Note differences in the styles of the 1853 declaration of Thomas Burns (figure 3-14) and that of Edward Tormey in 1868 (figure 3-19). Both declared their intentions in the same federal court. Some forms were not designed to accommodate any exceptions

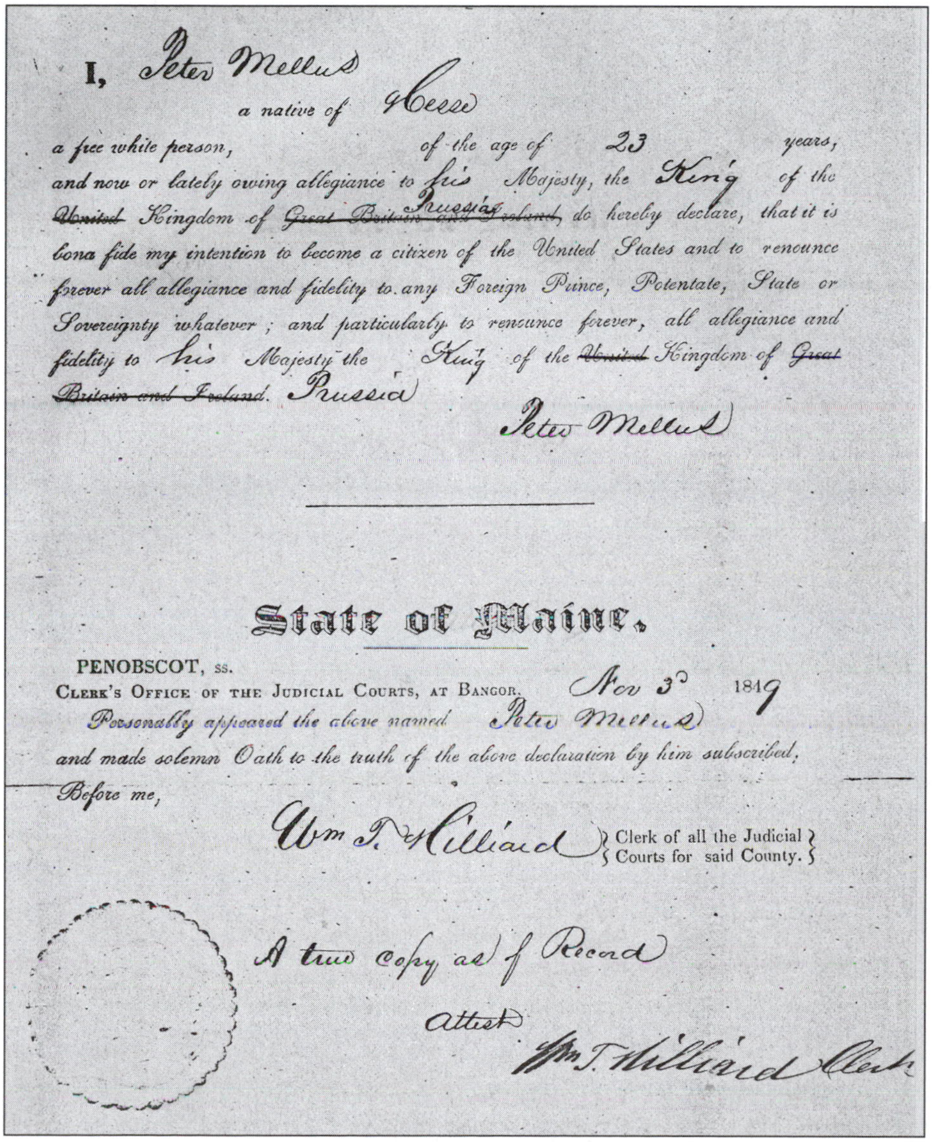

I, Peter Mellus

a native of Hesse

a free white person, of the age of 23 years, and now or lately owing allegiance to his Majesty, the King of the ~~United~~ Kingdom of ~~Great Britain and Ireland~~ Prussia, do hereby declare, that it is bona fide my intention to become a citizen of the United States and to renounce forever all allegiance and fidelity to any Foreign Prince, Potentate, State or Sovereignty whatever; and particularly to renounce forever, all allegiance and fidelity to his Majesty the King of the ~~United~~ Kingdom of ~~Great Britain and Ireland~~. Prussia

Peter Mellus

State of Maine.

PENOBSCOT, ss.

Clerk's Office of the Judicial Courts, at Bangor, Nov 3d 1849

Personally appeared the above named Peter Mellus and made solemn Oath to the truth of the above declaration by him subscribed,

Before me,

Wm T. Hilliard } Clerk of all the Judicial Courts for said County.

A true copy as of Record

attest Wm T. Hilliard Clerk

Figure 3-17. Declaration of intention of Peter Mellus, Clerk's Office of the Judicial Courts, at Bangor, Maine, 1849.

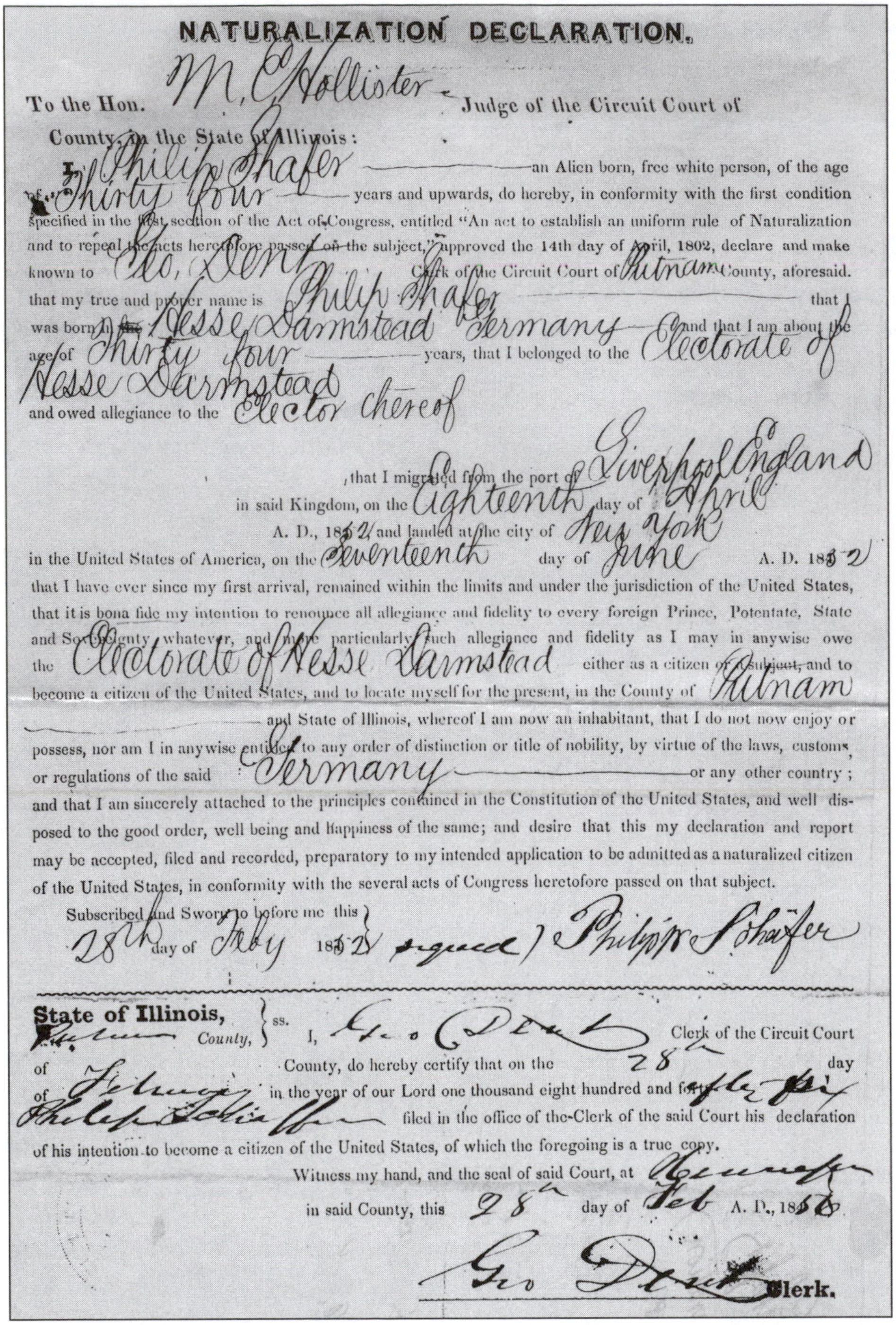

NATURALIZATION DECLARATION.

To the Hon. M. C. Hollister Judge of the Circuit Court of County, in the State of Illinois:

I, Philip Shafer an Alien born, free white person, of the age of Thirty four years and upwards, do hereby, in conformity with the first condition specified in the first section of the Act of Congress, entitled "An act to establish an uniform rule of Naturalization and to repeal the acts heretofore passed on the subject," approved the 14th day of April, 1802, declare and make known to Geo. Dent Clerk of the Circuit Court of Putnam County, aforesaid, that my true and proper name is Philip Shafer that I was born in Hesse Darmstead Germany and that I am about the age of Thirty four years, that I belonged to the Electorate of Hesse Darmstead and owed allegiance to the Elector thereof

, that I migrated from the port of Liverpool England in said Kingdom, on the Eighteenth day of April A. D., 1852 and landed at the city of New York in the United States of America, on the Seventeenth day of June A. D. 1852 that I have ever since my first arrival, remained within the limits and under the jurisdiction of the United States, that it is bona fide my intention to renounce all allegiance and fidelity to every foreign Prince, Potentate, State and Sovereignty whatever, and more particularly such allegiance and fidelity as I may in anywise owe the Electorate of Hesse Darmstead either as a citizen or subject, and to become a citizen of the United States, and to locate myself for the present, in the County of Putnam and State of Illinois, whereof I am now an inhabitant, that I do not now enjoy or possess, nor am I in anywise entitled to any order of distinction or title of nobility, by virtue of the laws, customs or regulations of the said Germany or any other country; and that I am sincerely attached to the principles contained in the Constitution of the United States, and well disposed to the good order, well being and happiness of the same; and desire that this my declaration and report may be accepted, filed and recorded, preparatory to my intended application to be admitted as a naturalized citizen of the United States, in conformity with the several acts of Congress heretofore passed on that subject.

Subscribed and Sworn to before me this 28th day of Feby 1852 (signed) Philip W Schäfer

State of Illinois, Putnam County, } ss. I, Geo Dent Clerk of the Circuit Court of County, do hereby certify that on the 28th day of February in the year of our Lord one thousand eight hundred and fifty two Philip Schafer filed in the office of the Clerk of the said Court his declaration of his intention to become a citizen of the United States, of which the foregoing is a true copy.

Witness my hand, and the seal of said Court, at Hennepin in said County, this 28th day of Feb A. D., 185[illegible].

Geo Dent Clerk.

Figure 3-18. 1852 declaration of Philip Shafer, Putnam County, Illinois.

to the norm. When twenty-three-year-old Peter Mellus, a native of Hesse (Germany), declared in 1849, the form had to be manipulated to work in the appropriate information (figure 3-17). It would appear that the Clerk's Office of Penobscot, Maine, was not prepared to provide citizenship to anyone except those from the "United Kingdom of Great Britain" because those words have been lined out on their printed form in favor of the word "Prussia." It seems unlikely that Peter Mellus signed his name in

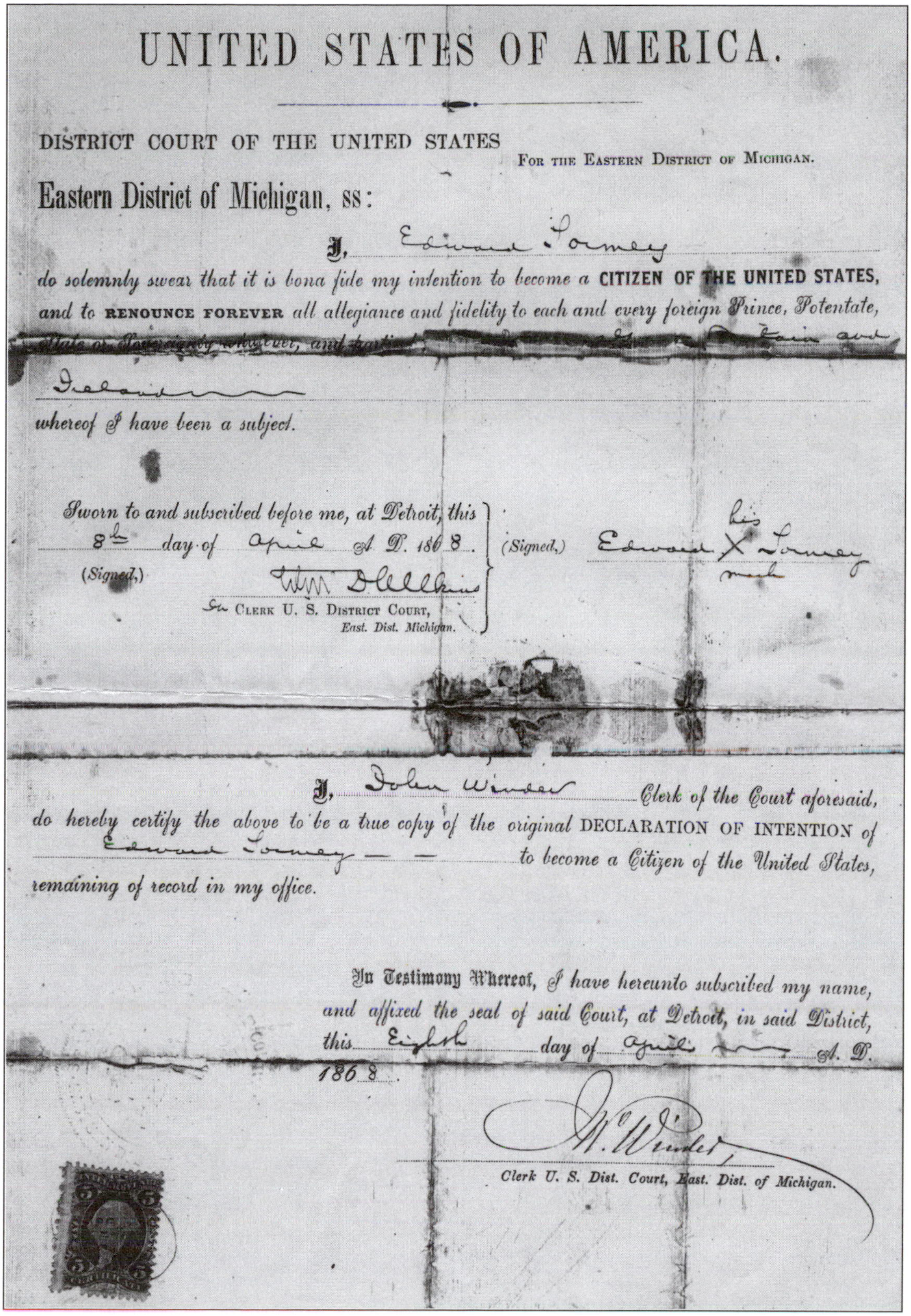

UNITED STATES OF AMERICA.

DISTRICT COURT OF THE UNITED STATES

FOR THE EASTERN DISTRICT OF MICHIGAN.

Eastern District of Michigan, ss:

I, Edward Tormey

do solemnly swear that it is bona fide my intention to become a CITIZEN OF THE UNITED STATES, and to RENOUNCE FOREVER all allegiance and fidelity to each and every foreign Prince, Potentate, State or Sovereignty whatever, and particularly [illegible] Great Britain and Ireland

whereof I have been a subject.

Sworn to and subscribed before me, at Detroit, this 8th day of April A. D. 1868.

(Signed,) Wm. D. Wilkins

Clerk U. S. District Court, East. Dist. Michigan.

(Signed,) Edward his X mark Tormey

I, John Winder Clerk of the Court aforesaid, do hereby certify the above to be a true copy of the original DECLARATION OF INTENTION of Edward Tormey to become a Citizen of the United States, remaining of record in my office.

In Testimony Whereof, I have hereunto subscribed my name, and affixed the seal of said Court, at Detroit, in said District, this Eighth day of April A. D. 1868.

Jn. Winder

Clerk U. S. Dist. Court, East. Dist. of Michigan.

Figure 3-19. 1868 declaration of Edward Tormey in the U.S. District Court, Eastern District of Michigan, Detroit.

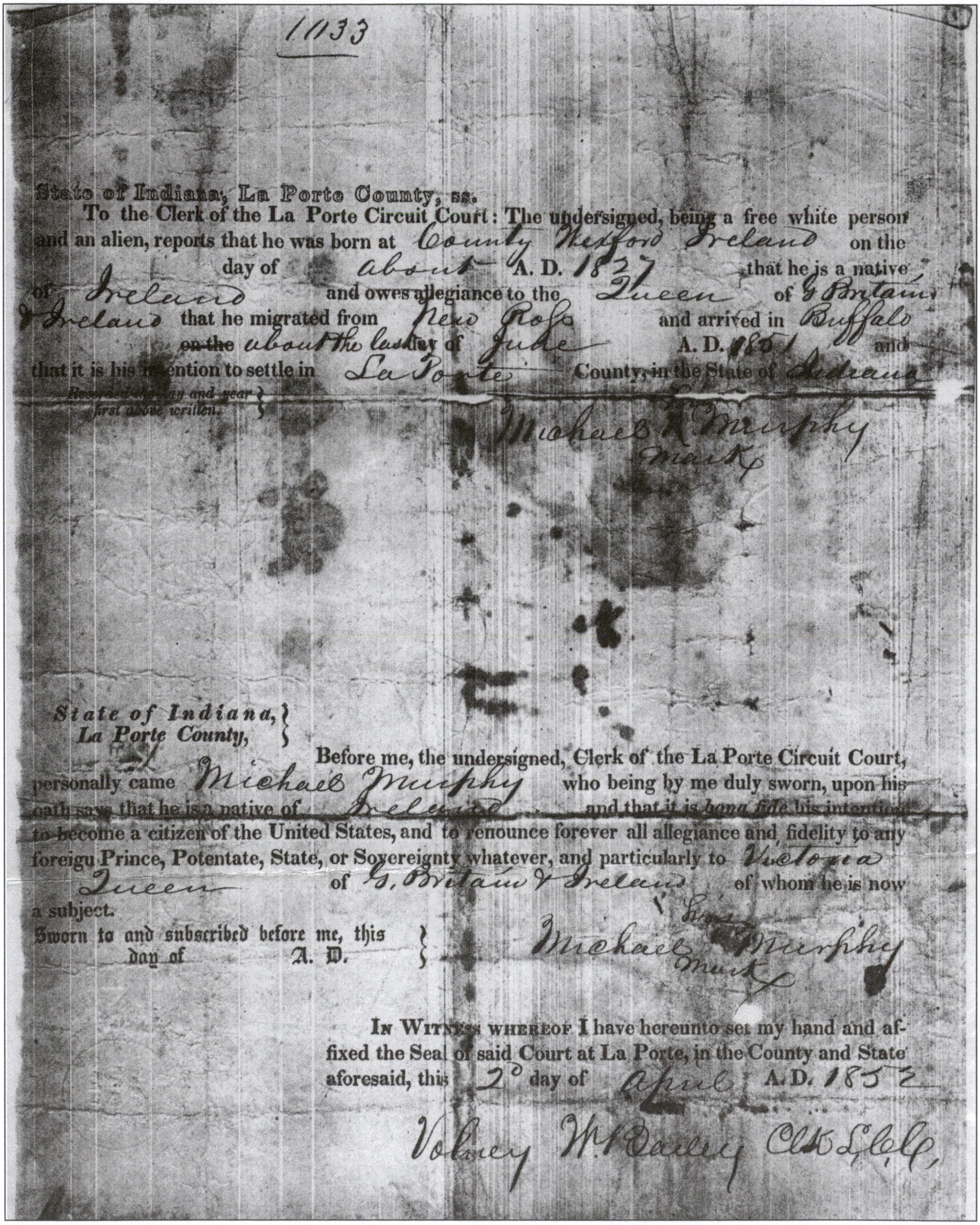

11133

State of Indiana, La Porte County, ss.

To the Clerk of the La Porte Circuit Court: The undersigned, being a free white person and an alien, reports that he was born at County Wexford Ireland on the day of about A. D. 1827 that he is a native of Ireland and owes allegiance to the Queen of G Britain & Ireland that he migrated from New Ross and arrived in Buffalo on the about the last day of June A. D. 1851 and that it is his intention to settle in La Porte County, in the State of Indiana

Recorded the day and year first above written.

Michael his X Murphy mark

State of Indiana, La Porte County,

Before me, the undersigned, Clerk of the La Porte Circuit Court, personally came Michael Murphy who being by me duly sworn, upon his oath says that he is a native of Ireland and that it is bona fide his intention to become a citizen of the United States, and to renounce forever all allegiance and fidelity to any foreign Prince, Potentate, State, or Sovereignty whatever, and particularly to Victoria Queen of G. Britain & Ireland of whom he is now a subject.

Sworn to and subscribed before me, this day of A. D.

Michael his Murphy mark

In Witness whereof I have hereunto set my hand and affixed the Seal of said Court at La Porte, in the County and State aforesaid, this 2d day of April A. D. 1852

Volney W. Bailey Clk L.C.C.

Figure 3-20. 1852 declaration of Michael Murphy of La Porte, Indiana.

either place on the document; the signature seems to match the handwriting of the clerk, William T. Hilliard.

A more common manipulation of the forms was the changing of dated forms. Philip Shafer, thirty-four, of Hesse Darmstadt (Germany), declared his intention to naturalize in Putnam County, Illinois, on 28 February 1852. The clerk of the court had apparently not yet used all of the "184_" forms (which required the user to fill in the year within the decade), so Philip's declaration had to be altered (figure 3-18).

The 1852 declaration of Michael Murphy is an interesting document in itself (figure 3-20). Tattered and ink-stained, the original document told of a man who was born "at County Wexford Ireland" about 1827; that he was a native of Ireland; migrated from New Ross; arrived in Buffalo about the last day of June in 1851; and that it was his intention to settle in La Porte County, Indiana. One of the problems that comes with working in old records is indecipherable handwriting. There are books on the subject, but I was able to remember that there is a New Ross in Ireland, and that there is an old style of writing in which

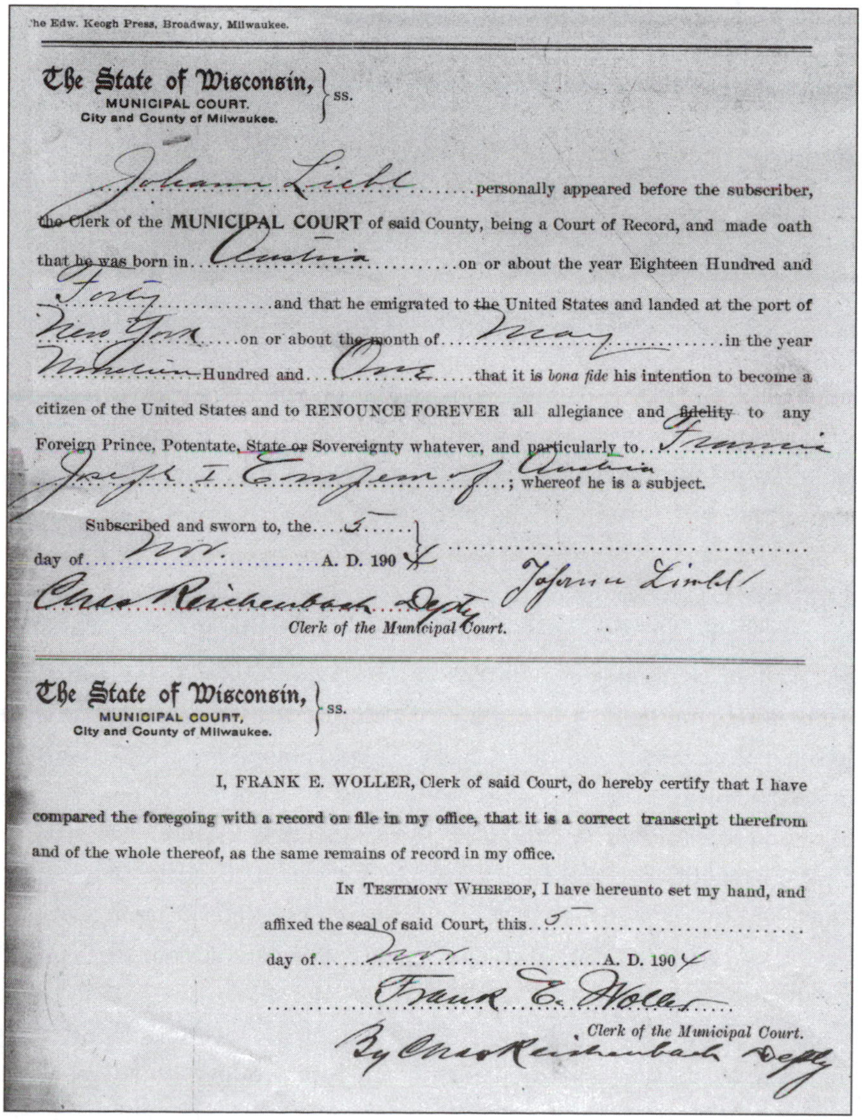

The Edw. Keogh Press, Broadway, Milwaukee.

The State of Wisconsin, }
MUNICIPAL COURT. } ss.
City and County of Milwaukee. }

Johann Liebl ....personally appeared before the subscriber, the Clerk of the MUNICIPAL COURT of said County, being a Court of Record, and made oath that he was born in ...Austria......... on or about the year Eighteen Hundred and Forty ....and that he emigrated to the United States and landed at the port of New York .....on or about the month of ....May.......... in the year Nineteen Hundred and ...One.......that it is *bona fide* his intention to become a citizen of the United States and to RENOUNCE FOREVER all allegiance and fidelity to any Foreign Prince, Potentate, State or Sovereignty whatever, and particularly to ...Francis Joseph I. Emperor of Austria......; whereof he is a subject.

Subscribed and sworn to, the....5.....
day of.........Nov.........A. D. 1904
Chas Reichenbach Depty
Clerk of the Municipal Court.

Johann Liebl

The State of Wisconsin, }
MUNICIPAL COURT, } ss.
City and County of Milwaukee. }

I, FRANK E. WOLLER, Clerk of said Court, do hereby certify that I have compared the foregoing with a record on file in my office, that it is a correct transcript therefrom and of the whole thereof, as the same remains of record in my office.

In Testimony Whereof, I have hereunto set my hand, and affixed the seal of said Court, this...5...........
day of.......Nov.............A. D. 1904
Frank E. Woller
Clerk of the Municipal Court.
By Chas Reichenbach Depty

Figure 3-21. 1904 declaration of Johann Liebl from the Municipal Court, Milwaukee, Wisconsin.

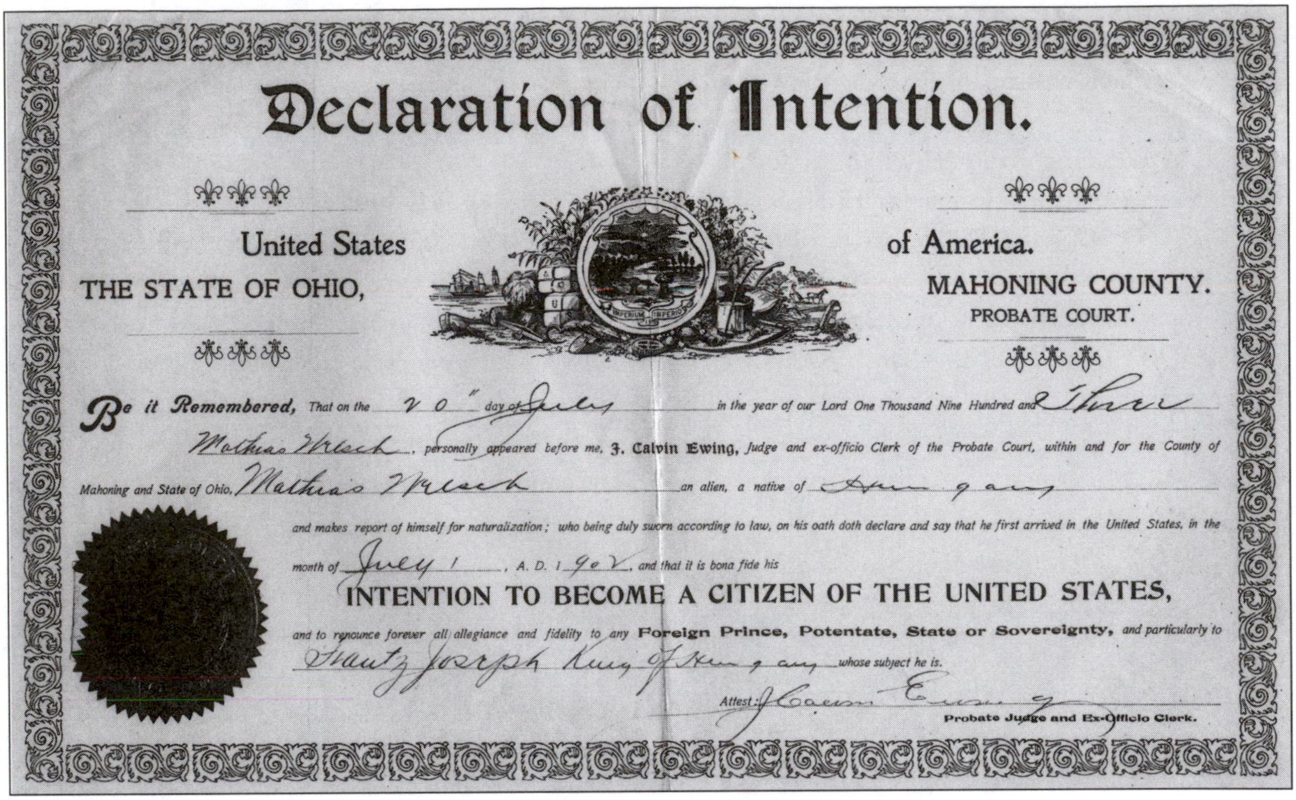

Declaration of Intention.

United States of America.

THE STATE OF OHIO, MAHONING COUNTY.

PROBATE COURT.

Be it Remembered, That on the 20" day of July in the year of our Lord One Thousand Nine Hundred and Three

Mathias Welsch, personally appeared before me, J. Calvin Ewing, Judge and ex-officio Clerk of the Probate Court, within and for the County of Mahoning and State of Ohio, Mathias Welsch an alien, a native of Hungary

and makes report of himself for naturalization; who being duly sworn according to law, on his oath doth declare and say that he first arrived in the United States, in the month of July 1, A. D. 1902, and that it is bona fide his

INTENTION TO BECOME A CITIZEN OF THE UNITED STATES,

and to renounce forever all allegiance and fidelity to any Foreign Prince, Potentate, State or Sovereignty, and particularly to Frantz Joseph King of Hungary whose subject he is.

Attest: J Calvin Ewing

Probate Judge and Ex-Officio Clerk.

Figure 3-22. 1902 declaration of Mathias Welsch, Mahoning County, Ohio.

a double "s" looks more like the letter "p." Note that the exact date of Michael Murphy's birth is not filled in. Presumably, he, like so many others of the time period, was not sure of his birth date, nor did he seem to be sure of the exact date of his arrival in Buffalo. Many of these old records are not going to give us precise answers—and if they do, the information may be less than reliable. Sometimes, incorrect answers were given quite innocently and only because the immigrant had honestly forgotten. Others may have provided the wrong dates of arrival in hopes that officials would not know the difference and that the wait to be eligible for naturalization would not be so long.

Some understanding of history is critical to the success of any investigation of this nature. On 1 November 1880, Jacob Kukowski went to the County Court at Winona, Minnesota, and declared his intention to become an American citizen. Unfortunately for anyone trying to trace Jacob's origins, the document says nothing more than that he renounced the "Reigning Sovereign of the Kingdom of Prussia." By the surname we can guess that Jacob was Polish. If Polish or Prussian history isn't your strength, even the brief history provided in any encyclopedia would probably help you to understand this document. In *Polish Surnames: Origins and Meanings*, William Hoffman states: "By the 19th century Prussia, Russia, and Austria had divided Poland among themselves, and now foreigners were trying to spell Polish names, with spectacularly dismal result. Poles who emigrated to the United States usually came by way of German ports, so the Germans filling out papers got another crack at mangling Polish emigrants' surnames."[1]

A declaration of intention from the Municipal Court of the city and county of Milwaukee, Wisconsin, provided little more in the way of biography for Johann Liebl, who appeared in that court on 5 November 1904 (figure 3-21). It is possible to discern

Figure 3-23. Overlaid on a map of the Austro-Hungarian Empire is a 1902 photograph of Janos Szucs, his wife, Teresa, and their son John with Teresa's brothers Andrew and Martin Skokan.

from the document, however, that Johann was born in Austria around 1840 and that he emigrated to the United States and landed at the port of New York on or about the month of May 1901. The arrival date may be the clue to finding Johann on a passenger list. There is a microfilmed index of passenger lists for the Port of New York covering the years 1897 to 1902 (see "Ship Passenger Arrival Lists" in chapter 2).

As late as 1902, the Probate Court of Mahoning County, Ohio, was issuing declarations of intention containing virtually no biographical detail. Such is the case for Mathias Welsch, a native of Hungary, who declared his intention in Youngstown (figure 3-22). Is there a chance that Mathias was part of a large migration of Hungarians who came into the United States around 1900? Many of the Hungarians,

such as Janos Szucs and his brothers-in-law, were attracted by jobs in Ohio mines.

After the establishment of the Bureau of Immigration and Naturalization in 1906, naturalization forms were standardized. In documents created after that date, you can expect to find certain required pieces of information, whether the declaration was filed in a court in Connecticut or California. The following example from the U.S. Circuit Court of the Northern District of Illinois provides a biographer or family historian with ideal information. The declaration of intention of Anton Matic not only provides his exact birth date and birthplace in Yugoslavia; his current address; the name of the vessel on which he emigrated from Trieste, Italy; his last foreign residence; his wife's name and birthplace (though it is noted only as "Jugoslavia"); and identifies his port of arrival in the United States; it also tells the reader that he was forty-four years of age; a laborer of white color; dark complexion; five feet six inches tall; 160 pounds; and that he has brown hair and brown eyes.

The federally mandated standard naturalization forms for declarations of intention changed slightly,

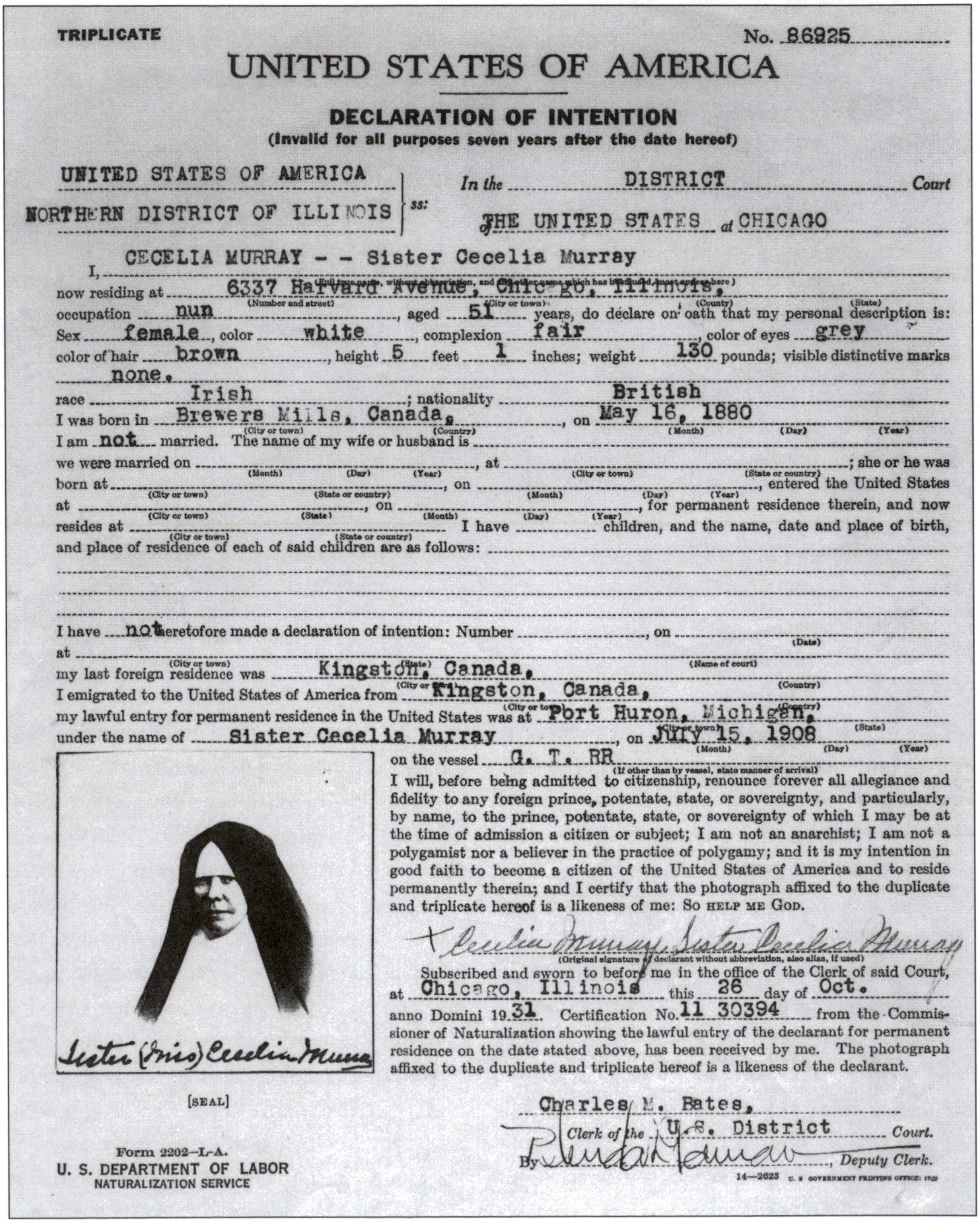

Figure 3-24. 1931 declaration of intention of Sister Cecilia Murray, U.S. District Court, Chicago.

but universally, over the next few years, to include more information and, in 1929, a photograph. Poor Sister Cecilia Murray would probably cringe to think that the well-kept secrets of her age, hair color, and weight would stay on public record for all the world to see (figure 3-24)! While photographs do not usually photocopy well, and the original naturalization records are rarely in places where they might be taken out to be photographed, an image such as the one shown on this 1931 document might be the only one available for an individual.

Aliens serious about becoming naturalized U.S. citizens had a specified time period in which to complete the naturalization process. If they did not comply, they had to start all over again. This statement was printed on the reverse side of copies of declarations of intention which aliens held until they returned to a court of record to complete the process.

Not less than 2 nor more than 7 years after the date the original of this declaration was made, and after you have lived in the United States for at least 5 years and in the State for at least 6 months, you may file a petition for naturalization (or second papers). You will not be notified by the Government or the clerk of court to file such petition. It will be necessary for you to make application, in person or by letter, to the nearest clerk of court exercising naturalization jurisdiction, or to a representative of the Immigration and Naturalization Service, for an application Form N-400. You should not wait to do this until near the close of the 7-year period, because if you do not file your petition with the court before the end of the 7-year period it will be necessary for you to file a new declaration of intention and wait at least another 2 years thereafter before you can file your petition for naturalization. However, a petitioner for naturalization who is married to a citizen of the United States is not required to make a declaration of intention as a basis for filing a petition for naturalization.

Applicants for naturalization, before being granted citizenship, must satisfy the judge of the naturalization court that they believe in the principles of the Constitution of the United States. The Immigration and Naturalization Service has prepared a citizenship textbook about the Constitution and Government of the United States which may be used by persons who have declared their intention to become citizens and who attend citizenship classes in public schools. This book and the classes will help applicants to prepare themselves for the duties and responsibilities of American citizenship.

Petition (Second or Final papers): Naturalization *petitions* were formal applications submitted to the court by individuals who had met the residency requirements and who had declared their intention to become citizens. As with the declarations of intention, their information content varied dramatically from one court to another. Most petitions created before 1906 offer little in terms of personal information. After 1906, the following might be found: name, address, occupation, date of emigration, birthplace, country from which emigrated, birth date or age, length of time in the United States, date of intention, name and age of spouse, names and ages of children, last foreign residence, port and mode of entry, name of ship, date of entry, names of witnesses, date of document, address of spouse, and photograph (after 1929).

When Giovanni Puccini of Borgo Abbuggiano, Italy, presented himself to the U.S. Circuit Court in Chicago on 13 April 1908, the petition for naturalization form on which he put his mark told a good deal about his life (figure 3-25). From the petition we see that he was born on the 28th of December in 1882, emigrated from Genoa on 24 September 1902, and entered the United States at the Port of New York. Giovanni lists his wife, Etrusca, and his

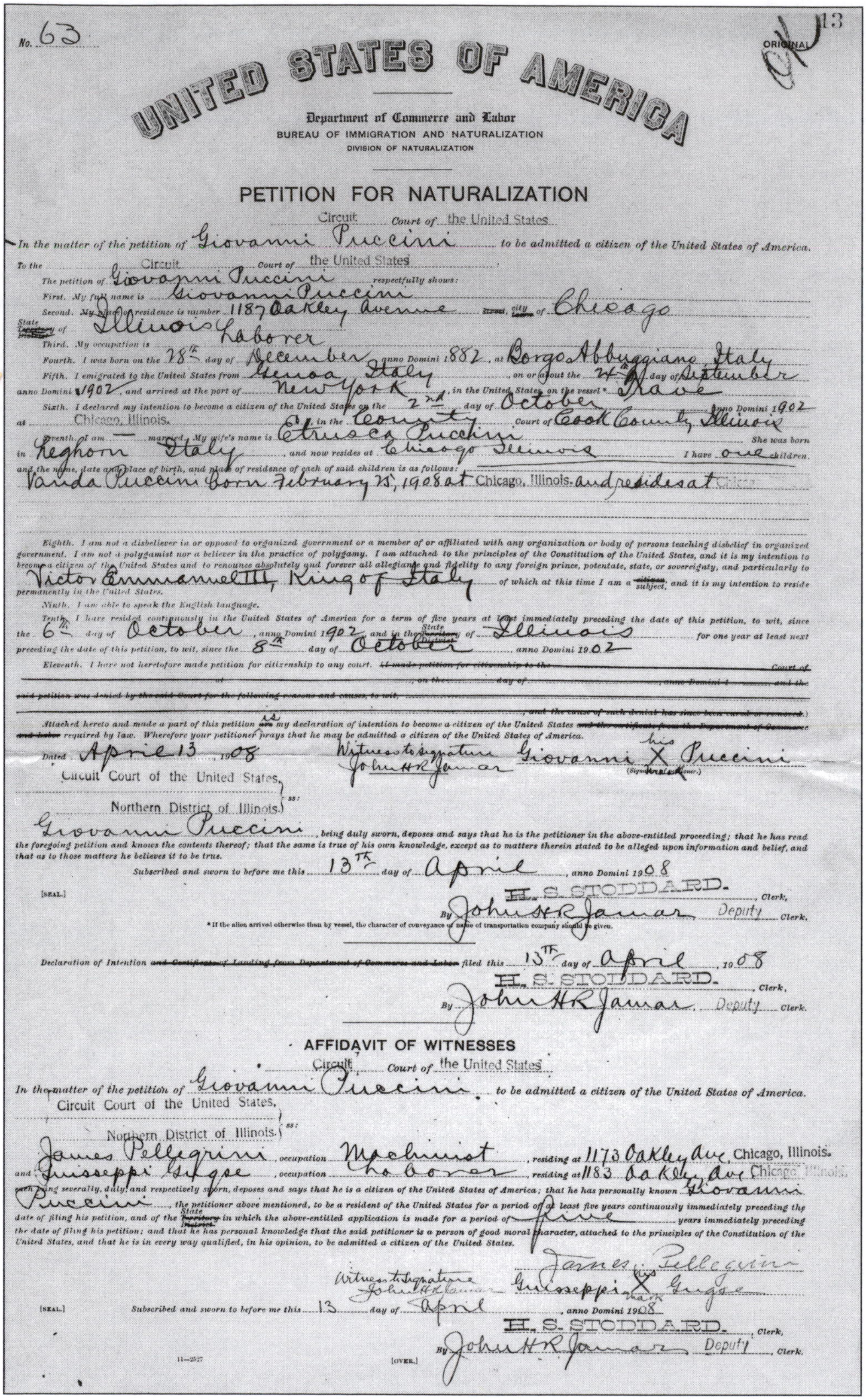

No. 63 ORIGINAL 13

UNITED STATES OF AMERICA

Department of Commerce and Labor
BUREAU OF IMMIGRATION AND NATURALIZATION
DIVISION OF NATURALIZATION

PETITION FOR NATURALIZATION

Circuit Court of the United States

In the matter of the petition of Giovanni Puccini to be admitted a citizen of the United States of America.

To the Circuit Court of the United States

The petition of Giovanni Puccini respectfully shows:

First. My full name is Giovanni Puccini

Second. My place of residence is number 1187 Oakley Avenue street, city of Chicago State of Illinois

Third. My occupation is Laborer

Fourth. I was born on the 28th day of December anno Domini 1882, at Borgo Abbuggiano Italy

Fifth. I emigrated to the United States from Genoa Italy, on or about the 24th day of September anno Domini 1902, and arrived at the port of New York, in the United States, on the vessel Trave

Sixth. I declared my intention to become a citizen of the United States on the 2nd day of October anno Domini 1902 at Chicago, Illinois, in the County Court of Cook County, Illinois

Seventh. I am married. My wife's name is Etrusca Puccini She was born in Leghorn Italy, and now resides at Chicago Illinois. I have one children, and the name, date and place of birth, and place of residence of each of said children is as follows: Vanda Puccini born February 25, 1908 at Chicago, Illinois, and resides at Chicago

Eighth. I am not a disbeliever in or opposed to organized government or a member of or affiliated with any organization or body of persons teaching disbelief in organized government. I am not a polygamist nor a believer in the practice of polygamy. I am attached to the principles of the Constitution of the United States, and it is my intention to become a citizen of the United States and to renounce absolutely and forever all allegiance and fidelity to any foreign prince, potentate, state, or sovereignty, and particularly to Victor Emmanuel III, King of Italy of which at this time I am a subject, and it is my intention to reside permanently in the United States.

Ninth. I am able to speak the English language.

Tenth. I have resided continuously in the United States of America for a term of five years at least immediately preceding the date of this petition, to wit, since the 6th day of October, anno Domini 1902, and in the State of Illinois for one year at least next preceding the date of this petition, to wit, since the 8th day of October anno Domini 1902.

Eleventh. I have not heretofore made petition for citizenship to any court. ~~(I made petition for citizenship to the ... Court of ... on the ... day of ..., anno Domini ..., and the said petition was denied by the said Court for the following reasons and causes, to wit, ..., and the cause of such denial has since been cured or removed.)~~

Attached hereto and made a part of this petition is my declaration of intention to become a citizen of the United States ~~and the certificate from the Department of Commerce and Labor~~ required by law. Wherefore your petitioner prays that he may be admitted a citizen of the United States of America.

Dated April 13 1908 Witness to signature John H R Jamar Giovanni his X mark Puccini (Signature of petitioner.)

Circuit Court of the United States, Northern District of Illinois, ss:

Giovanni Puccini, being duly sworn, deposes and says that he is the petitioner in the above-entitled proceeding; that he has read the foregoing petition and knows the contents thereof; that the same is true of his own knowledge, except as to matters therein stated to be alleged upon information and belief, and that as to those matters he believes it to be true.

Subscribed and sworn to before me this 13th day of April, anno Domini 1908

[SEAL.] H. S. STODDARD, Clerk,
By John H R Jamar Deputy Clerk.

* If the alien arrived otherwise than by vessel, the character of conveyance or name of transportation company should be given.

Declaration of Intention ~~and Certificate of Landing from Department of Commerce and Labor~~ filed this 13th day of April, 1908

H. S. STODDARD, Clerk,
By John H R Jamar Deputy Clerk.

AFFIDAVIT OF WITNESSES

Circuit Court of the United States

In the matter of the petition of Giovanni Puccini to be admitted a citizen of the United States of America.

Circuit Court of the United States, Northern District of Illinois, ss:

James Pellegrini, occupation Machinist, residing at 1173 Oakley Ave Chicago, Illinois, and Guisseppi Grgse, occupation Laborer, residing at 1183 Oakley Ave Chicago, Illinois, each being severally, duly, and respectively sworn, deposes and says that he is a citizen of the United States of America; that he has personally known Giovanni Puccini, the petitioner above mentioned, to be a resident of the United States for a period of at least five years continuously immediately preceding the date of filing his petition, and of the State in which the above-entitled application is made for a period of five years immediately preceding the date of filing his petition; and that he has personal knowledge that the said petitioner is a person of good moral character, attached to the principles of the Constitution of the United States, and that he is in every way qualified, in his opinion, to be admitted a citizen of the United States.

James Pellegrini
Witness to signature John H R Jamar Guisseppi his X mark Grgse

[SEAL.] Subscribed and sworn to before me this 13 day of April, anno Domini 1908

H. S. STODDARD, Clerk,
By John H R Jamar Deputy Clerk.

11—2527 [OVER.]

Figure 3-25. Petition for naturalization of Giovanni Puccini.

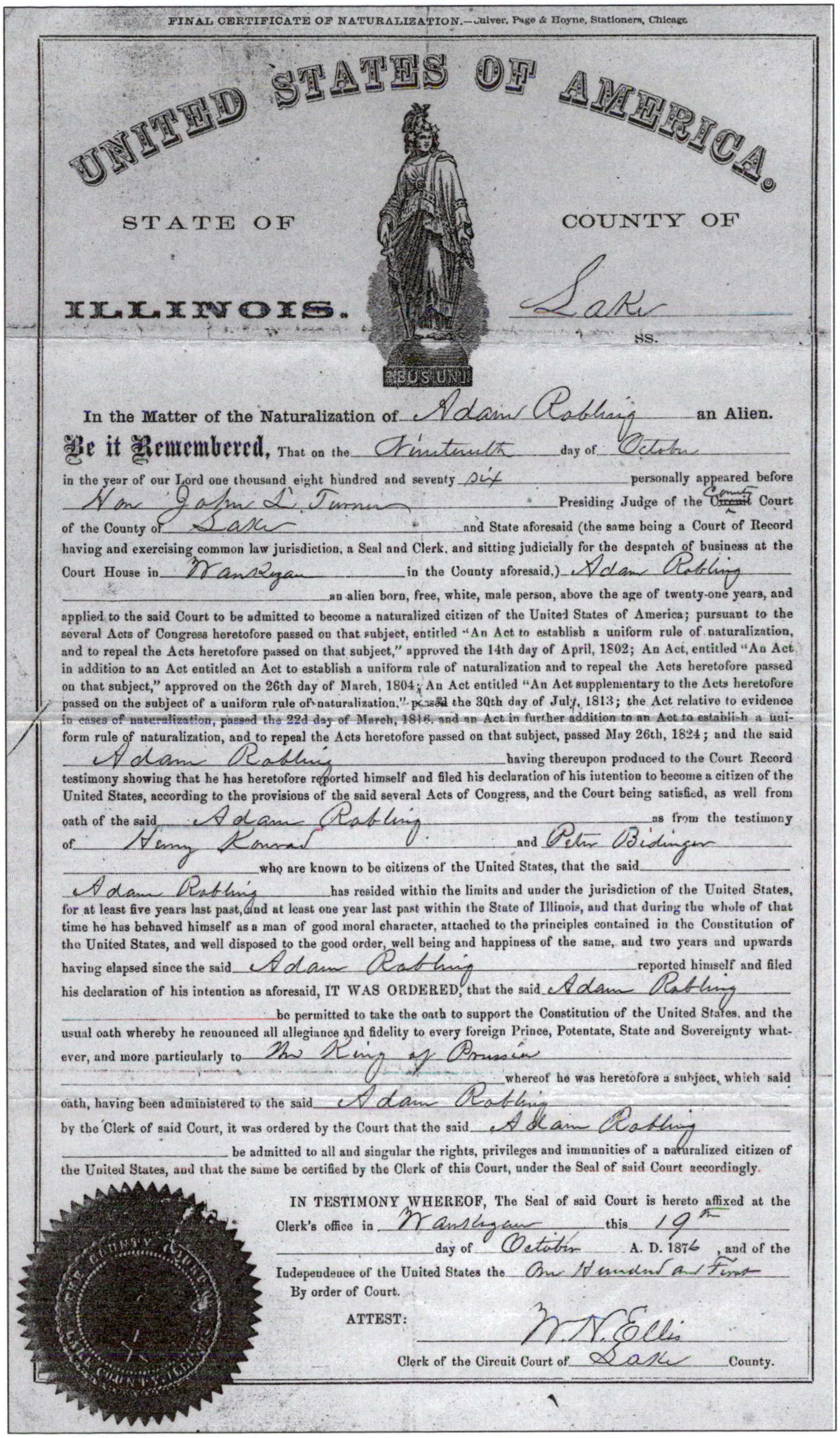

FINAL CERTIFICATE OF NATURALIZATION.—Culver, Page & Hoyne, Stationers, Chicago.

UNITED STATES OF AMERICA.

STATE OF ILLINOIS.

COUNTY OF Lake ss.

E PLURIBUS UNUM

In the Matter of the Naturalization of Adam Robling an Alien.

Be it Remembered, That on the Nineteenth day of October in the year of our Lord one thousand eight hundred and seventy six personally appeared before Hon John L. Turner Presiding Judge of the ~~Circuit~~ County Court of the County of Lake and State aforesaid (the same being a Court of Record having and exercising common law jurisdiction, a Seal and Clerk, and sitting judicially for the despatch of business at the Court House in Waukegan in the County aforesaid,) Adam Robling an alien born, free, white, male person, above the age of twenty-one years, and applied to the said Court to be admitted to become a naturalized citizen of the United States of America; pursuant to the several Acts of Congress heretofore passed on that subject, entitled "An Act to establish a uniform rule of naturalization, and to repeal the Acts heretofore passed on that subject," approved the 14th day of April, 1802; An Act, entitled "An Act in addition to an Act entitled an Act to establish a uniform rule of naturalization and to repeal the Acts heretofore passed on that subject," approved on the 26th day of March, 1804; An Act entitled "An Act supplementary to the Acts heretofore passed on the subject of a uniform rule of naturalization," passed the 30th day of July, 1813; the Act relative to evidence in cases of naturalization, passed the 22d day of March, 1816, and an Act in further addition to an Act to establish a uniform rule of naturalization, and to repeal the Acts heretofore passed on that subject, passed May 26th, 1824; and the said Adam Robling having thereupon produced to the Court Record testimony showing that he has heretofore reported himself and filed his declaration of his intention to become a citizen of the United States, according to the provisions of the said several Acts of Congress, and the Court being satisfied, as well from oath of the said Adam Robling as from the testimony of Henry Konrad and Peter Bidinger who are known to be citizens of the United States, that the said Adam Robling has resided within the limits and under the jurisdiction of the United States, for at least five years last past, and at least one year last past within the State of Illinois, and that during the whole of that time he has behaved himself as a man of good moral character, attached to the principles contained in the Constitution of the United States, and well disposed to the good order, well being and happiness of the same, and two years and upwards having elapsed since the said Adam Robling reported himself and filed his declaration of his intention as aforesaid, IT WAS ORDERED, that the said Adam Robling be permitted to take the oath to support the Constitution of the United States, and the usual oath whereby he renounced all allegiance and fidelity to every foreign Prince, Potentate, State and Sovereignty whatever, and more particularly to the King of Prussia whereof he was heretofore a subject, which said oath, having been administered to the said Adam Robling by the Clerk of said Court, it was ordered by the Court that the said Adam Robling be admitted to all and singular the rights, privileges and immunities of a naturalized citizen of the United States, and that the same be certified by the Clerk of this Court, under the Seal of said Court accordingly.

IN TESTIMONY WHEREOF, The Seal of said Court is hereto affixed at the Clerk's office in Waukegan this 19th day of October A. D. 1876, and of the Independence of the United States the One Hundred and First

By order of Court.

ATTEST: W. N. Ellis

Clerk of the Circuit Court of Lake County.

Figure 3-26. Final certificate of naturalization for Adam Robling, Lake County, Illinois. Similar certificates were given to individuals upon completion of the naturalization process, often becoming prized possessions that were handed down for generations within a family.

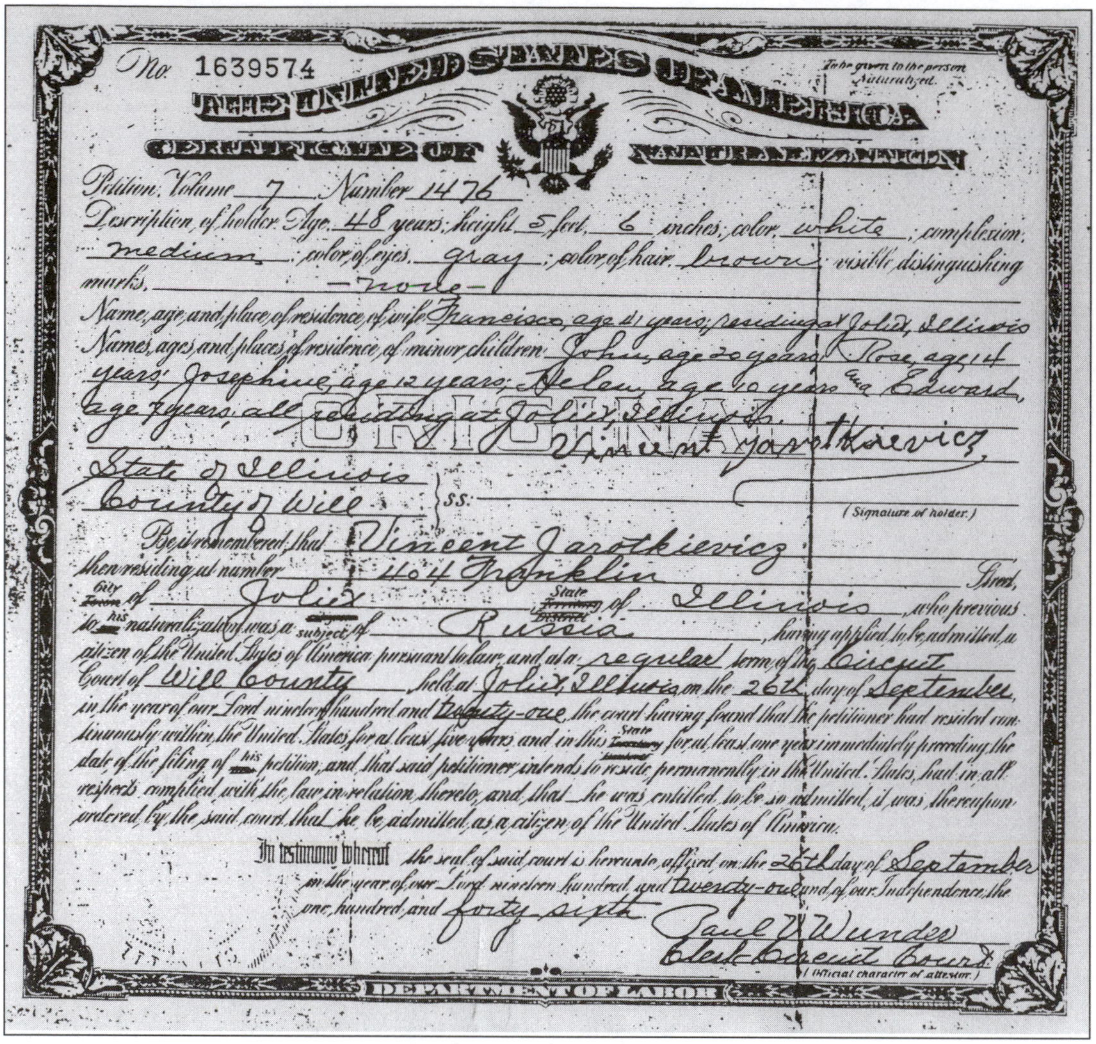

No. 1639574 — To be given to the person Naturalized.

THE UNITED STATES OF AMERICA

CERTIFICATE OF NATURALIZATION

Petition, Volume 7 Number 1476

Description of holder: Age, 48 years; height, 5 feet, 6 inches; color, white; complexion, medium; color of eyes, gray; color of hair, brown; visible distinguishing marks, — none —

Name, age, and place of residence of wife Francisco, age 41 years, residing at Joliet, Illinois

Names, ages, and places of residence of minor children John, age 20 years; Rose, age 14 years; Josephine, age 12 years; Helen, age 10 years and Edward, age 7 years, all residing at Joliet, Illinois.

ORIGINAL

Vincent Jarotkievicz (Signature of holder.)

State of Illinois
County of Will } SS:

Be it remembered, that Vincent Jarotkievicz then residing at number 404 Franklin Street, City of Joliet State of Illinois, who previous to his naturalization was a subject of Russia, having applied to be admitted a citizen of the United States of America pursuant to law, and at a regular term of the Circuit Court of Will County held at Joliet, Illinois on the 26th day of September in the year of our Lord nineteen hundred and twenty-one the court having found that the petitioner had resided continuously within the United States for at least five years and in this State for at least one year immediately preceding the date of the filing of his petition, and that said petitioner intends to reside permanently in the United States, had in all respects complied with the law in relation thereto, and that he was entitled to be so admitted, it was thereupon ordered by the said court that he be admitted as a citizen of the United States of America.

In testimony whereof the seal of said court is hereunto affixed on the 26th day of September in the year of our Lord nineteen hundred and twenty-one and of our Independence the one hundred and forty sixth.

Paul V. Wunder
Clerk Circuit Court (Official character of attestor.)

DEPARTMENT OF LABOR

Figure 3-27. Final certificate of naturalization for Vincent Jarotkievicz of Russia, who was naturalized in Joliet, Will County, Illinois, in 1946.

child, Vanda, with birth dates and places for each—among other important biographical notes.

Naturalization Oaths: Some naturalization oaths survive in separate files in courthouses and archives; however, most of them were interfiled with petitions or final papers. The majority of naturalization oaths contain little detail. As with every other kind of naturalization document, though, it may be worth the extra trouble to inquire about their existence in courts and archives and to examine them if they are found. An oath for John A. Drexel of Detroit revealed that he served in the "1st regiment of the Ohio Volunteer Cavalry from which he has been honorably discharged on January 8, 1853."

Certificate of Naturalization: Most certificates of naturalization contain only the name of the individual, the name of the court, and the date of issue. Certificates were issued to naturalized citizens upon completion of all citizenship requirements. As in the cases of the declarations of intention and the petitions, the amount of information provided on the certificate may vary greatly from one court to another and from one year to another. In some cases the certificate will provide the name; address; birthplace or nationality; country from which emigrated;

birth date or age; personal description; marital status; name of spouse; names, ages, and addresses of children; and date of document. Shown in figure 3-26 is a copy of the final certificate of naturalization for Adam Robling, who completed the naturalization process on 19 October 1876 in Lake County, Illinois.

Naturalization Certificate Stubs: Generally, the court did not retain copies of certificates issued to new citizens, but certificates were usually issued from bound volumes. Typical volumes were designed in a checkbook fashion, with the certificate to the right side of the page and a stub to the left to be kept as a permanent record of the person to whom the certificate was issued. These *naturalization stub books*, as they are sometimes called, also vary in content from one court to another and from one year to another, but they sometimes contain valuable genealogical information. Some court officials regarded stub books as a duplication of records that occupied needed space and ordered them destroyed. If certificate stubs survived, they might be found in the creating courts or in archives and historical agencies. See, for example, figure 3-28, a page from a stub book for the U.S. District Court, Northern District of Ohio, for Julius August Behnke. It shows his age, when and where he declared his intention to become a citizen, names, ages, and places of residence of his wife and children, and the date of issue of the certificate of naturalization. A disappointing feature of the stub books is that they are difficult to use because they are arranged by filing date and are rarely indexed.

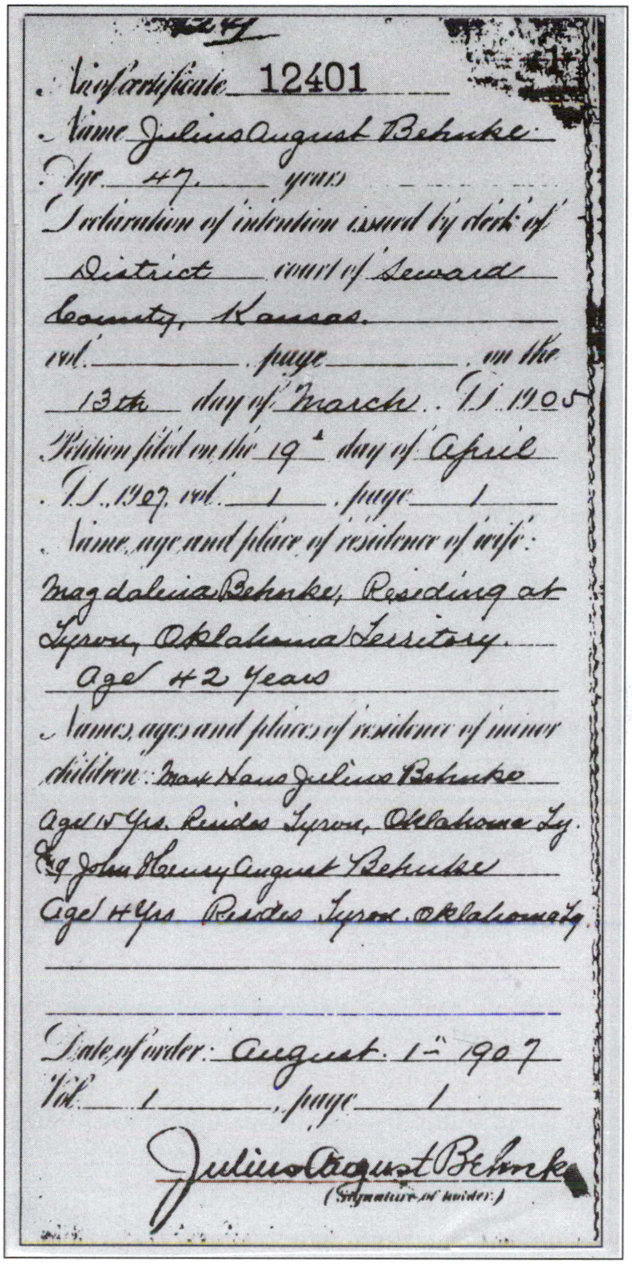

No. of certificate 12401

Name Julius August Behnke

Age 47 years

Declaration of intention issued by clerk of District court of Seward County, Kansas.

vol. ____ page ____ on the 13th day of March A.D. 1905

Petition filed on the 19th day of April A.D. 1907 vol. 1 page 1

Name, age and place of residence of wife: Magdalena Behnke, Residing at Tyrone, Oklahoma Territory. Age 42 Years

Names, ages and places of residence of minor children: Max Hans Julius Behnke Age 15 Yrs. Resides Tyrone, Oklahoma Ty. John Henry August Behnke Age 4 Yrs Resides Tyrone Oklahoma Ty.

Date of order: August 1st 1907

Vol. 1 page 1

Julius August Behnke

(Signature of holder.)

Figure 3-28. From a stub book for naturalization certificates. This one was issued to Julius August Behnke in the U.S. Court, Northern District of Ohio, Cleveland. The original stub book is now preserved at the National Archives–Great Lakes Region in Chicago.

Certificates of Arrival: Aliens arriving in the United States after 29 June 1906 were issued a *certificate of arrival* which verified their presence in the United States. These certificates were filed with subsequent citizenship papers. The Bureau of Immigration and Naturalization checked ship manifests to verify the legal admission of every applicant for citizenship who had arrived since the passage of the 1906 statute. INS historian Marian Smith explains the process:

Aliens submitted Declarations of Intention or Petitions to a naturalization court. On these forms, the immigrant named the port, date, and ship of his or her arrival. Copies of the form were forwarded to the appropriate ports of entry to be checked by

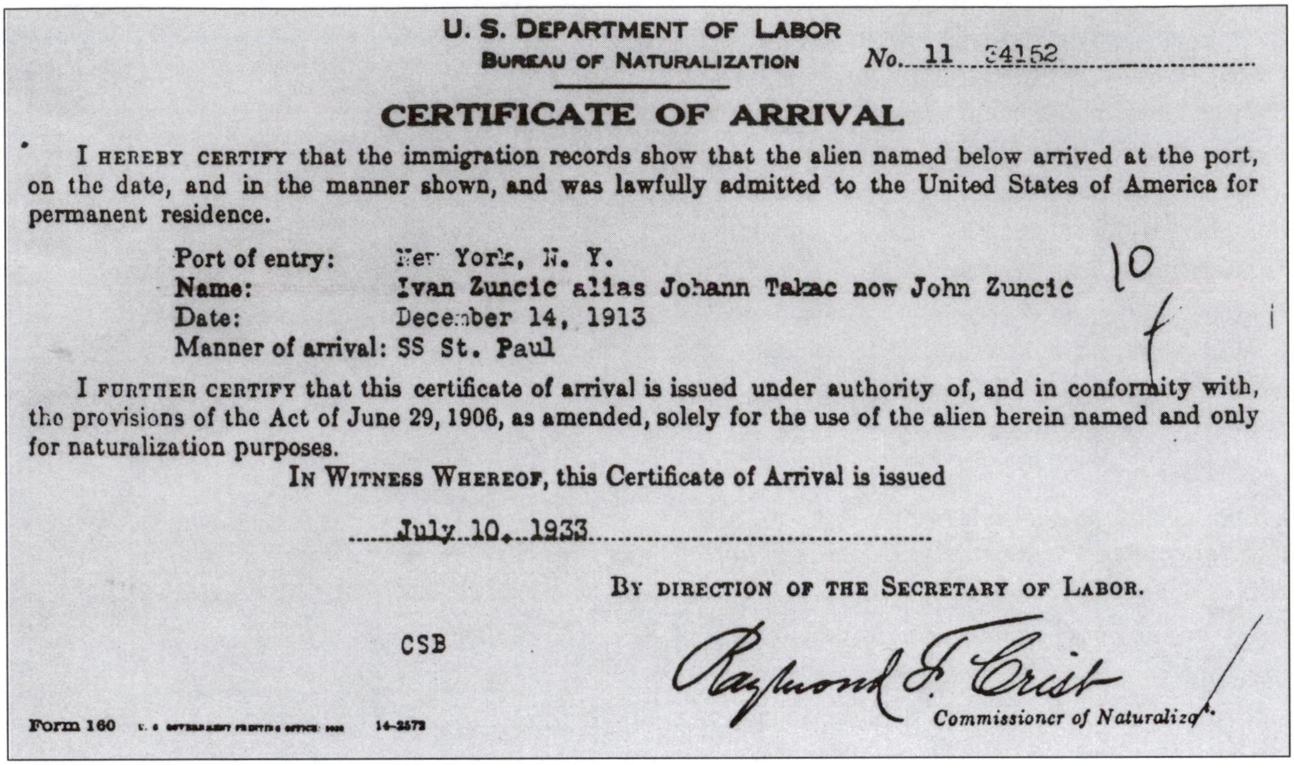
U. S. DEPARTMENT OF LABOR
BUREAU OF NATURALIZATION No. 11 34152

CERTIFICATE OF ARRIVAL

I HEREBY CERTIFY that the immigration records show that the alien named below arrived at the port, on the date, and in the manner shown, and was lawfully admitted to the United States of America for permanent residence.

Port of entry: New York, N. Y.
Name: Ivan Zuncic alias Johann Takac now John Zuncic
Date: December 14, 1913
Manner of arrival: SS St. Paul

I FURTHER CERTIFY that this certificate of arrival is issued under authority of, and in conformity with, the provisions of the Act of June 29, 1906, as amended, solely for the use of the alien herein named and only for naturalization purposes.

IN WITNESS WHEREOF, this Certificate of Arrival is issued

July 10, 1933

BY DIRECTION OF THE SECRETARY OF LABOR.

CSB

Raymond F. Crist
Commissioner of Naturalization.

Form 160 14-2573

Figure 3-29. Certificate of arrival of Ivan Zuncic.

verification clerks who located the immigrant's arrival record among their immigration manifests. If the record was found, INS issued a Certificate of Arrival and sent it back to the naturalization court.[2]

As Smith further explains in the article, the certificate of arrival was another crucial step in preventing naturalization fraud, "not only because it prevented ineligible aliens from becoming citizens, but also because it could prevent more than one person from using the same arrival record as the basis for naturalization." The certificate of arrival of "Ivan Zuncic, alias Johann Takac, now John Zuncic," demonstrates the attempts by the government to keep track of name changes (figure 3-29). For any number of reasons, immigrants often changed their names deliberately or had them changed inadvertently after arriving in the United States.

Finding Naturalization Records By Following Emigration Patterns

As mentioned earlier, there was a definite pattern in which immigrants took out first papers somewhere on the East Coast (where the vast majority of immigrants arrived in the United States) and completed the requirements in some county further inland; however, there were plenty of exceptions. Rudolph Schaefer, for example, appeared in St. Louis County Court to declare his intention to become a citizen on 1 November 1852. In October 1856, Rudolph was in the District Court of the United States for the Northern District of Ohio (Cleveland) pursuing his citizenship. Schaefer's declaration of intention and final papers are now located in the National Archives—Great Lakes Region in Chicago (figures 3-30 and 3-31).

In addition to county and federal courts, there may have been city or municipal courts, marine courts, criminal courts, police courts, or other courts having authority to naturalize in the area where an immigrant lived. Often it was a matter of the alien simply choosing to travel to the most conveniently located court—and the courthouse in an adjoining county might have been closer to home than the courthouse in his or her county of residence. The fact that thousands were naturalized in criminal courts does not mean they were criminals, but simply that the criminal courts were probably closest to home. The following examples demonstrate the differences in declarations of intention in forms used in four courts during the 1830s and 1840s.

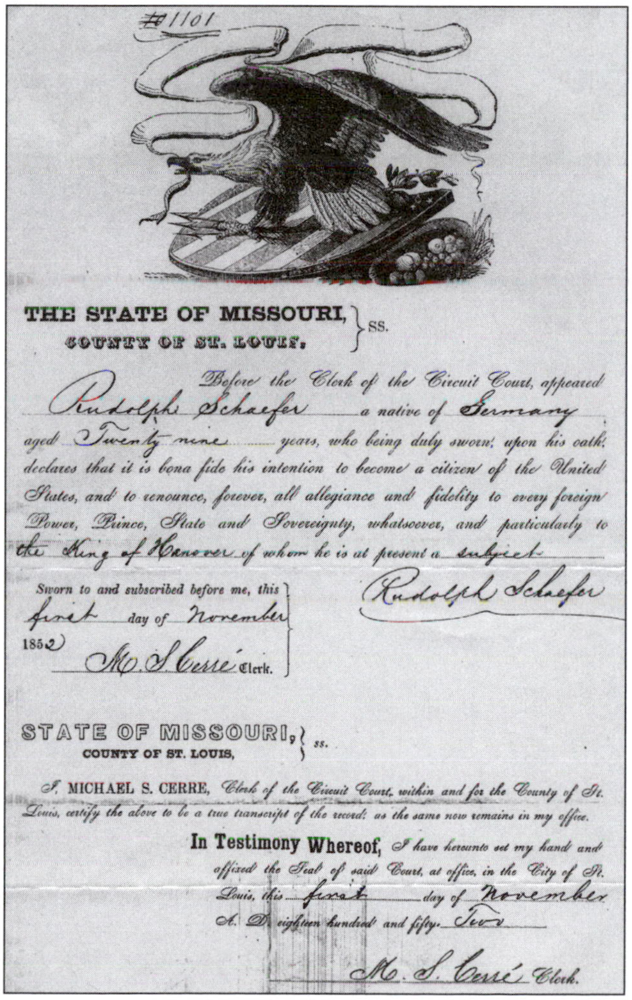
#1101

THE STATE OF MISSOURI, } ss.
COUNTY OF ST. LOUIS.

Before the Clerk of the Circuit Court, appeared Rudolph Schaefer a native of Germany aged Twenty nine years, who being duly sworn, upon his oath, declares that it is bona fide his intention to become a citizen of the United States, and to renounce, forever, all allegiance and fidelity to every foreign Power, Prince, State and Sovereignty, whatsoever, and particularly to the King of Hanover of whom he is at present a subject.

Sworn to and subscribed before me, this first day of November 1852
M. S. Cerre Clerk.

Rudolph Schaefer

STATE OF MISSOURI, } ss.
COUNTY OF ST. LOUIS,

I, MICHAEL S. CERRE, Clerk of the Circuit Court, within and for the County of St. Louis, certify the above to be a true transcript of the record; as the same now remains in my office.

In Testimony Whereof, I have hereunto set my hand and affixed the Seal of said Court, at office, in the City of St. Louis, this first day of November A. D. eighteen hundred and fifty-Two

M. S. Cerre Clerk.

Figure 3-30. Rudolph Schaefer's 1852 declaration of intention from the county of St. Louis, Missouri.

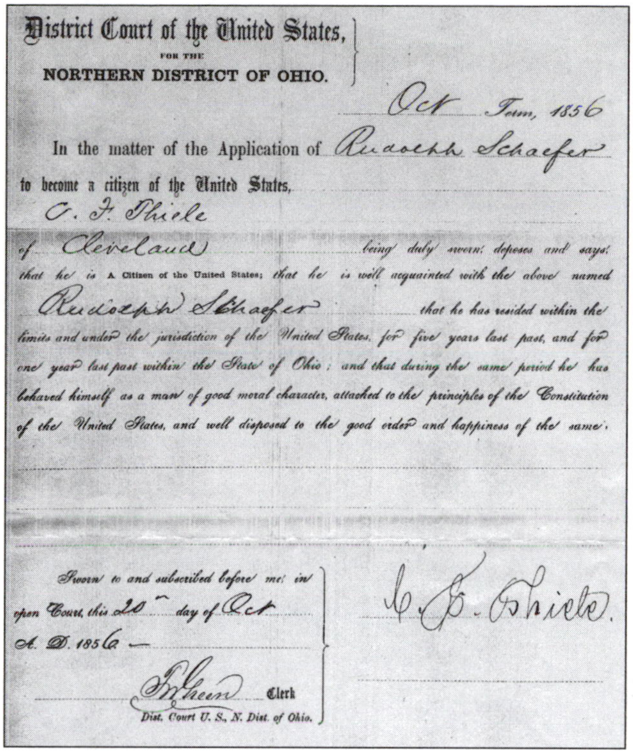
District Court of the United States, FOR THE NORTHERN DISTRICT OF OHIO.

Oct Term, 1856

In the matter of the Application of Rudolph Schaefer to become a citizen of the United States,

C. F. Thiele of Cleveland being duly sworn, deposes and says; that he is A Citizen of the United States; that he is well acquainted with the above named Rudolph Schaefer that he has resided within the limits and under the jurisdiction of the United States, for five years last past, and for one year last past within the State of Ohio; and that during the same period he has behaved himself as a man of good moral character, attached to the principles of the Constitution of the United States, and well disposed to the good order and happiness of the same.

Sworn to and subscribed before me, in open Court, this 20th day of Oct A. D. 1856 —

Clerk
Dist. Court U. S., N. Dist. of Ohio.

C. F. Thiele.

Figure 3-31. Rudolph Schaefer's 1856 certificate of naturalization from the U.S. District Court in Cleveland.

The Philadelphia City Court (figure 3-1) provides John Kopp's birth date, country of birth, and age, indicates that he was born a member of the German nation and owed allegiance to the king of Prussia, that he migrated from Bernambac to the United States, arrived at the port of Philadelphia on or about 16 July 1832, and intended to settle in Pennsylvania.

The declaration of Florence McCarthy gives us little help (figure 3-32). Is Florence male or female? The "United Kingdom of Great Britain and Ireland" is not specific enough to be of any help. The finder of this certificate will not even have Florence's signature to bring home—only the date and the name of the court in which the naturalization took place.

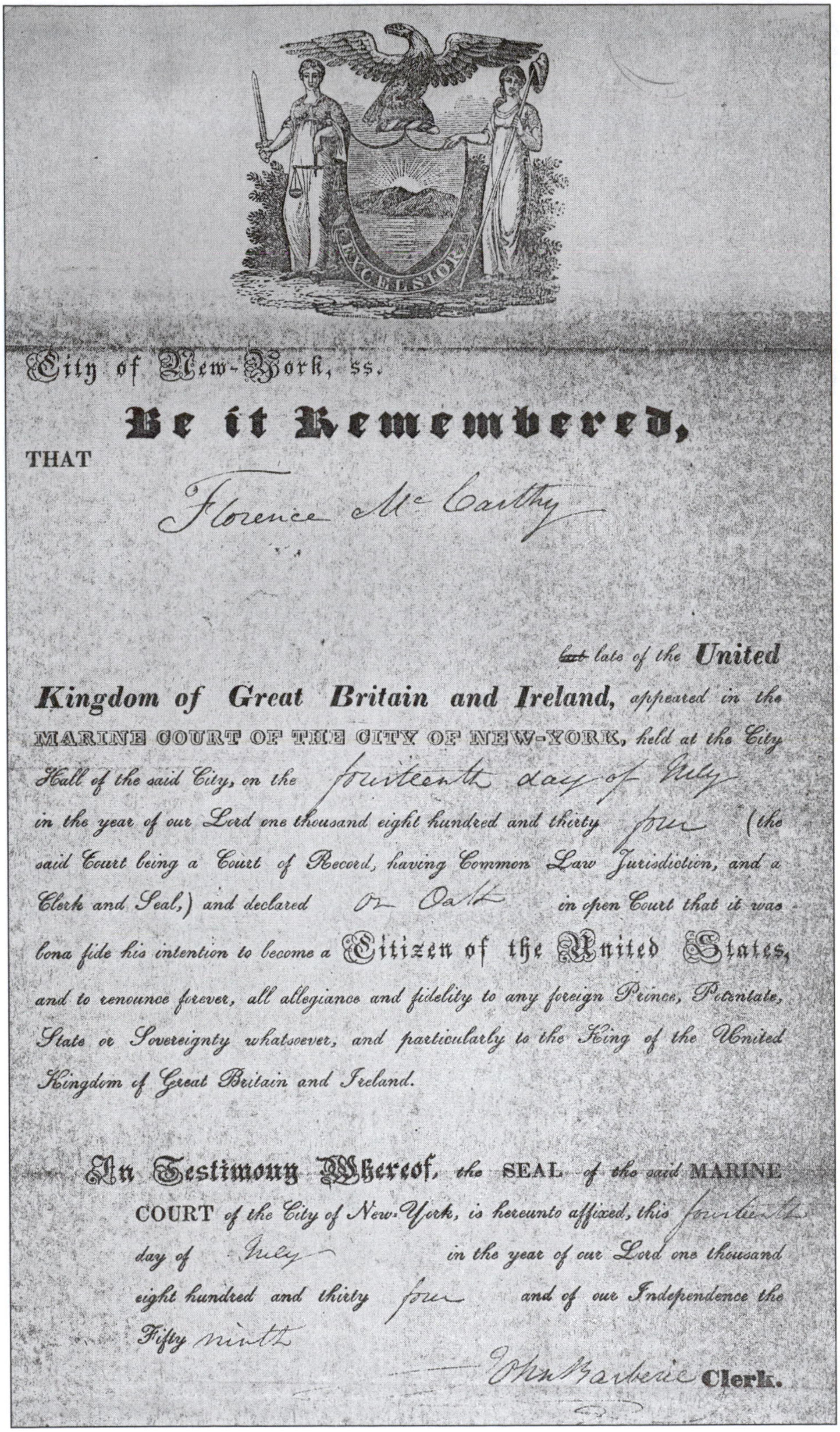
City of New-York, ss.

Be it Remembered,

THAT

Florence McCarthy

~~last~~ late of the **United Kingdom of Great Britain and Ireland,** *appeared in the* MARINE COURT OF THE CITY OF NEW-YORK, *held at the City Hall of the said City, on the* fourteenth day of July *in the year of our Lord one thousand eight hundred and thirty* four *(the said Court being a Court of Record, having Common Law Jurisdiction, and a Clerk and Seal,) and declared* On Oath *in open Court that it was bona fide his intention to become a* Citizen of the United States, *and to renounce forever, all allegiance and fidelity to any foreign Prince, Potentate, State or Sovereignty whatsoever, and particularly to the King of the United Kingdom of Great Britain and Ireland.*

In Testimony Whereof, *the* SEAL *of the said* MARINE COURT *of the City of New-York, is hereunto affixed, this* fourteenth *day of* July *in the year of our Lord one thousand eight hundred and thirty* four *and of our Independence the* Fifty ninth

John Barberie **Clerk.**

Figure 3-32. Declaration of intention for Florence McCarthy from the Marine Court of New York City, 1834.

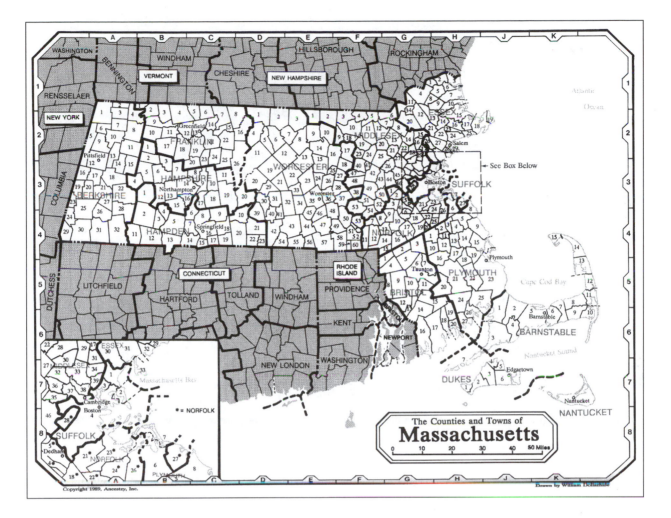

Figure 3-33. Counties and towns of Massachusetts from Ancestry's Red Book.

COURT BOUNDARIES AND JURISDICTIONS

A major challenge facing many researchers is finding the court in which a naturalization may have taken place. Boundaries and jurisdictions of courts have changed frequently over the years, usually due to population shifts. An individual who never changed his residence may have had his actions recorded in three or four different courts during his lifetime. With the enormous amounts of paper generated by courts every year and inevitable space limitations, older records are regularly moved to off-site warehouses or archives. Some court records have been moved several times and others have been deliberately or unintentionally destroyed.

In many counties there were several courts operating simultaneously. For example, there were at one time four courts handling naturalizations in Kane County, Illinois, with each court keeping its own set of records. "In 1965 all records were called into the Circuit Court office at Geneva. The Elgin City Court, the Aurora City Court and the Kane County Circuit Court records began in 1853 and ended in 1955. The Kane County Court located in Geneva processed naturalizations from 1872–1906."[3]

A good way to determine which courts served the people in the area where a specific person lived in a given time period is to consult *Ancestry's Red Book: American State, County and Town Sources*, rev. ed., edited by Alice Eichholz (Salt Lake City: Ancestry, 1992). Unique maps created by William

★　　★　　119　　★　　★

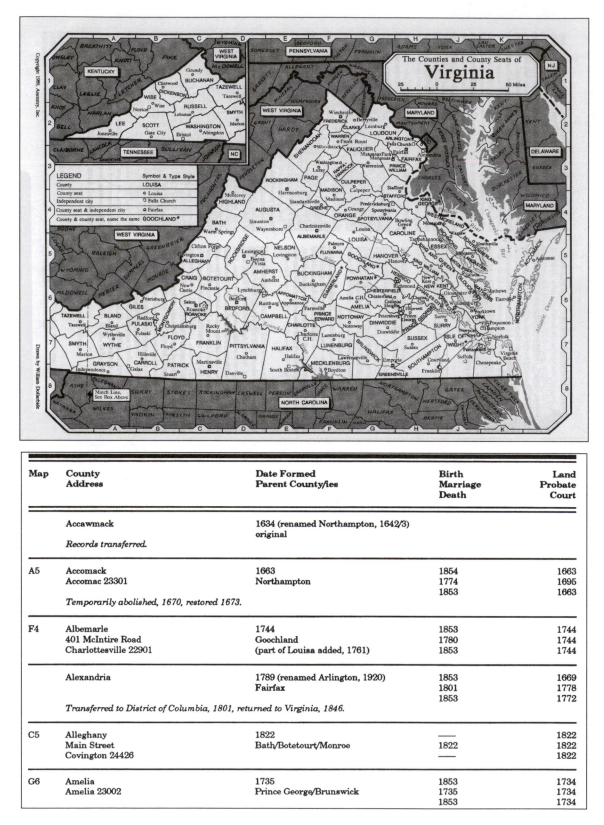

Map	County Address	Date Formed Parent County/ies	Birth Marriage Death	Land Probate Court
	Accawmack *Records transferred.*	1634 (renamed Northampton, 1642/3) original		
A5	Accomack Accomac 23301 *Temporarily abolished, 1670, restored 1673.*	1663 Northampton	1854 1774 1853	1663 1695 1663
F4	Albemarle 401 McIntire Road Charlottesville 22901	1744 Goochland (part of Louisa added, 1761)	1853 1780 1853	1744 1744 1744
	Alexandria *Transferred to District of Columbia, 1801, returned to Virginia, 1846.*	1789 (renamed Arlington, 1920) Fairfax	1853 1801 1853	1669 1778 1772
C5	Alleghany Main Street Covington 24426	1822 Bath/Botetourt/Monroe	—— 1822 ——	1822 1822 1822
G6	Amelia Amelia 23002	1735 Prince George/Brunswick	1853 1735 1853	1734 1734 1734

Figure 3-34. Map of the counties and county seats of Virginia, together with a portion of the table showing county addresses, formation dates and parent counties, and starting dates for vital records and land records from Ancestry's Red Book.

Dollarhide for the *Red Book* outline county boundaries for each state and include county seats. Tables that accompany the maps and descriptions of states provide an address for each clerk, the date the county was originally formed, and the name of the previous county or counties from which the current county was formed (figures 3-33 and 3-34). State chapters include sections on immigration/naturalization and special county resources. Eichholz, in her chapter on Massachusetts, for example, notes that

> the WPA developed an index of naturalizations found in numerous city, county, state, and federal courts in New England for the period 1786–1906, which is soundexed, microfilmed, and available through the National Archives

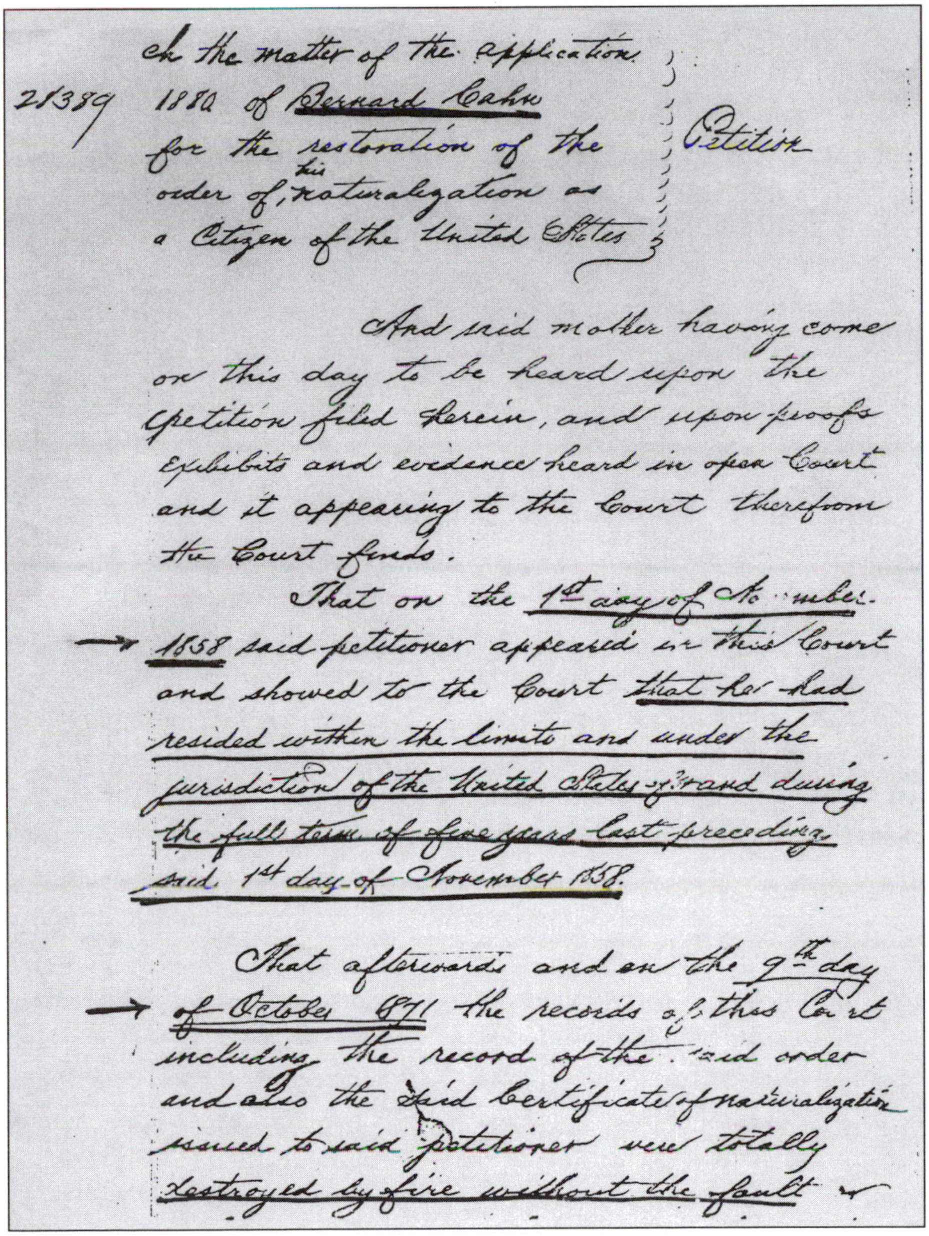

21389

In the matter of the application 1880 of Bernard Cahn for the restoration of his order of naturalization as a Citizen of the United States

Petition

And said matter having come on this day to be heard upon the petition filed herein, and upon proofs exhibits and evidence heard in open Court and it appearing to the Court therefrom the Court finds.

That on the 1st day of November 1858 said petitioner appeared in this Court and showed to the Court that he had resided within the limits and under the jurisdiction of the United States for and during the full term of five years last preceding said 1st day of November 1858.

That afterwards and on the 9th day of October 1871 the records of this Court including the record of the said order and also the said Certificate of naturalization issued to said petitioner were totally destroyed by fire without the fault or

Figure 3-35. When court records were lost due to fires, flood, or other disasters, many individuals returned to court to restore records. Such was the case of Bernard Cahn, whose 1858 naturalization was burned in the Great Chicago Fire of 1871.

(see more on the National Archives later in this book). The abstract cards used to create the microfilm for all of New England are at the National Archives–New England Region. In addition to the abstract cards and index, New England's regional branch of the archives holds dexigraphs of the actual records, making it possible to check the accuracy of the abstracts/index. Some have declarations of intention attached which may give more information about the immigrant.

The Massachusetts State Archives holds abstracts for state and local courts (1885–1931 with separate annual indexes), and also Essex County naturalization records (1901–82). Current petitions and index cards for the federal courts are at Immigration and Naturalization Service, U.S. Department of Justice, JFK Federal Building, Government Center, Boston Massachusetts 02203.[4]

In his description of New York naturalization records in the *Red Book*, Roger Joslyn states:

County naturalization records are kept by the county clerk. U.S. court records are in federal buildings in Buffalo and Albany, with most downstate records to the 1940s or 1950s at the National Archives–Northeast Region. At the latter is a WPA-created card index, arranged by Soundex, for all naturalizations (but not declarations of intention) performed in all courts in all five New York City boroughs, 1792–1906, together with dexigraphs (photostats) of the original records. Until the late 1800s and early 1900s, these records provide little information; upstate records up to the mid-1800s are generally more informative. For some early records, see two compilations by Kenneth Scott: *Early New York Naturalizations 1792–1840* (Baltimore, Md.: Genealogical Publishing Co., 1981), from federal, state, and local court records, and

with Kenn Stryker-Rodda, *Denizations, Naturalizations and Oaths of Allegiance in Colonial New York* (Baltimore, Md.: Genealogical Publishing Co., 1975). See also "Naturalizations in Federal Courts, New York District, 1790–1828," by Mrs. Edward J. Chapin in vol. 97 of *The New York Genealogical and Biographical Record* (1966); Kenneth Scott, "New York City Naturalizations, 1795–1799," *National Genealogical Society Quarterly* 71 (1983): 280–283; and "List of Immigrants 1802–1814" in the Emmet Collection in the New York Public Library manuscript department. A somewhat related work in this category is Kenneth Scott and Rosanne Conway, *New York Alien Residents*, 1825–1848 (1978; reprint, Baltimore, Md: Clearfield Co., 1991).[5]

While all naturalization records are supposed to be permanent records kept indefinitely by the courts, various circumstances have caused records to be lost, destroyed, or moved from their creating agencies. Natural disasters (such as floods and fires) as well as human acts (such as carelessness and politically based decisions) have destroyed some records and made others inaccessible. Over the years, some long-forgotten naturalization records have been rediscovered in warehouses, attics, and basements. Still other collections have been carefully maintained in museums, libraries, and historical and genealogical societies. The National Archives has custody of most of the older naturalization records that were created in federal circuit and district courts. State archives and historical agencies typically strive to preserve and catalog naturalization records that were recorded in state and local courts. If a record is not immediately found at the county level, an investigation of any such records kept at the state level may be in order.

Figure 3-36. The Great Chicago Fire of October 1871 destroyed court and other official county records (from Harper's Weekly, *11 November 1871).*

RE-RECORDED COURT RECORDS

If you are unsuccessful in locating naturalization documentation for an individual in what you think is the right court and time period, it may be worth looking at indexes or files for a later period. For any number of reasons, an individual may have had cause to re-register legal documents. Court fires, floods, and other courthouse mishaps were often the incentives that took aliens back into court long after they had first applied for citizenship. The following is a good example of a re-recording of a petition filed in Cook County Court, Illinois, in 1880 (see figure 3-35):

> In the matter of the application 28389-1180 of Bernard Cahn for restoration of the order of his naturalization as a Citizen of the United States

And said mother having come on this day to be heard upon the petition filed herein, and upon proofs exhibits and evidence heard in open Court and it appearing to the Court there from the Court finds

That on the 1st day of November 1858 said petitioner appeared in this Court and showed to the Court that he had resided within the limits and under the jurisdiction of the United States for and during the full term of five years last preceding said 1st day of November 1858.

That afterwards and on the 9th day of October 1871 the records of this Court including the record of the said order and also the said Certificate of naturalization issued to said petitioner were totally destroyed by fire without the fault of the petitioner.

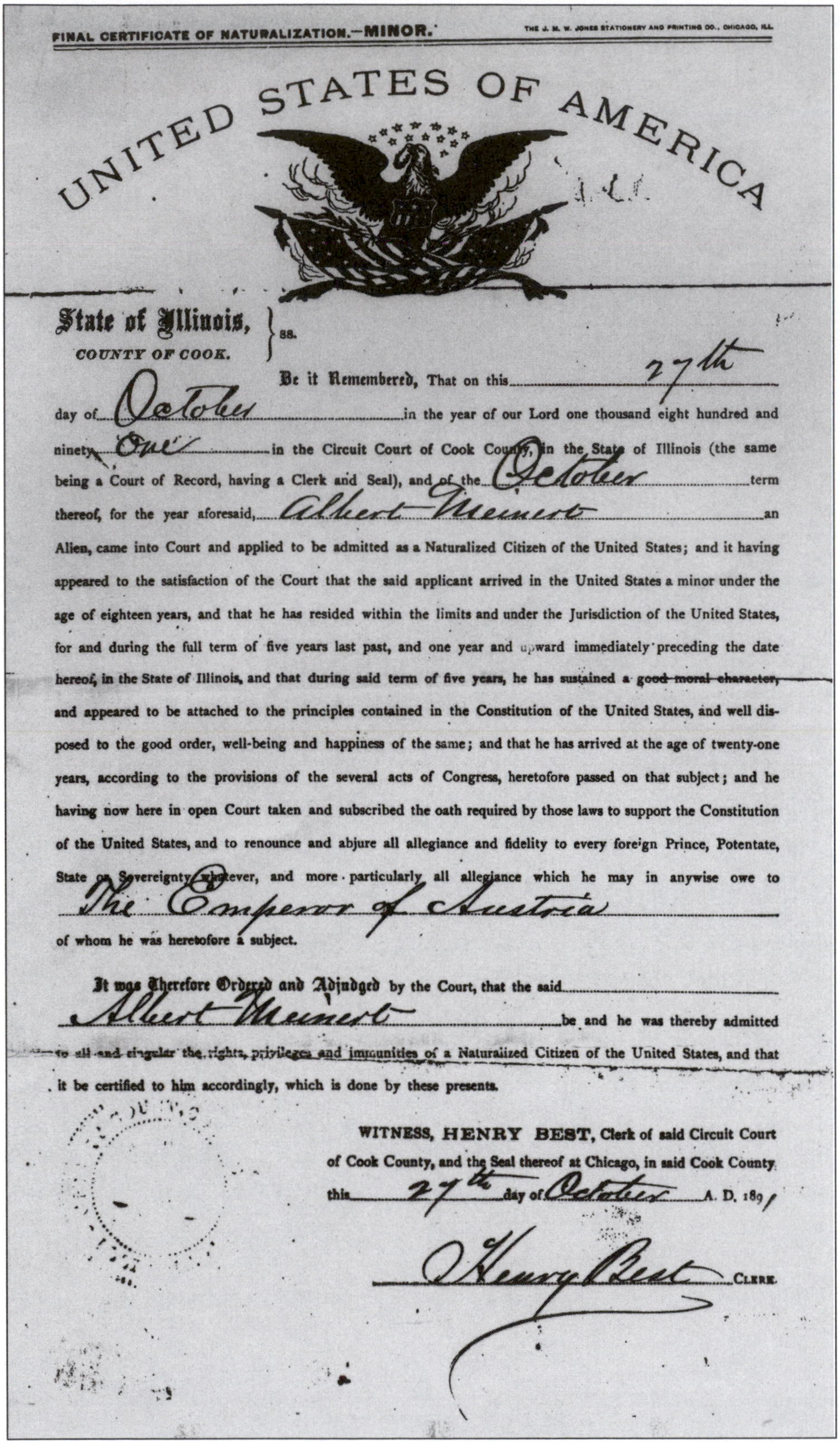

FINAL CERTIFICATE OF NATURALIZATION.—MINOR. THE J. M. W. JONES STATIONERY AND PRINTING CO., CHICAGO, ILL.

UNITED STATES OF AMERICA

State of Illinois, } ss.
COUNTY OF COOK. }

Be it Remembered, That on this 27th day of October in the year of our Lord one thousand eight hundred and ninety One in the Circuit Court of Cook County, in the State of Illinois (the same being a Court of Record, having a Clerk and Seal), and of the October term thereof, for the year aforesaid, Albert Meinert an Alien, came into Court and applied to be admitted as a Naturalized Citizen of the United States; and it having appeared to the satisfaction of the Court that the said applicant arrived in the United States a minor under the age of eighteen years, and that he has resided within the limits and under the Jurisdiction of the United States, for and during the full term of five years last past, and one year and upward immediately preceding the date hereof, in the State of Illinois, and that during said term of five years, he has sustained a good moral character, and appeared to be attached to the principles contained in the Constitution of the United States, and well disposed to the good order, well-being and happiness of the same; and that he has arrived at the age of twenty-one years, according to the provisions of the several acts of Congress, heretofore passed on that subject; and he having now here in open Court taken and subscribed the oath required by those laws to support the Constitution of the United States, and to renounce and abjure all allegiance and fidelity to every foreign Prince, Potentate, State or Sovereignty whatever, and more particularly all allegiance which he may in anywise owe to The Emperor of Austria of whom he was heretofore a subject.

It was Therefore Ordered and Adjudged by the Court, that the said Albert Meinert be and he was thereby admitted to all and singular the rights, privileges and immunities of a Naturalized Citizen of the United States, and that it be certified to him accordingly, which is done by these presents.

WITNESS, HENRY BEST, Clerk of said Circuit Court of Cook County, and the Seal thereof at Chicago, in said Cook County, this 27th day of October A. D. 1891

Henry Best CLERK.

Figure 3-37. Final certificate of naturalization—minor, for Albert Meinert, 27 October 1891, Cook County, Illinois.

INDEXES

Some courts have master naturalization indexes, but many have only separately indexed volumes of naturalization records that must be examined book by book. Frequently, the naturalizations of military personnel and of minors are in separate volumes and so can be easily overlooked. It is not unheard of to find naturalization records intermingled with other court records; some have even been found among land and property records. While originally filed and indexed in a separate minor's file, the document shown in figure 3-37 can now be located in the WPA-created index for the Northern District of Illinois. (See chapter 4 for further information about indexes.) In many cases, old naturalization files have been moved from the originating court to an archive.

UNEXPECTED TREASURES

While it must be emphasized that it is far from commonplace, unexpected treasures occasionally turn up in naturalization files. While I was indexing the naturalizations for the U.S. Circuit and District courts in Detroit and when I worked at the National Archives in Chicago, I saw enough of these to make me wish there were a way to let others know about them. Unfortunately, these buried nuggets don't show up in indexes. Even though the following naturalization file is indexed, the index format made no provision for "extras" that are included in the file. This is true of most naturalization indexes; they generally leave out all but the standard information, such as name of citizen, information about the court in which the naturalization took place, date of naturalization or declaration, and the petition number or declaration number. Given the enormous volume of records in most places where naturalizations are stored, chances are that most of these wonderful messages will never again see the light of day. One example is a personal letter found in the 1844 naturalization file of Elias Jones:

Detroit June 28, '44

Ins.

Mr. Elias W. Jones of this city is about applying to be admitted as a Citizen of the U.States—It is necessary that he prove his residence within the U.States for the past five years. At his request I send you an affidavit to be made by yourself and Mr. David Lewis before a Justice of the Peace—If Mr. Lewis be not at hand, any other person will answer. You will be careful to have all the blanks properly filled up by the Justice of the Peace. You will then take it to the proper office (I believe the Prothonotary) and have him Certify that the Justice of the Peace is duly commissioned and qualified & in the usual form.

I hope you will attend to this without delay & have the affidavit returned, directed to Elias W. Jones, Detroit, Michigan with all possible dispatch.

The fee, to the Officer, will be but trifling & I suppose it will fall on you to advance them for W. Jones who is able & willing to refund them to you. His [—] in this city is above reproach.

> Respectfully in your abl. servant
> Jno. Winder,
> Clerk U.S. Courts, Michigan

Dear Father

It is but a short time since I wrote before by Mr Major Flour merchant of Pottsville. This is the third letter since I received any from home. I have been anxiously waiting for answers, but have received none as yet, I hope you will write as soon as possible and let us know your state, You perceive by the foregoing that I am about becoming a citizen, I had thought of waiting for you, to become naturalized, & thereby save me the trouble, but I find on inquiry that it is just as short for me to become naturalized myself you will therefore immediately so that I can have my papers during the present session of the United States court, which will probably continue until that time, as above you will see what you have to do, You may have an opportunity of sending the affidavit by some person to [—ing] to have it certified by the Prothonotary or let Benjamin or yourself go down The reason I have for becoming naturalized myself is, that in case you become naturalized I should require a copy Certified to, which would be quite as expensive as this, get the justice to give you a copy of the affidavit herein contained on a letter short like this, so that on the last page you ["may" is lined out] can write me a letter. I am still with the same man and receive $150 per annum being pleased with the place I am inclined to remain. I hope you are and have been well let me know all when you write. Give my love to Benj & Nancy, to Lewis & family to W.V. Strout and fam and all friends the affidavit ["will" is lined out] and certificate will cost you a little I know you will not notice that if you have the means, Did I know that you ever destitute, all I have should be at your service. I told the Gentleman who wrote the affidavit and letter a little above that you lived at Pottsville, which is in the occasion of its being so filled [lined out] Dear parents I often think of you & my heart bounds with gratitude for your great kindness, which I can never repay, May heaven bless you, and bring you safely home to himself is my prayer. Direct your letter to the [G.D Crossman?] as usual

Your Dutiful son
Elias W. Jones

WHEN INFORMATION SOURCES DON'T MATCH

In almost every phase of genealogical and historical research, you will find information that does not correspond with previously collected data. You may find conflicting birth dates for (presumably) the same person, for example. When this happens, some detective work is in order. Sorting out and analyzing pieces of the puzzle is part of the intrigue of historical research. What is the source of each piece of information? When was the information recorded, by whom, and under what circumstances? Why is one source more likely to be credible than some other source? Unfortunately, it is sometimes virtually impossible to prove the birth date of an individual—occasionally because the person in question was himself not sure of a specific date or place. The following naturalization declaration for James Smith of Putnam County, Illinois, 1836, illustrates the problem:

To the Honorable Thomas Ford Presiding Judge of the Circuit Court in and for the County of Putnam & State of Illinois

I James Smith an alien born free white person of the age of forty five years last April do hereby in conformity with the first condition specified in the first section of the act of Congress entitled an act to establish an uniform rule of naturalization and to repeal the acts heretofore passed on that subject & approved the 14th day of April 1802 declare and make known to the said circuit court now sitting in and state aforesaid that my true and proper name is James Smith that I was born in (b)ramfield Township in the County of Suffolk and in the Kingdom of Great Britton sometime in the month of April A.D. 1791—and that I am about 45 years of age that I belonged to the Kingdom Great Britton [lined out] Brittish nation and owe allegiance to the King of Great Britton—that I migrated from the port of London in the said Kingdom of Great Britton on the 11th of May 1828 and landed on St. Johns Island first then some time in August 1829 I landed in the Town of White Hall in the state of [left blank] and in the United States of America, that I have ever since my first arrival remained within the limits and under the jurisdiction of the United States and that it bona fide my intention to renounce forever all allegiance and fidelity to every foreigner prince potentate state or sovereignty whatever and more particularly such allegiance and fidelity as I may in any wise owe to the King of Great Britton either as a citizen or subject of and to locate myself for the present in the county of Putnam and State of Illinois whereof I am now an inhabitant that I do not now enjoy or possess nor own nobility by virtue of the laws customs or regulations of the said Kingdom of Great Britton or any other country and that I am cincerely attached to the principals contained in the Constitution of the United States and well disposed to the good order well being and happiness of the same—and desire that this my declaration and report may be accepted and filed and recorded preparatory to my intended application to be admitted as a naturalized citizen of the United States in conformity with the required acts of Congress heretofore passed on that subjcct—Scpt 13th 1836.

James Smith
Sworn to and subscribed in open court
this 13th day of September 1836
Thomas Ford Judge

The above transcription of James Smith's declaration of intention presents a number of questions. The purpose of the transcription is to facilitate reading a document that does not reproduce particularly well. More importantly, it was chosen to demonstrate how vital it is to personally study original documents and not to depend entirely on the indexes or transcriptions of others. The spelling and punctuation have been left as they are in the original document; however, the author assumes responsibilities for any deciphering inaccuracies. A particular problem arose in trying to decipher the name of the township in Suffolk in which James Smith claims to have been born. The first letter of the town is where the question arises. My first guess at the name of the town was Cramfield. Consulting *A Topographical Dictionary of England* by Samuel Lewis (London, 1831; reprint; 4 vols. in 2; Baltimore: Genealogical Publishing Co., 1996), I found no reference to a Cramfield in Suffolk County. Looking at the township name again, I thought that it might be Bramfield, and that the writer of Smith's document had not capitalized the first letter. According to Lewis:

> Bramfield, a parish in the hundred of Blything, county of Suffolk, 2-miles (S.S.E.) From Halwsworth, containing 630 inhabitants. The living is a discharged vicarage in the archdeaconry of Suffolk, and diocese of Norwich.

Others looking at the township name suggested the possibility of its being "Framford." According to Lewis,

> Framfield, a parish in the hundred of Loxfield-Dorset, rape of Pevensey, county of Sussex, 1-miles (S.E.) From Uckfield, containing 1437 inhabitants.

The next step in this research project would be to investigate the availability of records for Bramfield and Framfield and to connect James Smith to one of these towns.

TIPS ON ACCESSING COURT RECORDS

Making sure that naturalization records are where you expect them to be may save you hours as well as money. Because so many records have been shifted around within and outside the courts (and continue to be moved), a telephone call, letter, e-mail, or check of the World Wide Web site of a court or an archives before a visit is wise. Some courts, especially in busy metropolitan areas, store records off-site. Because they can only be viewed and copied at the court, they must be ordered up from the warehouse in advance of your visit. Find out what the photocopy policy is at the court or archives you intend to visit. Because so many keepers of naturalization records now have Web sites and electronic capability, some ideas in chapter 7, "Naturalization Records and the Internet," may save you considerable time and effort whether you own a computer or not.

THE FAMILY HISTORY LIBRARY AND ITS FAMILY HISTORY CENTERS

Millions of naturalization records from counties all over the United States have been microfilmed by the Genealogical Society of Utah and are available at the Family History Library in Salt Lake City. Copies of the microfilm may be borrowed through the library's family history centers. It may be more convenient to access naturalization indexes and files through the Family History Library if the records have been microfilmed. Chapter 2 includes a lengthy discussion of the Family History Library and its holdings.

NOTES

1. William F. Hoffman, *Polish Surnames: Origins and Meanings* (Chicago: Polish Genealogical Society of America, 1992), 6.

2. Marian Smith, "Interpreting U.S. Immigration Manifest Annotations," *Avotaynu* 12 (1): 11 (Spring 1996).

3. *Kane County, Illinois Naturalization Index 1906–1955*, compiled and published by the Kane County Genealogical Society (Geneva, Ill., 1991), introduction.

4. Alice Eichholz, ed., *Ancestry's Red Book: American State, County and Town Sources*, rev. ed. (Salt Lake City: Ancestry, 1992), 344.

5. Ibid., 533.

Chapter Four Highlights

Published Naturalization Records and Indexes

PUBLISHED NATURALIZATION RECORDS

Few of the millions of naturalization processes that have been recorded in the United States have been published in printed form. The nature and volume of these records makes them impractical to print in their entirety. However, a significant number of printed indexes to naturalizations have been published; they are discussed later in the chapter.

RECORDS PUBLISHED IN MICROFORM

A bright spot for researchers is the fact that a significant number of naturalization records and indexes have been published in microform (microfilm or microfiche). The vast majority of microfilming has been done by the Genealogical Society of Utah for the Family History Library, by the National Archives, and by individual state archives and historical agencies. Other chapters in this book describe the holdings of the Family History Library and the National Archives and their access policies. Chapter 7, "Naturalization Records via the Internet," discusses some of the newest and most expeditious ways to learn more about state records. Names and addresses of state archives and historical agencies are listed in appendix B.

THE FAMILY HISTORY LIBRARY

Very often, the easiest place to begin a general search for a microfilmed naturalization record or index is at the Family History Library in Salt Lake City or at one of its family history centers near your home. A few major public libraries and genealogical societies also have the Family History Library Catalog, which is indexed by country, then by state, then by county. To use it, start searching in the county where the immigrant is known to have lived. Once you have found the county in the catalog, you will find topics (such as "Naturalization Records") arranged alphabetically. Within the category of naturalizations, you may find that the Genealogical Society of Utah has microfilmed all or part of a collection for the county of interest. Even if the actual naturalization papers or volumes have not been microfilmed, there may be a microfilm copy of an index to the records.

In many counties, the records of only some of the courts therein have been microfilmed; it may be misleading to look at a catalog that only partially reflects the records that are actually available. Sometimes permission is granted to microfilm only the records of certain courts or portions of court collections. Records created after 1920, for example, are often unavailable on microfilm. It's easy to look at a catalog, find a list of naturalizations for one or more courts, and then make the mistake of assuming that there are no other naturalization records available.

Microfilming is an ongoing project in many counties, so what is not available on microfilm one year may be the next. If you find that the records for the time and place you are interested in have been microfilmed, it is easier to view the microfilm copies at the Family History Library or one of its family history centers (if available from them) than to try to get the records from the originating court; this is especially true in large city courts, where indexes are sometimes off-limits to researchers, and when the records have been brought to the court from an off-site storage location. Also, it is often easier to

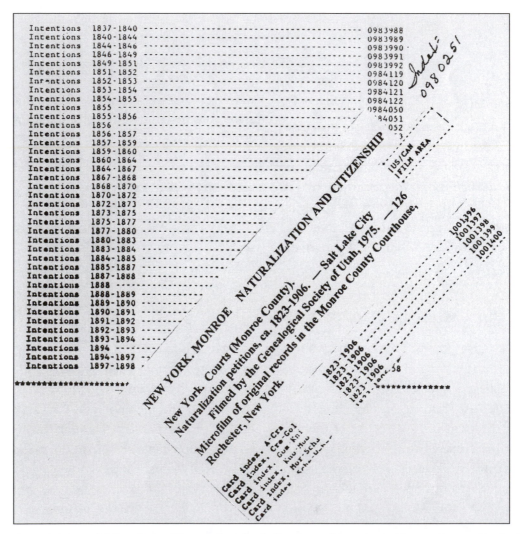

Figure 4-1. A partial list of microfilm numbers for declarations of intention in Monroe County, New York. They were microfilmed by the Genealogical Society of Utah and are available through the Family History Library and its family history centers.

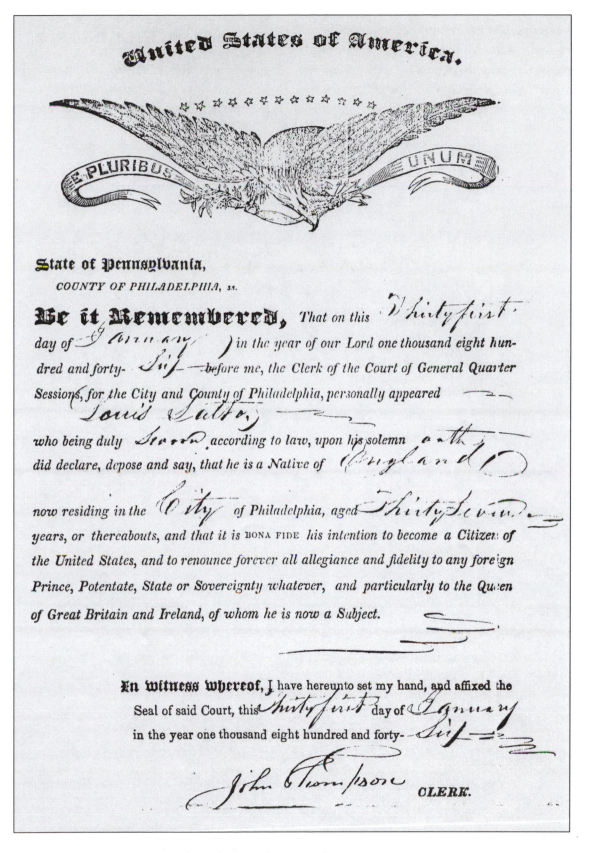

Figure 4-2. Declaration of intention for Louis Sutton or Sattor.

make photocopies of the records and indexes from the microfilm in a library than it is in a courthouse. Perhaps most importantly, being able to take time to study an index yourself can make the difference to your success.

THE PROBLEM WITH INDEXES

It makes no difference who may have created an index: every index is subject to error—particularly those that were created from handwritten records.

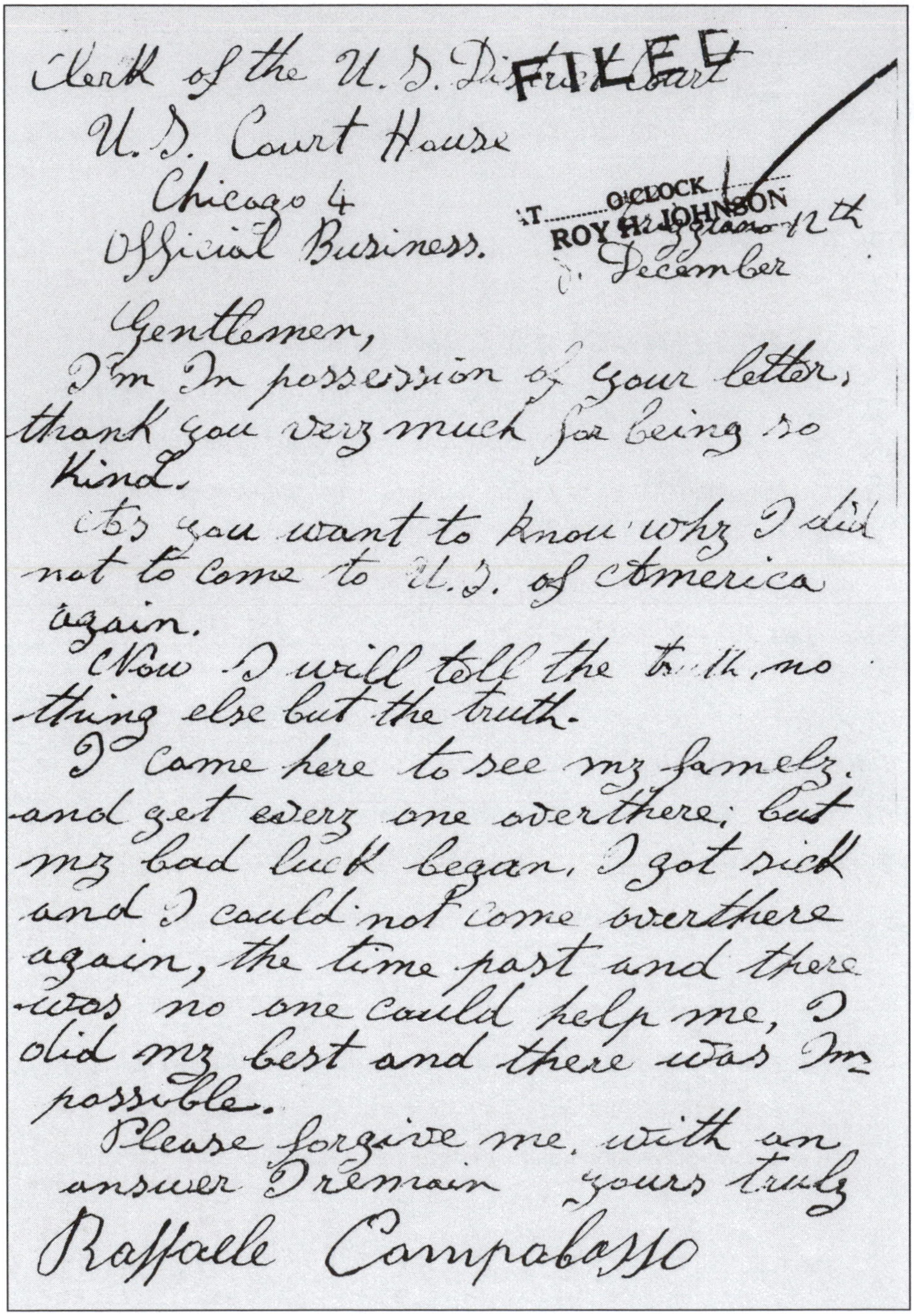

Figure 4-3. Letter from Raffaele Compobasso to the clerk of the U.S. District Court, U.S. Courthouse, Chicago.

For example, original records are sometimes overlooked during the indexing process. In other words, a person may actually have been naturalized, but if the clerk indexing documents skips a document for one reason or another, it obviously will not show up in the index. Some indexes to naturalization, such as those created by the WPA, were made on file cards. For decades these card files were searched by clerks and researchers. Along the way, some cards were lost, and others were mis-filed.

Archivist John Newman observed the following about the WPA works: "One must use these records with caution for the following reasons. First, not all records were searched." In Indiana, Newman says, "research employees, while usually hired locally and perhaps familiar with local names, had no training in deciphering spellings of names as they appeared in nineteenth-century court records. This was a special problem in interpreting names beginning with such letters as H, M, T, and W." Newman also points out that "no one in the Division of Community Service Programs showed any comprehensive understanding of the court system in Indiana. Thus records such as probate Complete Order books were searched, having no naturalization data, and other records, especially those created in the pre-1850 period and stored in attics or basements, were overlooked." Another, equally important, note that Newman makes is common to other states: "courts in the nineteenth century typically developed their own routine for procedures. Some counties, like Franklin, had virtually complete naturalization ledger books dating from the 1820s while most Indiana counties did not begin compiling these until the 1850s. Any court of record could naturalize, and the judge had to issue an order to that effect. While these court proceedings should be in order books, there is no guarantee that the information is available in that source."[1]

An example of a name that could easily have been misinterpreted is illustrated in figure 4-2. Is the name of the declarant Louis Sutton or Louis Sattor?

The indexer's guess may have been as bad as mine.

As Newman suggests, there are several places in court records where naturalization information may appear, and many of them may not be indexed as "naturalization records." While it may be impossible to find every case file that might contain evidence of an alien's attempts to become naturalized, some fascinating immigrant stories are hidden in court files. Consider the poignant letter of Raffaele Campobasso, reproduced in figure 4-3. Directed to the clerk of the U.S. District Court, U.S. Courthouse, Chicago, the letter is part of a U.S. Circuit Court file at the National Archives' Great Lakes Region (55C1731). The letter tells a story that will be overlooked if a search is confined to naturalization indexes:

Gentlemen,

I'm In possession of your letter, thank you very much for being so kind.

Its you want to know why I did not come to U.S. of America again.

Now I will tell the truth, no thing else but the truth.

I came here to see my famely and get every one over there; but my bad luck began, I got sick and I could not come over there again, the time past and there was no one could help me, I did my best and there was Impossible.

Please forgive me, with an answer I remain yours truly

Raffaele Campobasso

Even good indexes have their limitations. Some of the papers included in a file may not be included in an index, and index formats are traditionally rigid; selected identifying information is included in them, and nothing more. An example is a note found in a Cook County, Illinois, court file. Information provided in the note adds a personal dimension that is missing in a standard naturalization file or index. The note (figure 4-4), filed with the naturalization as proof of birth, was translated for the court as follows:

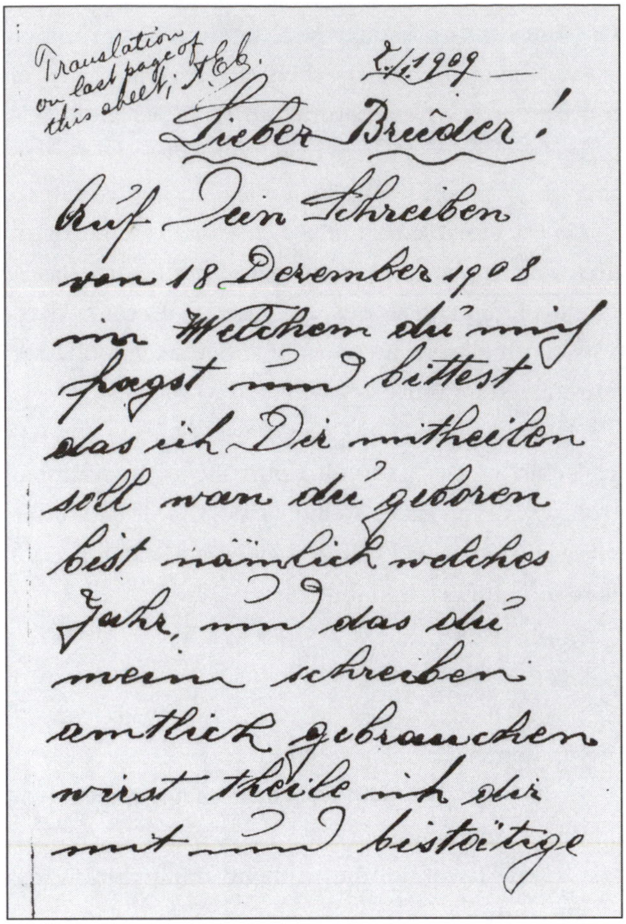

Translation on last page of this sheet;

7/1 1909

Lieber Brüder!

Auf Dein Schreiben
von 18 December 1908
in Welchem du mich
fragst und bittest
das ich Dir mittheilen
soll wan du geboren
bist nämlich welches
Jahr, und das du
mein schreiben
amtlich gebrauchen
wirst theile ich dir
mit und bistätige

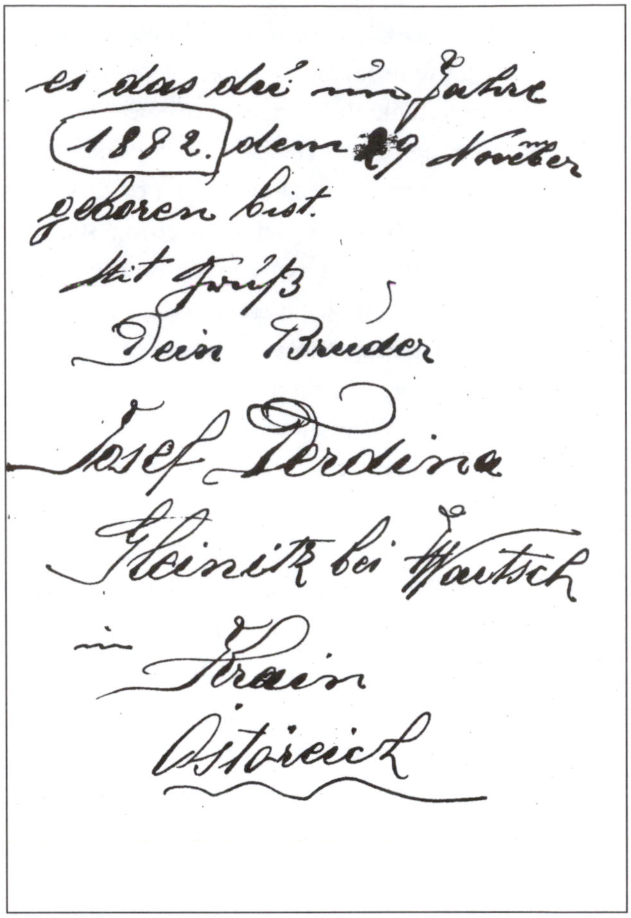

es das du im Jahre
1882. den 29 November
geboren bist.
Mit Gruß
Dein Bruder
Josef Terdina
Gleinitz bei Wartsch
in Krain
Östreich

Figure 4-4. 1908 letter from Joseph Terdina attesting to his brother Frank's birth date. This letter, folded into Frank Terdina's naturalization file, does not appear in the naturalization index.

Dear brother! To your letter of Dec. 18, 1908 in which you ask me and beg this I inform you when you were born, namely, what year, and that you desire to use this information legally, I have to inform you and testify there to that you were born in the year 1882, on the 29th of November. With greetings;

Your brother, Joseph Terdina

Gleinitz in Wartsch, Krain, Austria.

Many naturalization records are bound into volumes that are either self-indexed (each volume having its own index) or have no index at all. Order books were usually self-indexed (if at all); an example is shown in figure 4-6. Note the name changes shown in this index. A great many name changes will be found in naturalization documents. Sometimes, names and aliases are cross-referenced, and sometimes the new name is indexed and the aliases (often old names) are left out.

Genealogical Societies

Genealogical societies in the area where an immigrant lived are also prime candidates to have preserved and indexed naturalization records. In many cases, genealogists have literally saved these historical records from the garbage heap. Nine volumes of original Calumet City, Illinois, naturalization records were saved by the South Suburban Genealogical Society. The records, dating from around 1906 to 1952, were indexed by Joan Alguire, a member of the society.

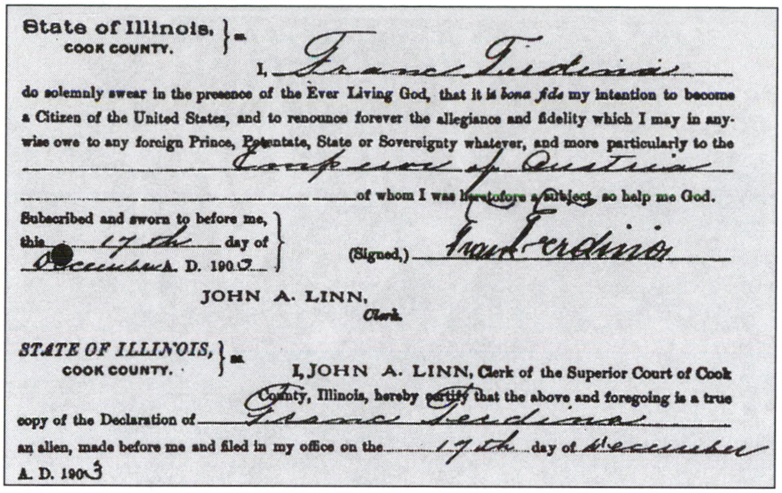

State of Illinois, } ss.
COOK COUNTY.

I, Franc Terdina

do solemnly swear in the presence of the Ever Living God, that it is *bona fide* my intention to become a Citizen of the United States, and to renounce forever the allegiance and fidelity which I may in anywise owe to any foreign Prince, Potentate, State or Sovereignty whatever, and more particularly to the Emperor of Austria of whom I was heretofore a subject, so help me God.

Subscribed and sworn to before me, this 17th day of December A. D. 1903

(Signed,) Franc Terdina

JOHN A. LINN,
Clerk.

STATE OF ILLINOIS, } ss.
COOK COUNTY.

I, JOHN A. LINN, Clerk of the Superior Court of Cook County, Illinois, hereby certify that the above and foregoing is a true copy of the Declaration of Franc Terdina an alien, made before me and filed in my office on the 17th day of December A. D. 1903

Figure 4-5. Declaration of intention of Franc Terdina, Cook County, Illinois, 1900.

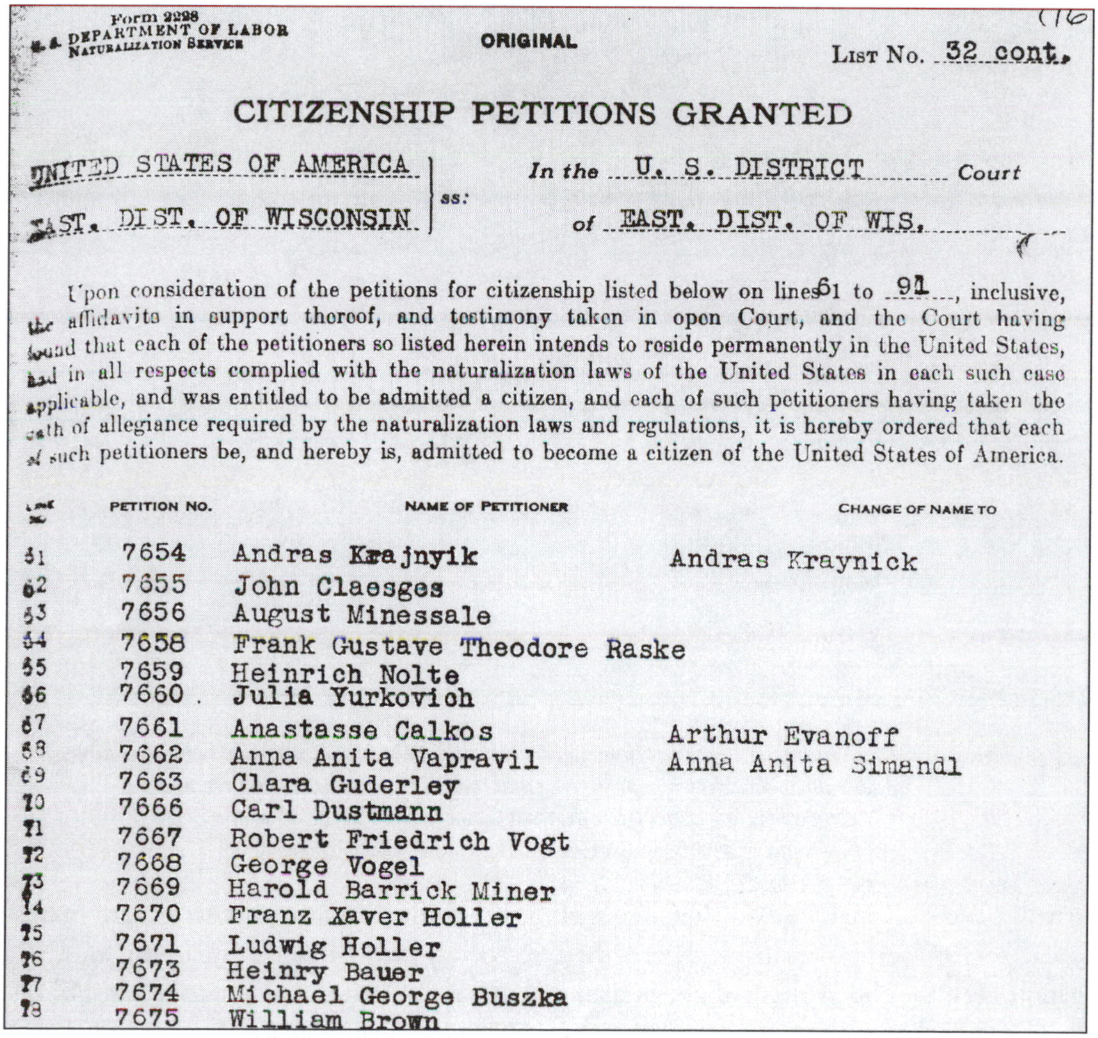

Form 2228
U. S. DEPARTMENT OF LABOR
NATURALIZATION SERVICE

ORIGINAL

LIST No. 32 cont.

CITIZENSHIP PETITIONS GRANTED

UNITED STATES OF AMERICA } ss: In the U. S. DISTRICT Court
EAST. DIST. OF WISCONSIN } of EAST. DIST. OF WIS.

Upon consideration of the petitions for citizenship listed below on lines 61 to 91, inclusive, the affidavits in support thereof, and testimony taken in open Court, and the Court having found that each of the petitioners so listed herein intends to reside permanently in the United States, and in all respects complied with the naturalization laws of the United States in each such case applicable, and was entitled to be admitted a citizen, and each of such petitioners having taken the oath of allegiance required by the naturalization laws and regulations, it is hereby ordered that each of such petitioners be, and hereby is, admitted to become a citizen of the United States of America.

Line No.	Petition No.	Name of Petitioner	Change of Name to
61	7654	Andras Krajnyik	Andras Kraynick
62	7655	John Claesges	
63	7656	August Minessale	
64	7658	Frank Gustave Theodore Raske	
65	7659	Heinrich Nolte	
66	7660	Julia Yurkovich	
67	7661	Anastasse Calkos	Arthur Evanoff
68	7662	Anna Anita Vapravil	Anna Anita Simandl
69	7663	Clara Guderley	
70	7666	Carl Dustmann	
71	7667	Robert Friedrich Vogt	
72	7668	George Vogel	
73	7669	Harold Barrick Miner	
74	7670	Franz Xaver Holler	
75	7671	Ludwig Holler	
76	7673	Heinry Bauer	
77	7674	Michael George Buszka	
78	7675	William Brown	

Figure 4-6. Citizenship petitions granted in the U. S. District Court of Wisconsin (from the National Archives–Great Lakes Region).

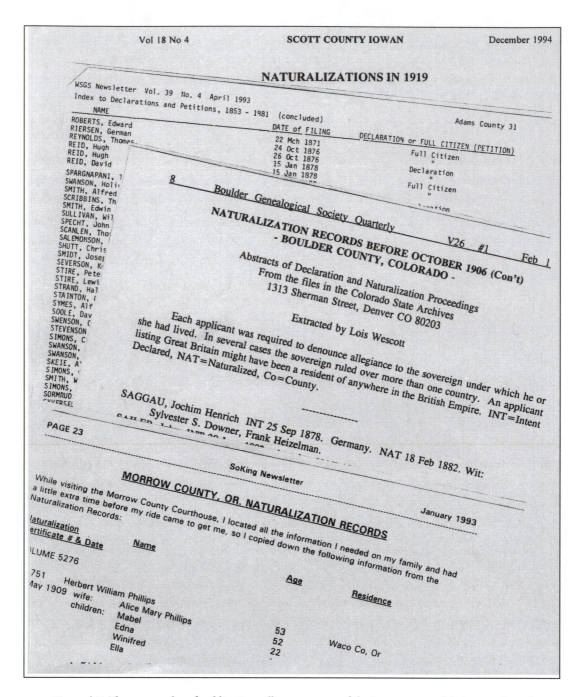

Figure 4-7. These examples of publications illustrate some of the important work being conducted
by genealogical societies in preserving and publishing naturalization records.
Shown here are pages from the Scott County Iowan, WSGS Newsletter,
Boulder Genealogical Society Quarterly, and SoKing Newsletter.

In virtually every corner of the United States, genealogical society volunteers have been saving naturalization records and making them available for public use. In county after county, societies have sponsored projects to index these materials. Some-times the final lists or abstracts are published in the society's newsletter or quarterly journal, and some-times the material is published in book form to be sold by the groups to augment other projects.

Shown in figure 4-7 is an example of the work

accomplished by just a few genealogical societies in their publications. In the December 1994 issue of the *Scott County Iowan* was transcribed a 1919 article from the *Davenport Democrat and Leader*. The newspaper had announced that sixty-five aliens were ready to take out their final papers, and noted that "all but 12 of those named are Germans and Austrians who were barred during the war from taking out the final papers." Those being sworn in on 19 January 1919 were listed with their addresses. Not only does the Scott County Genealogical Society do us a favor by listing the applicants, but, by including the "whole story," they remind us that the United States' involvement in wars affected the immigration and naturalization process and that many applications, such as these, were held up until the war had ended.

The Wisconsin State Genealogical Society has regularly published naturalization records in its *Newsletter*; many other genealogical organizations publish them in their quarterly journals. The example shown in figure 4-7 is an "Index to Declarations and Petitions, 1853–1881" for Adams County, Wisconsin. The Boulder Genealogical Society ran a series of abstracts of Boulder County, Colorado, declarations of intention and petition records over a period of time in its quarterly publication (figure 4-7).

Thoughtful genealogical society members regularly save bits of information, not just for their own families but often for strangers as well. The following note was published in the January 1993 *SoKing Newsletter* (South King County Genealogical Society, Kent, Washington) (figure 4-7). "While visiting the Morrow County Courthouse, I located all the information I needed on my family and had a little extra time before my ride came to get me, so I copied down the following information from the Naturalization Records." The article doesn't tell us how long the transcriber had to wait for a ride home, but it was long enough to copy quite a few names that were subsequently published. The quarterly publications of an organization are usually indexed and saved, but many newsletters are considered ephemeral: they are read and then discarded. The fact is significant because researchers often search quarterly publication indexes for the names they need, but seldom consider the historical information that might be preserved only in newsletters. Unfortunately, not all genealogical societies archive copies of their newsletters.

In figure 4-8 are pages showing extractions from naturalization records of Ventura County, California, extracted by Delores Pederson and published in *Rabbit Tracks*, the quarterly of the Conejo Valley Genealogical Society. The naturalization extracts were published with a good explanatory statement, noting that the material was taken from "Book 2," and "appears to consist of copies of certificates pasted onto pages, since the certificate number does not always match the page number." Another caveat given is that the book is divided into categories of records: "Alien pages 1–63, Minor pages 306–345, Soldier pages 397–398." The author additionally notes that "Names of witnesses are included [in the work] since they were normally friends and relatives or long-time acquaintances of the applicant. The spelling of the names are as they appear on the certificates unless additional information appears in the signature. Denied petitions are listed at the end. They are included to give names of applicant, if given, and witnesses." Indexers, abstracters, and extractors of naturalization and other records would do well to heed this example by providing adequate explanatory materials with the lists they publish.

Ethnic genealogical societies have also published good naturalization indexes of individuals, especially those living in ethnic enclaves. For example, the Polish Genealogical Society of Texas in the fall of 1993 published "Naturalization Records for Poles of Grimes County, Texas," *PGST News* 10 (3): 34–40.

PERIODICAL SOURCE INDEX

PERSI, the *Periodical Source Index*, is the best source for finding some of the hard-to-find publica-

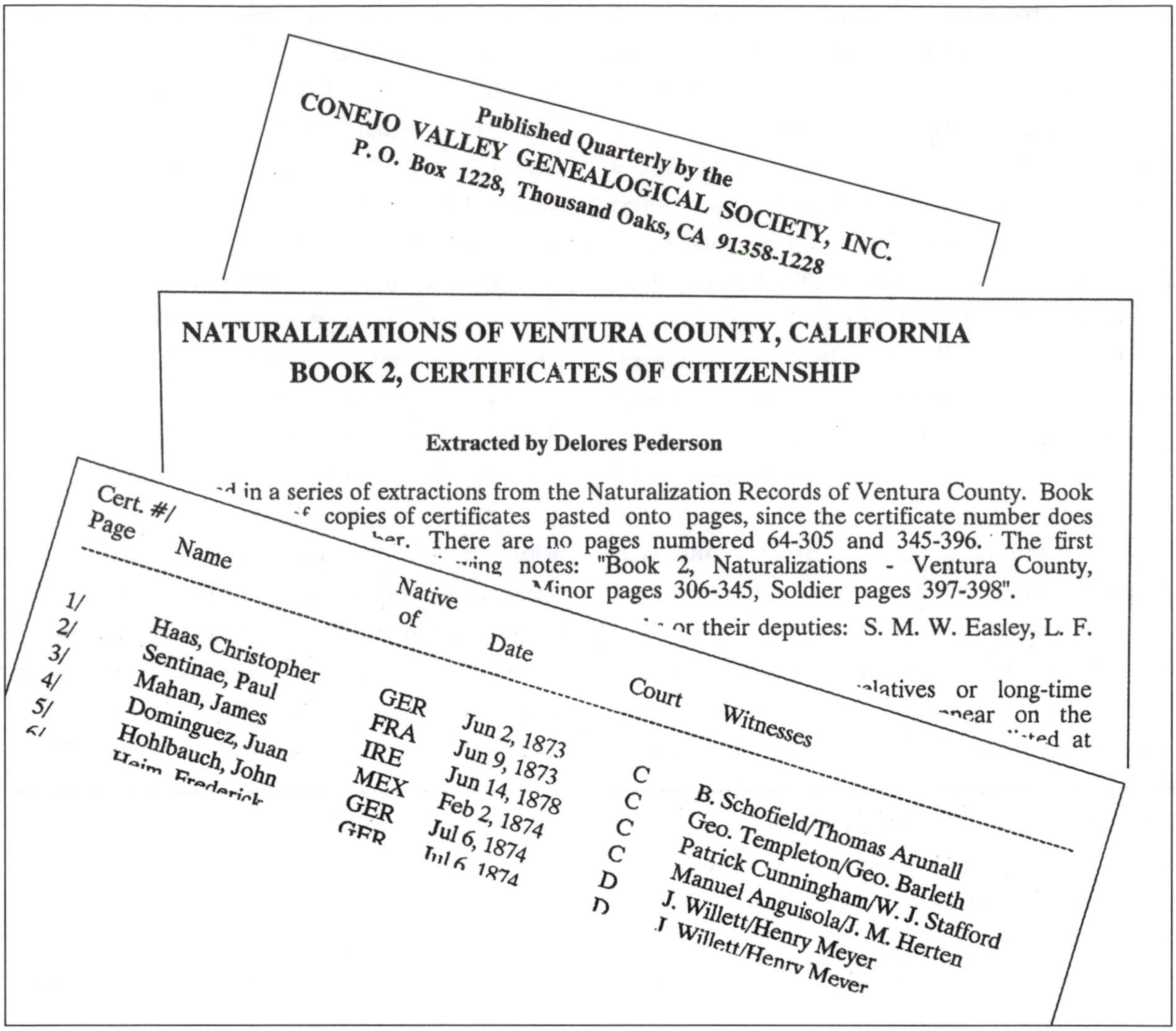

Published Quarterly by the
CONEJO VALLEY GENEALOGICAL SOCIETY, INC.
P. O. Box 1228, Thousand Oaks, CA 91358-1228

NATURALIZATIONS OF VENTURA COUNTY, CALIFORNIA
BOOK 2, CERTIFICATES OF CITIZENSHIP

Extracted by Delores Pederson

...d in a series of extractions from the Naturalization Records of Ventura County. Book ... copies of certificates pasted onto pages, since the certificate number does ...ber. There are no pages numbered 64-305 and 345-396. The first ...wing notes: "Book 2, Naturalizations - Ventura County, ...Minor pages 306-345, Soldier pages 397-398".

... or their deputies: S. M. W. Easley, L. F.

...elatives or long-time ...pear on the ...ted at

Cert. #/ Page	Name	Native of	Date	Court	Witnesses
1/	Haas, Christopher	GER	Jun 2, 1873	C	B. Schofield/Thomas Arunall
2/	Sentinae, Paul	FRA	Jun 9, 1873	C	Geo. Templeton/Geo. Barleth
3/	Mahan, James	IRE	Jun 14, 1878	C	Patrick Cunningham/W. J. Stafford
4/	Dominguez, Juan	MEX	Feb 2, 1874	C	Manuel Anguisola/J. M. Herten
5/	Hohlbauch, John	GER	Jul 6, 1874	D	J. Willett/Henry Meyer
6/	Heim, Frederick	GER	Jul 6, 1874	D	J. Willett/Henry Meyer

Figure 4-8. Extracts from naturalization records of Ventura County, California, published in the quarterly of the Conejo Valley Genealogical Society.

tions produced by genealogical societies. A number of historical and patriotic organizations have also published articles on the subject, and these have been indexed in *PERSI* as well.

Produced by the Allen County Public Library in Fort Wayne, Indiana, *PERSI* is a comprehensive subject index to genealogy and local history periodicals written in English or French-Canadian since 1800. It is a work in progress that includes more than 1 million citations to almost four thousand titles. *PERSI* lists articles according to locality, family (surname), and/or research methodology. It does not index every name in every article, nor does it include the full text of actual articles. This wonderful tool leads not only to naturalization records that have been published but to many ethnic and other records mentioned in this text. In addition to being available in book form in major libraries, *PERSI* is available on CD-ROM and on the Internet (http://www.ancestry.com) from Ancestry.

NATURALIZATION INDEXES IN BOOK FORM

There are relatively few indexes to naturalizations in book form, and only a handful are discussed here. These are described because they are among the most recognizable and are available in most libraries that have genealogical collections.

The largest and best-known work on the subject is *Philadelphia Naturalization Records: An Index to Records of Aliens' Declarations of Intention and/or Oaths of Allegiance, 1789–1880, in United States Circuit Court, United States District Court, Supreme Court of Pennsylvania, Quarter Sessions Court, Court of Common Pleas, Philadelphia*, edited by P. William Filby (Detroit: Gale Research, 1982). It is an index to the names of more than 113,000 aliens from nearly one hundred countries who applied for U.S. citizenship through the Philadelphia court system from 1789 to 1880. The index is based on an eleven-volume index compiled around 1940 by the WPA under the sponsorship of the Pennsylvania Historical Commission.

Newman's *An Index to Indiana Naturalization Records Found in Various Order Books of the Ninety-two Local Courts Prior to 1907* (Indiana Historical Society, 1981) begins with the caveat that "this index does not include names from the naturalization record books and related documents usually found in the clerk's office in each county "(page 1). In his introduction, Newman describes the WPA project: "From October, 1941, to April 1942, Indiana participated in a nationwide project, sponsored by the United States Department of Justice, to locate and photocopy naturalization records predating September 29, 1906" (page i). The purpose was to locate and inventory each naturalization proceeding (intention, petition, and/or order of the court) found in separate naturalization ledgers and in the various order books of the courts in Indiana that were authorized to naturalize citizens. Upon completion of the inventory, each record was to be microfilmed

or photocopied, and copies were to be collected in Washington, D.C. Newman states that "the war effort superseded completion of the project." The index "serves as an index to court records located in the proper courthouse. The records are not in the State Archives" (page 1).

Early New York Naturalization: Abstracts of Naturalization Records from Federal, State, and Local Courts, 1792–1840, compiled by Kenneth Scott (Baltimore: Genealogical Publishing Co., 1981), identifies ten thousand persons with name, age, place of residence and birth, and approximate date of arrival in America. With Kenn Stryker-Rodda, Kenneth Scott published *Denizations, Naturalization, and Oaths of Allegiance in Colonial New York* (Baltimore: Genealogical Publishing Co., 1975). It identifies several thousand denizations, licenses, and oaths of allegiance dating back as far as the seventeenth century.

Two other important works that cover early American history are *Names of Foreigners Who Took the Oath of Allegiance to the Province and State of Pennsylvania, 1727–1775*, edited by William H. Egle (Harrisburg, Pa.: E. K. Meyers, 1890; reprint; Baltimore: Genealogical Publishing Co., 1967), and Jeffrey and Florence L. Wyand's *Colonial Maryland Naturalization* (Baltimore: Genealogical Publishing Co., 1975; reprint; 1986), which documents almost two thousand naturalizations between 1660 and 1775.

COURT INDEXES

Court clerks compiled naturalization indexes—as they did all other court files—alphabetically by surname. Unfortunately for researchers, the vast majority of naturalization records that were indexed in old ledger books do not list surnames in strict alphabetical order; rather, they group names by the first letter of the surname. A certain number of lined pages in the oversized ledgers were reserved for each letter of the alphabet. As clerks found time, they penned in

| 1855-1903 | Se | Index to Cleveland U.S. District Court Naturalizations |

Szezabacki Martin	9800	Spero, Simon	10564		
Svec Vojtech	9822	Setak, John	10565		
Schreur, Jacob	9886	Seifert, Adolph	10568		
Steiner, Charles	9890	Scheuermann, Josef	10636		
Seifried Joseph	9960	Stefanski, Andrew	10717		
Seman Julius	9965	Schweitzer, George R.	10792		
Stein August	9966	Scherenbeck, Henry	10793		
Schneider Louis	9974	Schneider, Frederick	10866		
Steffen Frank	9975	Streik, Emil	10867		
Seiger, John	10035	Sebunek, Anton	10954		
Smeli, Josef	10088	Schneider, August	10955		
Steinke Louis	10089	Scherlofski, John	10956		
Seaman, Otto	10090	Steinert, Karl	11007		
Hettmish, Ludwig	10091	Schneidt, Edward	11008		
Seaman, August	10092	Steinbach Philipp	11068		
Scheldt, Julius	10171	Scheerline, John	11104		
Stendel, F.H. Charles	10191	Stedrowsky, James	11105		
Svek, Albert	10249	Schweitzer, George	11193		
Svetc, Charles	10250	Shea, Patrick	11214		
Stepanek, Vaclav	10251	Sweeney, John	11215		
Svec, John	10252	Stern, Bernard	11250		
Steinert, August	10303	Smetak, Joseph	11275		
Schmealatzki, Martin	10304	Svec Joseph	11296		
Sheehan John	10375	Spero Joseph	11297		
Semple, Robert	10376	Syba Josef	11350		
Shellew William	10377	Soderstrom John	11386		
Stejskal, Anton	10378	Sklounda Vaclav	11411		
Segenyer Henry	10407	Schneider Fred	11420		
Setzer, Henry	10561	Stener Louis	11455		
Steinz, Robert John	10562	Szemplewicz Andrew	11511		
Son, Samuel	10563	Smythe Alexander L	11482		

Figure 4-9. A handwritten page from a naturalization index ledger for the U.S. District Court, Northern District of Ohio, Cleveland, in which the names are grouped by the first letter of the surname—not completely alphabetized.

the names of applicants or new citizens. Each name entry was then assigned a file number for future reference. Declarations of intention and petitions were often arranged numerically and bound into volumes. Sometimes the declarations and petitions were bound together.

Indexes that are stored apart from the documents to which they refer can severely complicate a naturalization search. For example, the naturalization documents listed in some indexes in the National Archives system have been retained by the creating courts. Occasionally, the reverse is true: the court has kept indexes but retired the large old files and ledgers to an archive or historical agency for safekeeping. The splintered collection of naturalization records and indexes from the Detroit courts described in the introduction is just one example of a common problem.

Handwritten indexes can be time consuming to read through. Different handwriting styles can fool even a trained eye, and most record custodians these days simply do not have the time to study handwritten pages. Archivists and clerks are generally overworked, and some are less than delighted to have to lift heavy volumes off hard-to-reach shelves to find someone's great-grandfather's citizenship papers. For these and other reasons, it is always best to search indexes personally if at all possible.

With any index, there can be, and frequently are, omissions. Whenever possible, check several sources. For example, a researcher searched the Soundex index (explained later in this chapter) for the Northern District of Illinois for his grandfather's naturalization. Since several other sources indicated that the man had been naturalized in a Chicago court, the researcher felt he should continue his search there. When he checked an index of Chicago voters for the time period in question, he found that his grandfather had indeed been naturalized. The voter registration index also told him the name of the Chicago court in which his ancestor had been naturalized, and it gave him a date to work with.

With that precise information, he was able to go directly to Cook County court records and retrieve the document that had been filed by date of issue.

Custodians of naturalization records and researchers alike are often frustrated, believing that, somewhere among rows upon rows of boxes or ledgers of documents, a much-wanted citizenship paper resides with no way for them to know exactly where it is. In most archives, files are arranged numerically. No one is likely to take the time to search through millions of papers to find a specific document or file without the help of a good index. In cases where a declaration of intention and a petition are filed together, it is the petition number that is needed to retrieve the box or ledger.

NATURALIZATION INDEXES/ DATABASES ON THE INTERNET

One of the most exciting aspects about accessing naturalization records is that more and more naturalization indexes are becoming accessible on home computers via the Internet. For the present, there aren't too many, but some that are currently available are discussed in chapter 7, "Naturalizations and the Internet." Indexes, however, represent only the first steps. They help to locate records, but information taken from indexes can never take the place of the record itself. Hopefully, this chapter has shed some light on the many reasons why that is so.

THE SOUNDEX INDEX SYSTEM

During the 1930s and 1940s, most states participated in a nationwide project, sponsored by the U.S. Department of Justice and carried out by the WPA, to locate and photograph naturalization records predating 27 September 1906. Although all photostatic copies were to be deposited with the Immigration and Naturalization Service, few of the states or districts had been completed when the WPA was disbanded in 1942.

Figure 4-10. Index references or petition numbers are needed to retrieve naturalization files.

An index and filing system called the Soundex is the key to finding the names of individuals among the millions listed in the 1880, 1900, 1910, and 1920 federal censuses, as well as the WPA-created naturalization indexes. The Soundex indexes are coded surname (last name) indexes based on the progression of consonants rather than the spelling of the surname. This coding system was developed and implemented by the WPA in the 1930s for the Social Security Administration in response to that agency's need to identify individuals who would be eligible to apply for old-age benefits. Because early birth records are unavailable in a number of states, the 1880 federal census manuscripts became the most dependable means of verifying dates of birth for people who would qualify: those born in the 1870s. Widespread misspelling caused so many problems in matching names, however, that the Soundex system was adopted. Because locating eligible Social Security beneficiaries was the sole reason for creating the 1880 Soundex, only households with children ten years of age or under were included in that index. All households were included in the Soundex indexes for the 1900, 1910, and 1920 censuses. The Soundex system would work well, it was thought, in the naturalization indexes, because many foreign names were especially vulnerable to misspelling. Though like-sounding names are included in the Soundex, as the cards in figure 4-11 show, the names Wagenheim, Waxman, Wichman, Wagman, and Weisman don't sound much alike but are all coded as W-255. In another example, the names Cerny, Cheruen, Charon, Crummy, and Corn don't sound alike but are all coded as C650.

The New England states, New York City, and Chicago are blessed with comprehensive Soundex indexes which cover local and federal naturalizations. Besides Chicago, the Northern Illinois District index extends to courts in portions of Indiana, Iowa, and Wisconsin.

How the Soundex Works

Soundex index entries are arranged on cards, first in Soundex code order and then alphabetically by the first name of the person being naturalized. For each person, the Soundex card should show the family name, the country of birth or allegiance, the title and location of the court, the date of naturalization, the certificate or volume and page number, and the names of witnesses (usually two). Other spaces on the card ask for the address of the person being naturalized, age or when born, date and port of arrival in the United States, and addresses of the witnesses. Generally, if the information requested is on the actual naturalization documents, it will be reflected in the Soundex card. If the original papers do not provide biographical detail, the lines were left blank on the Soundex card. It is important to look at the reverse side of each card because additional information is sometimes added there. For several years the New York records were further indexed by national group (Germans, Italians, etc.). When the Soundex fails to supply a reference, as it occasionally does, ancillary records, such as order books (which show all naturalizations approved on a given day) and reg-

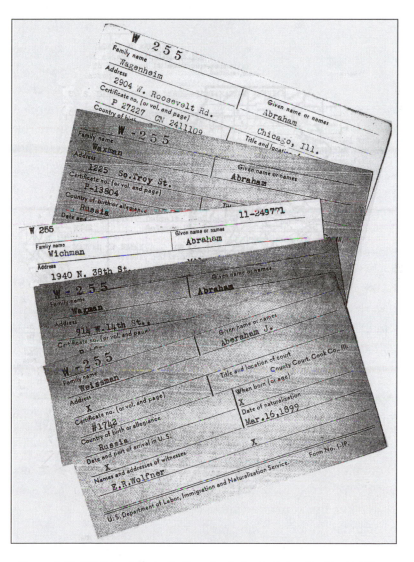

Figure 4-11. W255 cards from the Soundex Index to Naturalization Petitions for the United States District and Circuit Courts, Northern District of Illinois, and Naturalization District 9, 1840–1950.

★   ★   145   ★   ★

isters (which list petitioners by first letter of surname) may also exist.

CODING A SURNAME

To search for a name it is necessary to first determine its Soundex code. Every Soundex code consists of a letter and three numbers—for example, S655. The letter is always the first letter of the surname. The numbers are assigned according to the Soundex coding guide below.

Code key letters and equivalents:

1	B, P, F, V
2	C, S, K, G, J, Q, X, Z
3	D, T
4	L
5	M, N
6	R

The letters A, E, I, O, U, W, Y, and H are disregarded. Consonants in each surname which sound alike have the same code.

USE OF ZERO IN CODING SURNAMES

A surname that yields no code numbers, such as Lee, is L000; one yielding only one code number, such as Kuhne, takes two zeros and is coded as K500; and one yielding two code numbers takes just one zero; thus, Ebell is coded as E140. No more than three digits are ever used, so Ebelson would be coded as E142, not E1425.

NAMES WITH PREFIXES

Because the Soundex does not treat prefixes consistently, surnames beginning with, for example, Van, Vander, Von, De, Di, or Le may be listed with or without the prefix, making it necessary to search both. Search for the surname vanDevanter, for example, with and without the "van-" prefix. Mc- and Mac- are not considered prefixes.

NAMES WITH ADJACENT LETTERS HAVING THE SAME EQUIVALENT NUMBER

When two key letters or equivalents appear together or one key letter immediately follows or precedes an equivalent, the two are coded as one letter with a single number. (Surnames may have different letters that are adjacent and have the same number equivalent.) Pfeiffer, for example, is coded P160. Because the P and the F are both coded as 1, only one (P) is used. The letters E and I separate the coded Pf from the second and third appearance of the letter F, so one of these is coded. The double Fs again require that only one be considered in the code. The letter R is represented by 6, and in the absence of additional consonants, the code is rounded off with a zero. Other examples of double-letter names are Lennon (L550), Kelly (K400), Buerick (B620), Lloyd (L300), Schaefer (S160), Szucs (S200), and Orricks (O620). Occasionally the indexers themselves made mistakes in coding names, so it may be useful to look for a name in another code.

DIFFERENT NAMES WITHIN A SINGLE CODE

With this indexing formula, many different surnames may be included within the same Soundex code. For example, the similar-sounding surnames Scherman, Schurman, Sherman, Shireman, and Shurman are indexed together as S655 and will appear in the same group with other surnames, such as Sauerman or Sermon. Names that do not sound alike may also be included within a single code: Sinclair, Singler, Snegolski, Snuckel, Sanislo, San Miguel, Sungaila, and Szmegalski are all coded as S524.

ALPHABETICAL ARRANGEMENT OF FIRST OR GIVEN NAMES WITHIN THE CODE

As described above, multiple surnames appear within most Soundex codes. Within each Soundex code, the individual and family cards are arranged alphabetically by given name. Marked divider cards separate most Soundex codes.

MIXED CODES

Divider cards show most code numbers, but not all. For instance, one divider may be numbered 350 and the next one 400. Between the two divided cards there may be names coded 353, 350, 360, 365, and 355, but instead of being in numerical order they are interfiled alphabetically by given name.

SOUNDEX REFERENCE GUIDE

For those who are unsure of their Soundex skills, most genealogical libraries have a copy of Bradley W. Steuart's *The Soundex Reference Guide: Soundex Codes to Over 125,000 Surnames* (Bountiful, Utah: Precision Indexing, 1990).

There are several enormous naturalization indexes that should be consulted initially if the alien of interest lived in one of the areas covered by these compilations. One of the largest is *Index to Naturalization Petitions of the United States District Court for the Eastern District of New York 1865–1957*, described in a pamphlet of the same title (National Archives Trust Fund Board, 1991). The records which have been microfilmed consist of approximately 650,000 three- by five-inch cards that index bound and unbound naturalization petitions. The cards are arranged in three groups covering the periods July 1865 to September 1906, October 1906 to November 1925, and November 1925 to December 1957. The cards within each group are arranged alphabetically by the name of the person naturalized.

Index cards for the first group include the name of the naturalized individual, the date of naturalization, and the volume and record number of the naturalization petition. These cards may also contain such information as the address, occupation, birth date or age, former nationality, and port and date of arrival of the person naturalized, and the name of the witness to the naturalization.

The cards for the second and third groups show the name and the petition and certificate number of the person naturalized and generally include the address, age, and date of admission to citizenship. The petitions to which these microfilmed index cards relate are in the National Archives' Northeast Region (Pittsfield). They have not yet been microfilmed.

Petitions for the period from July 1865 to September 1906 are arranged in bound volumes. The information on each petition varies. Petitions dated 1 July 1865 to 5 July 1895 indicate the city of residence, former nationality of petitioner, name of witness, dates of petition, and admission to citizenship. Petitions dated from 5 July 1895 through 26 September 1906 may also contain information on the petitioner's occupation, date and place of birth, and port and date of arrival in the United States; the name, address, and occupation of the witness; and the signature of the alien.

Petitions filed after September 1906 are unbound and are arranged numerically by petition number. They usually indicate the occupation, place of embarkation, and date and port of arrival of the petitioner; name of the vessel or other means of conveyance into the United States; the court in which the alien's declaration of intention was filed and filing date; marital status; name and place of residence of each of the applicant's children; date of the beginning of the alien's continuous U.S. residence; length of residence in the United States; names, occupations, and addresses of witnesses; and signatures of alien and witnesses.

A caveat in the descriptive pamphlet states:

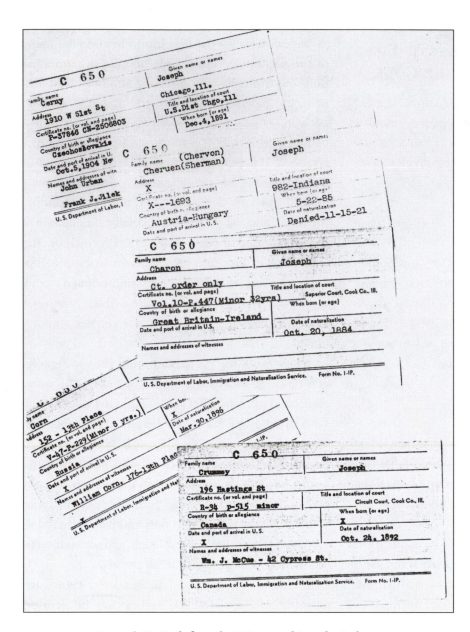

Figure 4-12. Cards from the WPA-created Soundex Index to Naturalization Petitions for the United States District and Circuit Courts, Northern District of Illinois and Immigration and Naturalization District 9, 1840–1950.

district to seek naturalization through the city or county courts in the counties in this district. This index, therefore, does not contain the names of all individuals naturalized in the counties of Kings, Queens, Richmond, Suffolk, and Nassau. The clerks of these county courts will, as a rule, have custody of the naturalization records of aliens who became citizens in their courts.

SOUNDEX INDEX AT THE NATIONAL ARCHIVES' GREAT LAKES REGION

The National Archives' Great Lakes Region in Chicago has in its custody the Soundex index to more than 1.5 million naturalization petitions from northern Illinois, northwestern Indiana, southern and eastern Wisconsin, and eastern Iowa. The microfilmed records are described in a pamphlet titled *Soundex Index to Naturalization Petitions for the United States District and Circuit Courts, Northern District of Illinois, and Immigration and Naturalization Service District 9, 1840–1950* (National Archives Trust Fund Board, 1991). The index consists of 162 cubic feet of three- by five-inch cards arranged in Russell-Soundex order and thereafter alphabetically by given name. The index includes civil and military petitions.

While the Soundex index includes references to naturalizations that took place in Illinois, Indiana, Wisconsin, and Iowa, a great portion of the records

The index reproduced on this microfilm publication refers only to those aliens who sought naturalization in the U.S. District Court for the Eastern District of New York, located in Kings County, New York. An alien, however, could become a naturalized citizen through any court of record, making it possible for those living in any of the five counties that make up the eastern

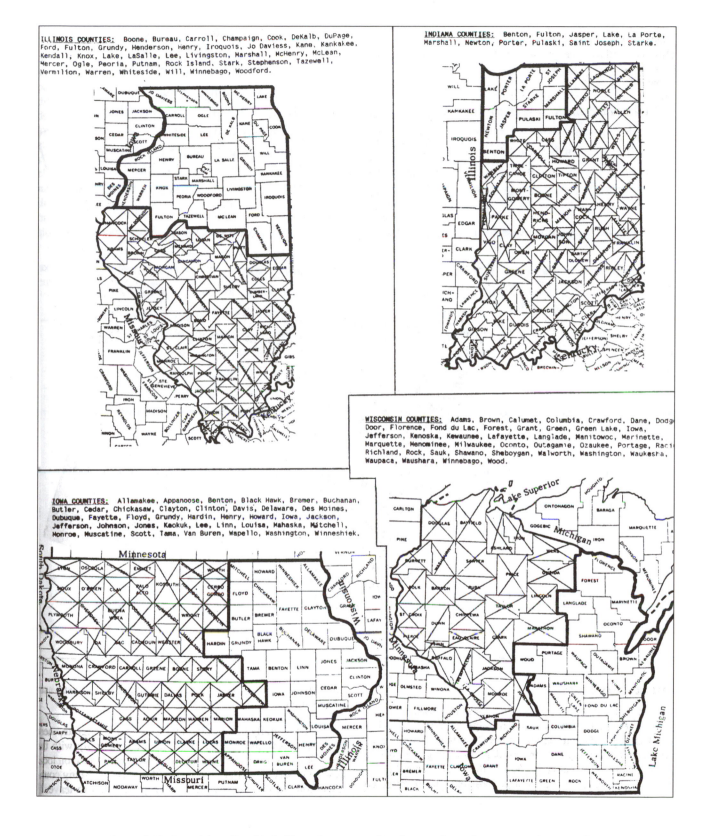

Figure 4-13. Counties outlined in bold are those covered in the Soundex index to naturalizations for parts of Illinois, Indiana, Iowa, and Wisconsin that together include more than a million and a half names.

cited in the index are not physically located at the National Archives. Naturalization records in the custody of the Great Lakes Region, with one exception, consist of records for persons naturalized in certain federal (not county or state) courts. Copies (not originals) of county naturalization records for 1871 through 1906 for Chicago/Cook County, Illinois, comprise the one exception. Examples from the Soundex index described above (figure 4-12) illustrate the standard format used for the cards and the kind of information about the individual that may or may not be included. Besides the name of the naturalized citizen, it is especially important to note the name of the court in which the naturalization took place and the petition number (when it is included on the card) when following through with a search for the actual naturalization documents. Normally, all biographical information recorded in the original document was copied to the Soundex card. If the spaces on the card for date of birth, birthplace, date and place of arrival in the United States, etc., are blank, it is likely that the original naturalization documents did not include that information.

While there is no comprehensive index to other naturalizations in its custody, the Great Lakes Region also has naturalization documents for other federal courts in Illinois, Indiana, Michigan, Minnesota, Ohio, and Wisconsin for certain years.

The National Archives' Northeast Region (Boston) has original copies of naturalization records of the federal courts for the six New England states. Individuals were also naturalized in state, county, and local courts. The branch has copies (dexographs—white-on-black photographs) of such court records between 1790 and 1906 for Maine, Massachusetts, Rhode Island, Vermont, and New Hampshire. For Connecticut there are originals of some state, county, and local naturalizations for the years 1790 to 1974. An index to naturalization documents filed in courts in Connecticut, Maine, Massachusetts, New Hampshire, and Rhode Island is also at the Northeast Region (Boston). The index contains some cards for New York and Vermont as well, but the records to which they refer are not among the photocopies at that regional archive. The New England WPA index consists of three- by five-inch cards arranged by name of petitioner and by the Soundex system. The index refers to the name and location of the court that granted citizenship and to the volume and page number of the naturalization record.

NOTE

1. Newman, John. *An Index to Indiana Naturalization Records Found in Various Order Books of the Ninety-two Local Courts Prior to 1907*. Indiana Historical Society, 1981, 4.

BIBLIOGRAPHY

Kane County Genealogical Society. *Kane County, Illinois Naturalization Index 1906–1955*. Geneva, Illinois: Kane County Genealogical Society, 1991.

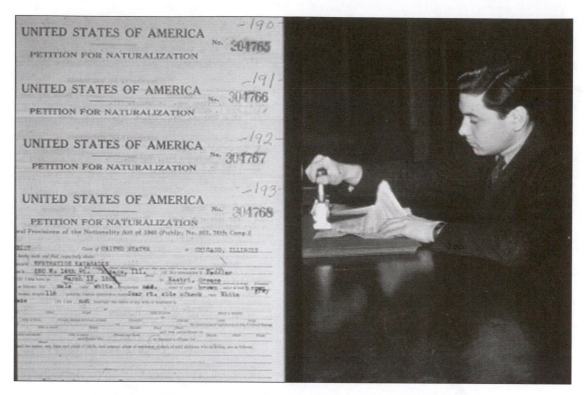

The forms used for naturalization documents have varied from one year to another and from one court to another. After September 1906, the INS standardized the naturalization forms to be distributed to court clerks.

Chapter Five Highlights

- *History of the INS*
- *Basic Naturalization Act of 1906*
- *Passenger lists and the INS*
- *Certificates of arrival*
- *Women's loss of citizenship and repatriation*
- *Visa files, 1924–1944*
- *Registry files, 1929–1944*

- *Alien registration records*
- *Table of Documents Issued by the INS since 1906 with abbreviations*
- *The Immigration Act of 1990*
- *Requests for records under the Freedom of Information Act (FOIA)*
- *Requests for records under the Privacy Act (PA)*
- *INS records in the National Archives*

Immigration and Naturalization Service
Department of Justice
425 I Street, N.W.
Washington, DC 20536
202-514-4316

You can also visit the INS home page on the World Wide Web at http://www.ins.usdoj.gov/

- The INS keeps duplicate copies of naturalization papers for those naturalized after 1906.

- Among other records, the INS also has visa files, registry files, alien registration files, and records relating to repatriation of American-born women.

Immigration and Naturalization Service

THE IMMIGRATION AND NATURALIZATION SERVICE (INS) has custody of more than 8 million citizenship-related records. As noted earlier, according to law, the Bureau of Immigration and Naturalization was to keep duplicate copies of declarations of intention and petitions for naturalization for every individual naturalized after 27 September 1906. When naturalization records can't be found elsewhere, INS files may be the only reliable source for obtaining copies of post-1906 naturalization files. Beyond the important duplicate naturalization files, the INS also maintains visa files, registry files, alien registration files, records relating to the repatriation of American-born women, and other records that are important to family historians, biographers, social historians, and other researchers.

HISTORY OF THE IMMIGRATION AND NATURALIZATION SERVICE

The first immigration office in the federal government was created in 1864; however, the federal government did not actually oversee immigration and naturalization until much later. Under the 1864 law, which was designed to encourage immigration, the president appointed a Commissioner of Immigration within the State Department to regulate the transportation and settlement of immigrants. The act provided that immigrants would not be compelled to enter military service during the Civil War unless they voluntarily renounced, under oath, their allegiance to their homelands and declared their intention to become citizens of the United States. "The said Commissioner established regulations whereby immigrants pledged the wages of their labor after their admission to this country, for a period not to exceed twelve months; such pledge was to repay the expenses of their emigration."[1]

The first immigrant office created no records of use to genealogists, for it did not record or regulate immigration. The 1864 law had no effect on the commissions, boards, or other officers responsible for immigration in each of the states. The commissioner's office was abolished when the law was repealed four years later.

In the meantime, a number of the states had begun to pass laws restricting immigration; notably New York, Massachusetts, California, and Louisiana; but their laws differed from each other. Each state had its own peculiar notion as to who should be excluded; and the problem soon became too big for the individual states to handle.[2]

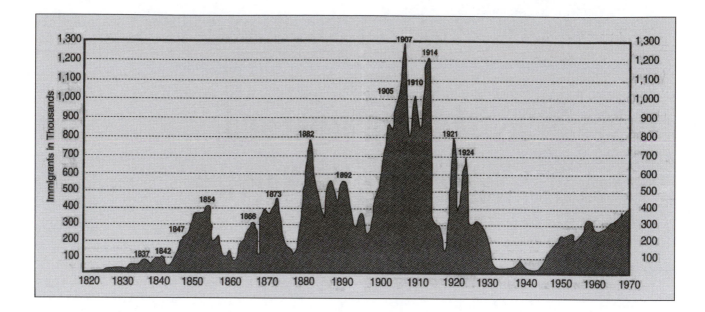

Figure 5-1. Immigration to the United States from 1820 to 1970.

Just as immigrant arrivals in the United States were reaching peak levels in the 1880s, new laws were being passed to control contract labor and to prevent the admission of undesirable aliens.

The first real control over immigration began in 1882; an act was passed requiring every immigrant who entered the United States to pay fifty cents (part of the collected funds were to be used to care for immigrants upon their arrival) and stipulating that all alien convicts were to be sent back to the ports from which they came. Passage expense was to be borne by the owner of the ship on which the convict had arrived in the United States.

Between 1882 and 1891, the secretary of the treasury had general supervision over immigration. In 1888, Congress established a committee to investigate immigration authority. The committee recommended consolidating this authority within a single federal agency. Congress enacted legislation drafted by the committee, calling it the Immigration Act of 1891. Signed by President Benjamin Harrison on 3 March 1891, the law established complete and definite federal control over immigration by providing

for an office: the superintendent of immigration under the Department of the Treasury. To implement the 1882 act, the Treasury Department contracted with state agencies to carry out the law.

As a result of this new law, all duties previously deferred to the states were transferred to the U.S. inspection officers by the end of fiscal year (June 30) 1891; the Bureau of Immigration began operations as part of the Treasury Department on 12 July 1891 as the first federal immigration agency. Besides its headquarters in Washington, D.C., the bureau began opening inspection stations (including Ellis Island, which opened in January 1892) at ports of entry along both borders and in major seaports. In 1893, the Marine Hospital Service began conducting medical inspections of arriving immigrants. From this early structure, the immigration side of the present Immigration and Naturalization Service evolved. In 1900, administration of the Chinese exclusion laws was added, and in 1903 the bureau became part of the Department of Commerce and Labor. It was designated a bureau in 1895, with responsibility for administering the alien contract labor laws.

THE BASIC NATURALIZATION ACT OF 1906

The naturalization side of the INS did not come into being until Congress created the Bureau of Immigration and Naturalization by passing the Naturalization Act of 29 June 1906 (32 Stat 596). The new agency became responsible for overseeing and supervising the courts in the naturalization of aliens and for keeping a duplicate of each court's final naturalization records. Prior to that date, naturalization was exclusively a function of the courts.

The intention of the Basic Naturalization Act was to provide a uniform rule for the naturalization of aliens throughout the United States. The law, effective 27 September 1906, was designed to provide "dignity, uniformity, and regularity" to the naturalization procedure. It established procedural safeguards and called for specific and uniform information regarding applicants and recipients of citizenship status. Rule Nine of the code required that all blank forms and records be obtained from and controlled by the Bureau of Immigration, "those alone being official forms. No other forms shall be used." The law also required that duplicate copies of declarations of intention and petitions for naturalization be sent to Washington, D.C.

The combined functions of immigration and naturalization lasted only seven years, however, and the Bureau of Naturalization became a separate bureau

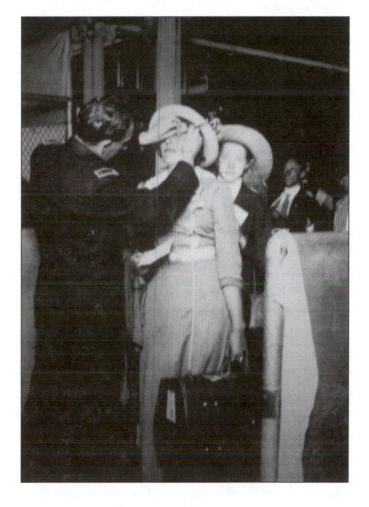

Figure 5-2. A physician at Ellis Island uses an instrument similar to a buttonhook to look for signs of trachoma, a blinding disease that for many years was the leading cause of deportation.

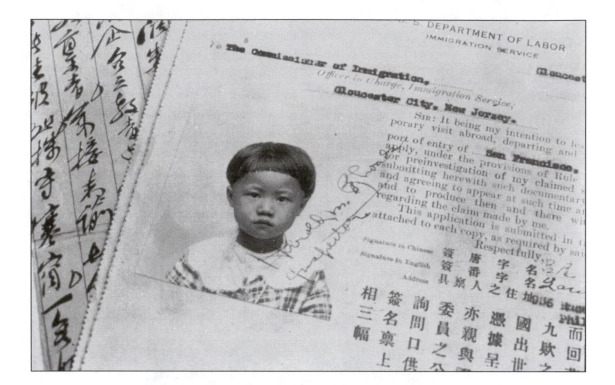

Figure 5-3. Certificate of residence from the Chinese Exclusion Files. In accordance with the Chinese exclusion laws (1882–1943), which were passed to restrict Chinese immigration to the United States, the Immigration and Naturalization Service barred Chinese from entering the United States between 1882 and 1924; the laws were designed especially to exclude laborers. Chinese residents of the United States who wished to visit China had to make formal application to the INS and establish their identity and occupation (students and merchants were exceptions to excluded occupations) to ensure they would be able to reenter the United States.

in 1913 when the Department of Commerce and Labor was split into two departments. Both functions moved to the new Department of Labor. The commissioner general continued to head the immigration agency, and the new Bureau of Naturalization was headed by a Commissioner of Naturalization. The bureaus remained separate until 1933, when they were consolidated by executive order to form the Immigration and Naturalization Service, still within the Labor Department. In a reorganization meant to provide more effective control over aliens at a time of increasing international tensions, the Immigration and Naturalization Service was separated from the Labor Department and placed under the jurisdiction of the Department of Justice in June 1940.

PASSENGER LISTS AND THE INS

An important aspect of immigration research is finding a specific individual on a passenger list. Most people are especially fascinated with the idea of how and when their immigrant ancestors first set foot on American soil. While research in passenger arrival records is discussed in chapter 2, "How to Find Immigration and Naturalization Records," it bears mention in this chapter. The INS played a role; notations containing valuable historical information were often added to passenger lists by immigration clerks as aliens began the naturalization process.

The first significant federal legislation relating to immigration was passed in 1819, when Congress approved an act regulating passenger ships and

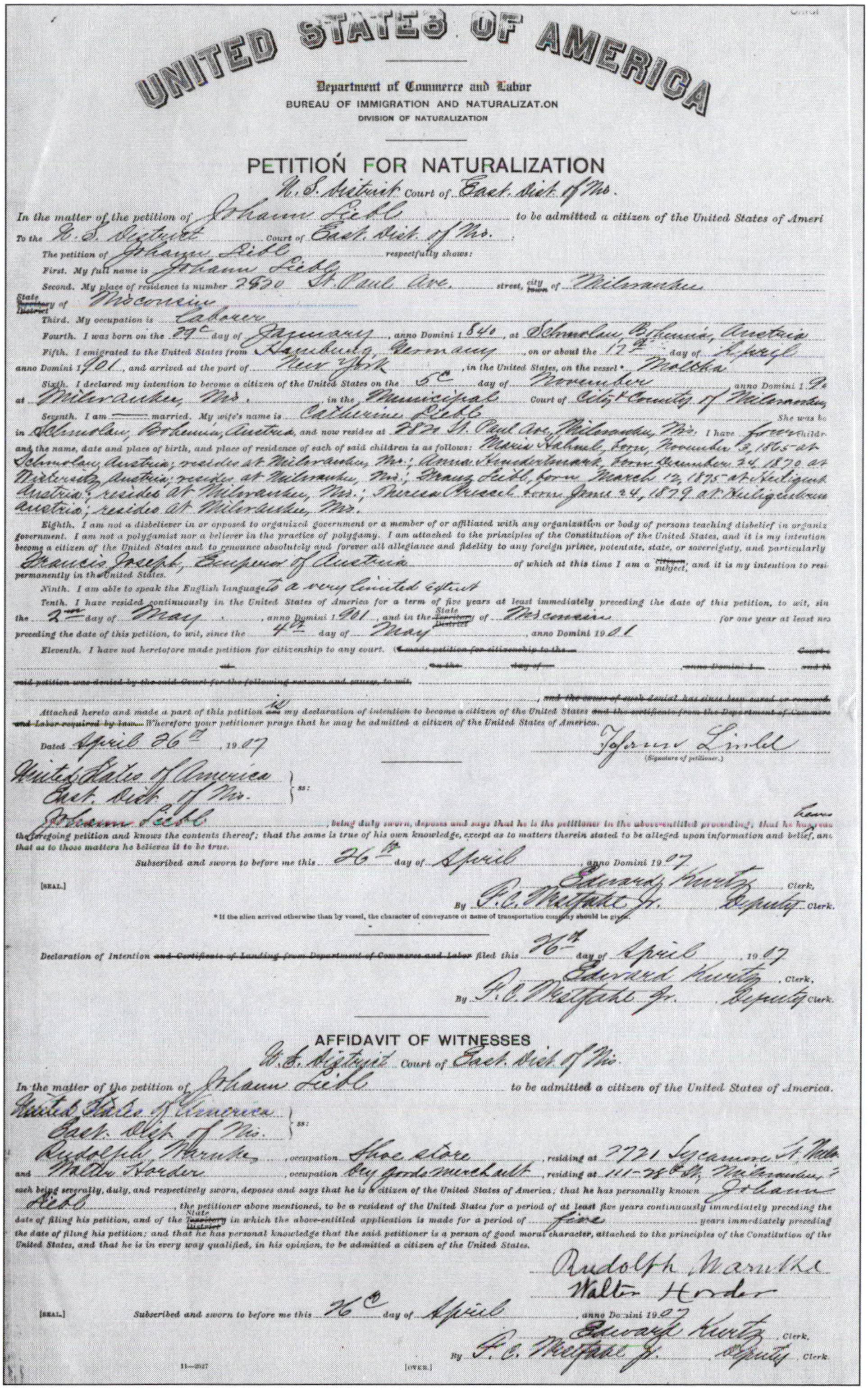

Figure 5-4. Petition for naturalization of Johann Liebl. On forms issued by the Bureau of Immigration and Naturalization under the Department of Commerce and Labor, this 1907 naturalization document was recorded in the U.S. District Court of the Eastern District of Michigan. The document reflects the 1906 move to a standardized form; a duplicate of this form was presumably sent to Washington, D.C.

TRIPLICATE   No. 83155

UNITED STATES OF AMERICA

DECLARATION OF INTENTION
(Invalid for all purposes seven years after the date hereof)

UNITED STATES OF AMERICA } ss: | In the _____ DISTRICT _____ Court

NORTHERN DISTRICT OF ILLINOIS | of THE UNITED STATES at CHICAGO, ILL.

I, _____ MOLLIE MEYEROWITZ _____
(Full true name, without abbreviation, and any other name which has been used, must appear here)
now residing at _____ 1667 North Richmond St. _____
(Number and street) (City or town) (County) (State)
occupation Saleslady _____, aged __29__ years, do declare on oath that my personal description is:
Sex Female _____, color White _____, complexion Dark _____, color of eyes Brown _____
color of hair Black _____, height 5 feet 2 inches; weight 125 pounds; visible distinctive marks
_____ None. _____
race Hebrew _____; nationality Russian _____
I was born in Kelem, Russia _____, on Dec. 25th, 1901 _____
(City or town) (Country) (Month) (Day) (Year)
I am not married. The name of my wife or husband is _____
we were married on _____, at _____; she or he was
(Month) (Day) (Year) (City or town) (State or country)
born at _____, on _____, entered the United States
(City or town) (State or country) (Month) (Day) (Year)
at _____, on _____, for permanent residence therein, and now
(City or town) (State) (Month) (Day) (Year)
resides at _____ I have __no__ children, and the name, date and place of birth,
(City or town) (State or country)
and place of residence of each of said children are as follows: _____
_____
_____
_____

I have not heretofore made a declaration of intention: Number _____, on _____
(Date)
at _____
(City or town) (State) (Name of court)
my last foreign residence was _____ Kelem, Russia _____
(City or town) (Country)
I emigrated to the United States of America from _____ Antwerp, Belgium _____
(City or town) (Country)
my lawful entry for permanent residence in the United States was at _____ New York, New York _____
(City or town) (State)
under the name of _____ Meierowicz, Bassie Malke _____, on _____ Nov. 13th, 1912 _____
(Month) (Day) (Year)
on the vessel _____ SS. Vaderland _____
(If other than by vessel, state manner of arrival)
I will, before being admitted to citizenship, renounce forever all allegiance and
fidelity to any foreign prince, potentate, state, or sovereignty, and particularly,
by name, to the prince, potentate, state, or sovereignty of which I may be at
the time of admission a citizen or subject; I am not an anarchist; I am not a
polygamist nor a believer in the practice of polygamy; and it is my intention in
good faith to become a citizen of the United States of America and to reside
permanently therein; and I certify that the photograph affixed to the duplicate
and triplicate hereof is a likeness of me: So HELP ME GOD.

_____ Mollie Meyerowitz _____
(Original signature of declarant without abbreviation, also alias, if used)
Subscribed and sworn to before me in the office of the Clerk of said Court,
at Chicago, Illinois _____ this 12th day of March _____
anno Domini 19_31_ Certification No. 11-34476 from the Commissioner of Naturalization showing the lawful entry of the declarant for permanent
residence on the date stated above, has been received by me. The photograph
affixed to the duplicate and triplicate hereof is a likeness of the declarant.

_____ CHARLES M. BATES _____
Clerk of the U. S. DISTRICT Court.
By _____ Marjorie Glass _____, Deputy Clerk.
14—2623 U. S. GOVERNMENT PRINTING OFFICE 1929

[SEAL]

Mollie Meyerowitz

Form 2202-L-A.
U. S. DEPARTMENT OF LABOR
NATURALIZATION SERVICE

Figure 5-5. Declaration of intention of Mollie Meierowicz.

ORIGINAL
(To be retained by clerk)

UNITED STATES OF AMERICA

No. 241

PETITION FOR CITIZENSHIP

No. 13874

To the Honorable the _____ DISTRICT _____ Court of _____ THE UNITED STATES _____ at _____ CHICAGO, ILL. _____

The petition of _____ MOLLIE MEYEROWITZ _____, hereby filed, respectfully shows:

(1) My place of residence is _____ 1536 N. Rockwell St., Chicago, Ill. _____ (2) My occupation is _____ Saleslady _____

(3) I was born in _____ Kelem, Russia _____ on _____ Dec. 25, 1901 _____ My race is _____ Hebrew _____

(4) I declared my intention to become a citizen of the United States on _____ Mar. 12, 1913 _____ in the _____ U.S.District

Court of _____ Northern Dist. of Ill. _____, at _____ Chicago, Ill.

(5) I am _____ not _____ married. The name of my wife or husband is _____; he was

we were married on _____ at _____; he was

born at _____ on _____; entered the United States

at _____ on _____ for permanent residence therein, and now

resides at _____ I have _____ no _____ children, and the name, date,

and place of birth, and place of residence of each of said children are as follows: _____

_____

_____

_____

(6) My last foreign residence was _____ Kelem, Russia _____ I emigrated to the United States of

America from _____ Antwerp, Belgium _____ My lawful entry for permanent residence in the United States

was at _____ New York, N. Y. _____, under the name of _____ Bassie Malke Mt Meierowicz _____

on _____ November 13, 1912 _____, on the vessel _____ Vaderland _____
as shown by the certificate of my arrival attached hereto.

(7) I am not a disbeliever in or opposed to organized government or a member of or affiliated with any organization or body of persons teaching disbelief in or opposed to organized government. I am not a polygamist nor a believer in the practice of polygamy. I am attached to the principles of the Constitution of the United States and well disposed to the good order and happiness of the United States. It is my intention to become a citizen of the United States and to renounce absolutely and forever all allegiance and fidelity to any foreign prince, potentate, state, or sovereignty, and particularly to _____

THE STATE OF RUSSIA

of whom (which) at this time I am a subject (or citizen), and it is my intention to reside permanently in the United States. (8) I am able to speak the English language. (9) I have resided continuously in the United States of America for the term of five years at least immediately preceding the date of this petition, to wit, since _____ November 13, 1912 _____ and in the County of _____ Cook _____

this State, continuously next preceding the date of this petition, since _____ August, 1917 _____, being a residence within said county of at least six months next preceding the date of this petition.

(10) I have _____ not _____ heretofore made petition for citizenship: Number _____, on

at _____ and such petition was denied by that Court for the following reasons and causes, to wit: _____

and the cause of such denial has since been cured or removed.

Attached hereto and made a part of this, my petition for citizenship, are my declaration of intention to become a citizen of the United States, certificate from the Department of Labor of my said arrival, and the affidavits of the two verifying witnesses required by law.

Wherefore, I, your petitioner, pray that I may be admitted a citizen of the United States of America, and that my name be changed to _____

I, your aforesaid petitioner being duly sworn, depose and say that I have { read heard read } this petition and know the contents thereof; that the same is true of my own knowledge except as to matters herein stated to be alleged upon information and belief, and that as to those matters I believe it to be true; and that this petition is signed by me with my full, true name.

Mollie Meckerowitz
(Complete and true signature of petitioner)

No. 68875

AFFIDAVITS OF WITNESSES

William Lipman _____, occupation _____ Leather & Shoe findings
residing at _____ 1541 N. Fairfield, Chicago, Illinois _____ business _____, and

Ernest J. Landon _____, occupation _____ Cash Register business
residing at _____ 1507 N. Washtenaw, Chicago, Illinois

each being severally, duly, and respectively sworn, deposes and says that he is a citizen of the United States of America; that he has personally known and has been acquainted in the United States with

MOLLIE MEYEROWITZ _____, the petitioner above mentioned, since _____ Jan. 1, 1928

and that to his personal knowledge the petitioner has resided in the United States continuously preceding the date of filing this petition, of which this affidavit is a part, to wit, since the date last mentioned, and at _____ Chicago, Illinois _____, in the County of _____ Cook

this State, in which the above-entitled petition is made, continuously since _____ Jan. 1, 1928 _____, and that he has personal knowledge that the petitioner is and during all such periods has been a person of good moral character, attached to the principles of the Constitution of the United States, and well disposed to the good order and happiness of the United States, and that in his opinion the petitioner is in every way qualified to be admitted a citizen of the United States.

William Lipman
(Signature of witness)

Ernest Landon
(Signature of witness)

Subscribed and sworn to before me by the above-named petitioner and witnesses in the office of the Clerk of said Court at _____ Chicago, Ill. _____ this _____ 29th _____ day of _____ October _____, Anno Domini 19 35. I hereby certify that certificate of arrival No. _____ 11-34476 _____ from the Department of Labor, showing the lawful entry for permanent residence of the petitioner above named, together with declaration of intention No. _____ 83155 _____ of such petitioner, has been by me filed with, attached to, and made a part of this petition on this date.

HENRY W. FREEMAN

jma

By _Marjorie Showerman_
Clerk.

Deputy Clerk.

(SEAL)

Form 2204—L-A
U. S. DEPARTMENT OF LABOR
IMMIGRATION AND NATURALIZATION SERVICE
14—2611

Figure 5-6. Petition for naturalization for Mollie Meierowicz.

vessels. The law provided that the captain or master of any ship or vessel that arrived in the United States or its territories had to report to the collector of the port of arrival and deliver the following information for each passenger he had taken on board at any foreign port: age, sex, occupation, country of origin, and where they intended to become inhabitants. Subsequent laws were enacted over the years limiting number of passengers to be carried, and regulating food provisions, ventilation of steerage, sanitation, etc.

After the 1906 establishment of the Bureau of Immigration and Naturalization, all immigration stations in the United States required each alien arriving in the United States to provide the following information for a registry: name, age, occupation, personal description (including height, complexion, color of hair and eyes), place of birth, last residence, intended place of residence in the United States, date of arrival, and port of arrival.

A significant number of passenger arrival lists have been microfilmed and are available for research. John P. Colletta, Ph.D., clearly describes passenger lists and how to use them in *They Came in Ships: A Guide to Finding Your Immigrant Ancestor's Arrival Record*, 2nd ed., rev. and enl. (Salt Lake City: Ancestry, 1993). Marian L. Smith, historian for the INS, provides the fascinating story of "The Creation and Destruction of Ellis Island Immigration Manifests" in two parts in *Prologue: Quarterly of the National Archives* 28 (3): 240–45 (Fall 1996) and 28 (4): 314–18 (Winter 1996). A quick reference list of seventy-nine American ports of entry together with date spans that are available on microfilm is included in appendix C.

As Marian L. Smith suggests in "Interpreting U.S. Immigration Manifest Annotations" in *Avotaynu: The International Review of Jewish Genealogy* 12 (1): 10–13 (Spring 1996), "Immigration manifests have been essential to the work of the U.S. Immigration and Naturalization Service since 1892." Smith suggests that by learning and understanding more about early twentieth-century U.S. immigration laws and procedures, researchers can learn to interpret immigration manifest notations. Using a lit-

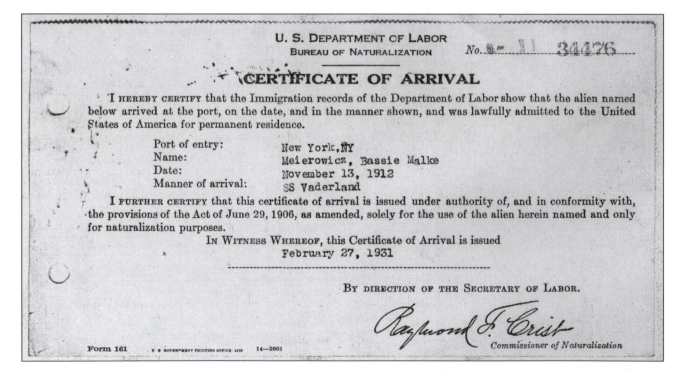

Figure 5-7. Certificate of arrival for Bassie Malke Meierowicz.

tle logic, one can surmise that if the INS retrieved an old passenger list and made notes next to an individual's record, there must have been renewed interest in that individual's case. Smith says that

> most after-arrival annotations stem from three categories of activity. One is reentry, an INS term for the readmission of aliens previously admitted for permanent residence; another is certification of arrival, a step in the naturalization process designed to prevent fraud. Last is a routine activity called verification of arrival that was and is generally the first step in handling immigrant cases that range from provision of benefits to the prosecution of legal violations. Once one learns more about each of these procedures, it is possible to recognize and interpret most after-arrival annotations.[3]

CERTIFICATES OF ARRIVAL

Probably the most common reentry annotations are related to an immigrant's first step toward naturalization. Verifying that all petitioners for naturalization were legally admitted immigrants was one of the reforms instituted by the Basic Naturalization Act of 1906. Smith further notes that

> under the 1906 statute, the naturalization procedure required a step whereby the Bureau of Immigration and Naturalization checked ship manifests to verify the legal admission of every applicant for citizenship who had Declarations of Intention or Petitions to a naturalization court. On these forms, the immigrant named the port, date, and ship of his or her arrival. Copies of the form were forwarded to the appropriate ports of entry to be checked by verification clerks who located the immigrants' arrival record among their immigration manifests. If the record was found, INS issued a Certificate of Arrival and sent it back to the naturalization court.[4]

Between 1906 and 1924, the certificate of arrival was a critical identifying factor connecting the immigrant to the port of arrival. Beginning 1 July 1924, the INS began collecting immigrant visas, which subsequently became the official arrival records. One could not be admitted for permanent residence without an immigrant visa, and only a permanent admission could be used to issue a Certificate of Arrival, which would support a naturalization. According to INS historian Smith, an immigrant visa leads to permanent admission, which leads to a certificate of arrival, which leads to naturalization. The alien's immigrant visa file then became the first place to search for proof of legal entry into the United States.

WOMEN'S LOSS OF CITIZENSHIP AND REPATRIATION

According to English common law, upon which American law was based in the early nineteenth century, women's citizenship was generally recognized. However, certain laws led to confusion over whether a woman's nationality was derived from that of her father or husband. Most often a woman's nationality was assumed to be determined by her husband's when she married. The courts usually held that an alien wife of an alien husband could not herself be naturalized. The practice had its origins in the act of 10 February 1855 (U.S. Stat. 604), which declared that every alien woman who married a U.S. citizen, or whose husband became a U.S. citizen, automatically obtained citizenship (consequently, the act of marriage served to automatically naturalize any alien woman who married a U.S. citizen). In 1860, Congress modified the language of the law so that native-born and other U.S. citizen women would lose their U.S. citizenship if they left the United States to take up foreign residence with an alien husband.[5]

An act of 2 March 1907 (Statutes at Large, 34, sec. 3) spelled out even more clearly that a woman

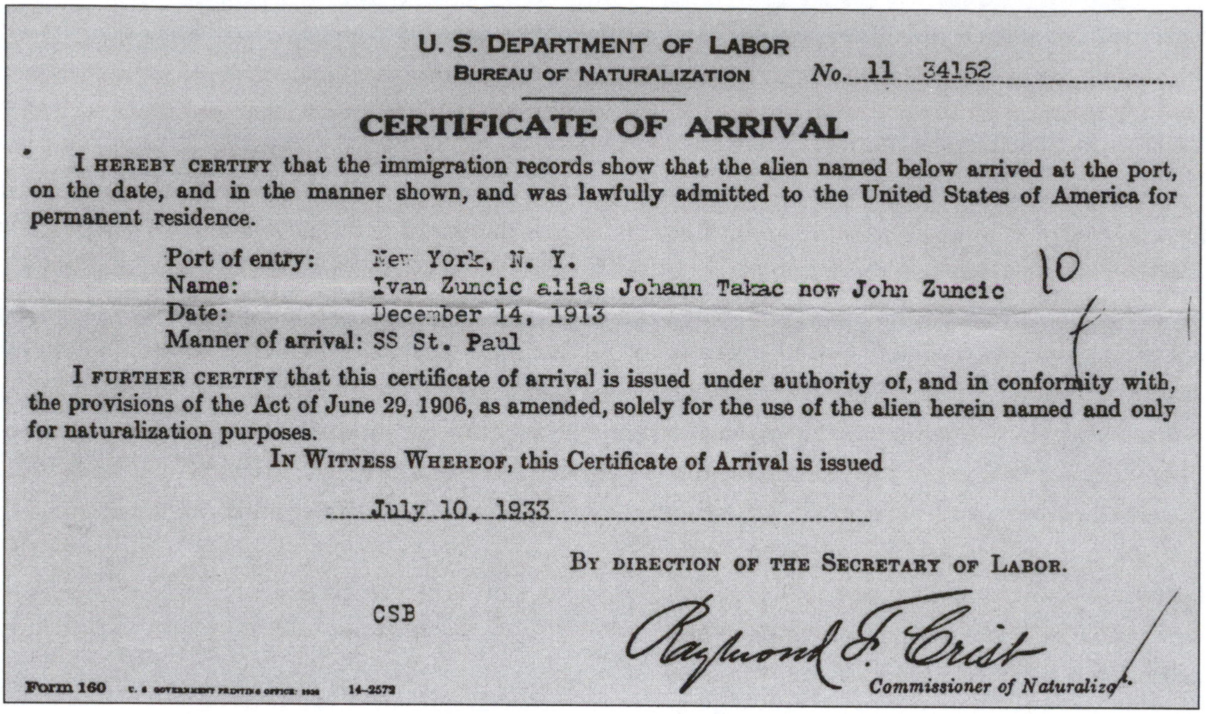
U. S. DEPARTMENT OF LABOR
BUREAU OF NATURALIZATION No. 11 34152

CERTIFICATE OF ARRIVAL

I HEREBY CERTIFY that the immigration records show that the alien named below arrived at the port, on the date, and in the manner shown, and was lawfully admitted to the United States of America for permanent residence.

Port of entry: New York, N. Y.
Name: Ivan Zuncic alias Johann Takac now John Zuncic 10
Date: December 14, 1913
Manner of arrival: SS St. Paul

I FURTHER CERTIFY that this certificate of arrival is issued under authority of, and in conformity with, the provisions of the Act of June 29, 1906, as amended, solely for the use of the alien herein named and only for naturalization purposes.

IN WITNESS WHEREOF, this Certificate of Arrival is issued

July 10, 1933

BY DIRECTION OF THE SECRETARY OF LABOR.

CSB

Raymond F. Crist
Commissioner of Naturalizat

Form 160 14-2573

Figure 5-8. Certificate of arrival of Ivan Zuncic. The INS issued a certificate of arrival and sent it back to the naturalization court. From 1906 to1924, the certificate of arrival was a critical identifying factor connecting the immigrant to the port of arrival.

would lose her U.S. citizenship if she married an alien—regardless of her age, the couple's country of residence, or whether her husband's homeland recognized her as one of its own. However, the new law continued to allow an alien's wife to gain or reacquire U.S. citizenship if her husband became naturalized.

In 1918, the Constitution was amended to grant women the right to vote.

The Act of September 22, 1922, known as the Cable Act or the Married Women's Act, repealed provisions of the 1907 statute and prohibited expatriation of a U.S. citizen by any marriage contracted after that date to an alien eligible for citizenship. Congress acted again on March 2, 1931, to prohibit such expatriation by marriage to an alien even if the husband was racially ineligible to naturalize. To restore citizenship to women who lost their nationality by marriage prior to 1922, Congress provided for resumption of citizenship under the Act of June 25 1936, if her marriage had terminated on or before that date. Not until July 2, 1940, did Congress provide the same relief to women whose marriages had not terminated. While the act itself restored the women's U.S. citizenship, they could not resume or exercise their rights as citizens until taking an oath of allegiance before a naturalization court or a legation or embassy secretary.[6]

VISA FILES, 1924 TO 1944

While the first quantitative immigration law of 1921 set temporary annual quotas according to nationality, the National Origins Act of 1924 (49 Stat. 153) was the first permanent immigration quota law to be passed. The act established a discriminatory quota system, non-quota status, and a consular control system; it also required all aliens arriving in the United States to present a visa. The visas were foreign service forms issued to immigrants by a U.S. Consul at a U.S. embassy office abroad. Children could be issued visas, but they usually traveled on the visa of a parent. Aliens wishing to move

APPLICATION TO TAKE OATH OF ALLEGIANCE TO THE UNITED STATES UNDER THE ACT OF JUNE 25, 1936, AS AMENDED, AND FORM OF SUCH OATH

To the Honorable, the .... DISTRICT .... Court of .... THE UNITED STATES ....

This application, hereby made and filed, respectfully shows:

(1) My full, true, and correct name is .... SOLEDAD VARGAS GARCIA ....
(Full, true name, without abbreviation, and any other name which has been used, must appear here)

(2) My present place of residence is .... 3220 E. 4th St., Los Angeles, Calif. .... (County) (State)

(3) My occupation is .... housewife ....

(4) I am .... 48 .... years old. (5) I was born on .... May 10, 1894 .... (Year) in .... El Paso (Co.) Texas, U.S.A. ....

.... (County, district, province, or state) (Country)

(6) My personal description is as follows: Sex .... fem. ....; color .... wh. ...., complexion .... dk. ....
color of eyes .... brn. ...., color of hair .... dk.brn. ...., height .... 5 .... feet .... 2 .... inches, weight .... 190 .... pounds;
visible distinctive marks .... scar l. temple; mole center front of throat ....

(7) I am .... married; the name of my husband is .... Ramon R. Garcia ....; we were married
on .... May 17, 1912 .... (Year) at .... El Paso, Tex. (State) (Country); he was born
at .... Juarez, Chih., Mex. .... on .... Sept. 5, 1891 .... (Day) (Year); and now resides
(City or town) (County, district, province, or state) (Country)
at .... with me .... (Number and street) (City or town) (State) (Country)

(8) I lost, or believe that I lost, United States citizenship solely by reason of my marriage on .... March 17, 1912 .... (Year)
to .... Ramon R. Garcia .... then an alien, a citizen or subject of .... Mexico ....
and my marital status with such person was .... not .... terminated on .... (Month) (Day) (Year)
.... (State by what means marital status terminated)

(9) I have .... resided continuously in the United States since the date of my marriage shown in paragraph 8 hereof,
to wit, since .... May 10, 1894 .... (Month) (Day) (Year)

(10) I hereby apply to take the oath of renunciation and allegiance as prescribed in Section 335 (b) of the Nationality
Act of 1940 (54 Stat. 1157) to become repatriated and obtain the rights of a citizen of the United States.

Soled Vargas Garcia
(Full, true, and correct signature of applicant, without abbreviation)

Subscribed and sworn to before me by the above-named applicant, in the office of the clerk of said court at ....
.... Los Angeles .... this .... 2nd .... day of .... Mar. ...., Anno Domini 19.43

.... SMITH ....
Clerk.

By .... [SEAL]
Deputy Clerk.

STATE OF CALIFORNIA
} ss:
COUNTY OF LOS ANGELES
In the .... DISTRICT .... Court
of .... THE UNITED STATES ....

Upon consideration of the foregoing, it is hereby ORDERED and DECREED that the above application be granted; that
the applicant named therein be repatriated as a citizen of the United States, upon taking the oath of renunciation and
allegiance to the United States; and that the clerk of this court enter these proceedings of record.

By the Court: .... LEON R. YANKWICH .... Judge.

Figure 5-9. It was under the 1936 Act, as amended in 1940, that Soledad Vargas de Garcia resumed her U.S. citizenship on 2 March 1943. Mrs. Garcia filed a triplicate form N-415 with the U.S. District Court in Los Angeles, made an oath of allegiance before that court, and was repatriated. The original N-415 remained with the court's records while the second and third copies were forwarded to the INS.

Figure 5-10. Old County Court house, El Paso, Texas.

permanently to the U.S. applied for an immigrant visa. Those traveling to the U.S. for a limited time (such as foreign students, those on temporary business matters, and vacationers) applied for a non-immigrant visa.

Aliens had to present their visas to an immigration inspector as they arrived in the United States. The visas were subsequently filed; non-immigrant visas were filed at the port and immigrant visas were forwarded for filing at INS headquarters in Washington, D.C.

REGISTRY FILES, 1929 TO 1944

Registry files are a result of the Registry Act of 1929 (when the National Origins Act came into effect). The law allowed the INS to create arrival records for aliens of good moral character who had been in the United States since before 3 June 1921. Approved cases resulted in at least three documents: certificate of registry, record of registry, and registry file. Registry files are arranged by registry file number at INS head-

quarters in Washington, D.C. (Registry files contain the original application, report of investigation, correspondence, extra photographs, and other miscellaneous items. These files can be requested from the INS only if the registry file number can be provided.)

ALIEN REGISTRATION RECORDS, 1940 TO 1944

In response to the threat of war, the United States began the Alien Registration Program in July 1940. Pursuant to the Alien Registration Act of that year (also known as the Smith Act), every alien resident living in the United States had to register at a local post office. Aliens entering the United States had to register as they applied for admission. Alien registration requirements applied to all aliens over the age of fourteen, regardless of nationality and regardless of immigration status.

American Consular Service

at RIGA, LATVIA.

QUOTA

Immigration Visa

* Nonpreference ☐

Preference ☒

Passport No. 31014 585822, issued by Soviet authorities, Kiev, Russia on the 20th day of December, A. D. 1926, valid until the 30th day of January, A. D. 1928.

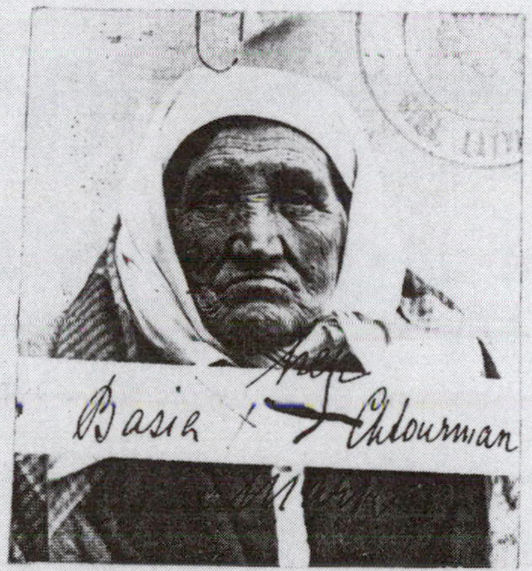

1—1096 GOVERNMENT PRINTING OFFICE

No. 840

Russian (Quota.) Russian (Nationality.)

Date: February 2nd, 1927

For the journey to the United States.

SEEN:

The Bearer, Basia CHTOURMAN (Ternoff Schturman), who is of Russian (Citizen or subject.) nationality, having been seen and examined, is classified as a Quota Immigrant and is granted this Immigration Visa, pursuant to the Immigration Act of 1924.

The validity of this Immigration Visa expires on the 2nd day of June, A. D. 1927.

AMERICAN CONSULAR SERVICE $9.00 FEE STAMP

Vice Consul of the United States of America.

Fee $9.00.

Fee No. 284

NOTE: This Immigration Visa will not entitle the person to whom issued to enter the United States if, upon arrival in the United States, he is found to be inadmissible to the United States under the Immigration Laws. (Subdivision (g), Section 2, Immigration Act of 1924.)

* Check appropriate classification.

Figure 5-11. Front of the visa packet issued to Basia Chtourman, who was born in 1850 in Ustingrad, Russia. She left Kiev in 1926 to join her son in Buffalo, N.Y. Tragically, she never reached her destination; she became ill and died in Halifax, Nova Scotia. Her visa, however, remains on file with the INS.

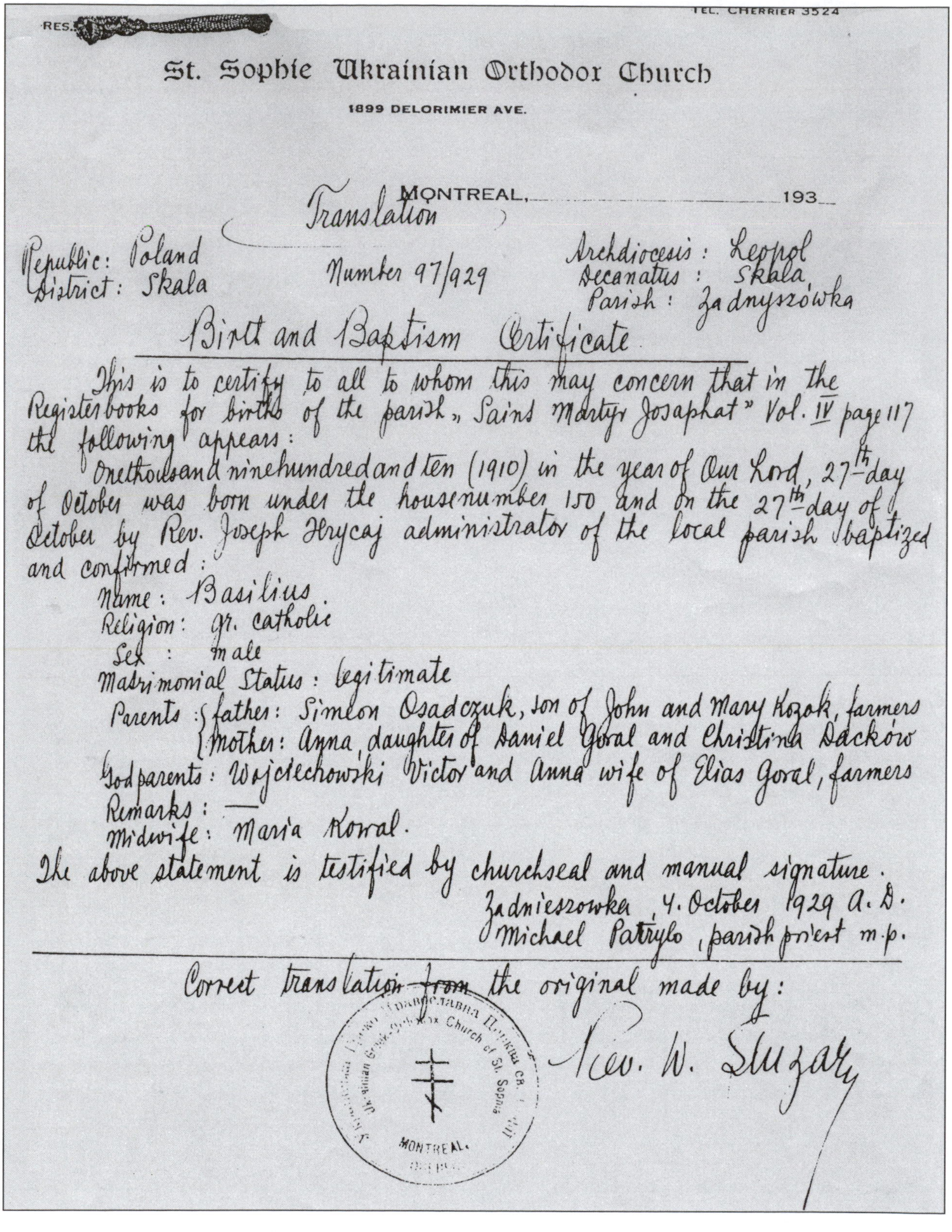

RES.

TEL. CHERRIER 3524

St. Sophie Ukrainian Orthodox Church

1899 DELORIMIER AVE.

MONTREAL,_____ 193_

Translation

Number 97/929

Republic: Poland
District: Skala

Archdiocesis: Leopol
Decanatus: Skala
Parish: Zadnyszówka

Birth and Baptism Certificate

This is to certify to all to whom this may concern that in the Register books for births of the parish „Saint Martyr Josaphat" Vol. IV page 117 the following appears:

One thousand nine hundred and ten (1910) in the year of Our Lord, 27th day of October was born under the house number 150 and on the 27th day of October by Rev. Joseph Hrycaj administrator of the local parish baptized and confirmed:

Name: Basilius.
Religion: Gr. Catholic
Sex: male
Matrimonial Status: legitimate
Parents: father: Simeon Osadczuk, son of John and Mary Kozak, farmers
mother: Anna, daughter of Daniel Goral and Christina Dacków
Godparents: Wojciechowski Victor and Anna wife of Elias Goral, farmers
Remarks: —
Midwife: Maria Kowal.

The above statement is testified by churchseal and manual signature.
Zadnieszówka, 4. October 1929 A.D.
Michael Patrylo, parish priest m.p.

Correct translation from the original made by:

Rev. W. Sluzar

Figure 5-12. A birth and baptism certificate for Basilius Osadczuk
is just one of many supporting documents found attached to INS visa files.

★   ★   166   ★   ★

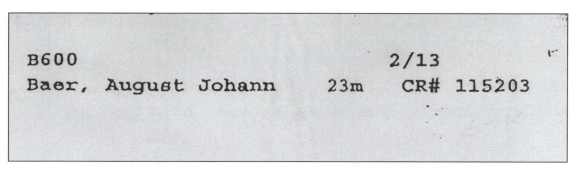

```
B600                              2/13
Baer, August Johann    23m    CR# 115203
```

Figure 5-13. The registry problem: this index card to passenger arrivals at Boston does not refer to a ship, but only to the cryptic "CR#" (certificate of registry number).

Figure 5-14. Certificate of registry, 1929–1940. This two-sided document has an "R" number, which is not the same as a "CR" number.

DUPLICATE

PRESENT NAME ZENTOS (SURNAME) NICKOLAS (MIDDLE) JOHN (FIRST) 44 (AGE)

NAME AT TIME OF ENTRY Zenetos (SURNAME) Nickolas (MIDDLE) Joanis (FIRST)

July 26, 1915 (DATE OF ARRIVAL) New York, New York (PLACE OF ARRIVAL)

(MANNER OF ARRIVAL)

Arcadia, Greece (COUNTRY OF BIRTH)

5 feet 5 inches (PRESENT HEIGHT) medium fair (COMPLEXION) brown (EYES) black

DATE OF REGISTRY February 27, 1940 FILE NO. R-124505

(SIGNATURE OF ALIEN)

APR 26 1940 8-189154 (SIGNED IN PRESENCE OF) (TITLE OF GOVT. OFFICER)

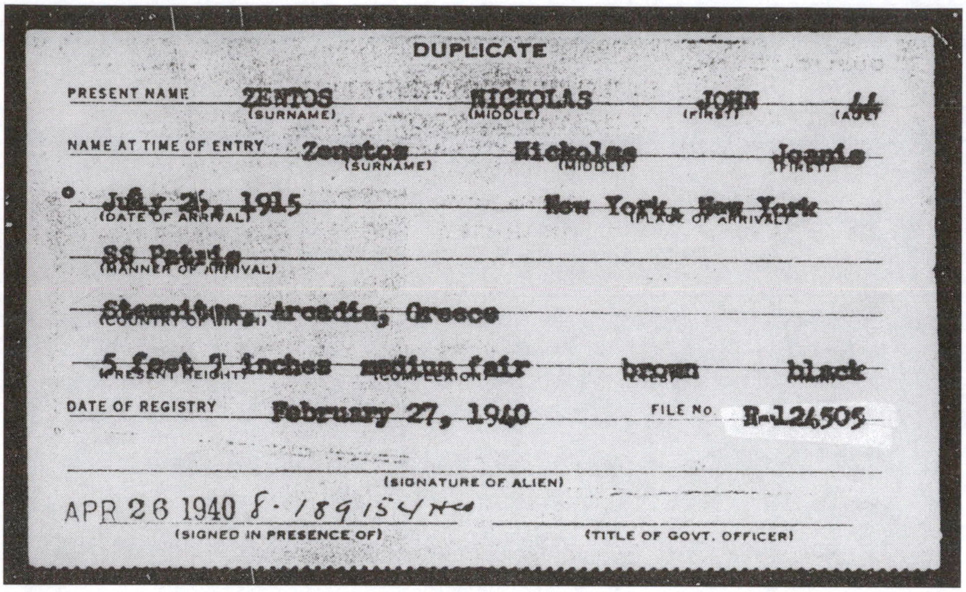

Figure 5-15. Copy of a duplicate card given to the immigrant. The card shown for John Nickolas Zentos indicates that his name, at the time of entry, was Joanis Nickolas Zenetos. This card is on file at the INS. If an alien was never naturalized, this document might be found among family papers. If the individual did go through the process of becoming a naturalized citizen, the INS took the registry certificate upon naturalization. The naturalization papers have no reference to the certificate of registry.

As part of the registration process, aliens were fingerprinted and asked to fill out a two-page form. Each set of forms was numbered with an alien registration number. The completed forms were forwarded to the INS for statistical coding, indexing, and filing. The alien carried the alien registration receipt card to show compliance with the law.

Early registrations (ca. July 1940 to April 1944) are on microfilm in INS custody. They are searchable by name, date of birth, and place of birth. The records are subject to the Freedom of Information Act/Privacy Act.

As John Newman notes in *American Naturalization Processes and Procedures 1790-1985* (Indiana Historical Society, 1981), page 1, "Many aliens lived their lives as positive contributors to their community and new nation without formally acquiring citizenship."

The foregoing information on visa files, registry files, and alien registration records was adapted from a leaflet titled "Ellis Islands en la Frontera: US/Mexican Border Arrival Manifests and other INS Records for Hispanic Family History Research" by INS historian Marian Smith (April 1997).

The Immigration Act of 1990

The Immigration Act of 1990 (8 U.S.C. 1101) represents a major overhaul of immigration laws, amending the Immigration and Nationality Act. Changes included revisions to the numerical limits and preference system regulating immigration; administrative naturalization, empowering the attorney general to issue final determinations on applications for U.S. citizenship; and the issuing of certificates of naturalization. Since 1990, the courts have no longer been involved in conferring citizenship, so they do not have records for naturalizations that have taken place since 1990.

Requests for Records Under the Freedom of Information Act (FOIA)

All requests for naturalization and alien-related records must be submitted to the INS in writing. Any person can request access to INS records not previously made available to the public.

TABLE 5-1. SOME DOCUMENTS ISSUED BY THE INS SINCE 1906, WITH ABBREVIATIONS

Some naturalization certificates have letter abbreviations preceding the certificate number. The following list defines some of the more frequently used abbreviations.

"A" Files	Alien files
"DERIV.A" and/or "DA" Files	Certificate of citizenship documenting derivative or "acquired" citizenship by birth outside the United States or its possessions (i.e., child of U.S. citizen born abroad). Not A-files.
"OM" Files	Naturalization files related to persons naturalized overseas while members of the armed forces of the United States during World War II. All on microfilm.
"OS" Files	Naturalization files created for persons naturalized outside the United States under the act of 30 June 1953. A file of this series bears the same number that appears on the certificate issued to the person.
"B" Files	Certificates of naturalization or repatriation issued to persons who regained U.S. citizenship before 13 January 1941, either by taking the prescribed oath of renunciation and allegiance before a naturalization court in the U.S. or before a U.S. diplomatic or consular officer abroad, following loss of citizenship by reason of service in the armed forces of an allied foreign country in World War I or World War II, or by voting in a foreign political election during World War II. Not duplicated in court records.
"C" Files	Certificate files
"D" Files	Certificates of naturalization or repatriation issued to persons who regained U.S. citizenship on or after 13 January 1941, either by taking the prescribed oath of renunciation and allegiance before a naturalization court in the U.S. or before a U.S. diplomatic or consular officer abroad, following the loss of citizenship by reason of service in the armed forces of an allied foreign country in World War I or World War II, or by voting in a foreign political election during World War II. Not duplicated in court records.
"OL" Files	"Old Law" naturalization certificates issued by the INS to replace naturalization certificates that were lost, destroyed, or mutilated, where the original naturalization certificate was issued under the procedure in effect prior to the act of 29 June 1906 (which became effective 27 September 1906).
"3904/-" Files	Containing applications to resume citizenship by persons who lost citizenship as described under "B" and "D" files above, but who never applied for a certificate and for whom no prior certificate file exists.
"15/-" Files	Files relating to persons expatriated before 1945. Files in National Archives (Washington, D.C.)
"24/-" Files	Files relating to persons expatriated before 1945. Files in National Archives (Washington, D.C.)
"72/-" Files	Files relating to persons expatriated before 1945. Files in National Archives (Washington, D.C.)
"129/-" Files	Files documenting the repatriation of women who lost U.S. citizenship by marriage to an alien before 1922 and who resumed U.S. citizenship under the act of 25 June 1936. All on microfilm.

Figure 5-16. Certificates of lawful entry for Marcin Andrew Zientek and Paul Hugo Gustav Ziesler, providing a photograph on one side of the card and biographical information and the critical "R" number on the reverse side of the card.

DUPLICATE

PRESENT NAME	ZIENTEK	ANDREW	MARCIN
	(SURNAME)	(MIDDLE)	(FIRST)
NAME AT TIME OF ENTRY	Zientek	Andrew	Marcin
	(SURNAME)	(MIDDLE)	(FIRST)

April 8, 1911
(DATE OF ARRIVAL)

New York, New York
(PLACE OF ARRIVAL)

SS unknown
(MANNER OF ARRIVAL)

Jablono, Lubel, Poland
(PLACE OF BIRTH)

October 12, 1889
(DATE OF BIRTH)

5 feet 9 inches	medium dark	brown	brown
(PRESENT HEIGHT)	(COMPLEXION)	(EYES)	(HAIR)

DATE OF ISSUE May 23, 1941

FILE No. R-157343

JUN 4 1941

(SIGNATURE OF ALIEN)

(SIGNED IN PRESENCE OF)   8-16   (TITLE OF GOVT. OFFICER)

DUPLICATE

PRESENT NAME	ZIESLER	HUGO GUSTAV	PAUL
	(SURNAME)	(MIDDLE)	(FIRST)
NAME AT TIME OF ENTRY	Ziesler	Hugo Gustav	Paul
	(SURNAME)	(MIDDLE)	(FIRST)

September 15, 1915
(DATE OF ARRIVAL)

San Francisco, California
(PLACE OF ARRIVAL)

SS William Chatham
(MANNER OF ARRIVAL)

Berlin, Germany
(PLACE OF BIRTH)

August 31, 1891
(DATE OF BIRTH)

5 feet 8 inches	sallow	blue	brown
(PRESENT HEIGHT)	(COMPLEXION)	(EYES)	(HAIR)

DATE OF ISSUE September 30, 1943

FILE No. R-224689

(SIGNATURE OF ALIEN)

(SIGNED IN PRESENCE OF)   (TITLE OF GOVT. OFFICER)

Figure 5-16 (cont.). Opposite sides of certificates of lawful entry for Zientek and Ziesler.

alien reg # 2176791

19:1270

MINNEAPOLIS NO. 53730
Page 1

Form 659
U.S. DEPARTMENT OF JUSTICE
IMMIGRATION AND NATURALIZATION SERVICE

No. R_____

District File No. 43530/140

APPLICATION FOR REGISTRY OF AN ALIEN

NOTE.—This application form and instructions on page 4 should be carefully studied before preparation and when prepared should be typewritten and submitted in duplicate either in person or by mail at the immigration and naturalization office located nearest alien's place of residence. Strike out words or parts not applicable. Be sure to answer every applicable question fully and accurately, as failure to give correct and satisfactory answer may result in delay, or even in the denial of your application.

To the Commissioner of Immigration and Naturalization,
                    Washington, D. C.

Through the immigration and naturalization officer in charge at ___Minneapolis, Minnesota___

I, __Emil Smith__   __109 Nicollet Avenue__   __Minneapolis,__   __Minnesota__
        (Name)   (Number and street)   (City)   (State)

an alien, believing that there is no record showing that I am now a lawful permanent resident of the United States, hereby request that under the provisions of the act of Congress of March 2, 1929, as amended, a record of registry of my arrival in the United States be made. I hereby agree to appear in person at such time and place as may be designated for examination regarding the claims made by me. This application is submitted in duplicate together with two photographs of myself, 2 by 2 inches in size, and money order in the sum of $10, payable to the Commissioner of Immigration and Naturalization, Washington, D. C., and documents to prove my residence in the United States and good character.

In support of my application I make the following statements:

THE FACTS IMMEDIATELY FOLLOWING ARE GIVEN AS OF THE DATE OF THE ENTRY UPON WHICH I BASE THIS APPLICATION

(1) (1) My name given at birth was ___Milan___   (Schmitz) SHIMITZ
                                        (First)   (Middle)   (Last)

(4) (2) I entered under the name of ___Milan (Shmitz) SHIMITZ___
                                        (First)   (Middle)   (Last)

(3) (3) My occupation was __student__   (4) My race or people is __Sracan WHITE__

(5) My last place of residence before entry was ___Kettefl, Hungary___
                                                    (Give as of present location—Country)
_____
        (Province)   (City or town)

(6) I arrived in the United States on (Date) ___November 18, 1912___
                                            (Month)   (Day)   (Year)

At the port of ___New York___
                (Seaport or land border port)

(7) I came on the vessel ___Prz. Fred. Wilhelm___   (8) I {was/were} inspected and
                            (Name of vessel)
admitted by an immigrant inspector.

(If means of conveyance to the United States was other than by vessel, describe such conveyance)

_____
(If entry occurred at other than regular seaport or land border port, describe the circumstances of entry (including date) as accurately as possible, naming the State in which, and the city or town at or near which you entered.)

(9) I was born at ___Kettefl, Hungary___   on ___June 16, 1898___
                    (Place and country)   (Month) (Day) (Year)

(10) My destination was ___Minneapolis, Minnesota___
                            (City or town and State)

(11) I was coming to join ___step brother, William Petrof___
                    (State name and whether friends or relatives, and if the latter, the relationship)

(12) I was coming to remain ___permanently___
                            (State whether temporarily or permanently)

(13) I was accompanied by ___do not remember the man's name___
                            (State name and relationship, if any)

THE FACTS IMMEDIATELY FOLLOWING ARE GIVEN AS OF THE DATE OF THIS APPLICATION

(14) My present name is (print full name) ___Emil   Smith___
                                            (First)   (Middle)   (Last)

(15) I now reside at ___109 Nicollet Avenue___

(4) (16) My occupation is __laborer__   (17) My personal description is as follows:

Height __5__ __5__   __medium__   __brown HAZEL__ __brown__
        (Feet) (Inches) (Complexion)   (Color of eyes) (Color of hair)

Marks of identification ___scar on first finger of right hand___

(18) My nationality is ___Hungarian___   (19) My sex is ___male___
                    (Country of which citizen or subject)

16—13451

Figure 5-17. Three-page application for registry of an alien for Milan Shimitz/Emil Smith.

Page 2

(20) I {have~~X~~ / have never} heretofore filed application for registry _____

(21) I {have ~~no~~ / ~~have never~~} heretofore filed a declaration of intention to become a citizen *Aug. 1940*

(22) I {~~did~~ / did not} withdraw my declaration of intention during the World War to avoid military service.

(23) I am _____not_____ married.   The name of my wife or husband is _____

We were married on _____ at _____
          (Month)   (Day)   (Year)   (City or town)   (State)

(24) She or he was born at _____
                 (City or town)   (State or country)

on _____, arrived in the United States at _____
   (Month)   (Day)   (Year)   (City or town)

on _____, for permanent residence, and now resides at _____
   (Month)   (Day)   (Year)   (City or town)

_____ was _____ naturalized on _____
     (State or country)   (Month)   (Day)   (Year)

at _____ and certificate No. _____ issued.
   (City or town)   (County)   (State)

* If applicant has been previously married give facts relative to each such marriage as to dates, places, name of spouse, and manner and date of termination of marriage.

_____

_____

_____

(25) * I have _____no_____ children, whose names, ages, places of birth, and places of residence are as follows:

Name	Age	Place of Birth	Now Residing At—

(26) * Since the date of entry upon which this application is based I have resided in the United States as follows:

Street and Number	City or Town	State	From— Month	From— Year	To— Month	To— Year
912 Marshall St. N. E.	Minneapolis	Minn.		1912		1916
119 University Ave. S. E.	"	"		1916		1919
115 E. Hennepin	"	"		1919		1920
U.S. Army				1920		1923
119 University Ave. S. E.	"	"		1923		1933
109 Nicollet	"	"		1933		date

* *Use separate sheet for additional entries.* During the season, worked on various farms for month or so at a time, always returning to Mpls. and keeping it as headquarters.

16—13451

Figure 5-17 (cont.).

Page 4

NOTE CAREFULLY.—This application must be sworn to before an officer of the Immigration and Naturalization Service.

(Application not to be signed on this page until applicant appears before an officer of the Immigration and Naturalization Service for a hearing on the application.)

I, _____ EMIL SMITH _____, do swear (affirm) that I know the contents of this application for registry subscribed by me, that the same are true to the best of my knowledge, except as to matters therein stated to be alleged upon information and belief, and that as to those matters I believe them to be true, and that corrections numbered (1) to (4) were made by me or at my request, and that this application was signed by me with my full, true name: So help me God.

Emil Smith
_____
(Complete and true signature of applicant)

Subscribed and sworn to before me by the above-named applicant at _____ MINNEAPOLIS, MINNESOTA. _____

this _____ 18th _____ day of _____ NOVEMBER _____, Anno Domini 19 41

Royall Storey
ROYALL H. STOREY
Immigrant Inspector designated
Naturalization Examiner.
(Title of officer)

PHOTOGRAPHS.—You are required to send with this application two photographs of yourself taken within 30 days of the date of this application. These photographs must be 2 by 2 inches in size, and the distance from top of head to point of chin should be approximately 1¼ inches. They must not be pasted on cards or mounted in any other way, must be on thin paper, have a light background, and clearly show a front view of your face without hat. Snapshots, group or full-length portraits will not be accepted. Both of these photographs must be signed by you on the margin and not on the face or the clothing.

MONEY ORDER.—You are required to send with this application a money order in the sum of $10, payable to the Commissioner of Immigration and Naturalization, Washington, D. C.

DOCUMENTS.—In support of your application you should send with it photostatic or typewritten copies of documentary evidence to prove that you have resided continuously in the United States since prior to July 1, 1924, and also to prove good character. These documents may consist of bank books, leases, deeds, licenses, receipts, letters, birth records, marriage records, church records, school records, employment records, affidavits, and police records, etc. The originals of such documentary evidence must be brought with you when you are notified to appear for a hearing on this application.

IMPORTANT.—Paragraph (c) of section 1 of the act of Congress approved March 2, 1929, entitled "An act to supplement the naturalization laws, and for other purposes," under which this application is made, reads:

"The provisions of section 76 of the act entitled 'An act to codify, revise, and amend the penal laws of the United States,' approved March 4, 1909, shall apply in respect of the record of registry authorized by this section in the same manner and to the same extent, including penalties, as they apply in respect of the oaths, notices, affidavits, certificates, orders, records, signatures, and other instruments, papers, or proceedings specified in such section 76."

Said section 76 of the Criminal Code provides a penalty of not more than $1,000, or imprisonment of not more than 5 years, or both, in the case of any person who shall knowingly impersonate any person other than himself, or shall falsely appear in the name of a deceased person, or in an assumed or fictitious name; or whoever shall falsely make, forge, or counterfeit any oath, notice, affidavit, certificate, order, record, signature, or other instrument, paper, or proceeding required or authorized by any law, relating to or providing for the naturalization of aliens; or whoever shall utter, sell, dispose of, or shall use as true or genuine, for any unlawful purpose, any false, forged, antedated, or counterfeit oath, notice, certificate, order, record, signature, instrument, paper, or proceeding above specified; or whoever shall sell or dispose of to any person other than the person for whom it was originally issued any certificate of citizenship or certificate showing any person to be admitted a citizen.

Figure 5-17 (cont.).

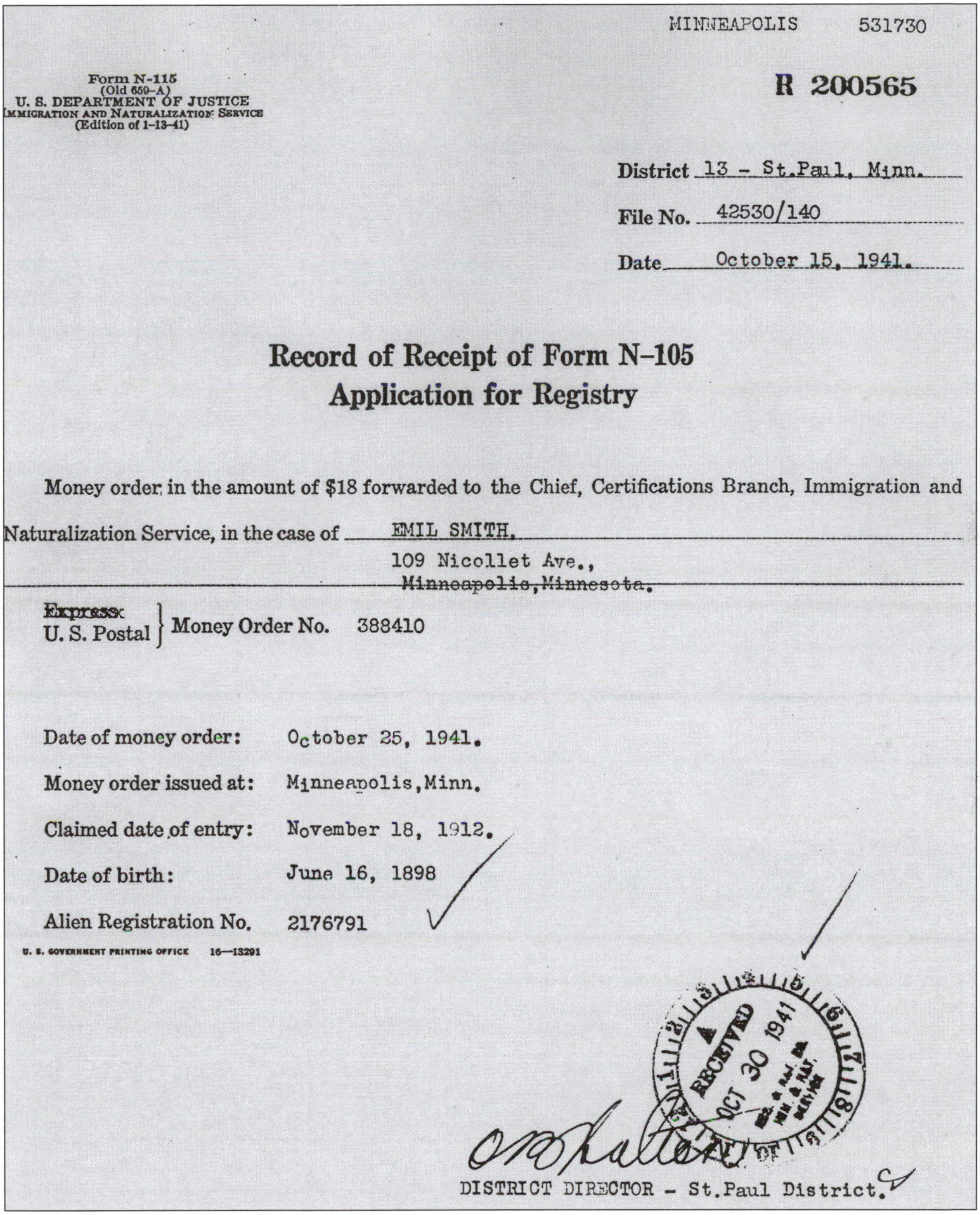

MINNEAPOLIS   531730

R 200565

Form N-115
(Old 659-A)
U. S. DEPARTMENT OF JUSTICE
IMMIGRATION AND NATURALIZATION SERVICE
(Edition of 1-13-41)

District _13 - St.Paul, Minn._

File No. _42530/140_

Date _October 15, 1941._

Record of Receipt of Form N-105
Application for Registry

Money order in the amount of $18 forwarded to the Chief, Certifications Branch, Immigration and

Naturalization Service, in the case of _____ EMIL SMITH,

109 Nicollet Ave.,
Minneapolis,Minnesota.

Express
U. S. Postal } Money Order No.   388410

Date of money order: October 25, 1941.

Money order issued at: Minneapolis,Minn.

Claimed date of entry: November 18, 1912.

Date of birth: June 16, 1898

Alien Registration No.   2176791

U. S. GOVERNMENT PRINTING OFFICE   16—13291

RECEIVED OCT 30 1941

DISTRICT DIRECTOR - St.Paul District.

Figure 5-18. Record of receipt of form N-105 for Emil Smith.

Form N-130
(Old 659-D)
U. S. DEPARTMENT OF JUSTICE
IMMIGRATION AND NATURALIZATION SERVICE
(Edition of 1-13-41)

MINNEAPOLIS FILE NO. 531730

RECORD OF INVESTIGATION OF APPLICANT FOR REGISTRY

COMMISSIONER OF IMMIGRATION AND NATURALIZATION,
Washington, D. C.

District No. 13 St.Paul,Minn.
District file No. 42530/140
C. O. file No. TP-200565
November 25, 1941.

Transmitted herewith is record of investigation in the case of the following-named applicant for registry.

DATA AS OF DATE OF ARRIVAL

Name ___SHIMITZ___ — ___MILAN___
(Surname)   (Middle name)   (First name)

Occupation ___Student.___ Race ___White (Serbian)___

Last residence before entry ___Kettefl, Hungary.___

Date of arrival in United States ___November 18, 1912___ Place of arrival ___New York, N.Y.___

Manner of arrival ___S.S. Prinz Frederick Wilhelm.___

Place of birth ___Kettefl, Hungary___ Date of birth ___June 16, 1898___

DATA AS OF DATE OF REGISTRY

Name ___SMITH___ — ___EMIL___
(Surname)   (Middle name)   (First name)

Place of residence ___109 Niclllet Ave., Minneapolis,Minnesota.___

Occupation ___Laborer___ Personal description ___5' 5"___ ___Medium___
                                                        (Height)   (Complexion)

___Hazel___ ___Brown___ ___Scar on first finger of right hand.___
(Color of eyes)   (Color of hair)   (Visible distinctive marks)

Recommendation: That a Certificate of Lawful Entry be ___GRANTED___ (A.R.A. No. 2176791)

ENCLOSURES: Form 659
                Record of Investigation,
                Two photographs

Form N-115 for'd C.O. Oct. 15, 1941.

(Photostat copy of A.R.A. record received and examined.)

DISTRICT DIRECTOR of St. Paul District.

It is ordered that Certificate of Lawful Entry be

February 6, 1942

Certificate of Lawful Entry No. ___178130___ sent to ___St. Paul___ on _____

Copy of this order sent to _____ E.I. on _____
1b

U. S. GOVERNMENT PRINTING OFFICE   16—13320

Figure 5-19. Record of investigation.

Form N-120
(Old 659-B)
U. S. DEPARTMENT OF JUSTICE
IMMIGRATION AND NATURALIZATION SERVICE
(Edition of 1-13-41)

Affidavit of Witness in Registry Proceeding

MPLS FILE   531730

In the Matter of the Application of

EMIL SMITH.

To be registered under the provisions of section 328 (b) of the Nationality Act of 1940 (54 Stat. 1152).

No. R _____

District File No. ___42530/140___

AFFIDAVIT

CLARENCE PETERSON _____, occupation ___WOODWORKER.___

residing at ___2319 Cole Ave., S.E. Minneapolis, Minnesota.___
(Number and street)   (City or town)   (State)

being duly sworn, deposes and says that (s)he { is / is not } a citizen of the United States of America; that

(s)he has personally known and has been acquainted in the United States with _____

___EMIL SMITH._____, the applicant above mentioned;

that to { his / her } personal knowledge the applicant has resided in the United States as follows:

___MINNEAPOLIS, MINN._____ from ___Sometime in 1920___ to ___DATE.___
(City, town, and State)   (Month)   (Year)   (Month)   (Year)

_____ from _____ to _____
(City, town, and State)   (Month)   (Year)   (Month)   (Year)

_____ from _____ to _____
(City, town, and State)   (Month)   (Year)   (Month)   (Year)

_____ from _____ to _____
(City, town, and State)   (Month)   (Year)   (Month)   (Year)

that (s)he has personal knowledge that the applicant is a person of good moral character, and that the

longest period during the residence described in which (s)he has not seen the applicant is ___0___
(Years)

___TWO OR THREE MONTHS.___
(Months)

     I first met Emil Smith here in Minneapolis when he was living at the
Florence Hotel, sometime in 1920.   I worked with Smith at the Minneapolis Bedding
Company for several years until they went out of business, in 1929.   Since
first meeting Smith in 1920, I have known him as a friend and we have continued
the friendship up to the present time.   I know that he goes out of Minneapolis
during the summer to work on various farms for a few months at a time but he always
comes back to Minneapolis when he is out of a job and as far as I know he con-
siders Minneapolis his home - working out of here.   As far as I know he has
never been out of the United States and has never had any trouble with the
police that I know of.

Clarence Peterson
(Signature of witness)

Subscribed and sworn to before me by the above-named witness at ___MINNEAPOLIS, MINN.___

this ___21st___ day of ___NOVEMBER___ Anno Domini 19__41__

Royal H Storey

ROYAL H. STOREY
Immigrant Inspector - designated
Naturalization Examiner.

U. S. GOVERNMENT PRINTING OFFICE   16—13455

Figure 5-20. Affidavit of witness in registry proceeding.

★   ★   177   ★   ★

```
                        LIST OF EXHIBITS:

1.    Statement of Police Department, City of Minneapolis,Minn.,
      showing absence of any record against EMIL SMITH.

2.    Certificate of Clerk of the Hennepin County District Court,
      Minneapolis,Minneta., showing absence of any criminal record
      against applicant.

3.    Affidavit of one C. O. Peterson, relative to employment of
      applicant by the Minneapolis Bedding Co., in Minneapolis,Minn.,
      from 1924 to 1929.

4.    Statement of Motor Vehicle Department, Dept. of State, State
      of Minnesota, St.Paul,Minn., showing that one EMIL SMITH of Minneapolis,Minn.
      registered a car in Minnesota in 1927, 1928 and 1929.

5.    Letter of Mrs. F. D. Thielen, Prop. of Florence Hotel, 119
      University Ave., S E. Minneapolis,Minn., relative to residence of
       applicant in that Hotel between July 1, 1923 and July, 1933.

6.    Letter of J. B. Anderson, Clerk at the Old Columbia Hotel,
      109 Nicollet Ave., Minneapolis,Minn., relative to residence of
      applicant at that Hotel from 1933 to date.

7.    Residence Evidence exhibited.
```

Figure 5-21. List of exhibits for alien registration of Emil Smith.

INS form G-639, the Freedom of Information/Privacy Act Request (appendix A), is recommended for rapid identification and to ensure expeditious handling; however, requests may be made in any written form. The Freedom of Information Act requires the INS to allow public access unless the information is exempt from mandatory disclosure under the act (for example, classified national security, business proprietary, personal privacy, investigative). Requests must be for access to records that already exist, and requesters cannot require the INS to "create" records.

The request should adequately describe the specific records sought (naturalization, visa, registry, and alien registration records) to enable the INS staff to conduct a search for the requested records with a reasonable amount of effort. The immigrant's experience will determine what records are available. The minimum information required to initiate a search of INS records is the alien's full name (with any alternate spellings or aliases) and date and place of birth. Include a request for any records that INS may have that pertain to that particular immigrant. When requesting records of immigrants who arrived, were naturalized, and otherwise encountered the INS before ca. 1955, mail your request to:

INS Freedom of Information
2nd Floor, ULLB
425 I Street, N.W.
Washington, DC 20536
202-514-1722

Beginning in 1955, the INS distributed most Alien Files (A-Files) to its various District Offices throughout the United States. Records of immigrants who had dealings with the INS after about 1955–1960 are contained in A-Files, and Freedom of Information (FOIA) and Privacy Act (PA) requests should be

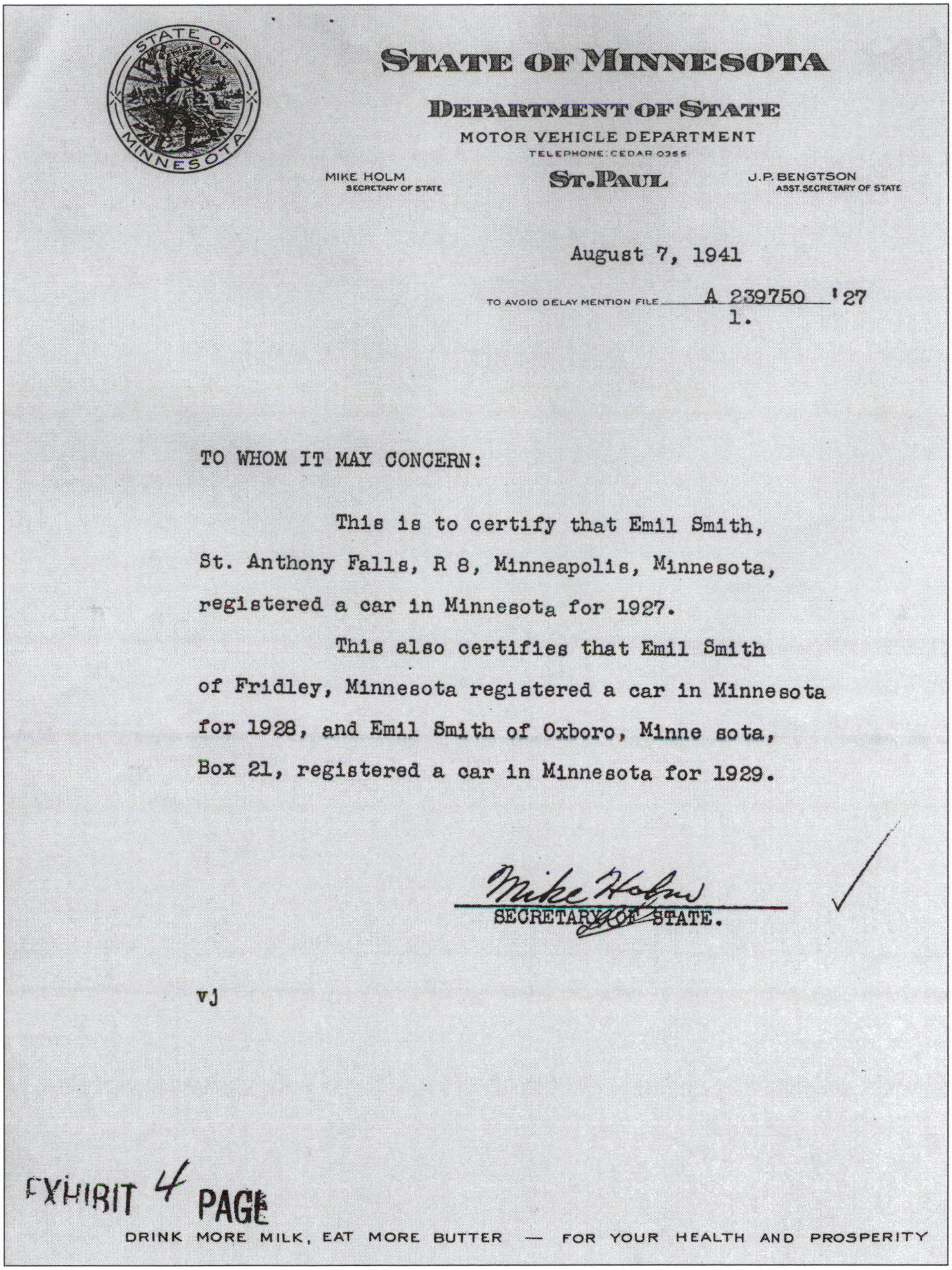

STATE OF MINNESOTA

DEPARTMENT OF STATE

MOTOR VEHICLE DEPARTMENT
TELEPHONE: CEDAR 0355

MIKE HOLM
SECRETARY OF STATE

ST. PAUL

J.P. BENGTSON
ASST. SECRETARY OF STATE

August 7, 1941

TO AVOID DELAY MENTION FILE   A 239750   '27
1.

TO WHOM IT MAY CONCERN:

This is to certify that Emil Smith,
St. Anthony Falls, R 8, Minneapolis, Minnesota,
registered a car in Minnesota for 1927.

This also certifies that Emil Smith
of Fridley, Minnesota registered a car in Minnesota
for 1928, and Emil Smith of Oxboro, Minnesota,
Box 21, registered a car in Minnesota for 1929.

Mike Holm
SECRETARY OF STATE.

vJ

EXHIBIT 4 PAGE

DRINK MORE MILK, EAT MORE BUTTER — FOR YOUR HEALTH AND PROSPERITY

*Figure 5-22. Certification from the state of Minnesota, Department of State, Motor Vehicle Department,
that Emil Smith registered a car in 1927, 1928, and 1929.*

RESIDENCE EVIDENCE EXHIBITED.

1. HONORABLE DISCHARGE from U.S. Army, dated October 27, 1923, issued at Fort Mc Dowell, California, Serial No. 6491470, Company L, 15th Infantry, in name EMIL SMITH - Enlisted Fort Snelling, Minnesota, November 22, 1920.   Character Excellent

2. Alien Registration Receipt Card No. 2176791, issued to Emil Smith, 109 Niclllet Ave., Minneapolis,Minn.

(This man appears to be sincere in all of his statements. He lives at a very cheap hotel in the Gateway district,Minneapolis, and claims to have no letters, receipts, postcards, or other evidence of residence to submit.   Has no insurance policies and never attended school in the U.S. except a night school for a short period in 1916.   Has never been married.)

European and American Styles   Phone: Dinsmore 1784

FLORENCE HOTEL

Mrs. F. ———— Prop.

119 UNIVERSITY AVENUE S. E.

Minneapolis, Minn._____Sept 13_____1924 1

This is to say that I have known Mr Emil Smith

for about 18 years he lived at my Hotel from

July 1 st 1923 until July 1933 and has been

at my Hotel at various times since that time,

Mrs. F. D. Thielen
proprietor Florence Hotel
119 - University ave. S. E.
Minneapolis
Minnesota

Figure 5-23. Residence evidence exhibited for Emil Smith.

MPLS FILE NO. 531730

Form N-125
(Old 659-C)
U. S. DEPARTMENT OF JUSTICE
IMMIGRATION AND NATURALIZATION SERVICE
(Edition of 1-13-41)

District 13 - St. Paul, Minn.

File No. 42530/140

Date November 25, 1941.

Findings in Application for Registry

(Under Nationality Act of 1940)

In re: EMIL SMITH.

From a consideration of the foregoing record, it is found that:

1. The applicant is an alien __NOT__ ineligible to citizenship.

2. There is __NO__ record of the applicant's admission for permanent residence.

3. The applicant __DID__ enter the United States prior to July 1, 1924.

4. The applicant has __—__ resided continuously in the United States since prior to July 1, 1924.

5. The applicant is __—__ a person of good moral character.

6. The applicant is __NOT__ subject to deportation.

RECOMMENDATION:

It is recommended that application for registry be GRANTED (A.R.A.No. 21 76791)

NO application for C/A is pending. Closed St.Paul Naturalization file 14-51725 shows that refund of C/A fee was recommended March 25, 1941.

Applicant was born June 16, 1898 in Hungary and closed file indicates inability of the Ellis Island office to verify claimed arrival at that Port November 18, 1912 ex S.S.Prinz Frederick Wilhelm.

Exhibits 3 to 7 bear out applicant's claim of continuous residence in the U.S. from a date prior to July 1, 1924, and testimony of witnesses is favorable.

Royall H. Storey

ROYALL H. STOREY
Immigrant Inspector designated Naturalization Examiner.
(Title of examining officer)

(If recommendation is for denial, a statement in support thereof must be made.)

U. S. GOVERNMENT PRINTING OFFICE 16—13293

Figure 5-24. Findings in application for registry.

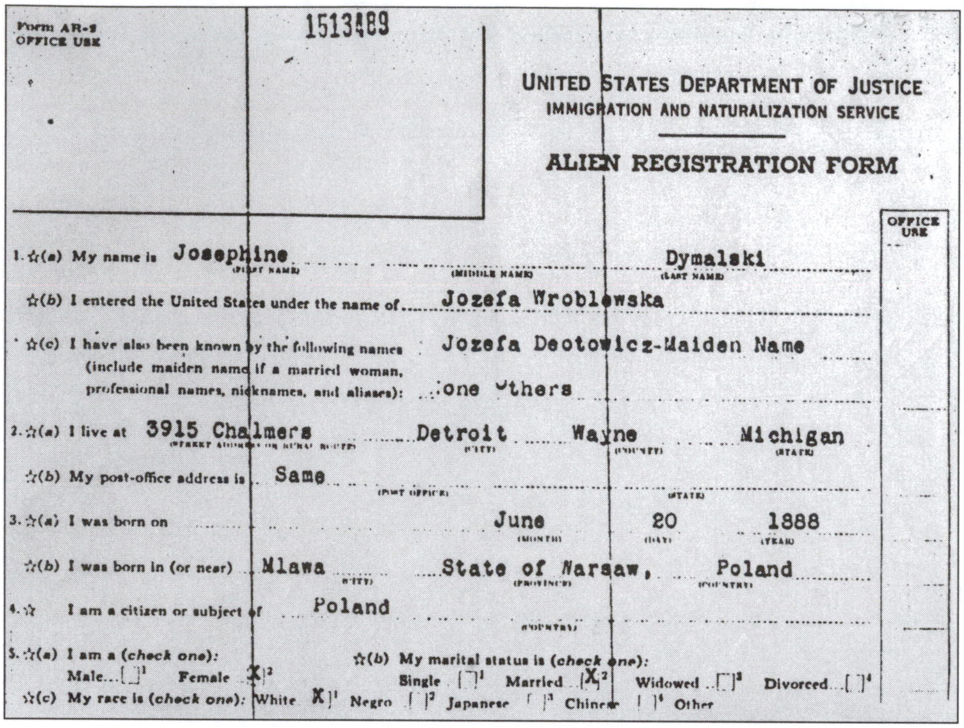
Form AR-2
OFFICE USE
1513489

UNITED STATES DEPARTMENT OF JUSTICE
IMMIGRATION AND NATURALIZATION SERVICE

ALIEN REGISTRATION FORM

OFFICE USE

1. ☆(a) My name is Josephine (FIRST NAME) (MIDDLE NAME) Dymalski (LAST NAME)
☆(b) I entered the United States under the name of Jozefa Wroblewska
☆(c) I have also been known by the following names (include maiden name if a married woman, professional names, nicknames, and aliases): Jozefa Deotowicz-Maiden Name; one Others
2. ☆(a) I live at 3915 Chalmers (STREET ADDRESS OR RURAL ROUTE) Detroit (CITY) Wayne (COUNTY) Michigan (STATE)
☆(b) My post-office address is Same (POST OFFICE) (STATE)
3. ☆(a) I was born on June (MONTH) 20 (DAY) 1888 (YEAR)
☆(b) I was born in (or near) Mlawa (CITY) State of Warsaw, (PROVINCE) Poland (COUNTRY)
4. ☆ I am a citizen or subject of Poland (COUNTRY)
5. ☆(a) I am a (check one): Male [ ]¹ Female [X]²
☆(b) My marital status is (check one): Single [ ]¹ Married [X]² Widowed [ ]³ Divorced [ ]⁴
☆(c) My race is (check one): White [X]¹ Negro [ ]² Japanese [ ]³ Chinese [ ]⁴ Other

Figure 5-25. Alien registration form for Jozefa Wroblewska.

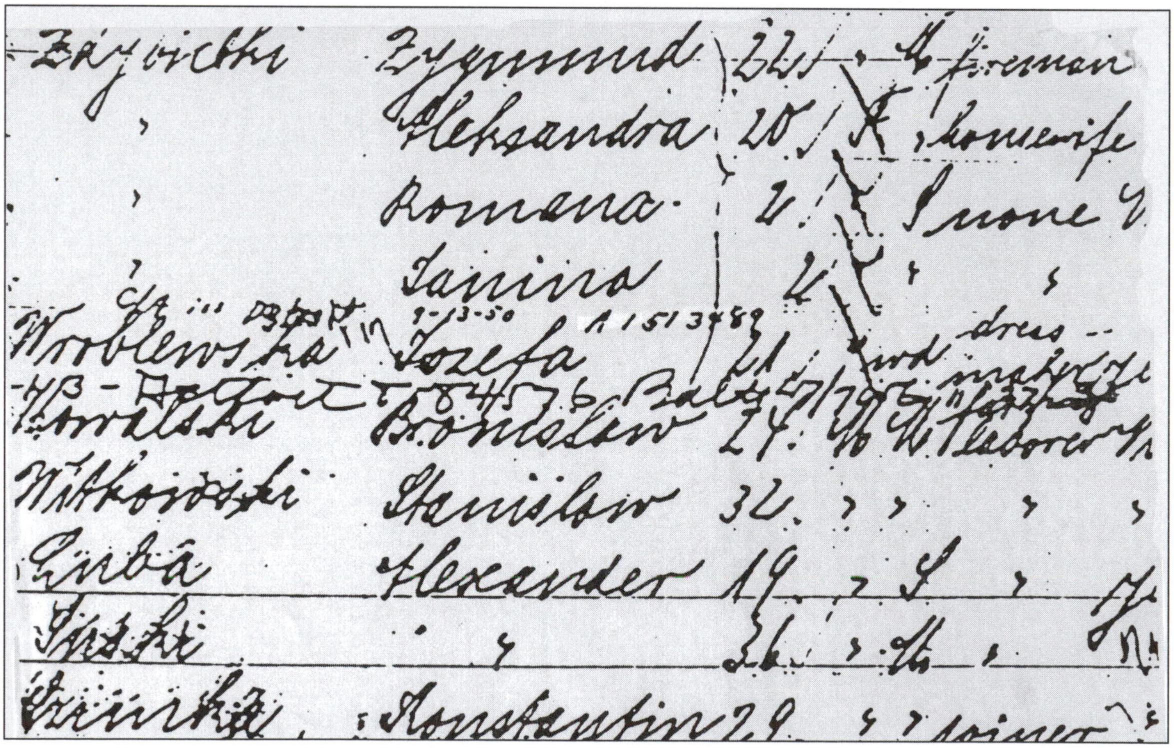
Zajoriski Zygmund 22 M foreman
Aleksandra 20 F housewife
Romana 2 F none
Janina 2
Wroblewska Jozefa 21 dress maker
9-13-50 A1513489
Kowalski Bronislaw 24 M laborer
Witkowski Stanislaw 32
Guba Alexander 19 S
Konstantin 29 joiner

Figure 5-26. Portion of a passenger list showing the "A" number that was added by the name of passenger Josefa Wroblewska. The "A" was added forty years after she arrived in the United States.

mailed to the INS district office in possession of the desired A-File. (Note: Records of some immigrants who entered the U.S. during the early twentieth century may have been moved to an A-File.)[7]

A requester may be required to pay fees for the privilege of searching, reviewing, and copying records. A requester will be notified beforehand if fees will exceed twenty-five dollars.

VERIFICATION OF IDENTITY

Verification of identity is not required for access to records available under the Freedom of Information Act. However, individuals requesting records protected under the Privacy Act must provide a privacy waiver from the subject of the record unless the Freedom of Information Act requires release of the records.

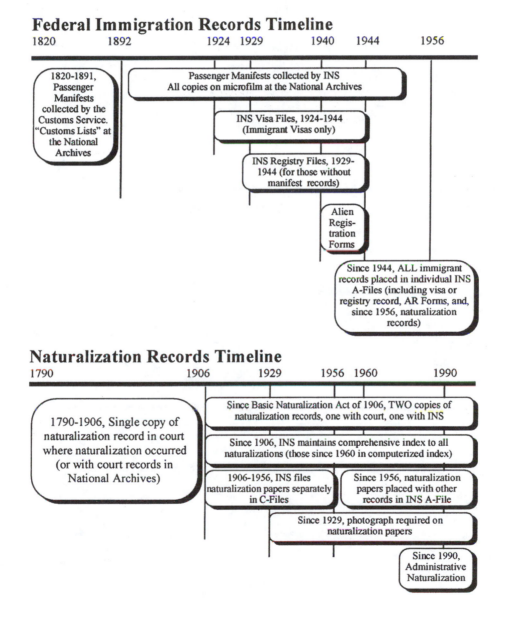

Figure 5-27. Federal Immigration and Naturalization Timelines.
Courtesy of Immigration and Naturalization Service.

Figure 5-28. Records of Mexican border entries are being microfilmed.
There are more than five hundred reels for El Paso spanning the years 1903 to 1954.

REQUESTS FOR RECORDS UNDER THE PRIVACY ACT (PA)

All requests must be submitted in writing. Under the Privacy Act, an individual who is a U.S. citizen or legal permanent resident may seek access to records that are retrieved by his or her own name or other personal identifier, such as Social Security number or employee identification number contained in INS records. Such records will be made available unless they fall within the exemptions of the Privacy Act and Freedom of Information Act.

The Privacy Act also gives individuals who are U.S. citizens or legal permanent residents a legal right to request correction or amendment of information pertaining to themselves in INS records. INS form G-639, Freedom of Information/Privacy Act Request, is again recommended for rapid identification and to ensure expeditious handling; however, requests may also be made in any written form. The request should adequately describe the types of records that the agency staff should search.

INS RECORDS IN THE NATIONAL ARCHIVES

Records no longer needed by an agency for administrative purposes and which have been judged by the National Archives staff to be of permanent (archival) value are transferred from the agency to the regional archives of the National Archives and Records Administration. The INS recently transferred all of its passenger manifests to the National Archives. Passenger lists are no longer available for research from the INS. Naturalization records at the National Archives are not INS records but are those that were created by the courts.

See chapter 6, "Naturalization Records in the National Archives," for an overview of where to find records within the National Archives' regional archives and how to use the records most effectively.

NOTES

1. Kansas, Sidney. *U.S. Immigration Exclusion and Deportation and Citizenship of the United States of America.* 3rd ed. New York: Matthew Bender Co., 1948, 3.
2. Ibid., 4.
3. Smith, Marian L. "Interpreting U.S. Immigration Manifest Annotations." *Avotaynu: The International Review of Jewish Genealogy* 12 (1): 10–13 (Spring 1996), 10.
4. Ibid., 11.
5. Smith, Marian L. "Repatriation of American-Born Women who Lost U.S. Citizenship by Marriage to an Alien." *Somos Primos: A Quarterly Publication of the Society of Hispanic Historical and Ancestral Research* 8 (1): 10–11 (Winter 1997).
6. Ibid., 11.
7. Smith, Marian. "Ellis Islands en la Frontera: U.S./Mexican Border Arrival Manifests and other INS Records for Hispanic Family History Research." Leaflet. Washington, D.C., April 1997.

BIBLIOGRAPHY

Colletta, John P. *They Came in Ships: A Guide to Finding Your Immigrant Ancestor's Arrival Record.* 2nd ed., rev. and enl. Salt Lake City: Ancestry, 1993.

Kansas, Sidney. *U.S. Immigration Exclusion and Deportation and Citizenship of the United States of America.* 3rd ed. New York: Matthew Bender Co., 1948.

Smith, Marian L. "Interpreting U.S. Immigration Manifest Annotations." *Avotaynu: The International Review of Jewish Genealogy* 12 (1): 10–13 (Spring 1996).

_____. "Repatriation of American-Born Women who Lost U.S. Citizenship by Marriage to an Alien." *Somos Primos: A Quarterly Publication of the Society of Hispanic Historical and Ancestral Research* 8 (1): 10–11 (Winter 1997).

_____. "Ellis Islands en la Frontera: U.S. Mexican Border Arrival Manifests and other INS Records for Hispanic Family History Research." Leaflet. Washington, D.C., 1997.

Chapter Six Highlights

CHAPTER SIX

Naturalization Records in the National Archives

By FAR THE GREATEST NUMBER OF NATURALIZATION records in the National Archives and its regional archives come from the district courts of the United States (Record Group, or RG, 21). Because of the close relationship of the record groups containing naturalization information, researchers should also consider the records of the Immigration and Naturalization Service (RG 85).

The exceptionally high research value of these records, coupled with the many exceptions and variances in the naturalization holdings and indexes in the National Archives regional system, dictates a special treatment of this record category. Some of the regional archives have naturalization records and indexes from local (non-federal) courts. In addition, many have acquired indexes created by the WPA that combine local and federal court records and, in some cases, those created by the Immigration and Naturalization Service.

Some courts have relinquished most of their naturalization records to the National Archives while retaining custody of the indexes, making it still necessary to consult the court for a file number to access a document. A state-by-state listing of naturalization records and indexes held by the National Archives and its regional archives appears at the end of this discussion.

Naturalization documents are among the most heavily used textual records in the National Archives system. America is a nation of immigrants, and, through naturalization records, genealogists, historians, and other scholars can document histories of individuals and groups of immigrants. Additionally, naturalization records often contain information that cannot be found in any other source. The destruction of the 1890 census makes naturalization records a source of unparalleled value for the two-decade gap between the 1880 and 1900 censuses.

As noted earlier in this book, under the First Naturalization Act of 26 March 1790 (1 Stat. 103), an alien's application could be filed in any common law court of record. Under this and various other laws, aliens were naturalized regularly in local courts until 1906. Although the following listing attests to the occurrence of naturalizations in the federal courts, the greater number took place in local courts, so a search of county courts could be more productive for a specialized search.

Further, a researcher should understand that while the naturalization process may have begun in one place, an individual's move to another state or county may have dictated its completion in another court. Under these circumstances, records may be found in two or more different locations. Very often, the naturalization procedure began with the declaration of intention in the county where the immigrant first took up residency in the United States, and the petition for naturalization and final oath being completed in another county, often geographically distant from the first court. An example is that of Mathias Welsch, who declared his intention to become a naturalized citizen in the Probate Court of Mahoning County, Ohio in 1903, and completed the naturalization process with the filing of his petition for naturalization in the U.S. Circuit Court, Chicago, Illinois, in 1908 (figures 6-1 and 6-2).

THE NATIONAL ARCHIVES, WASHINGTON, D.C.

Microfilm Research Room (Room 400)
Eighth and Pennsylvania Avenue NW
Washington, DC 20408

Telephone: 202-501-5400
202-501-5410 (genealogical staff)
E-mail: inquire@arch1.nara.gov
URL: http://www.nara.gov/nara/dc/Archives1_info.html
Fax: 301-713-6905 (fax-on-demand information)

The Microfilm Research Room (Room 400) in the National Archives building in downtown Washington, D.C., has some microfilmed federal court naturalization indexes, declarations, and petitions. However, as Claire Prechtel-Kluskens notes in "The Location of Naturalization Records" in *The Record: News from the National Archives and Records Administration* 3 (2): 22 (November 1996), "it is by no means a complete collection of these records. To repeat, most Federal naturalization records are found in the National Archives Regional Archives serving the state in which the Federal court is located."

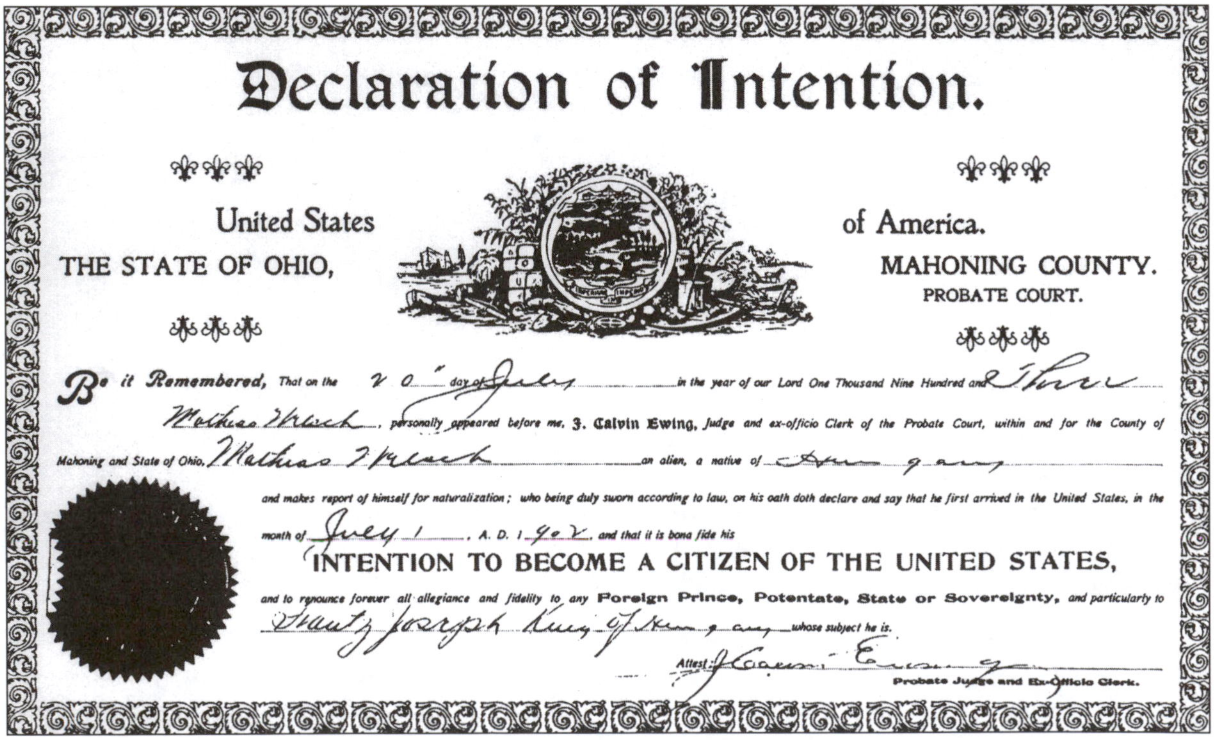

Declaration of Intention.

United States of America.
THE STATE OF OHIO, MAHONING COUNTY.
PROBATE COURT.

Be it Remembered, That on the 20th day of July in the year of our Lord One Thousand Nine Hundred and Three Mathias Welsch, personally appeared before me, J. Calvin Ewing, Judge and ex-officio Clerk of the Probate Court, within and for the County of Mahoning and State of Ohio, Mathias Welsch an alien, a native of Hungary and makes report of himself for naturalization; who being duly sworn according to law, on his oath doth declare and say that he first arrived in the United States, in the month of July 1, A. D. 1902, and that it is bona fide his

INTENTION TO BECOME A CITIZEN OF THE UNITED STATES,

and to renounce forever all allegiance and fidelity to any Foreign Prince, Potentate, State or Sovereignty, and particularly to Frantz Joseph King of Hungary whose subject he is.

Attest: J. Calvin Ewing
Probate Judge and Ex-Officio Clerk.

Figure 6-1. Declaration of intention for Mathias Welsch from Probate Court, Mahoning County, Ohio, 1903.

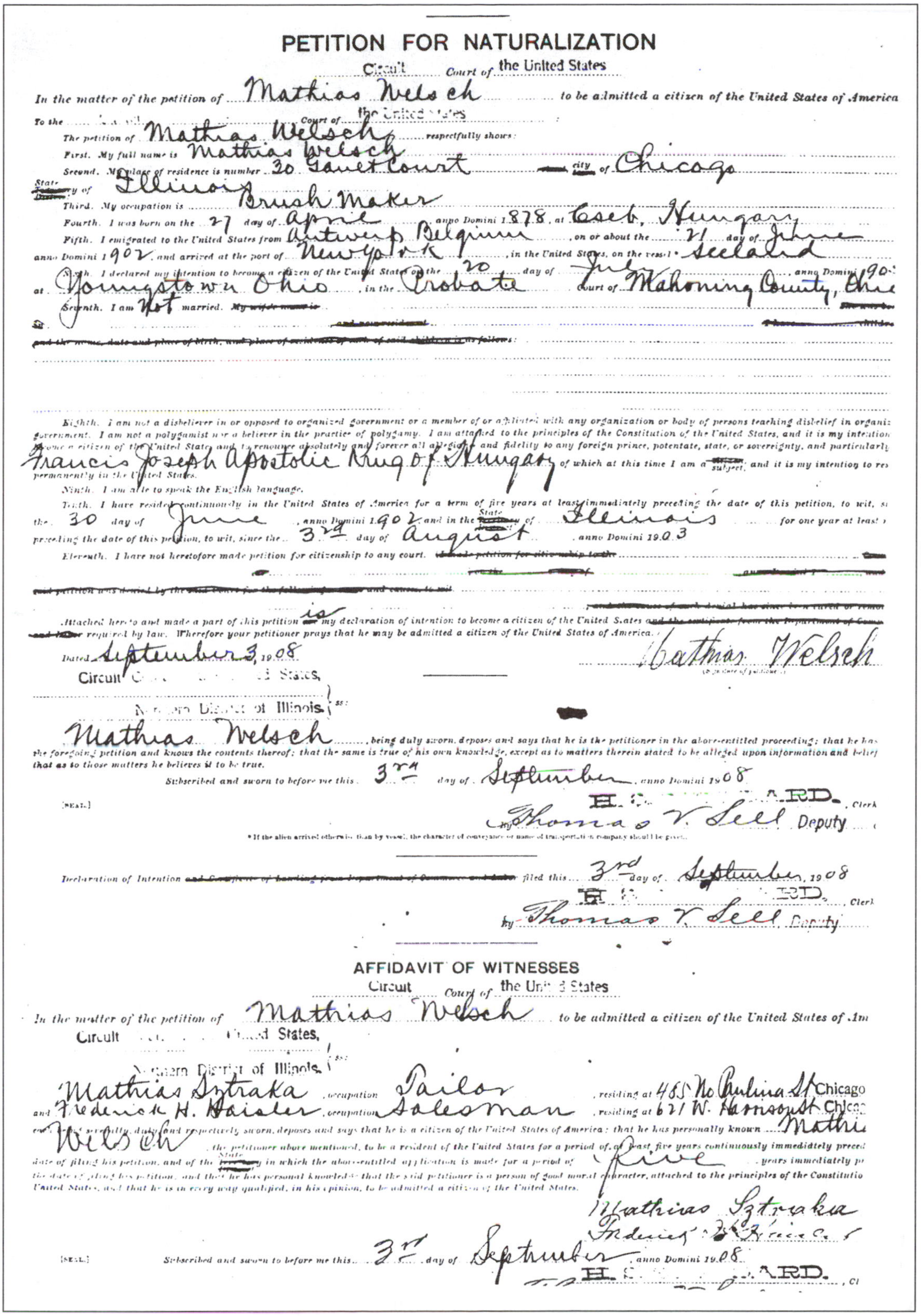

PETITION FOR NATURALIZATION

Circuit Court of the United States

In the matter of the petition of Mathias Welsch to be admitted a citizen of the United States of America

To the Circuit Court of the United States

The petition of Mathias Welsch respectfully shows:

First. My full name is Mathias Welsch

Second. My place of residence is number 30 Gault Court city of Chicago State of Illinois

Third. My occupation is Brush Maker

Fourth. I was born on the 27 day of April anno Domini 1878, at Cseb, Hungary

Fifth. I emigrated to the United States from Antwerp, Belgium on or about the 21 day of June anno Domini 1902, and arrived at the port of New York, in the United States, on the vessel* Seeland

Sixth. I declared my intention to become a citizen of the United States on the 20 day of July anno Domini 1903 at Youngstown Ohio in the Probate Court of Mahoning County, Ohio

Seventh. I am not married. ~~My wife's name is~~ ~~and now resides~~ ~~I have~~ ~~children, and the name, date and place of birth, and place of residence of said children is as follows:~~

Eighth. I am not a disbeliever in or opposed to organized government or a member of or affiliated with any organization or body of persons teaching disbelief in organized government. I am not a polygamist nor a believer in the practice of polygamy. I am attached to the principles of the Constitution of the United States, and it is my intention to become a citizen of the United States and to renounce absolutely and forever all allegiance and fidelity to any foreign prince, potentate, state, or sovereignty, and particularly to Francis Joseph Apostolic King of Hungary of which at this time I am a subject, and it is my intention to reside permanently in the United States.

Ninth. I am able to speak the English language.

Tenth. I have resided continuously in the United States of America for a term of five years at least immediately preceding the date of this petition, to wit, since the 30 day of June anno Domini 1902 and in the State of Illinois for one year at least immediately preceding the date of this petition, to wit, since the 3rd day of August anno Domini 1903

Eleventh. I have not heretofore made petition for citizenship to any court. ~~I made petition for citizenship to the~~ ~~Court of~~ ~~and said petition was denied by the said Court for the following reasons and causes, to wit:~~ ~~and the cause of such denial has since been cured or removed.~~

Attached hereto and made a part of this petition is my declaration of intention to become a citizen of the United States ~~and the certificate from the Department of Commerce and Labor~~ required by law. Wherefore your petitioner prays that he may be admitted a citizen of the United States of America.

Dated September 3, 1908 — Mathias Welsch (Signature of petitioner.)

Circuit Court of the United States, Northern District of Illinois, } ss:

Mathias Welsch, being duly sworn, deposes and says that he is the petitioner in the above-entitled proceeding; that he has read the foregoing petition and knows the contents thereof; that the same is true of his own knowledge, except as to matters therein stated to be alleged upon information and belief, and that as to those matters he believes it to be true.

Subscribed and sworn to before me this 3rd day of September, anno Domini 1908

[SEAL.] H. C. [illegible]ARD, Clerk. By Thomas V. Sell Deputy

* If the alien arrived otherwise than by vessel, the character of conveyance or name of transportation company should be given.

Declaration of Intention ~~and Certificate of Arrival from Department of Commerce and Labor~~ filed this 3rd day of September, 1908

H. C. [illegible]ARD, Clerk. By Thomas V. Sell Deputy

AFFIDAVIT OF WITNESSES

Circuit Court of the United States

In the matter of the petition of Mathias Welsch to be admitted a citizen of the United States of America

Circuit Court of the United States, Northern District of Illinois, } ss:

Mathias Sztraka occupation Tailor, residing at 485 No. Paulina St. Chicago and Frederick H. Haisler occupation Salesman, residing at 621 W. Harrison St. Chicago each being severally, duly, and respectively sworn, deposes and says that he is a citizen of the United States of America; that he has personally known Mathias Welsch the petitioner above mentioned, to be a resident of the United States for a period of at least five years continuously immediately preceding the date of filing his petition, and of the State in which the above-entitled application is made for a period of five years immediately preceding the date of filing his petition, and that he has personal knowledge that the said petitioner is a person of good moral character, attached to the principles of the Constitution of the United States, and that he is in every way qualified, in his opinion, to be admitted a citizen of the United States.

Mathias Sztraka

Frederick H. Haisler

[SEAL.] Subscribed and sworn to before me this 3rd day of September, anno Domini 1908

H. C. [illegible]ARD, Cl

Figure 6-2. Petition for Naturalization for Mathias Welsch from U.S. Circuit Court, Chicago, 1908.

REGIONAL ARCHIVES

You don't have to go to Washington, D.C., to visit the National Archives. The National Archives and Records Administration (NARA) has regional archives in Boston, Pittsfield (Massachusetts), New York, Philadelphia, Atlanta, Chicago, Kansas City, Fort Worth (Texas), Denver, Laguna Niguel (Los Angeles), San Francisco, Seattle, and Anchorage. These are national resources in local settings.

In 1969 the archivist of the United States established a regional archives system to make regionally created, historically valuable federal records more accessible to the public. Each regional archives in the system has historical records from federal courts and from regional offices of federal agencies in the geographic areas each serves.

Records preserved at regional archives (except Pittsfield) document federal government policies and programs at the local and regional levels. They are kept because of their permanent historical, fiscal, and legal value and for their importance to the continuing work of the U.S. government.

Records transferred to any of the regional offices of the National Archives are controlled by the National Archives and Records Administration (NARA), which is responsible for the use of the records in its custody. Archival holdings are made available to agency staff and the public unless access is restricted on recommendation of the transferring agency (such as the U.S. courts). All such restrictions must be consistent with exemptions listed in the Freedom of Information Act. Some INS records in the National Archives (RG 85) are of particular interest to family historians.

As with any other archive or library, it is wise to call in advance of a visit to check on hours of operation and research policies; they vary somewhat from region to region. If you plan to use microfilmed records, you may need to call ahead to make an appointment because the availability of microfilm readers is limited at some facilities.

Before using original records (such as original naturalization papers), every researcher must obtain a researcher identification card. An applicant must show identification that includes a photograph, such as a driver's license, school or business identification, or passport, and complete a short form giving name, address, telephone number, and brief description of the proposed research topic. A researcher ID card, valid for two years and renewable, is then issued. It must be presented during each research visit.

NARA NORTHEAST REGION (BOSTON)

Frederick C. Murphy Federal Center
380 Trapelo Road
Waltham, MA 02154-6399
Telephone: 781-647-8100
E-mail: archives@waltham.nara.gov
Fax: 781-647-8460

The National Archives' Northeast Region (Boston) has more than twenty-five thousand cubic feet of historical records dating from 1789 to the 1970s, including some photographs, maps, and architectural drawings. These records were created or received by the federal courts and more than eighty federal agencies in Maine, New Hampshire, Vermont, Massachusetts, Rhode Island, and Connecticut.

Records of naturalization proceedings in federal courts are usually among the records of the district in which such proceedings took place. As stated, these records may still be in the custody of the court or may have been transferred to the National Archives. In a few cases, the National Archives has copies of local court naturalizations. The Northeast Region (Boston), for example, has five- by eight-inch photographic copies of naturalization declarations, petitions, and records from a number of federal, state, and local courts in Maine, Massachusetts, New Hampshire, Rhode Island, and Vermont which were made by the WPA in the 1930s. The copies are for naturalization proceedings which took place from 1787 to 1906. An accompanying card index covers the six New England states (including all Connecticut courts to 1940). The index is also available on microfilm.

ALIEN REGISTRATION

Registration of aliens with a local court of record was required from 1802 to 1828. (Customs officers in Salem and Beverly, Massachusetts, recorded passenger lists with aliens clearly marked, 1798–1800. These records are in the National Archives.) Enforcing this law during the War of 1812 has given us some valuable data for persons immigrating after 1800. Many of these are indexed in the Passenger and Immigration Lists Index (see chapter 2).

Under the 1929 Alien Registration Act, aliens were again required to register their current residence and place of employment annually with the federal government. Immigrant identification cards, certificates of registry, certificates of lawful entry, certificates of arrival, and alien registration cards are forms of identification. All aliens were required to carry one of these identification cards with them to be considered legal aliens; any alien without one of them could be deported without a hearing. If they still exist, these cards or certificates are usually found among home sources.

NARA NORTHEAST REGION (PITTSFIELD)

10 Conte Drive
Pittsfield, MA 01201-8230
Telephone: 413-445-6885
E-mail: archives@pittsfield.nara.gov
Fax: 413-445-7599

The National Archives' Northeast Region (Pittsfield) has almost sixty thousand rolls of National Archives microfilm publications, created to allow access to

Figure 6-3. Records found in the National Archives' regional archives offer a host of potential research uses, both general and specific.

information while preserving original documents from deterioration and damage from handling. Microfilm holdings include an index to New England naturalization petitions, 1791 to 1906; an index to naturalization petitions and records of the U.S. District Court, 1906 to 1966, and the U.S. Circuit Court, 1906 to 1911, for the District of Massachusetts; and petitions and other naturalization records of the U.S. District Court and Circuit Courts of the District of Massachusetts, 1906 to 1929.

NARA Northeast Region (New York City)

201 Varick Street
New York, NY 10014-4811
Telephone: 212-337-1300
E-mail: archives@newyork.nara.gov
Fax: 212-337-1306

The National Archives' Northeast Region (New York City) has more than sixty-three thousand cubic feet of historical records dating from 1685 to the 1980s, among them photographs, maps, and architectural drawings. These records were created or received by the federal courts and more than sixty federal agencies in New Jersey, New York, Puerto Rico, and the U.S. Virgin Islands.

The Northeast Region (New York City) has photocopies of naturalization documents filed in federal, state, and local courts located in New York City, 1792 to 1906; photocopies of court indexes to the naturalization records; and a comprehensive card index to the naturalization records. The card index is arranged by name of individual naturalized according to the Soundex system. The photocopies and original index were made by the WPA. The branch also has case files relating to Chinese immigrants and the Exclusion Act of 1902. The case files include correspondence, reports, interrogations,

STATE OF PENNSYLVANIA
County of Philada.
being first duly

UNITED STATES OF AMERICA
ORIGINAL
Certificate of Residence.
Issued to Chinese Laborer, under the Provisions of the Act of May 5, 1892, as amended by the Act approved November 3, 1893.

This is to Certify That Mrs. Toy Yee, a Chinese Laborer, now residing at Philada has made application No. 837 to me for a Certificate of Residence, under the provisions of the Act of Congress approved May 5, 1892, as amended by the Act approved November 3, 1893, and I certify that it appears from the affidavit of witness submitted with said application that said Mrs. Toy Yee was within the limits of the United States at the time of the passage of said Act, and was then residing at Philadelphia, and that he was at that time lawfully entitled to remain in the United States, and that the following is a descriptive list of said Chinese Laborer, viz:

Name: Mrs. Toy Yee — Age: 28 years
Local Residence: 918 Race St.
Occupation: Housekeeper — Height: 5 ft. 1" — Color of Eyes: Black
Complexion: Bright — Physical Marks or Peculiarities for Identification: Heavy scar alongside of right eye

And as a further means of identification I have affixed hereto a photographic likeness of said Mrs Toy Yee

Given under my hand and seal this ... of April 1894 at Philadelphia, State of Penna.

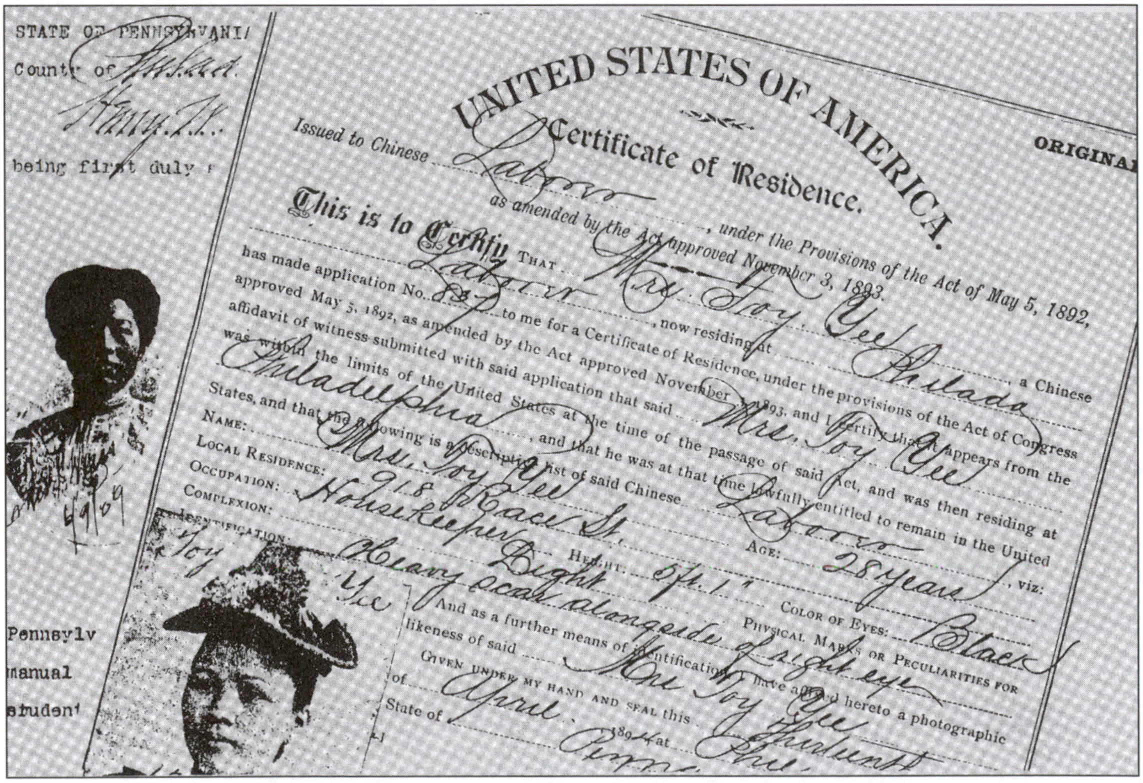

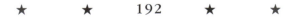

Figure 6-4. Certificate of residence. From the Immigration and Naturalization Service, RG 85, National Archives–Mid-Atlantic Region, Philadelphia.

1616.

PRINTED BY J. WILSON, WILMINGTON.

At a Special District court of the United States, holden at Wilmington in and for the District of Delaware, on the Second day of September in the year of our Lord, one thousand eight hundred and Two and of the Independence of the United States of America the Twentyseventh before the honorable Gunning Bedford Esquire Judge of the Court aforesaid.

Be it remembered, that on the day and year aforesaid, came into Court Elenthere Frénée dupont aged years, or thereabouts, a native of France subject to the French Republic residing in Wilmington in the District aforesaid, and his occupation a and made oath in open court, that it was bona fide his intention to become a citizen of the United States, and to renounce forever all allegiance and fidelity to any foreign, prince, potentate, state or sovereignty whatever, and particular to the Republic of France whereof he was before a subject. Pursuant to the provision of the Act of Congress of the United States, passed April 14th, 1802, entitled "An Act to establish an uniform rule of naturalization, and to repeal the Acts heretofore passed on that subject."

By the Court.

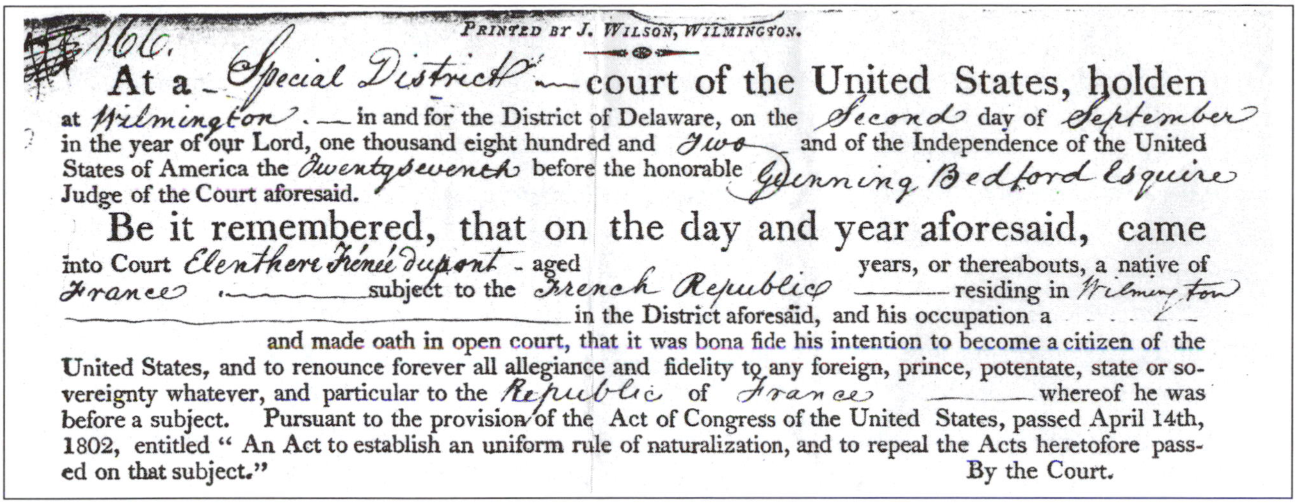

Figure 6-5. 1802 naturalization of Elenthere Frénée Dupont. From the Special District Court of Wilmington, Delaware. The original record is at the National Archives—Mid-Atlantic Region, Philadelphia.

transcripts of testimony, and exhibits; they cover the period 1921 to 1944.

NARA Mid-Atlantic Region (Center City Philadelphia)

900 Market Street
Philadelphia, PA 19107-4292
Telephone: 215-597-3000
E-mail: archives@philarch.nara.gov
Fax: 215-597-2303

The National Archives' Mid-Atlantic Region (Center City Philadelphia) has more than fifty thousand cubic feet of historical records, among them photographs, maps, and architectural drawings, dating from 1789 to 1989. These records were created or received by the federal courts and more than fifty federal agencies in Delaware, Maryland, Pennsylvania, Virginia, and West Virginia.

The records of the Immigration and Naturalization Service in the Mid-Atlantic Region include those of the District 4 Field Office, headquartered in Philadelphia. The records of the Office of the Commissioner of Immigration include office diaries, 1882 to 1903; a register of immigrant arrivals, 1892; a register of detained immigrants, 1901 to 1912; aliens' applications for permission to depart the United States, 1918 to 1919; manifests debarred and returned to foreign ports, 1891 to 1917; departure reports of aliens, 1942 to 1951; lists of deported immigrants from the ports of Philadelphia, New York, Boston, and Baltimore; and records of the Special Board of Inquiry—Philadelphia, 1893 to 1909. With the exception of aliens' applications to depart the United States, all are unindexed.

The Mid-Atlantic Region has registers of aliens, 1798 to 1812, for the U.S. District Court for the Eastern District of Pennsylvania. The registers of aliens record primarily those French immigrants required to register with the clerk of the court during the Quasi-War with France. The records which are indexed provide a rich source of personal information for the individuals registered; taken as a whole, they provide a unique source for the study of that segment of society.

Of special interest are the records of the Special Board of Inquiry. They provide interrogation testimony of immigrant arrivals who were detained and who requested to appear before the Special Board of Inquiry. The region also has passenger lists for the airship Hindenburg leaving Lakehurst Naval Air Station in New Jersey. Chinese case files in the possession of the Mid-Atlantic Region date from 1895 to

1920; however, some files include material from as late as 1952. These cases concern attempts to enforce the various Chinese exclusion laws. Included are applications for permission of Chinese merchants and laborers to depart and return to the United States, applications for certificates of residence and certificates of identity, illegal entry and Chinese student reports, and the report of the Chinese census of 1905 for parts of Pennsylvania, New Jersey, Delaware, Maryland, Virginia, and West Virginia. Almost all of the case files pertaining to individual Chinese contain still photographs of the individuals.

The Mid-Atlantic Region has the following microfilm publications: *Index to Naturalization Petitions for Eastern District Court of Pennsylvania, 1795–1951; Index to Naturalization Petitions for the Middle District of Pennsylvania, 1901–1990; Index to Naturalization Petitions for the Western District Court of Pennsylvania, 1820–1906; Index to Naturalization Petitions for the District of Delaware, 1795–1926; Index to Naturalization Petitions for the District of Maryland, 1795–1951; Records of the Special Board of Inquiry from District No. 4, Philadelphia, 1893–1909;* and *Records of Chinese Case Files from District No. 4, Philadelphia, 1900–1923*.

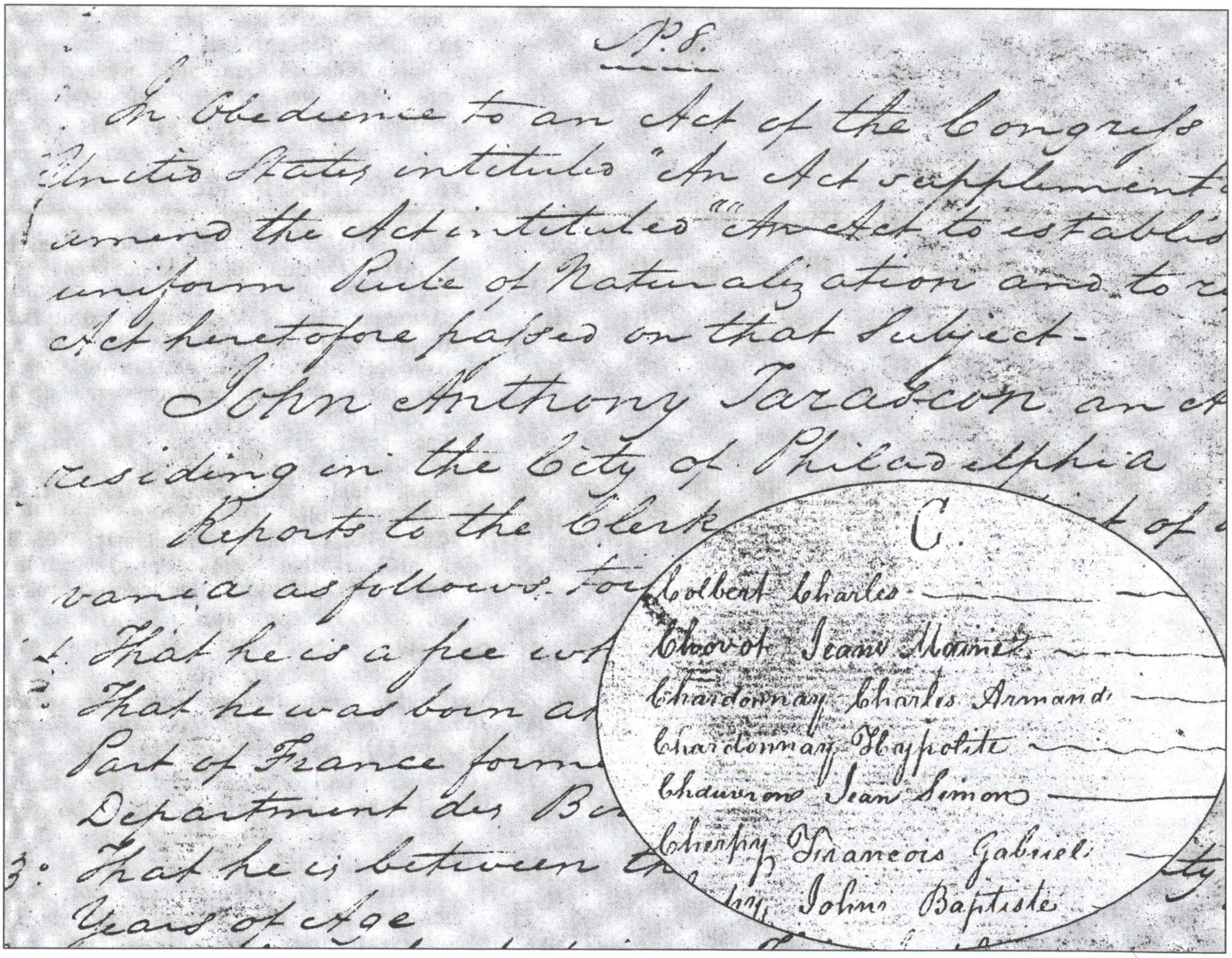
N°. 8.
In Obedience to an Act of the Congress
United States intituled "An Act supplement
amend the Act intituled "An Act to establi
uniform Rule of Naturalization and to r
Act heretofore passed on that Subject.
John Anthony Tarascon an
residing in the City of Philadelphia
Reports to the Clerk
vania as follows: to
1. That he is a free wh
2. That he was born a
Part of France form
Department des B
3. That he is between th
Years of Age

C.
Colbert Charles
Chardonnay Charles Armand
Chardonnay Hypolite
Chauvron Jean Simon
John Baptiste

Figure 6-6. 1798 French alien registration and index. From U.S. District Court for the Eastern District of Pennsylvania (RG 21).

Figure 6-7. Microfilmed census records in the National Archives' regional archives often form the starting point for finding ethnic origins.

NARA SOUTHEAST REGION

1557 St. Joseph Avenue

East Point, GA 30344-2593

Telephone: 404-763-7477/7383

E-mail: archives@atlanta.nara.gov

Fax: 404-763-7033

The National Archives' Southeast Region has approximately seventy thousand cubic feet of archival holdings dating from 1716 to the 1980s—primarily textual records but also maps, photographs, and architectural drawings. These records were created or received by the federal courts and more than one hundred federal agencies; they are unique evidence of the impact of federal government policies and programs in Alabama, Florida, Georgia, Kentucky, Mississippi, North Carolina, South Carolina, and Tennessee.

The Southeast Region has naturalization petitions and indexes to naturalizations in some federal courts from throughout the southeastern states listed above. See the detailed listings by state for more information. Most of the naturalization petitions which the Southeast Region does not have (after 1906) are still held by the clerk's offices of various federal courts. Contact them directly for reference service.

The Southeast Region has the following microfilm publications: M1183 (1 roll), Record of Admissions to Citizenship, District of South Carolina, 1790–1906; M1547 (107 rolls), Naturalization Records of U.S. District Courts in the Southeast, 1790–1958. (Few of the microfilm records date past 1945. Not all courts are included.)

The Southeast Region has a copy of the WPA Index to Naturalization Records in State and Local Courts for Mississippi, 1798 to 1906. These are arranged by county and thereunder alphabetically. The index cites state and local records. Copies of most of these are held by the Mississippi State Archives.

NARA CENTRAL PLAINS REGION

2312 East Bannister Road
Kansas City, MO 64131-3011
Telephone: 816-926-6272
E-mail: archives@kansascity.nara.gov
Fax: 816-926-6982

The National Archives' Central Plains Region has more than thirty-five thousand cubic feet of historical records, among them photographs, maps, and architectural drawings, dating from around 1820 to the 1980s. These records were created or received by the federal courts and more than seventy federal agencies in Iowa, Kansas, Minnesota, Missouri, Nebraska, North Dakota, and South Dakota.

The Central Plains Region maintains some naturalization records for the U.S. district courts for the districts of southern Iowa, Kansas, Minnesota, and eastern and western Missouri. Although records of these proceedings are in the custody of the Central Plains Region, the indexes necessary to use the records generally remain with the courts.

NARA GREAT LAKES REGION

7358 South Pulaski Road
Chicago, IL 60629-5898
Telephone: 773-581-7816
E-mail: archives@chicago.nara.gov
Fax: 312-353-1294

The National Archives' Great Lakes Region has more than sixty-five thousand cubic feet of historical records dating from 1800 to the 1980s, including textual records and non-textual records (such as maps and photographs) from federal courts and some eighty-five federal agencies in Illinois, Indiana, Michigan, Minnesota, Ohio, and Wisconsin.

The Great Lakes Region has two general groups of Immigration and Naturalization Service records. One is a card index (using the Soundex system) of individuals naturalized in county and federal courts in what was INS District 9 (northern Illinois, including Chicago and Cook County; southern and eastern Wisconsin; eastern Iowa; and northwest Indiana). The index covers the period 1840 to 1950 (except Cook

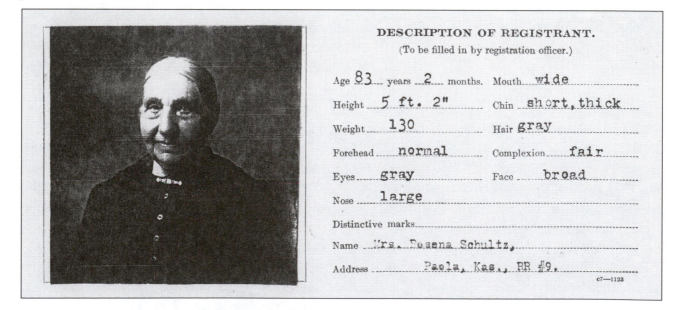

Figure 6-8. An alien registration card from the National Archives' Central Plains Region.

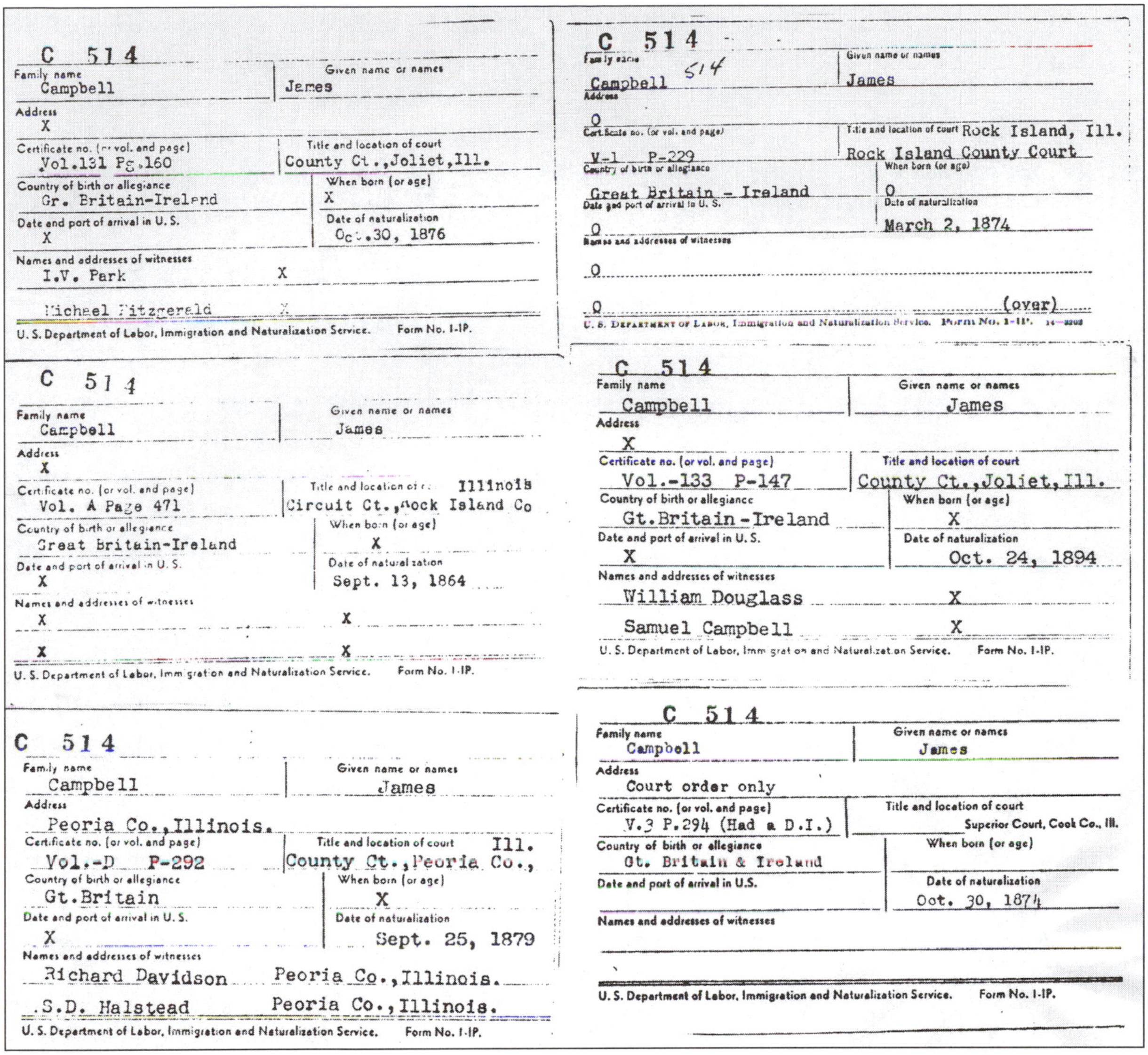

C 514
Family name: Campbell
Given name or names: James
Address: X
Certificate no. (or vol. and page): Vol.131 Pg.160
Title and location of court: County Ct.,Joliet,Ill.
Country of birth or allegiance: Gr. Britain-Ireland
When born (or age): X
Date and port of arrival in U. S.: X
Date of naturalization: Oct.30, 1876
Names and addresses of witnesses: I.V. Park X
Michael Fitzgerald X
U. S. Department of Labor, Immigration and Naturalization Service. Form No. 1-IP.

C 514
Family name: Campbell 514
Given name or names: James
Address: 0
Certificate no. (or vol. and page): V-1 P-229
Title and location of court: Rock Island, Ill. Rock Island County Court
Country of birth or allegiance: Great Britain - Ireland
When born (or age): 0
Date and port of arrival in U. S.: 0
Date of naturalization: March 2, 1874
Names and addresses of witnesses: 0
0 (over)
U. S. Department of Labor, Immigration and Naturalization Service. Form No. 1-IP.

C 514
Family name: Campbell
Given name or names: James
Address: X
Certificate no. (or vol. and page): Vol. A Page 471
Title and location of court: Illinois Circuit Ct.,Rock Island Co
Country of birth or allegiance: Great Britain-Ireland
When born (or age): X
Date and port of arrival in U. S.: X
Date of naturalization: Sept. 13, 1864
Names and addresses of witnesses: X X
X X
U. S. Department of Labor, Immigration and Naturalization Service. Form No. 1-IP.

C 514
Family name: Campbell
Given name or names: James
Address: X
Certificate no. (or vol. and page): Vol.-133 P-147
Title and location of court: County Ct.,Joliet,Ill.
Country of birth or allegiance: Gt.Britain-Ireland
When born (or age): X
Date and port of arrival in U. S.: X
Date of naturalization: Oct. 24, 1894
Names and addresses of witnesses: William Douglass X
Samuel Campbell X
U. S. Department of Labor, Immigration and Naturalization Service. Form No. 1-IP.

C 514
Family name: Campbell
Given name or names: James
Address: Peoria Co.,Illinois.
Certificate no. (or vol. and page): Vol.-D P-292
Title and location of court: Ill. County Ct.,Peoria Co.,
Country of birth or allegiance: Gt.Britain
When born (or age): X
Date and port of arrival in U. S.: X
Date of naturalization: Sept. 25, 1879
Names and addresses of witnesses: Richard Davidson Peoria Co.,Illinois.
S.D. Halstead Peoria Co.,Illinois.
U. S. Department of Labor, Immigration and Naturalization Service. Form No. 1-IP.

C 514
Family name: Campbell
Given name or names: James
Address: Court order only
Certificate no. (or vol. and page): V.3 P.294 (Had a D.I.)
Title and location of court: Superior Court, Cook Co., Ill.
Country of birth or allegiance: Gt. Britain & Ireland
When born (or age):
Date and port of arrival in U.S.:
Date of naturalization: Oct. 30, 1874
Names and addresses of witnesses:
U. S. Department of Labor, Immigration and Naturalization Service. Form No. 1-IP.

Figure 6-9. With so little identifying biographical information provided on these Soundex cards, it is virtually impossible to distinguish one James Campbell from another. Common names are especially problematical. There are probably close to fifty cards for individuals by the name of James Campbell in the index, but there is little information to be found on most cards reflecting pre-1906 naturalizations. Note that the cards generally reflect the degree of information provided in the actual naturalization documents. If there is no date or place of birth or date and port of arrival, it is usually because the actual documents do not contain this information.

County, which dates from 1871 because of the loss of records in the Great Chicago Fire of that year).

The second series of INS records at the Great Lakes Region consists of segregated Chinese case files and correspondence generated as a result of the Chinese exclusion laws. These are from the Chicago District Office (1898 to 1940) and the St. Paul District Office (1906 to 1942). The files document investigations of individuals and contain considerable biographic data. They are a good source for the history of social and economic life in the Chinese community at the turn of the century.

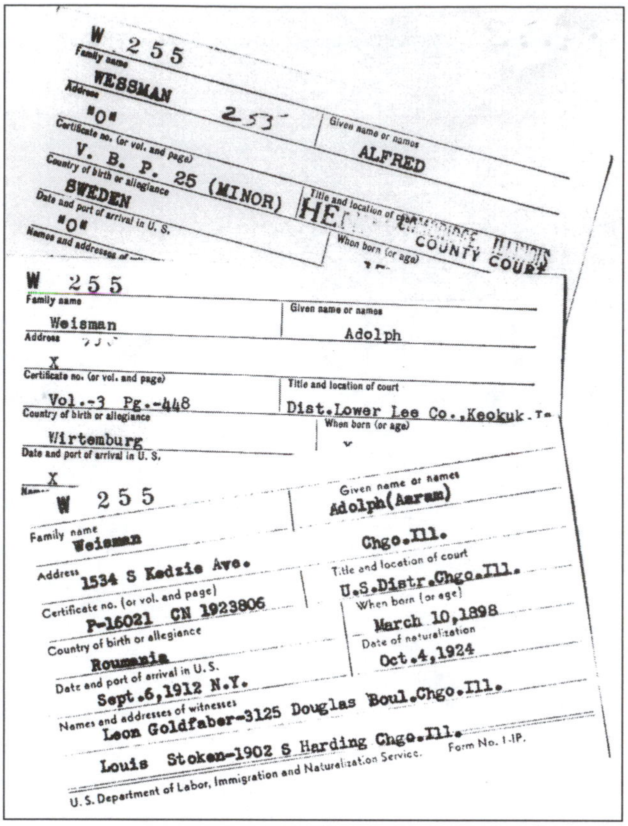
W 255
Family name
WESSMAN
Address
"O" 253
Given name or names
ALFRED
Certificate no. (or vol. and page)
V. B. P. 25 (MINOR)
Country of birth or allegiance
SWEDEN
Title and location of court
HENRY COUNTY COURT
Date and port of arrival in U. S.
"O"
When born (or age)
Names and addresses of witnesses

W 255
Family name
Weisman
Given name or names
Adolph
Address
X
Certificate no. (or vol. and page)
Vol.-3 Pg.-448
Title and location of court
Dist.Lower Lee Co.,Keokuk
Country of birth or allegiance
Wirtemburg
When born (or age)
Date and port of arrival in U. S.
X

W 255
Family name
Weisman
Given name or names
Adolph(Aaram)
Chgo.Ill.
Address
1534 S Kedzie Ave.
Title and location of court
U.S.Distr.Chgo.Ill.
Certificate no. (or vol. and page)
P-16021 CN 1923806
When born (or age)
March 10,1898
Country of birth or allegiance
Roumania
Date of naturalization
Oct.4,1924
Date and port of arrival in U.S.
Sept.6,1912 N.Y.
Names and addresses of witnesses
Leon Goldfaber-3125 Douglas Boul.Chgo.Ill.
Louis Stoken-1902 S Harding Chgo.Ill.
Form No. 1-IP.
U. S. Department of Labor, Immigration and Naturalization Service.

Figure 6-10. While the three naturalization records are in the index at the National Archives' Great Lakes Region, the naturalization for Adolph (Aaram) Weisman is the only actual record at the Great Lakes Region. To obtain the naturalization records for Alfred Wessman, it is necessary make a request to the Henry County, Illinois County Court. To obtain the record for Adolph Weisman of Wirtemburg, it is necessary to request the record from the District Court, Lee County, Iowa.

NARA SOUTHWEST REGION

501 West Felix Street, Building 1
Fort Worth, TX 76115-3405

P.O. Box 6216
Fort Worth, TX 76115-0216

Telephone: 817-334-5525
E-mail: archives@ftworth.nara.gov
Fax: 817-334-5621

The National Archives' Southwest Region has more than sixty-six thousand cubic feet of historical records dating from 1806 to the 1980s, including photographs and maps. These records were created or received by the federal courts and eighty-five federal agencies in Arkansas, Oklahoma, Louisiana, and Texas.

The Southwest Region has a card index to certificates of naturalization issued between 1831 and 1906 by federal, state, and local courts in Louisiana. There is also a bound index to naturalization records in federal, state, and county courts in Texas which covers most Texas counties for the period 1853 to 1939. Both indexes were compiled by the WPA in the 1930s and were subsequently used by the INS.

NARA ROCKY MOUNTAIN REGION

Denver Federal Center, Building 48
Denver, CO 80225

P.O. Box 25307
Denver, CO 80225-0307

Telephone: 303-236-0817
E-mail: archives@denver.nara.gov
Fax: 303-236-9354

The National Archives' Rocky Mountain Region has in its custody more than thirty-five thousand cubic feet of historical records dating from about 1860 to the 1980s, among them photographs, maps, and architectural drawings. These records were created or received by the federal courts and more than seventy-five federal agencies in Colorado, Montana, New Mexico, North Dakota, South Dakota, Utah, and Wyoming.

In addition to the naturalization records held for the states covered in the region, the Rocky Mountain Region has microfilmed Colorado naturalization records.

NARA PACIFIC REGION (LAGUNA NIGUEL)

24000 Avila Road, First Floor—East Entrance
Laguna Niguel, CA 92677-3497

P.O. Box 6719
Laguna Niguel, CA 92607-6719

Telephone: 949-360-2641
E-mail: archives@laugna.nara.gov
Fax: 949-360-2624

The National Archives' Pacific Region (Laguna Niguel) has more than twenty-eight thousand cubic feet of historical records dating from around 1850 to the 1980s. In addition to textual records there are architectural drawings, maps, and photographs. These records were created or received by the federal courts and more than fifty federal agencies in Arizona, southern California, and Clark County, Nevada.

In addition to the naturalization records for the states covered in the region, the Pacific Region (Laguna Niguel) has some microfilmed naturalization records.

NARA PACIFIC REGION (SAN FRANCISCO)

1000 Commodore Drive
San Bruno, CA 94066-2350
Telephone: 650-876-9009
E-mail: archives@sanbruno.nara.gov
Fax: 650-876-9233

The National Archives' Pacific Region (San Francisco) has in its custody more than forty-four thousand

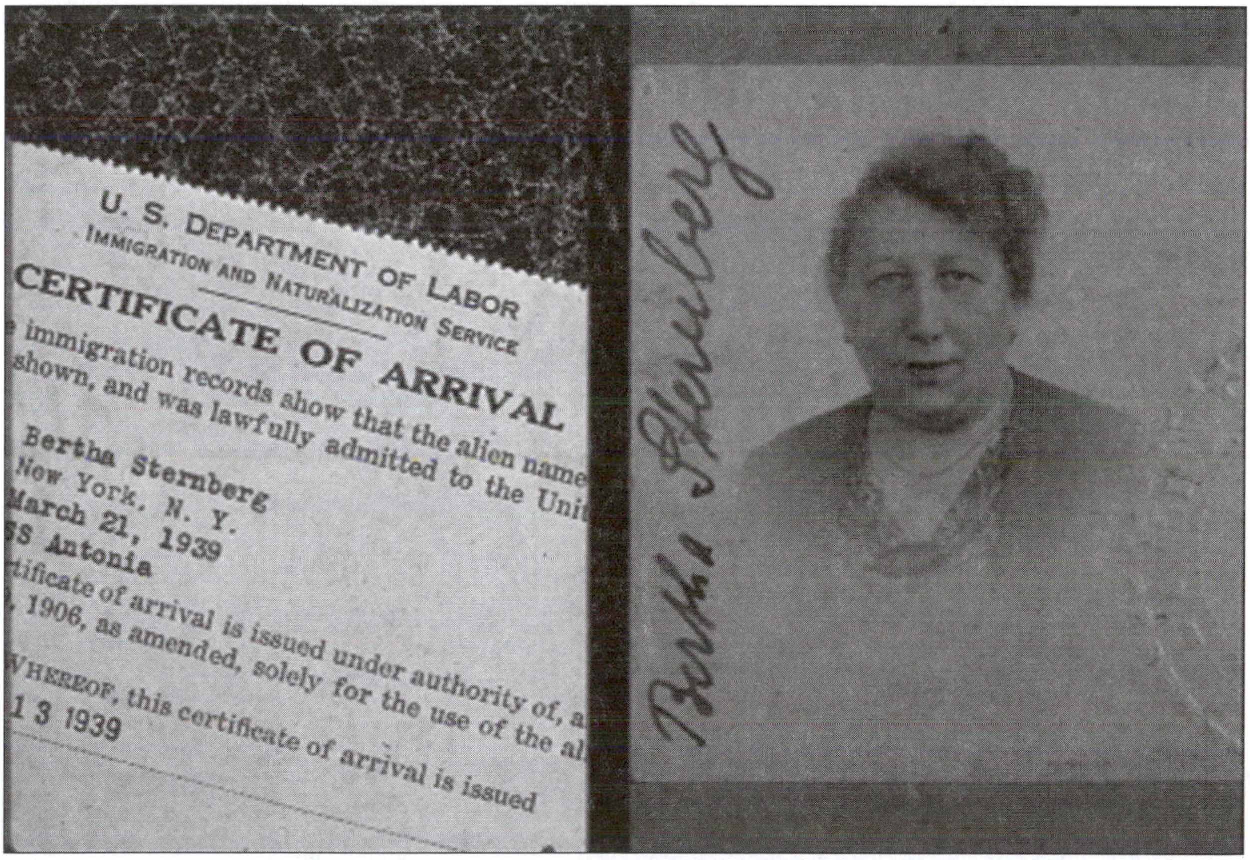

Figure 6-11. The regional archives of the National Archives preserve and make available millions of original naturalization records.

Figure 6-12. Beginning in 1929, declarations of intention included a photograph of the individual.

cubic feet of historical records dating from 1850 to the 1980s. Among them are photographs, maps, architectural drawings, and other nontextual documentation. The records were created or received by the federal courts and more than one hundred federal agencies in northern California, Guam, Hawaii, Nevada (except Clark County), American Samoa, and the Trust Territory of the Pacific Islands.

Court naturalization records for the Pacific Region (San Francisco) were almost entirely originated by U.S. courts, including records from federal courts in San Francisco (1852–1971); Sacramento (1917–56); Reno, Nevada (1868–1929; declarations of intention only, 1907–29, all on microfilm); and Honolulu, Hawaii (1900–1960). State, city, and county government-originated naturalization records remain in the custody of state, city, and county courts, archives, and clerks' offices, with only a few exceptions: the Pacific Region (San Francisco) has a few such records from local courts, including some naturalization records from the

Marin County, California, Superior Court (1852–1957; declarations of intention only, 1951–57) and non-federal Nevada district courts in Fallon (1877–1956; declarations of intention only, 1877–1907) and Reno (1853–1949; declarations of intention only, 1853–76).

In addition to court naturalization records, the Pacific Region (San Francisco) has Asian immigration case files of the Immigration and Naturalization Service for the San Francisco District Office, 1884–1955 (a database index is in progress) and the Honolulu District Office, 1900–1955 (with a database index). The cases cover mostly Chinese immigrants and some Japanese and a few other ethnic Asian immigrant groups. A few cases cover Russians (mostly Jewish) immigrating to San Francisco from Asian ports. The majority of cases document investigations under the Chinese Exclusion Acts (1882–1943). There is also a small collection of records of the government of American Samoa related to immigration and naturalization in American Samoa (1933–65).

In addition to naturalization records for the states covered in the region, the Pacific Region (San Francisco) has National Archives microfilm publication T1220, *Selected Indexes to Naturalization Records of the U.S. Circuit and District Courts, Northern District of California, 1852–1928*, and microfilm publication M1744, *Index to Naturalizations of the U.S. District Court for the Northern District of California, ca. 1860–1989.*

NARA Pacific Alaska Region (Seattle)

6125 Sand Point Way, N.E.
Seattle, WA 98115-7999
Telephone: 206-526-6507
E-mail: archives@seattle.nara.gov
Fax: 206-526-4344

The National Archives' Pacific Alaska Region (Seattle) has more than thirty thousand cubic feet of historical records, among them photographs, maps, and architectural drawings, dating from the 1850s to the 1980s. These records were created or received by the federal courts and more than sixty federal agencies in Idaho, Oregon, and Washington.

The Pacific Alaska Region (Seattle) has naturalization records for Ada County, Idaho, 1883 to 1919; indexes to naturalization records of the Montana courts; indexes to naturalization records of the U.S. courts for the District of Oregon; indexes to naturalization records of King County, Washington, courts; indexes to naturalization records of the Snohomish County, Washington, territorial and superior courts; indexes to naturalization records of the Thurston County, Washington, courts; indexes to naturalization records of the Pierce County, Washington, territorial and superior courts; indexes to naturalization

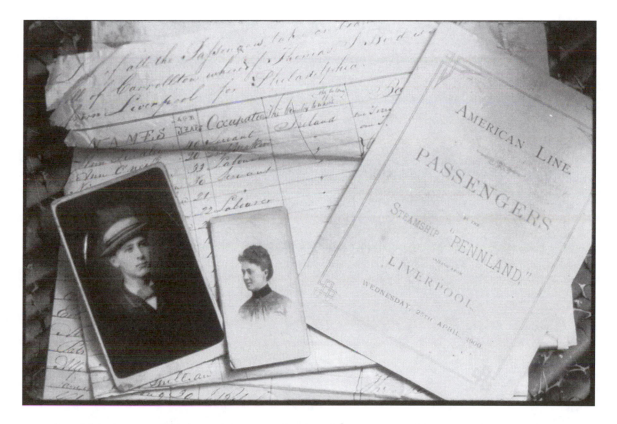

Figure 6-13. While the regional archives of the National Archives have some microfilm copies of passenger lists, it is best to call in advance to determine if the regional archive you plan to visit has the microfilm you need to search.

records of the U.S. District Court, Western District of Washington, Northern Division (Seattle); and indexes to naturalization records of the U.S. District Court, Western District of Washington, Southern Division (Tacoma).

The INS records held by the Pacific Alaska Region (Seattle) are those of the Portland, Oregon, office of the INS and the Portland Collector of Customs; they primarily concern the enforcement of the Chinese Exclusion Act.

NARA Pacific Alaska Region (Anchorage)

654 West Third Avenue
Anchorage, AK 99501-2145
Telephone: 907-271-2443
E-mail: archives@alaska.nara.gov
Fax: 907-271-2442

In addition to the naturalization records it holds for the state of Alaska, the National Archives' Pacific Alaska Region (Anchorage) has original federal court naturalization records, microfilm copies of some records, and indexes that range in dates from around 1901 to 1929.

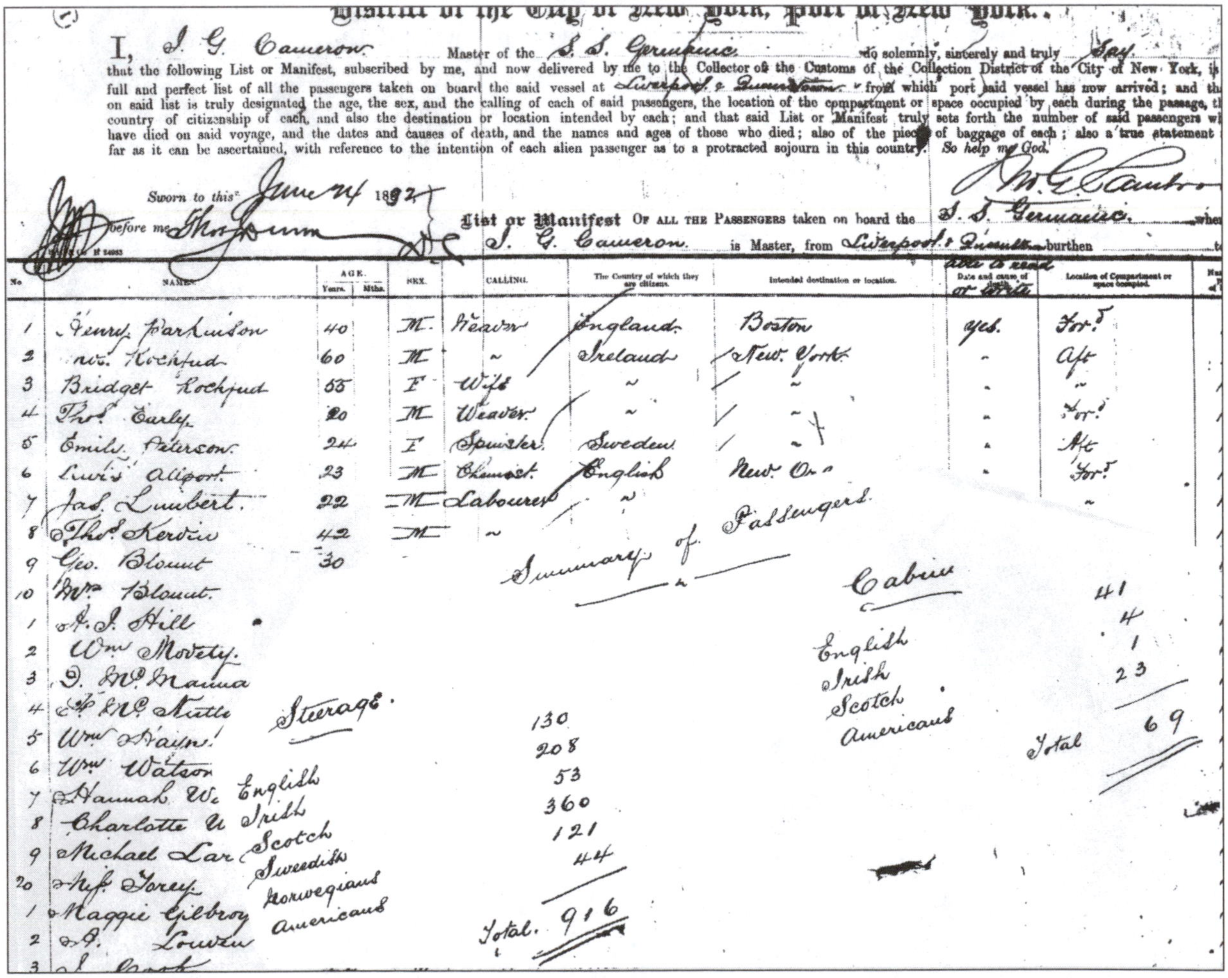

District of the City of New York, Port of New York.

I, J. G. Cameron Master of the S. S. Germanic do solemnly, sincerely and truly say that the following List or Manifest, subscribed by me, and now delivered by me to the Collector of the Customs of the Collection District of the City of New York, is a full and perfect list of all the passengers taken on board the said vessel at Liverpool & Queenstown from which port said vessel has now arrived; and that on said list is truly designated the age, the sex, and the calling of each of said passengers, the location of the compartment or space occupied by each during the passage, the country of citizenship of each, and also the destination or location intended by each; and that said List or Manifest truly sets forth the number of said passengers who have died on said voyage, and the dates and causes of death, and the names and ages of those who died; also of the pieces of baggage of each; also a true statement so far as it can be ascertained, with reference to the intention of each alien passenger as to a protracted sojourn in this country. So help me God.

Sworn to this June 24 1892 before me

List or Manifest of all the Passengers taken on board the S. S. Germanic whereof J. G. Cameron is Master, from Liverpool & Queenstown burthen

No.	Names.	Age: Years.	Age: Mths.	Sex.	Calling.	The Country of which they are citizens.	Intended destination or location.	Date and cause of death	Location of Compartment or space occupied.
1	Henry Parkinson	40		M	Weaver	England	Boston	yes	For
2	Wm. Rochford	60		M	"	Ireland	New York	"	Aft
3	Bridget Rochford	55		F	Wife	"	"	"	"
4	Thos. Early	20		M	Weaver	"	"	"	For
5	Emily Peterson	24		F	Spinster	Sweden	"	"	Aft
6	Louis Allport	23		M	Chemist	English	New Or "	"	For
7	Jas. Lambert	22		M	Labourer	"			"
8	Thos. Kerdin	42		M	"				
9	Geo. Blount	30							
10	Wm. Blount								
1	A. J. Hill								
2	Wm. Moselty								
3	D. McManna								
4	A. McNuttle								
5	Wm. Hain								
6	Wm. Watson								
7	Hannah W.								
8	Charlotte W.								
9	Michael Lar								
20	M. Torey								
1	Maggie Gilbroy								
2	A. Lowen								

Summary of Passengers.

Cabin

English	41
Irish	4
Scotch	1
Americans	23
Total	69

Steerage.

English	130
Irish	208
Scotch	53
Swedish	360
Norwegians	121
Americans	44
Total.	916

Figure 6-14. On the last page of a passenger list, the ship's master usually summarized the total number of passengers. Any passengers who had died on the voyage were also noted.

Figure 6-15. Passenger lists prior to 1900 rarely provide the exact town of origin, but only the country of origin.

NATURALIZATION RECORDS IN THE NATIONAL ARCHIVES' REGIONAL ARCHIVES BY STATE

Alabama

NARA Southeast Region

Southern District of Alabama, Mobile

Declarations of Intention, 1855–1986 (includes
Confederate declarations, 1861–62)
(indexed)

Petitions, 1906–69 (indexed)

Southern District of Alabama, Selma

Declarations of intention, 1909–41 (indexed)

Petitions, 1909–43 (indexed)

Middle District of Alabama

Declarations of Intention, 1907–Feb. 1960
(indexed)

Petitions, 1912–60 (indexed)

Military Petitions, 1917–18 (indexed)

Northern District of Alabama, Birmingham

Declarations of intention, 1911–59 (indexed)

Petition Index, 1911–63

Petitions, 1909–63 (indexed)

Military petitions, 1918–24

Northern District of Alabama, Florence

Declarations of intention, 1923–29 (indexed)

Petitions, 1922–26 (indexed)

Northern District of Alabama, Huntsville

Declarations of intention, 1923–25 (indexed)

Petitions, 1924–26 (indexed)

Alaska

NARA Pacific Alaska Region (Anchorage)

Juneau

Declarations of intention, 1900–29 (indexed)

Special court orders, 1914–32

Military petitions for naturalization, 1918–46

Depositions for military petitions for naturalization, 1933–48

Records relating to repatriation, 1922–52 (unindexed)

Petitions for military repatriations, 1922–46

Overseas military petitions for naturalization, 1942–54

Naturalization depositions, 1925–71

U.S. District Court, San Diego (Southern Division)

Petitions for naturalization, 1955–66

Declarations of intention, 1955–66

Naturalization depositions, 1955–66

Naturalization court orders, 1955–66

Naturalization repatriations, 1966–73

Superior Court, County of San Diego

Index to naturalizations, 1929–56

Index to declarations of intention, 1853–1956

Index to citizens naturalized, 1853–1956

Declarations of intention, 1941–66

Petitions for naturalization, 1906–56

Certificates of citizenship, 1883–1903

California—Northern

NARA Pacific Region (San Francisco)

Northern District of California, San Francisco

Declarations of intention and petitions, 1923–38

Naturalization depositions, 1906–57

Index to naturalizations, 1853–67

Naturalization correspondence, 1907–42

Admiralty case files, 1882–1902

Declarations of intention, 1851–1955

Index to declarations of intention, 1851–1906

Index to declarations and petitions, 1906–28

Register of applications, 1853–67

Petitions and affidavits, 1903–06

Petitions and records, 1907–56

Military petitions, 1918–46

Overseas military petitions, 1944–47 and 1954–55

Recommendations of naturalization examiner, 1949–55

Petition for naturalization files, 1924–56

Certificates of naturalization, 1852–06

Index to certificates of naturalizations, 1857–1906

Certificate of naturalization stubs, 1908–26

Records of repatriations, 1919–41 and 1936–69

Naturalization depositions, 1907–58

Eastern District of California, Sacramento

Declaration of intention, 1917–56

Petitions (military), 1944–46

Petitions, 1922–56

Petitions recommended to be granted/denied, 1928–58

Overseas military certificates of naturalization, 1944–45

U.S. Circuit Court, Ninth Circuit

Index to naturalization certificates, 1868

Declarations of intention, 1855–1911

Applications for naturalization, 1879–1903 (microfilmed)

Petitions and affidavits, 1903–06

Petition and record of naturalization, 1907–11

Certificates of naturalization, 1855–1906

Certificate of naturalization stubs, 1907–12

Index to certificates and petitions for naturalization, 1855–1912 (microfilmed)

Records of naturalization, 1880

Naturalization case records, 1869–1901

Naturalization records of minors, 1867–84

Colorado

NARA Rocky Mountain Region

U.S. District Court, Denver

Declarations of Intention, 1877–1952

Naturalization Dockets, 1906–16

Petition and Record, 1906–50

U.S. District Court, Pueblo

Declarations of Intention, 1906–49

Petition and Record, 1912–49

Soldiers' Petition and Record, 1919–28

Miscellaneous Naturalization Records, 1883–1922

Connecticut

NARA Northeast Region (Boston)

Connecticut naturalization records transferred to the Northeast Region (Boston) between December 1984 and January 1985 are classified under RG 200. City court records that were accessioned along with federal court records are under RG 21. The Soundex index for Connecticut, located in the Reading Room, covers all naturalizations between 1790 and 1940.

U.S. Circuit Court, Hartford

Declarations of Intention, 1906–11

Record of Naturalization, 1893–1906

Petition and Record of Naturalization, 1906–11

U.S. District Court, Hartford

Record of Naturalization (Hartford and New Haven), 1842–1903

Declarations of Intention, 1911–55

Petition and Record, 1911–73

Depositions of Witnesses, 1926–55

U.S. Circuit Court, New Haven

Declarations of Intention (with Petitions), 1893–1906

Declarations of Intention, 1906–11

Petition and Record of Naturalization, 1906–11

U.S. District Court, New Haven

Declarations of Intention, 1911–63

Petition and Record Book, 1911–65

Petition and Record for Military, January–June 1919

Petition and Record for Military Overseas, 1942–56

Military Repatriations, 1920–31

Women's Applications for Repatriation, 1936–72

Court Lists of Petitions Granted/Denied, 1928–62

Depositions of Witnesses, 1923–68

Name Index to Petitions, 1906–49

City Court, Ansonia

Record of Declarations Filed, 1893–1906

Petitions and Records of Naturalizations, 1904–06

Naturalization Record Books, 1893–1906

Register of Declarations and Petitions Filed, 1900–06

City Court, Bridgeport

Record of Declarations of Intention, 1852–77

Record of Naturalizations, 1852–76

Ledger of Witnesses, 1875–77

County Court, Fairfield

Record of Naturalization, 1839–54

Naturalization Petition, 1795

Court of Common Pleas, Fairfield

Record of Declarations of Intention, 1874–1906

Record of Declarations and Naturalizations, 1880–87 and 1896

Superior Court, Fairfield

Record of Declarations of Intention, 1854–1905

Declarations of Intention, 1906–62

Record of Naturalizations, 1842–1905

Petition and Record, 1906–55

Military Naturalizations, 1918–24

Naturalization Ledgers, 1860–88

Naturalization Witness Ledger, 1890–1903

Declarations and Naturalizations Ledgers, 1884–1905

Certificate Books, 1907

Certificate Stubs, 1910–55

Naturalizations Cash Book, 1913–16

Depositions, 1925–55

Name Index, Superior Court Declarations, 1906–42

Loss of Citizenship Notices, 1963–66

Petitions Granted, 1930–58

Repatriation Cases, 1937–55

Transfer of Petitions, 1955

City Court, Hartford

Naturalization Record Book, 1875–76

Court at Hartford, Hartford County

Record of Naturalizations, 1834–66

Petitions and Applications, 1829–66

Court of Common Pleas, Hartford

Record of Declaration of Intention, 1876–1906

Record of Testimony of Witnesses, 1876–1903

Superior Court, Meriden
Declarations of Intention, 1936–54
Petition and Record, 1939–54
Repatriation Lists, 1940–53
Enemy Alien List, 1942–50
Petitions Granted/Denied, 1939–55
Monthly Reports, 1951–57
Lists of Fees Collected and Quarterly Abstracts, 1951–57

County Court, New Haven
Naturalization Petitions, 1795–1868
Record of Naturalizations, 1836–58

Court of Common Pleas, New Haven
Record of Declarations of Intention, 1876–1906
Record of Naturalizations, 1874–1906

Superior Court, New Haven
Record of Declarations of Intention, 1852–1903
Record of Naturalizations, 1859–92

District Court, Waterbury
Record of Declarations of Intention, 1880–1906
Record of Naturalizations, 1880–1906
Declarations of Intention, 1906–27
Petition and Record, 1906–27
Index Book, 1868–88
Index to Declarations and Naturalizations, 1926–70

Court of Common Pleas, Waterbury
Declarations of Intention, 1927–41
Petition and Record, 1927–41

Superior Court, Waterbury
Declarations of Intention, 1941–71
Petition and Record, 1941–71
Certificates of Naturalization, 1907–20
Certificates of Arrival, 1920s
Index to Declarations of Intention, 1928–71
Transfers from Waterbury, 1960
Transfers to Waterbury, 1964–70
Repatriations, 1938–70
Petitions Granted/Denied, 1930–72
Declarations of Intention, 1919–72
Naturalization Sessions, 1955–58
Name Index to Waterbury Courts, 1880–1972

Court of Common Pleas, New London County
Records of Declarations of Intention, 1875–1906
Record of Naturalizations, 1874–1906
Applications and Petitions, 1875–1905

Superior Court, New London
Record of Declaration of Intention, 1872–1906
Record of Naturalizations, 1856–1906
Declarations of Intention, 1909–74
Petition and Record, 1910–74
Affidavits of Witnesses/Declarations, 1805–95
Applications and Petitions, to 1890
Petitions Granted/Denied, 1929–55 and 1971–73
Applications for Transfer of Petitions, 1953–74
Orders of Cancellation, 1934–42
Depositions, 1945–48
Sessions for Naturalizations, 1918–30
Depositions of Witnesses, 1910–45
Forms Relating to Declarations, 1926–29
Repatriations, 1936–63
Transfer of Petitions, 1952–74
Lists of Petitions Granted/Denied, 1929–75
Name Index, 1856–1906 and 1906–73

County Court, Tolland
Record of Declaration of Intention, 1853–1906
Record of Naturalizations, 1853–80
Naturalization Petitions, 1825–95

Superior Court, Tolland
Record of Declarations and Naturalizations, 1880–1902
Declarations of Intention, 1906–49
Record of Naturalizations, 1896–1906
Petition and Record, 1914–55
Record of Witnesses and Testimony, 1880–92, 1894, and 1898
Petitions Granted/Denied, 1930–55
Repatriations, 1941–45
Naturalization Stubs, 1907–24
Tolland Name Index, 1853–1955

City Court, Waterbury
Record of Naturalizations, 1854–67

Superior Court, Windham County
Record of Declarations, 1855–81 and 1884–1906

Record of Naturalizations, 1855–63 and
1866–1906
Petition and Record, 1906–74
Declarations of Intention, 1906–74
Index to Petitions, 1906–27
Petitions Granted/Denied, 1929–74
Transfers of Petitions, 1956–69
Repatriation Cases, 1937–66
Certificates of Naturalization, 1907–26
Petitions for Citizenship, 1808–84 and
1891–1900
Petitions Pending of Enemy Aliens, 1941–51
Windham Name Index, 1927–74

Delaware

NARA Mid-Atlantic Region (Center City Philadelphia)
Wilmington
Name Index, 1795–1926
Petitions, 1797–1844
Petitions, 1845–1929
Petitions, 1930–53
Military Petitions, 1918–19
Declarations of Intention, 1818–41
Declarations of Intention, 1842–1936

Florida

NARA Southeast Region
Southern District, Key West
Declarations of Intention, 1867–1956 (indexed)
Petitions, 1847–1969 (indexed to May 1959)
Naturalization Petitions of Minors, 1862–88
Military Petitions and Certificates, Overseas,
1945–54
Southern District, Miami
Declaration of Intention, 1913–67 (indexed to
September 1950)
Petitions, 1913–70 (indexed to January 1959)
Naturalization Petition Transfers, 1953–60
*Middle District, Tampa (in Southern District,
1879–1962)*
Naturalization Index, 1906–60
Petitions, 1907–60

Declarations of Intention, 1909–63 (indexed to
1960)
Application to Take Oath of Allegiance,
1937–63 (indexed)
Naturalization Outside the U.S., 1944–55 (very
few)
*Middle District, Jacksonville (in Southern District
until 1962)*
Declarations of Intention, 1892–1975 (indexed
to February 1961)
Petitions, 1895–1975 (indexed to September
1954)
Military Petitions, June 1918–Dec. 1923
(indexed)
Northern District, Pensacola
Declarations of Intention, 1906–45 (indexed)
Petitions, 1903–72 (indexed)
Military Petitions, 1918–22 (unindexed)

Georgia

NARA Southeast Region
Southern District, Savannah
Petitions, 1790–1861; later petitions retained in
Clerk's office
Middle District, Athens
Declarations of Intention, 1907–28 (indexed)
Petitions, 1910–25 (indexed)
Northern District, Rome
Declaration of Intention, 1907–64 (indexed)
Petitions, 1909–26 (indexed)
Military Petitions, Mar.–Nov. 1918 (unindexed)
Northern District, Atlanta
Declarations of Intention, 1907–61 (indexed to
1950)
Petitions, 1907–64 (indexed to 1950)
Military Petitions, 1918–24 (unindexed)

Hawaii

NARA Pacific Region (San Francisco)
U.S. District Court, Hawaii
Naturalization Case Files, 1927–59
Records of Naturalization, 1900–06

Declarations of Intention, 1900–29

Index to Military-Civil Petitions and Naturalizations, 1900–29

Civil Petitions, 1903–60

Military Petitions, 1918–21

Certificate of Naturalization Stubs, 1907–61

Illinois

NARA Great Lakes Region

The National Archives' Great Lakes Region has the original Soundex-style index to naturalizations which occurred in local and federal courts from 1840 to 1950, as well as a microfilm copy. Although the vast majority of the indexed records are for Cook County, Illinois, there are some for other counties in northern Illinois, northwestern Indiana, eastern Iowa, and Wisconsin. Petitions filed in Chicago prior to 1871 were destroyed by the Great Chicago Fire and do not appear in the index. The naturalization index has been microfilmed. Copies of this microfilm are available through the Family History Library and at the Cook County Circuit Court Archives, at the Illinois Regional Archives Depository, and at some libraries with genealogical collections.

U.S. Circuit Court, Northern District, Chicago

Declarations of Intention, 1906–11

Index to Declarations of Intention, 1906–11

Index to Naturalization Petitions, 1906–11

Petition Books, 1906–11

Certificate of Naturalization Stubs, 1907–11

U.S. District Court, Northern District, Chicago

Index to Declarations, 1906–60

Declarations of Intention, 1872–1982

Naturalization Orders, 1872–1903

Naturalization Order Books, 1921–76

Naturalization Depositions, 1909–64

Naturalization Journals, 1925–59

Records of Repatriation, 1936–69

Index to Petition Books, 1906–60

Military Petition and Record Books, 1918–26, 1942–46, and 1954–55

Certificate of Naturalization Stubs, 1912–18

Petitions, 1872–1975

Naturalization Case Files, 1928–78

Designations of Examiner or Officer, 1918–35

Naturalization Transfer Case Files, 1953–64

Overseas Military Petition Books, 1942–56

Repatriation Order Books, 1940

Records of Soldier Repatriations, 1918–41

Register of Transfer Cases, 1953–64

U.S. District Court, Southern District, Peoria

Index to Declaration of Intention and Petition Books, 1905–54

Declaration of Intent Books, 1905–51

Naturalization Petition and Record Books, 1908–54

Certificate of Naturalization Stubs, 1903–26

Repatriation Certificates, 1937–59

Naturalization Order Book, 1921–57

Overseas Naturalization Certificates, 1943–55

U.S. District Court, Southern District, Springfield

Naturalization Declaration Books, 1856–1902

Naturalization Record Book, 1862–1903

Index to Declarations and Petitions, 1906–52

Declarations of Intention, 1903–50

Naturalization Records, 1856–1903

Naturalization Records, Minors, 1856–1964

Naturalization Order Book, 1929–55

Naturalization Petition and Order Books, 1906–66

Military Petition and Record Book, 1943–57

U.S. District Court, Eastern District, Danville

Petition and Record Books, 1906–62

Records of Repatriations, 1938–50

Naturalization Order Book, 1930–58

Naturalization Depositions, 1942–51

Military Petitions, 1944–54

Declarations of Intention, 1906–51

Indiana

NARA Great Lakes Region

See Illinois. (The Great Lakes Region's Soundex-style index includes northwestern Indiana.)

U.S. District Court, Northern District, Hammond
   Declarations of Intention, 1906–21
   Naturalization Depositions, 1932–45
U.S. District Court, Southern District, Indianapolis
   Declarations of Intention, 1906–48
   Naturalization Record Book, 1903–06
   Petition and Record Books, 1907–45
   Military Petition and Record Books, 1918
   Naturalization Application Files, 1865–1954
   Naturalization Military Petition Certificate Stubs,
      1917–24

Iowa
NARA Central Plains Region
*U.S. District Court, Northern District. Cedar
Rapids Division, Cedar Rapids*
   Declarations of Intentions, 1910–1981
      (indexed)
   Petitions, 1913–78 (indexed)
   Certificate Stubs, 1917–27
U.S. District Court, Northern District, Central Division, Ft. Dodge
   Declarations of Intention, 1917–77 (indexed)
   Petitions, 1909–77 (indexed)
   Oath of Allegiance, 1938–63 (indexed)
U.S. District Court, Northern District, Central Division, Mason City
   Declarations of Intention, 1944–61
   Orders of Admissions, Continuance, and
      Denials, 1944–61
   Military Petitions, 1954
   Oath of Allegiance, 1944–58
*U. S. District Court, Northern District, Eastern
Division, Dubuque*
   Declarations of Intention, 1914–62
   Petitions, 1915–62
   Petitions, Recommended and Granted, 1934–36
   Repatriation Cases, 1937–59
   Orders of Admissions, Continuance, Denials,
      1934–63

*U.S. District Court, Northern District, Eastern
Division, Waterloo*
   Declaration of Intention, 1944–58
   Petitions, 1944–62
   Petitions for Naturalization Transfers, 1954–59
   Orders of Admission, Continuance, Denials, 1955–62
   Military Petitions in Foreign Countries, 1943
      (indexed)
*U.S. Superior Court, Cedar Rapids Division, Linn
County, Cedar Rapids*
   Declarations of Intention, 1886–1947
   Petitions and Naturalization Record, 1891–1947
   List of Petitions Granted, 1929–48
   Repatriations, 1940–47
*U.S. District Court, Southern District, Eastern
Division, Keokuk*
   Declarations of Intention and Misc., 1849–1888
   List of Persons Naturalized, 1853–1874
U.S. District Court, Southern District, Central Division, Ottumwa
   Declarations of Intention, 1916–51
   Petitions and Records, 1916–51
   Repatriation of Native-Born, Sept. 1938–Sept. 1951
   Copies of Petitions and Certificate Naturalization, March 1942
   Certificates of Naturalization, 1921–26
*U.S. District Court, Southern District, Southern
Division, Creston*
   Declarations of Intention, 1930–50
   Petitions for Citizenship, 1940–51
U.S. District Court, Southern District, Central Division, Des Moines
   Declarations of Intention, 1915–35 (indexed)
   Declarations of Intention, 1936–88
   Petitions and Records, 1915–84
U.S. District Court, Northern District, Sioux City
   Declarations of Intention, 1932–83
   Petitions for Naturalization, 1930–88
   Naturalization Court Orders, 1932–85
   Naturalization Petitions Transferred "In," 1954–75
   Oath Allegiance, 1940–63
   Naturalization Proceedings, 1964–92

Kansas

NARA Central Plains Region

U.S. District Court, First Division, Topeka

Index to Naturalization Cases, 1856–1897

Letters Relating to Indian Naturalization, 1856–1892

Records of Indians Naturalized, 1865–1874 (Including Delaware, Kickapoo, Miami, and Pottowattomie)

Declaration of Intention, 1862–1921

Petitions and Naturalization, 1868–1984

Certificate Stubs, 1908–21

Repatriation Proceedings and Military Petitions for Naturalization, 1940–55

Naturalization Orders Recommended and Granted, 1933–58

U.S. District Court, Second Division, Wichita

Declarations of Intention, 1909–47

Petitions and Naturalization, 1909–79

Transferred Petitions, 1954–63

Naturalization Certificate Stubs, 1909–25

Military Petitions/Naturalization Outside U.S., 1942–53

Repatriation Proceedings, 1940–56

Records of Naturalization Recommended and Granted, 1927–55

U.S. District Court, Third Division, Ft. Scott

Declarations of Intention, 1915–64

Naturalization Certificate Stubs, 1916–29

Naturalization Petitions and Records, 1916–66

Naturalization Petitions/Orders, 1941–66

U.S. District Court, Kansas City, Kansas

Naturalization Petitions, 1939–70

Kentucky

NARA Southeast Region

Western District, Louisville

Declarations of Intention, 1906–51 (indexed)

Petitions, 1906–57 (indexed)

Military Naturalization Petitions, 1918–21 (unindexed)

Western District, Bowling Green

Declarations of Intention, 1915–78 (indexed)

Petitions, 1915–76 (indexed)

Eastern District, Catlettsburg/Ashland

Petitions, 1913–29 (indexed)

Eastern District, Covington

Declarations of Intention, 1911–29 (indexed)

Petitions, 1910–56 (indexed)

Eastern District, Frankfort

Declarations of Intention, 1910–28; 1931–52 (indexed)

Petitions, 1912–29; 1932–51 (indexed)

Eastern District, Lexington

Declarations of Intention, 1922–29 (indexed)

Petitions, 1922–43 (indexed)

Eastern District, London

Declarations of Intention, 1913–72 (indexed)

Petitions, 1913–73 (indexed to 1949)

Eastern District, Pikeville

Declarations of Intention, 1938–42 (indexed)

Petitions, 1942–59 (indexed)

Eastern District, Richmond

Petitions, 1913–28 (indexed)

Louisiana

NARA Southwest Region

Western District, Alexandria

Declarations of Intention, 1919–20

Petitions, 1922–64

Lists of Petitions Granted, Continued, or Denied, 1930–59

Western District, Opelousas

Declarations of Intention, 1918–56

Petitions, 1922–64

Lists of Granted Petitions, 1930–55

Western District, Shreveport

Declarations of Intention and Petitions, 1885–91

Declarations of Intention, 1906–42

Petitions, 1902–67

Lists of Petitions Granted, 1929–56

Eastern District, Baton Rouge, District Court

Declarations of Intention, 1907–51

Maryland

NARA Mid-Atlantic Region (Center City Philadelphia)

Baltimore

Name Index, 1797-1951

Petitions, 1906-29

Petitions, 1930-72

Military Petitions, 1918-23

Naturalization Registers, 1792-1906

Declarations of Intention, 1906-31

Massachusetts

NARA Northeast Region (Boston)

U.S. District Court, District of Massachusetts

Declarations of Intention (clerk's copies), 1798-1874

Declarations of Intention (originals), 1804-74

Declarations of Intention, 1874-1906 and 1906-50

Petitions and Records of Naturalization, 1790-1868

Name Indexes to Naturalizations, 1790-1911

Naturalization Record Books, 1790-1868

Petitions and Records of Naturalizations, 1868-1950

Declarations of Intention (with Petitions), 1884-1909

Petitions and Records of Naturalization for Personnel, 1919

Depositions of Witnesses, 1911-50

Court Lists of Naturalization Hearings, 1927-51

Naturalization Certificate Stub Books, 1906-15

Naturalization Case Files, 1912-49

U.S. Circuit Court, District of Massachusetts

Declarations of Intention (originals), 1845-75

Records of Declarations Filed, 1845-75

Declarations of Intention, 1875-1911

Petitions and Records of Naturalization, 1845-64 and 1864-1911

Name Index to Naturalization Record Books, 1845-71

Naturalization Record Books, 1845-64

Declarations of Intention (with Petitions), 1864-1909

Depositions of Witnesses, 1908-11

Michigan

NARA Great Lakes Region

U.S. Circuit Court, Eastern District, Detroit

Declarations of Intention, 1874-1912

Naturalization Application File, 1837-1906

Register (Index) of Declarations of Intention, 1837-1916

Register (Index) of Final Papers Issued, 1837-1916

Naturalization Certificate Stubs, 1908-11

Register of Aliens, 1837-1906

Naturalization Petition Book, 1908-11

U.S. District Court, Eastern District, Detroit

Naturalization Application Files, 1837-97

Declarations of Intention, 1856-1984

Naturalization Petition and Record Books, 1906-80

Overseas Military Petitions and Records, 1942-56

Naturalization Hearing Dockets, 1912-20

Naturalization Depositions, 1906-70

Register (Index) of Declarations of Intention, 1837-1916

Register (Index) of Final Paper Issued, 1837-1916

Naturalization Certificate Stubs, 1909-25

Naturalization Order Book, 1932-35

Repatriation Records, 1918-70

Naturalization Transfer Case Files, 1953-87

Naturalization Monthly Reports, 1969-75

U.S. District Court, Western District, Marquette

Declarations of Intention, 1887-1909

Naturalization Petition and Record, 1888-1915

Duplicate Military Petitions and Certificates, 1943-46

Index to Naturalization Records, 1887-1915

U.S. District Court, Western District, Grand Rapids

Declarations of Intention, 1865-1978

Naturalization Petition and Record, 1868-1972

Minnesota (Part)

NARA Great Lakes Region

U.S. District Court, Fifth Division, Duluth

Index to Declarations of Intent and Petitions, 1906–44

Declarations of Intention, 1894–1943

Petition Books, 1897–1955

Certificate of Naturalization Stubs, 1906–23

Naturalization Depositions, 1950–59

Certificates of Loyalty, 1949–51

Reports of Naturalization Proceedings, 1949–59

Naturalizations of Foreign Soil, 1943–54

Repatriate Oaths of Allegiance, 1936–69

Alien Enemy Notices to Commissioner of Naturalizations, 1942–49

Naturalization Certificate Stubs, 1907–26

Naturalization Orders, 1929–69

Repatriation Records, 1938–66

U.S. Circuit Court, Fifth Division, Duluth

Index to Declarations of Intention and Petitions for Naturalization, 1906–11

Declarations of Intention, 1891–1911

Petitions for Naturalization, 1847–1911

Certificates of Naturalization Stubs, 1906–11

U.S. District Court, Third Division, St. Paul

Naturalization Petitions and Records, 1952–79

Repatriation Records, 1936–75

Record of Transfers of Naturalization Petitions, 1953–77

Record of Declarations of Intention, 1955–69

Declarations of Intention Filed in Various Minnesota Counties, 1861–97

Naturalization Certificate Stubs, 1907–26

U.S. District Court, Sixth Division, Fergus Falls

Index to Naturalization Petitions and Declarations of Intention, 1890–1959

Naturalization Petitions and Records, 1944–78

Record of Declarations of Intention, 1947–50

Minnesota (Part)

NARA Central Plains Region

U.S. District Court, First Division, Winona

Declarations of Intention, 1896–1924

Naturalization Petitions, 1896–1920

Certificate Stubs, 1909 and 1916–20

U.S. District Court, Second Division, Mankato

Declarations of Intention, 1906–40

Naturalization Papers, 1893–1919

Naturalization Petitions, 1897–1944

U.S. District Court, Third Division, St. Paul

Declaration of Intention, 1859–1955

Naturalization Petitions, 1897–1951

Naturalization Petitions Military, 1918

Overseas Naturalization Petitions, 1943–54

U.S. District Court, Fourth Division, Minneapolis

Declaration of Intention, 1906–62

Petitions and Naturalization Records, 1897–1965

Naturalization Petitions–Military, 1918

Naturalization Order Books, 1929–60

Naturalization Certificate Stubs, 1917–27

Naturalization Certificate Stubs for Soldiers, 1918–19

Repatriation Records, 1919–42

U.S. District and Circuit Court, Fourth Division, Minneapolis

Naturalization Certificate Stubs, 1907–12

U.S. District Court, Sixth Division, Fergus Falls

Declaration of Intention, 1896–1944

Repatriation Applications and Orders, 1938–46

U.S. Circuit Court, First Division, Winona

Declaration of Intention, 1910

Naturalization Petitions, 1897–1899

U.S. Circuit Court, Second Division, Mankato

Declaration of Intention, 1900–11

Naturalization Petitions, 1897–1911

U.S. Circuit Court, Third Division, St. Paul

Declaration of Intention, 1875–1911

Naturalization Petitions, 1897–1911

U.S. Circuit Court, Fourth Division, Minneapolis

Declaration of Intention, 1890–1911

Naturalization Petitions, 1897–1911

U.S. Circuit Court, Sixth Division, Fergus Falls

Declaration of Intention, 1890–1911

Naturalization Petitions, 1897–1911

Mississippi

NARA Southeast Region

Southern District, Biloxi

Petition and Record, 1908-28 (indexed)

Index to Petitions, ca. 1929-60

Petitions, 1928-65 (indexed to 1960)

Declarations of Intention, 1906-45 (indexed)

Transfer Petitions, 1953-56 (unindexed)

Southern District, Jackson

Declarations of Intention, 1911-58 (indexed)

Petition and Record, 1911-29 (indexed)

Petitions, 1929-53 (indexed)

Northern District, Clarksdale

Declarations of Intention, 1913-55 (indexed)

Petitions, 1913-55 (indexed)

Northern District, Aberdeen

Petitions, 1930-43 (indexed)

Missouri

NARA Central Plains Region

U.S. District Court, Eastern District, Northern Division, Hannibal

Declarations of Intention, 1871-1951

Naturalization Petitions, 1907-36

Naturalization Certificate Stubs, 1907-19

Petitions Transferred, 1963-76

Repatriation Book, 1954-55

Court Orders, 1929-77

U.S. District Court, Eastern Division, St. Louis

Index to Declarations, 1849-1956

First Papers, 1855-1906

Declaration of Intention, 1906-69

Military Petitions, 1846-1930

Petitions Indexed, 1956

Petition and Record, 1906-92

Naturalization Final Paper Minor II, 1890-1895

Decree Minors, 1905-06

Proofs General, 1905-06

Decrees General, 1905-06

Proofs Minor, 1905-06

Minors Final Papers, 1890-99

Decrees Soldiers, 1906

Soldiers Petitions, 1917-19

Index to Declarations, 1849-1925

Index to Petitions, 1931-56

World War II Naturalization Transfers, 1942-85

Unnumbered Depositions and Misc. Papers, 1912-41

Naturalization Certificate Stubs, 1907-26

Court Orders, 1917-30

Certificate Stubs, 1931-79

Oath of Allegiance, 1938-72

Naturalization Transfers, 1985-89

Petition and Decree Cont., 1969-91

Oversea Letters Korea, 1954-55

Transfers, 1988-93

U.S. Circuit Court, Eastern Division, St. Louis

Index to Petitions, 1846-1910

Declarations of Intention, 1849-1911

Petition and Record, 1907-13

Final Papers: Index, 1846-1930

Naturalization card index, 1890-1991

U.S. District Court, Eastern District, Southeastern Division, Cape Girardeau

Petitions, 1908-29

Declarations, 1908-19

Transferred Petitions, 1908-29

Court Order, 1930-87

U.S. District Court, Western District, Central Division, Jefferson City

Index to Naturalization, 1876-1906

Index to Naturalization, 1938-74

Declaration of Intention, 1938-80

Naturalization Petitions, 1938-82

Naturalization Recommended To Be Granted, 1964-82

Transfer Petitions, 1955-82

U.S. District Court, Western District, Western Division, Kansas City, Missouri

Declaration of Intention, 1906-87

Index to Transfers, 1958-63

Index to Petitions, 1848-1950

Index to Certificate Stubs, 1914-76

Naturalization Petitions, 1909-91

Military Petitions, 1918
Military Petitions, 1942–46
Repatriation-Expatriation, 1937–42
Transfer Petitions and Misc., 1989–91

U.S. District Court, Western District,
Northern Division, St. Joseph
Declarations of Intention, 1907–08
District and Circuit Court Naturalization Petitions, 1907–76
Naturalization Petitions Denied, 1927–55
Transferred Petitions, 1959–63
Application: Oath of Allegiance, 1941–45
Military and Overseas Petitions, 1943–55
Certificate Stubs, 1907–26
Naturalization Orders, 1927–55
Transfers, 1959–63
Repatriation Petitions, 1941–45

U.S. District Court, Western District,
Southern Division, Springfield
Declarations of Intention, 1895–1899
Declarations of Intention, 1917–85
Naturalization Petitions and Records, 1911–83
Citizenship Petitions Granted, 1930–36
Naturalization Transfers, 1946–83
Overseas Petitions for Naturalization, 1955–54
Naturalization Certificate Stubs, 1916–27
Certificates of Loyalty, 1944–47
Misc. Correspondence, 1945–46
Court Orders, 1966–85

U.S. District Court, Southwestern Division, Joplin
Declaration of Intention, 1907–73
Naturalization Petitions, 1930–74
Naturalization Petitions Granted/Denied/
  Transfers, 1930–75
Repatriation, 1937–39
Lists, 1930–75

Montana

NARA Pacific Alaska Region (Seattle)
Territorial Court Journals
Manuscript Entries Regarding Naturalizations, 1878–89
U.S. Circuit Court, Helena
Index to Naturalizations, 1891–98
Declarations of Intention, 1891–93
Record of Citizenship (Petitions), 1891–98
U.S. District Court, Helena
Certificate Stub Books, 1907–27
Declarations of Intention, 1892–1929
Index to Naturalization Record, 1894–1902
Naturalization Petitions, 1907–27
U.S. District Court, Butte
Index to Declarations of Intention, 1894–1902
Declarations of Intention, 1894–1902
Petition and Record, 1910–29
Index to Record of Citizenship, 1894–1903
Record of Citizenship (Petitions), 1894–1903
U.S. District Court, Great Falls
Declarations of Intention, 1924
Petition and Record, 1926

Nebraska

NARA Central Plains Region
U.S. District Court, Chadron Division, Chadron
Declarations of Intention, 1930–49
Naturalization Petitions, 1930–47
Naturalization Petitions Granted, Continued, and
  Denied, 1930–47
U.S. District Court, Grand Island Division, Grand
Island
Declarations of Intention, 1930–51
Naturalization Petitions Combined, 1932–44
Naturalization Petitions, 1942–50
Repatriations, 1941
Naturalization Granted, Continued, and Denied, 1931–51
U.S. District Court, Hastings Division, Hastings
Declarations of Intention, 1931–51
Naturalization Petitions and Records, 1931–51
Repatriations, 1941–42

U.S. Circuit Court, Southeastern Division, Fargo
Declaration of Intention, 1890–1918
Naturalization Petitions, 1906–24
U.S. District Court, Southeastern Division, Fargo
Certificate Stubs, 1907–24
U.S. Circuit Court, Northwestern Division, Devils Lake
Declarations of Intention, 1891–1906

Ohio

NARA Great Lakes Region
U.S. District Court, Northern District, Toledo
Index to Declarations of Intention, 1869–84
Declarations of Intention, 1869–84 and 1907–29
Declarations of Intention—Minors, 1875–80
Index to Naturalization Journal, 1875–1900
Naturalization Journal, 1875–1900
Naturalization Index, 1875–ca. 1940
U.S. District Court, Northern District, Cleveland
Index to Naturalization Journals, 1855–1903
Naturalization Journals, 1855–1902
Index to Declarations of Intention, 1855–1906
Declarations of Intention—Minors, 1856–1902
Declarations of Intention, 1855–1943
Naturalization Petitions, 1855–1903
Certificate of Naturalization Stubs, 1907–25
U.S. Circuit Court, Southern District, Cincinnati
Naturalization Journals, 1852–1905
Final Petitions for Naturalization, 1888–1964
U.S. District Court, Southern District, Cincinnati
Index to Naturalization Records, 1852–1906
Declarations of Intention, 1861–1906
Naturalization Final Papers, 1859–1906
Naturalization Journals, 1858–1906
Index to Declarations of Intention and Petitions, 1906–42
Naturalization Petition and Record Books, 1906–29
Declarations of Intention, 1905–56
Naturalization Depositions, 1909–29
Naturalization Certificate Stubs, 1907–26
U.S. District Court, Southern District, Columbus
Naturalization Certificate Stubs, 1916–25

Naturalization Briefs, 1945–51
U.S. District Court, Southern District, Dayton
Naturalization Certificate Stubs, 1916–27
Declarations of Intention, 1906–30

Oklahoma

NARA Southwest Region
Indian Territory, Northern District, Muskogee
Certificates of Naturalization, 1889–1906
Indian Territory, Southern District, Ardmore
Naturalization Records, 1896–1906
Indian Territory, Central District, South McAlester
Declarations of Intention, 1891–1906
Petitions, Oaths of Witnesses, and Orders Granting Citizenship, 1904–06
Orders Granting Citizenship, 1890–1903
Petitions and Orders of Naturalization for Persons Who Arrived in the U.S. as Minors, 1891–1903
Western District, Oklahoma City
Correspondence and Notices, 1909–60
Eastern District, Muskogee
Index to Declarations of Intention and Petitions, ca. 1908–36
Declarations of Intention, 1909–88
Petitions, 1908–87
Petitions of Military Servicemen, 1944–45
Transferred Petitions, 1954–78
Naturalization Certificate Stubs, 1894–1929
Applications to Regain Citizenship and Repatriation Oaths, 1940–44

Oregon

NARA Pacific Alaska Region (Seattle)
U.S. Circuit Court, Oregon
Index to Declarations and Admissions, 1870–1907
Declarations of Intention, 1906–11
Index to Admissions to Citizenship, 1870–1906
Journal of Admission to Citizenship, 1903–06
Petition and Record, 1906–11
U.S. District Court
Index to Declarations of Intention, 1859–92

Declaration of Intention, 1906-62

Index to Declarations and Admissions,
    1859-1907

Index to Admissions to Citizenship, 1859-1906

Journal of Admissions to Citizenship, 1904-06

Index to Declarations and Petitions, 1906-56

Petitions and Records, 1906-70

Military Petitions for Naturalization, 1918

Pennsylvania

NARA Mid-Atlantic Region (Center City
Philadelphia)

Philadelphia, Eastern District of Pennsylvania

Name Index, 1795-1951

Petitions, 1790-1929

Petitions, 1930-66

Declarations of Intention, 1834-1929

See P. William Filby's *Philadelphia Naturalization
    Records: An Index to Records of Aliens' Declara-
    tions of Intention and/or Oaths of Allegiance,
    1789-1880, in the United States Circuit Court,
    United States District Court, Supreme Court of
    Pennsylvania, Quarter Sessions Court, Court of
    Common Pleas, Philadelphia* (Detroit: Gale
    Research Co., 1982).

Pittsburgh, Western District of Pennsylvania

Name Index, 1820-1906

Name Index, 1906-90

Petitions, 1820-1929

Petitions, 1930-79

Erie, District Court Petitions, 1940-72

Declarations of Intention, 1859-1931

Harrisburg, Scranton, Wilkes-Barre, Williamsport;
Middle District of Pennsylvania

Name Index, 1901-90

Petitions, 1901-29

Scranton, District Court Petitions, 1901-90

Wilkes-Barre, District Court Petitions, 1943-72

Williamsport, 1909-13

Harrisburg, 1911-17

Declarations of Intention, 1906-31

Puerto Rico

NARA Northeast Region (New York City)

U.S. District Court for Puerto Rico, San Juan

1898-1972 (alphabetical index only for 1917-29)

Rhode Island

NARA Northeast Region (Boston)

U.S. District Court, District of Rhode Island

Declarations of Intention, 1835-1950 and
    1900-25

Petitions and Records of Naturalization,
    1842-1906 and 1911-50

Naturalization Record Books, 1842-1903

Depositions of Witnesses, 1941-60

Naturalization Certificate Stubs, 1911-57

Record of Depositions, 1916-27

U.S. Circuit Court, District of Rhode Island

Record of Declarations Filed, 1888-97

Petitions and Records of Naturalization,
    1843-1911

Naturalization Record Books, 1842-1901

Declarations of Intention (with Petitions),
    1850-1911

Naturalization Certificate Stubs, 1907-11

South Carolina

NARA Southeast Region

U.S. District Court, Eastern District, Charleston

Index to Naturalization Proceedings, 1790-1906

Declarations of Intention, 1907-65 (indexed)

Petitions, 1866-1953 (indexed)

Military Petitions, 1918-24 (indexed)

U.S. Circuit Court, Charleston

Naturalization Index, 1790-1906

Declarations of Intention, 1906-11 (indexed)

Petitions, 1867-1911 (indexed)

Eastern District, Columbia

Declarations of Intention, 1910-41 (indexed)

Petitions, 1910-53 (indexed)

Index to Military Petitions, 1918-20 (Camp
    Jackson)

Military Petitions, 1918-20 (Camp Jackson)

Eastern District, Florence
    Declarations of Intention, 1910–56 (indexed)
    Petitions, 1917–43 (indexed)
Eastern District, Aiken
    Petitions, 1917–26 (indexed)
Eastern District, Orangeburg
    Declarations of Intention, 1938–55 (indexed)
    Petitions, 1939–41 (indexed)
Western District, Greenville
    Petitions, Oct. 1911–65 (indexed)

South Dakota

NARA Central Plains Region
U.S. Circuit Court, Southwestern Division, Bismark
    Declarations of Intention, 1903–29
U.S. District Court, Second Judicial District, South Dakota
    Territorial Journal, 1862–1873
    Territorial Index (All Districts), 1882–1904
    Declarations of Intention (All Districts), 1876–1904
    Declarations of Intention, 1870
    Declarations of Intention Out of State, 1851–1886
    Declarations of Intention, 1883–1911
    Final Naturalization Certificates, 1892–1905
    Naturalization of Austrians and Hungarians, 1904
U.S. District Court, Deadwood
    Declarations of Intention, 1890–1900
U.S. District Court, Pierre
    Declarations of Intention, 1892
U.S. District Court, Sioux Falls
    Declarations of Intention, 1906–24
    Petitions and Records, 1906–28
    Naturalization Records, 1905–06
U.S. Circuit Court, Sioux Falls
    Declarations of Intention, 1892–1906
    Naturalization Certificates, 1907–23

Tennessee

NARA Southeast Region
Eastern District, Knoxville
    Declarations of Intention and Depositions, 1891–1928 (unindexed)

    Declarations of Intention, 1907–88 (indexed)
    Index to Petitions, 1908–41
    Petitions, 1908–70 (indexes in volumes to December 1957)
Eastern District, Chattanooga
    Petition Index Cards, 1890–1955
    Declarations, 1907–57 (indexed)
    Petitions, 1907–74 (indexed)
    Military Petitions, August 1918–December 1918 (indexed)
    Military Petitions, World War II, 1941–45 (few)
Eastern District, Greenville
    Declarations of Intention, 1914–74 (indexed)
    Petitions, 1911–64 (indexed)
Middle District, Nashville
    Petitions Retained at Clerk's Office in Nashville
Western District, Memphis
    Declarations of Intention, 1906–61 (indexed)
    Index to Petitions, 1954–67
    Petitions, 1907–63 (indexes except for December 1940–November 1954)
    Military Naturalization Petitions, 1918–19, 1953–55 (indexed)
Western District, Jackson
    Declarations of Intention, 1909–42 (indexed)
    Petitions, 1921–29 (indexed)
    (After March 1929, only declarations of intention were filed at Jackson; petitions were all filed at Memphis.)

Texas

NARA Southwest Region
Northern District, Abilene
    Declarations of Intention, 1909–83
    Petitions, 1911–84
    Transferred Petitions, 1955–84
    Lists of Granted Petitions, 1929–87
    Stubs of Naturalization Certificates, 1918–29
    Petitions by Military Servicemen, 1943–44
    Applications to Regain Citizenship and Repatriation Oaths, 1941–61

Transferred Petitions, 1948-80

Index to Petitions by Military Servicemen,
ca. 1918-44

Petitions by Military Servicemen, 1918-55

Applications to Regain Citizenship and
Repatriation Oaths, 1940-70

Lists of Granted Petitions, 1928-82

Orders Granting Citizenship, 1880

Eastern District, Paris

Petitions, 1908-28

Eastern District, Texarkana

Declarations of Intention, 1908-60

Petitions, 1930-60

Lists of Granted, Denied, or Continued Petitions,
1931-60

Transferred Petitions, 1954-57

Utah

The National Archives does not have naturalization
records for Utah. The records are in the custody of
the U.S. District Court, District of Utah, 350 S. Main
Street, Room 150, Salt Lake City, UT 84101. Older
records may be found in the Utah State Archives and
Record Service, Archives Building, State Capitol, Salt
Lake City, UT 84114.

Vermont

NARA Northeast Region (Boston)

U.S. District Court, District of Vermont

Name Indexes to Declarations and Petitions,
1801-1964

Name Index to Naturalization Petitions, 1951-83

Record Books of Declarations Filed, 1801-1906

Declarations Filed, 1907-45

Record Books of Petitions Filed, 1842-1906

Petitions for Naturalization, 1904-06

Petitions and Records of Naturalization,
1842-1972; 44 rolls

Declarations of Intention (with Petitions),
1840-1908

Depositions of Witnesses, 1932-62

Virginia

NARA Mid-Atlantic Region
(Center City Philadelphia)

Alexandria, Eastern District of Virginia

Petitions, 1909-29

Petitions, 1930-81

Military Petitions, Camp Humphreys, 1918

Declarations of Intention, 1867-1938

Richmond, Eastern District of Virginia

Petitions, 1906-29

Petitions, 1930-56

Military Petitions, Camp Lee, 1918-24

Abingdon, Western District of Virginia

Petitions, 1913-29

Charlottesville, Western District of Virginia

Petitions, 1910-29

Petitions, 1930-57

Declarations of Intention, 1908-29

Washington

NARA Pacific Alaska Region (Seattle)

*U.S. Circuit Court, Eastern District,
Northern Division, Spokane*

Declarations of Intention, 1903-06

Record of Naturalizations, 1903-06

Petition and Record, 1908

*U.S. District Court, Eastern District, Northern
Division, Spokane*

Index to Naturalizations, 1906-47

Declarations of Intention, 1890-1964

Petitions for Naturalization, 1907-60

Naturalization Record, 1892-1902

*U.S. District Court, Western District, Northern
Division*

Naturalization Indexes, 1890-1952

Declarations of Intention, 1890-1950

Naturalization Petitions, 1906-50

Naturalization Record, Adult (Petitions),
1890-1906

Naturalization Record, Minor (Petitions),
1892-1906

Naturalization Depositions, 1911-53

Naturalization Certificate Stubs, 1907-25

Statements of Fact for Petitions, 1911-14

*U.S. District Court, Western District,
Southern Division*

Naturalization Indexes, 1912-53

Partial Indexes to Military Petitions, 1918-19

Naturalization Petitions and Records, 1912–52

Declarations of Intention, 1907–57

Naturalization Records, 1896–1900

Orders of the Court of Naturalization, 1929–59

Overseas Naturalization Petitions, 1954–55

Repatriation Petitions, 1936–43

Soldiers' Repatriation Petitions, 1919–43

Naturalization Certificate Stubs, 1913–19

U.S. District Court, Southern Division, Walla Walla

Declaration of Intentions, 1907–50

Petition for Naturalization, 1907–50

U.S. District Court, Southern Division, Yakima

Declarations of Intention, 1907–42

Petitions for Naturalization, 1907–72

County Court, King County

Territorial Court Index, 1864–89

Naturalization Index, 1906–28

Declarations of Intention, 1854–1924

Petitions for Naturalization, 1906–28

Naturalization Records (Petitions), 1889–1906

County Court, Pierce County

Naturalization Indexes, 1853–1922

Declarations of Intention, 1853–1922

Record of Citizenship (Petitions), 1854–81

Petitions for Naturalization, 1889–1923

County Court, Snohomish County

General Index to Naturalization, 1892–1975

Card Index to Naturalization, 11950–74

Declarations of Intention, 1876–1973

Petitions for Naturalization, 1890–1974

Repatriation Petitions, 1939–55

Citizenship Record (Petition), 1890–1906

Citizenship Petitions Granted, 1929–75

County Court, Thurston County

Card Index to Naturalization, 1850–1974

Declarations of Intention, 1883–1974

Petitions for Naturalization, 1902–74

Certificate Stub Books, 1907–24

Deposition Case Files, 1844–1907

Interrogatories and Deposition Notices,
   1929–41

Repatriation Petitions, 1940–64

Transferred Naturalization Petitions, 1852–74

Naturalization Court Orders, 1930–74

Naturalization Journals (Petitions), 1891–1906

West Virginia

NARA Mid-Atlantic Region

(Center City Philadelphia)

Clarksburg, Northern District of West Virginia

Petitions, 1908–50

Declarations of Intention, 1908–52

Elkins, Northern District of West Virginia

Petitions, 1926–56

Petitions, 1970–80

Declarations of Intention, 1930–53

Declarations of Intention, 1972–85

Fairmont, Northern District of West Virginia

Petitions, 1944–74

Declarations of Intention, 1942–74

Phillipi, Northern District of West Virginia

Petitions, 1910–25

Declarations of Intention, 1920–29

Wheeling, Northern District of West Virginia

Name Index, 1844–75

Naturalization Records, 1844–75

Naturalization Records, 1876–1935

Charleston, Southern District of West Virginia

Name Index, 1904–62

Petitions, 1906–29

Military Petitions, 1918

Declarations of Intention, 1906–52

Wisconsin

NARA Great Lakes Region

U.S. District Court, Western District, LaCrosse

Declarations of Intention, 1870–1900

Naturalization Docket Book, 1871–1900

U.S. District Court, Western District, Madison

Naturalization Docket Book, 1873–1906

Declarations of Intention, 1876–1902

Naturalization Petitions, 1941–69

Records Relating to Repatriation, 1961

Index to Declarations of Intention, 1848–99

Duplicate Petitions and Duplicate Certificates of Naturalization for Members of the Armed Forces Serving Overseas, 1941–56

U.S. District Court, Western District, Superior
Naturalization Petition and Record Book, 1910–18
Declarations of Intention, 1902–21
Certificates of Naturalization Stubs, 1910–20
Naturalization Petitions, 1955
Duplicate Petitions and Duplicate Certificates of Naturalization of World War II Veterans, 1954

U.S. District Court, Eastern District, Milwaukee
Naturalization Petition and Record Books, 1848–1970
Index to Declarations of Intention, 1943–54
Declarations of Intention, 1848–1971
Repatriation Order Book, 1940
Orders Granting or Denying Citizenship, 1929–57
Naturalization Depositions, 1908–42
Naturalization Index, 1848–1990

Wyoming

The National Archives does not have naturalization records for Wyoming. The records are in the custody of the U.S. District Court, P.O. Box 727, Cheyenne, WY 82003. The Wyoming State Archives, Barrett Building, Cheyenne, WY 82002, has old naturalizations.

WPA NATURALIZATION INDEXES

During the 1930s and 1940s, most states participated in a nationwide project, sponsored by the U.S. Department of Justice and carried out by the Work Projects Administration (WPA), to locate and photograph naturalization records predating 27 September 1906. Although all photostatic copies were to be deposited with the Immigration and Naturalization Service, few of the states or districts had been completed when the WPA was disbanded in 1942.

There are several enormous naturalization indexes that should be consulted initially if the alien of interest lived in one of the areas covered by these compilations.

One of the largest is *Index to Naturalization Petitions of the United States District Court for the Eastern District of New York 1865–1957*, described in a pamphlet of the same title (National Archives Trust Fund Board, 1991). The records which have been microfilmed consist of approximately 650,000 three- by five-inch cards that index bound and unbound naturalization petitions. The cards are arranged in three groups covering the periods July 1865 to September 1906, October 1906 to November 1925, and November 1925 to December 1957. The cards within each group are arranged alphabetically by the name of the person naturalized.

Index cards for the first group include the name of the naturalized individual, the date of naturalization, and the volume and record number of the naturalization petition. These cards may also contain such information as the address, occupation, birth date or age, former nationality, and port and date of arrival of the person naturalized, and the name of the witness to the naturalization.

The cards for the second and third groups show the name, petition, and certificate number of the person naturalized and generally include the address, age, and date of admission to citizenship.

The petitions to which these microfilmed index cards relate are in the National Archives' Northeast Region (New York City). They have not yet been microfilmed.

Petitions for the period from July 1865 to September 1906 are arranged in bound volumes. The information on each petition varies. Petitions dated 1 July 1865 to 5 July 1895 indicate the city of residence, former nationality of petitioner, name of witness, dates of petition, and admission to citizenship. Petitions dated from 5 July 1895 through 26 September 1906 may also contain information on the petitioner's occupation, date and place of birth, and port and date of arrival in the United States; the name, address, and occupation of the witness; and the signature of the alien.

Petitions filed after September 1906 are unbound and are arranged numerically by petition number. They usually indicate the occupation, place of embarkation, and date and port of arrival of the petitioner; name of the vessel or other means of conveyance into the United States; the court in which the alien's declaration of intention was filed and filing date; marital status; name and place of residence of each of the applicant's children; date of the beginning of the alien's continuous U.S. residence; length of residence in the United States; names, occupations, and addresses of witnesses; and signatures of alien and witnesses.

A caveat in the descriptive pamphlet states:

The index reproduced on this microfilm publication refers only to those aliens who sought naturalization in the U.S. District Court for the Eastern District of New York, located in Kings County, New York. An alien, however, could become a naturalized citizen through any court of record, making it possible for those living in any of the five counties that make up the eastern district to seek naturalization through the city or county courts in the counties in this district. This index, therefore, does not contain the names of all individuals naturalized in the counties of Kings, Queens, Richmond, Suffolk, and Nassau. The clerks of these county courts will, as a rule, have custody of the naturalization records of aliens who became citizens in their courts.

The National Archives' Great Lakes Region in Chicago has in its custody the Soundex index to more than 1.5 million naturalization petitions from northern Illinois, northwestern Indiana, southern and eastern Wisconsin, and eastern Iowa. The microfilmed index is described in a pamphlet titled *Soundex Index to Naturalization Petitions for the United States District and Circuit Courts, Northern District of Illinois, and Immigration and Naturalization Service District 9, 1840–1950* (National Archives Trust Fund Board, 1991). The index consists of 162 cubic feet of three- by five-

inch cards arranged in Russell-Soundex order and thereafter alphabetically by given name. The index includes civil and military petitions.

While the Soundex index includes references to naturalizations that took place in parts of Illinois, Indiana, Wisconsin, and Iowa, a great portion of the records cited in the index are not physically located at the National Archives. Naturalization records in the custody of the Great Lakes Region, with one exception, consist of records for persons naturalized in certain federal (not county or state) courts. The one exception is copies (not originals) of county naturalization records for 1871 through 1906 for Chicago/Cook County, Illinois. A sampling of the Soundex index described above (see figure 4-11, chapter 4) illustrates the standard format used for the cards and the kind of information about the individual that may or may not be included. Besides the name of the naturalized citizen, it is especially important to note the name of the court in which the naturalization took place and the petition number (when it is included on the card) when following through with a search for the actual naturalization documents. Normally, much of the biographical information recorded in the original document was copied to the Soundex card. If the spaces on the card for date of birth, birthplace, date and place of arrival in the United States, etc., are blank, it is likely that the original naturalization documents did not include that information. (For additional information on the origin and organization of the Soundex, see chapter 4, "Published Naturalization Records and Indexes.")

While there is no comprehensive index to other naturalizations in its custody, the Great Lakes Region also has naturalization documents for other federal courts in Illinois, Indiana, Michigan, Minnesota, Ohio, and Wisconsin for certain years.

The Northeast Region (Boston) has original copies of naturalization records of the federal courts for the six New England states. Individuals were also naturalized in state, county, and local courts. The branch has copies (dexographs—white-on-black photographs) of such court records between 1790 and 1906 for Maine, Massachusetts, Rhode Island, Vermont, and New Hampshire. For Connecticut there are originals of some state, county, and local naturalizations for the years 1790 to 1974. An index to naturalization documents filed in courts in Connecticut, Maine, Massachusetts, New Hampshire, and Rhode Island is also at the Northeast Region (Boston). The index contains some cards for New York and Vermont as well, but the records to which they refer are not among the photocopies at that regional archive. The New England WPA index consists of three- by five-inch cards arranged by name of petitioner and by the Soundex system. The index refers to the name and location of the court that granted citizenship and to the volume and page number of the naturalization record.

The naturalization process began with the declaration of intention (first papers) and concluded with the petition for citizenship and the naturalization certificate. The normal eligibility waiting period for citizenship was five years. If favorably judged, a court order admitting the petitioner to citizenship was entered in the record book. Although the court kept naturalization certificate stubs or another record of the event, the actual naturalization certificate was given only to the new citizen; copies of certificates were not retained by the court.

Because of derivative citizenship, naturalization records for women and children are rarely found for early years. Since 1790, children under the age of twenty-one years have become citizens automatically by naturalization of the parent. Until 1922, a wife became naturalized upon citizenship conferred to her husband, and no separate filings were necessary. After an act of 22 September 1922, a married woman had to be naturalized on her own.

BIBLIOGRAPHY

Kansas, Sidney. *U.S. Immigration Exclusion and Deportation and Citizenship of the United States of America*. 3rd ed. New York: Matthew Bender Company, 1948.

Newman, John J. American *Naturalization Processes and Procedures, 1790–1985*. Indianapolis: Indiana Historical Society, 1985.

Guide to Genealogical Research in the National Archives. Rev. ed. Washington, D.C.: National Archives Trust Fund Board, 1985.

Szucs, Loretto Dennis, and Sandra Hargreaves Luebking. *The Archives: A Guide to the National Archives Field Branches*. Salt Lake City: Ancestry, 1988.

_____, *The Source: A Guidebook of American Genealogy*. Rev. ed. Salt Lake City: Ancestry, 1997.

CHAPTER SEVEN

Finding Naturalization Information on the Internet

A WHOLE NEW WORLD OF RESEARCH IS OPENING UP VIA the Internet; genealogists and historians, like researchers in every other field, are reaping this technological harvest. The World Wide Web contains a wealth of information useful for finding naturalization records, both in the U.S. and abroad. Although only a handful of searchable databases are available online now, virtually all federal, state, and county agencies have Web sites that outline their holdings and provide key information on how to access their records. Some have forms that can be downloaded, and some even have indexes to collections that can be searched online.

Going beyond the offerings of government and historical agencies, the Internet offers tools and useful information. Computers allow us access to places that we couldn't reach before; they let us store and retrieve information quickly and efficiently. But that is only the beginning; this new technology allows libraries, archives, genealogical and historical societies, genealogical publishers, government agencies, and museums, as well as individuals, to share their wealth of information. Genealogical societies and publishers have posted a vast array of guides and databases on their home pages. With the click of a button, you have the power to see into the card catalog of a distant library, exchange research notes with a newly found cousin, download files from some sleepy town halfway across the world, or examine photographs taken in the very place and time your ancestors lived.

As Laurie and Steve Bonner note in *Searching for Cyber-Roots: A Step-by-Step Guide to Genealogy on the World Wide Web* (Salt Lake City: Ancestry, 1997), "The Internet isn't replacing the days of rooting through the files in a dusty corner of a small-town courthouse, or wading through high grass to run cold fingers over a faded tombstone, or squinting at microfiche amidst the hum of a big library. But it will add a new dimension to your journey, and soon the flicker of a computer screen will become as familiar to you as your notebooks, file folders, and index cards." And don't worry if you don't have a computer at home; many public libraries are now online and allow the public to use their computers at no charge. Some even offer classes on using the Internet.

Where you begin your Internet investigation depends a great deal on your level of experience in conducting research and your level of experience with the Internet. Your goals will probably make your decision quite easy. Is the information you seek likely to be found in a federal, state, or local agency? Could a genealogical or historical society help guide you to specific resources? Are you seeking help to research a specific surname? In any case, a well-planned strategy can save both the experienced and novice researcher valuable time. With literally millions of people and sources now on the Internet and more being added daily, a visit to the Internet can be like a visit to the jungle; it's easy to get lost. As the editor of *Genealogical Computing* quarterly, Jake Gehring, pointed out in *Ancestry* 15 (2) (March/April 1997),

> Without some guidance, using the World Wide Web to find information is an exercise in educated guessing. In a way, the same problems often exist in print. A large and valuable manuscript collection is a daunting obstacle if no one has taken the time to index its contents. Indexes and catalogs help us to find information quickly because they lend additional organization to the data they describe. Fortunately, similar finding aids exist on the Internet. These indexes are called search engines. Each search engine is different in terms of organization and coverage; each indexes Web sites in a slightly different manner; and each interprets your request differently. Dozens of search engines now exist, yet only a handful stand out as fast, comprehensive powerful tools.

It is important to find a search engine you are comfortable with. Experiment with several to find the one that works best for you. And remember, as my father always told me, "If all else fails, follow directions." Most search engines come with specific directions and tips on how to best use their valuable tools. Here is a list of major search engines that Jake Gehring presented in the same issue of *Ancestry*.

Alta Vista
http://www.altavista.digital.com/
(Indexes USENET news groups as well as the World Wide Web and is updated often.)

Excite
http://www.excite.com/
(Big on features, speed, and accuracy; very comprehensive.)

Hot Bot
http://www.hotbot.com/
(Fully automated; fast growing; good search features.)

Lycos
http://www.lycos.com/
(Complete searching; includes additional features such as PeopleFind and CityGuide.)

Meta Crawler
http://www.metacrawler.com/
(Searches Lycos, Excite, Yahoo, Hot Bot and other search engines simultaneously.)

Yahoo!
http://www.yahoo.com/
(Hierarchically organized; extremely popular.)

Bear in mind that all search engines are not equal. In doing a search, it is important to note that the criteria you enter may bring up different results in different search engines. Many search engines are equipped with "smart" functions capable of looking for variations of a word, determining that Robert equals Bob, or even establishing relationships between words or phrases (for example, "elderly people" are the same as "senior citizens"); nevertheless, a search for "naturalizations" may produce different results than a search for "naturalization records." So don't give up if your first search doesn't uncover the exact information that you need. Try some variations, or experiment with a different search engine.

In order to do a more localized search, you will need to enter more information. For example, using the criteria "minnesota naturalization records," I did a search using the search engine Meta Crawler. I specified that I wanted to use "all," meaning that I wanted all the criteria that I entered to be in the results. The search resulted in thirty-six references, including *Naturalization Records in Minnesota* by Park Genealogical Books (http://www.parkbooks.com/Html/res_nat.html). I visited the site and was rewarded with a page of information on Minnesota naturalizations. From this I learned that the naturalization records for Minnesota are located in three major repositories: the Minnesota Historical Society houses a large collection received from the Minnesota courts; the federal court records for Minnesota are divided between the National Archives' Central Plains Region (pre-1971) and Great Lakes Region (after 1971).

Many of the records from the Minnesota Historical Society are available through interlibrary loan, and the society's page contained a link to PALS, an online catalog for libraries in Minnesota, so I decided to pursue this channel. I did a search of "All PALS Libraries" using the keywords "naturalization records" and was rewarded with 753 matches to the word "naturalization" and 287 matches to "naturalization records." There were naturalizations by county, declarations of intention, and some family histories, as well as some how-to books and various other references. I was also given the option to "Limit Search." Each item had a number which could be clicked on to display more information. This information included the library, location (microfilm number), author, title, publisher, description, summary, subject, and genre-heading. There were also more options for browsing to the previous/next record, a results list, submitting an interlibrary loan request, a long display, and "suggest purchase."

Feeling confident now, I moved on. Suppose that the ancestor in question was not located in the naturalization records found on this search. What next?

The same search on Meta Crawler could be made for the ancestor's ethnic origins. A previous search that I had done using the terms "naturalization records" had turned up a link to "NOIS-Norway Online Information Service." I decided to pursue this avenue, since I was unfamiliar with Norwegian research (as I was with Minnesota research), and I wanted to be able to view the search as a newcomer to genealogy or to this type of genealogical research would. The page that came up was titled "How to Trace Your Ancestors in Norway" (http://www.norway.org/ancestor.htm), and this page contained sections on emigration lists and migration records. Armed with this new information, I performed another search using the more specific terms "emigration lists Norway"; this provided more links to information in Norway. Besides the site I had just visited, I found one titled "Emigration Archives" (http://fjordinfo.vestdata.no/offentleg/sffarkiv/sffut1.htm). It turned out to be information on the county (*fylke*) Son og Fjordane. The site contains an online migration database, 1839 to 1924, as well as other information on emigrants from Norway. A great site, but suppose our ancestors are not from Son og Fjordane? Let's move on. The next site was titled "Department of History," which turned out to be the University of Bergen's

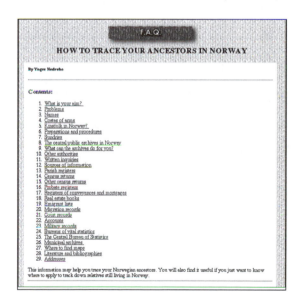

Figure 7-1. Norway Online Information Service offers twenty-two pages of information on Norwegian genealogy.

Department of History (http://www.uib.no/hi/1801page.html). This page had links to an emigration list for Bergen Dpty. for 1874 to 1924 and also the 1801 Census of Norway. These are both searchable databases and great resources.

But let's say we would rather find a source a little closer to home. The search also turned up a link to the Vesterheim Genealogical Center and Naeseth Library in Madison, Wisconsin (http://fjordinfo.vestdata.no/offentleg/sffarkiv/sffutvgc.htm). Some of the center's holdings include microfilms, genealogical databases, passenger lists, and censuses.

This is just one example of what the researcher can find in a relatively short period of time on the Web. Keep in mind though, that just as every researcher's needs are different, so may be the results. You may not find the same type of information as easily for your state or region of interest as I did for this one; then again, you might have even better luck. Maybe one of your ancestors is out there in a database right now, just waiting for you to find him or her from the comfort of your own home or local library.

As noted previously, genealogical and historical organizations and genealogical companies have been building vast databases, any of which may contain the unique piece of information you need to com-plete the biography of an individual or the history of a family. Below is a list of some of these resources. In addition to providing entry to the databases, the following home pages are doorways to other sources and tools that can be useful in various other stages of research. This list includes not only sites for information on the naturalization records themselves, but also some alternative sites to provide more valuable information about your immigrant ancestors. Also, remember to keep an open mind; sometimes the original source may not be the best source of information. A good example of that is the Immigration and Naturalization Service. Although its home page has some information and forms available upon request, I found a site for Jewish Genealogy (http://www.jewishgen.org/faqinfo.html) that explained the process of requesting forms from the INS and offered viable alternatives that could yield faster results. Another thing to keep in mind is that information on the Internet is not monitored and is not always accurate; consequently, it is wise to check several sites to verify information. Also, by referencing other sites, you enhance the picture you are assembling of your ancestors and compensate for naturalization records that may be unavailable.

Figure 7-2. Immigration and Naturalization Service home page.

GOVERNMENT AGENCIES

The Immigration and Naturalization Service (INS)
http://www.ins.usdoj.gov/
Forms Download
http://www.ins.usdoj.gov/forms/index.html
Request Forms by Mail
http://www.ins.usdoj.gov/exec/forms/formsbymail.asp
(Downloadable forms; list of local offices; and regulatory information)

The National Archives and Records Administration (NARA)
Immigrant and Passenger Arrivals
http://www.nara.gov/publications/microfilm/immigrant/immpass.html

(This site contains some general information about the NARA Microfilm Publication Program; Records of the U.S. Customs Service, 1820–ca.1891; Records of the Immigration and Naturalization Service, 1891–1957.)

Records of the Immigration and Naturalization Service
http://www.us.net/upa/guides/insa3.htm
(Information regarding INS.)

Libraries and Museums

Balch Institute for Ethnic Studies
http://www.libertynet.org/~balch/
(Research in Ethnic Studies and Immigration; Description of Collections; Educational Programs.)

Ellis Island
http://www.ellisisland.org/
(Immigrant Museum, American Family Immigration Center, Immigrant Wall of Honor, Links)

Immigration History Research Center (IHRC) at the University of Minnesota
http://www.umn.edu/ihrc/
(Information about archival and library collec-

tions; search IHRC collections online; information on genealogical research.)

Leo Baeck Institute
http://www.users.interport.net/~lbi1/
(Information on facilities and collections available.)

Library of Congress
http://lcweb.loc.gov/
(American Memory Project; exhibitions; access to Library of Congress and other library catalogs; research tools; copyright records; ethnic/country studies)

New York Public Library
http://www.nypl.org/research/chss/lhg/research.htm
(Description of collections, including naturaliza-

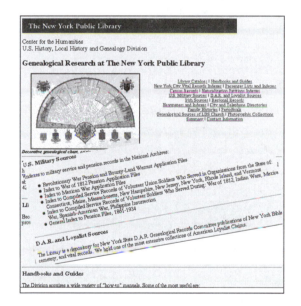

tion petition indexes; access to CATNYP online catalog; mail reference inquiries; links to other resources both inside and outside of the library.)

Some Regional Links

This small cross-section is intended to demonstrate what is available in various states.

Free Library of Philadelphia
http://www.library.phila.gov/central/ssh/waltgen/
pass1.htm
(Very informative site on passenger lists, immigration, emigration, naturalization, oaths of allegiance, and passports with outside resources.)

Naturalization Records in the Milwaukee Urban Archives
http://www.uwm.edu/Library/arch/citizen.htm
(Information on the naturalization process in the nineteenth and early twentieth centuries; records available for Ozuakee, Sheboygan, and Washington counties.)

Nemaha County Genealogical Society (Kansas)
http://ukanaix.cc.ukans.edu/kansas/seneca/gensoc/
courths/natural.html
(Inventory of naturalization records available in the Nemaha County District Court)

Ohio Historical Society/About Naturalizations in Ohio
http://www.ohiohistory.org/natural.html
(Information about naturalization records in Ohio; which records are held by Ohio Historical Society; other resources for naturalization records.)

Oregon State Archives
http://arcweb.sos.state.or.us/natural.html
(Information about the types of naturalization records; lists records available by county; recommends some published resources.)

Pennsylvania GenWeb Project-Naturalization and Immigration Page
http://www.chartiers.com/pages/nat.html
(Basic information on naturalizations; lists of Pennsylvania persons naturalized in 1760 and 1761 and Pennsylvania Quakers naturalized in 1760; links to other sources.)

U.S. GenWeb Project Home Page
http://www.usgenweb.com/
(This valuable resource has listings for each county by state. Many of the sites contain information, lists, or databases of naturalization records.)

Westchester County Archives
http://nyslgti.gen.ny.us/Westchester/arcintro.html
(A great resource for county records.)

GENEALOGICAL/HISTORICAL SOCIETIES

Federation of Genealogical Societies
http://www.fgs.org/~fgs/
(Links and information on the various members from all across the U.S.; current events; news on records preservation issues)

Immigrant Genealogical Society
http://feefhs.org/igs/frg-igs.html
(First immigrants list, databases, research services)

National Genealogical Society
http://www.genealogy.org/~ngs/
(Genealogical forms and research aids; genealogists' guide to the Internet; tips for beginners; Journal of Online Genealogy; links.)

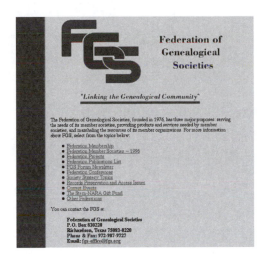

U.S. Internet Genealogical Society
http://www.usigs.org/
(Resources listed national and by state.)

ETHNIC GENEALOGICAL RESOURCES

Association of European Migration Institutions
http://users.cybercity.dk/~ccc13652/
(From the home page, "Institutions and organizations in Europe, whose fields of interest concern migration, research, and exhibitions portraying emigration, and who seek to promote understanding of common goals …" addresses and links to members which include museums, archives, institutes, etc. from across Europe.)

Australian Archives' Genealogical Records
http://www.aa.gov.au/AA_WWW/AA_Holdings/
ΛΛ_Genie/Genie.html
(Information on records available, including naturalization, passenger lists, migrant selection documents; database to allow users access to detailed information about the records held and the agencies that created them.)

Australian Migration and Naturalizations-LDS Microform Copies
http://www.zeta.org.au/~feraltek/lists/ldsmigr.htm
(Migration and naturalization records available through LDS libraries.)

Avotaynu
http://www.avotaynu.com/
(Information on publications, maps, links.)

Cunard Archives: information on passengers and emigrants
http://www.liv.ac.uk/~archives/cunard/chome.htm
(Archives of the Cunard Steamship Company, established in 1840, which carried many immigrants to America.)

Federation of East European Family History Societies (FEEFHS)
http://feefhs.org/
(A great resource page with many valuable links, Internet Journal, maps and more)

GENUKI—Genealogy in the U.K. and Ireland
http://midas.ac.uk/genuki/
(Tips on getting started; great links to resources in U.K. and Ireland, including information on immigration/emigration resources and much more)

German and American Sources for German Emigration to America
by Michael P. Palmer
http://www.genealogy.com/gene/www/emig/
emigrati.htm
(List of German emigrant resources.)

Irish Emigrants
http://genealogy.org/~ajmorris/ireland/ireemg1.htm
(List of Irish emigrants.)

Jewish Genealogy
http://www.jewishgen.org/
(Answers some basic questions about Jewish genealogy; databases; Jewish Cemetery Project online; Jewish Family Finder; includes information on naturalizations.)

Norway/Son og Fjordane: The Emigration Archives
http://fjordinfo.vestdata.no/offentleg/sffarkiv/sffut1.htm
(This site contains an online migration database, 1839 to 1924, as well as other information on emigrants from Norway.)

ODESSA . . . A German-Russian Genealogical Library
http://pixel.cs.vt.edu/library/odessa.html
(A great site—library and repository with extensive information including immigration, naturalization, and ship records; also, some declarations of intention listed online)

ODIN—Ministry of Foreign Affairs
How to trace your ancestors in Norway
http://odin.dep.no/ud/publ/96/ancestors/
(Contains general information on preparation and procedures, and lists various sources of information.)

Palatines to America
http://genealogy.org/~palam/
(This organization has an "On-line Immigrant Ancestor Register," a quarterly journal, a newsletter, and regional publications; also links to other sites.)

Swenson Swedish Immigration Research Center
http://www2.augustana.edu/admin/swenson/
(Information about collections and publications; links to other sites, including some Scandinavian immigration.)

LINKS TO PASSENGER LISTS/ IMMIGRANT INFORMATION

Emigration/Ship Lists and Resources
http://www.geocities.com/Heartland/5978/Emigration.html
(Links to various passenger lists and immigrant/emigrant information.)

Genealogy Resources on the Internet
Passenger Lists; Ships; Ship Museums
http://www-personal.umich.edu/~cgaunt/pass.html
(Links to Information about researching passenger lists, information in archives, information about ships, individual ships, and disasters.)

Library of Michigan—Bibliography of Immigrant/Passenger Lists
http://www.libofmich.lib.mi.us/genealogy/immigration.html
(Lists various printed sources.)

The Olive Tree Genealogy-Index to Passenger Lists
http://www.rootsweb.com/~ote/indexshp.htm
(Index to various ships passenger lists, as well as information and links to other books and resources.)

OTHER GENERAL GENEALOGICAL SITES

American Genealogical Lending Library (AGLL)
http://www.agll.com/
(Seven steps to a family tree; newsletter.)

Ancestry.com
http://www.ancestry.com/
(Lots of searchable databases, several with immigration information; links to other sources; online genealogy newsletters; National Archives Research Guide; PERSI—Online Genealogical Periodical Search; Community Tree; Genealogy

Academy with genealogy classes; Social Security Death Index Online; links to professional researchers; information on publications and sales online; new database added daily; and more.)

Cyndi's List of Genealogical Sites on the Internet
http://www.CyndisList.com
(Categorized links to more than twenty thousand genealogy-related sites.)

Everton's Genealogical Helper
http://www.everton.com/
(Online searches; databases; newsletter online; links.)

Family Tree Maker
http://www.familytreemaker.com/
(Beginners' class online; Family Finder indexes and searches; orders for record look-ups.)

Frontier Press
http://www.doit.com/frontier/
(Information on publications and book sales online.)
Genealogy Home Page
http://genhomepage.com/
(Categorized links to resources.)

Rand Genealogy Club
http://www.rand.org/personal/Genea
(Categorized links, including some immigration resources.)

Immigration Chronology

1562: French Huguenots established a colony on Parris Island near Beaufort, South Carolina, but abandoned it within two years.

1565: The earliest Hispanic settlers within the area of the United States settled Saint Augustine, Florida in 1565.

1598: Hispanics settled in New Mexico.

1607: Jamestown, Virginia, was founded by English colonists.

1614: The first major Dutch settlement was founded near Albany, New York.

1619: The first black slaves arrived at Jamestown.

1620: The Mayflower, carrying Pilgrims, arrived in Massachusetts.

1623: New Netherland (Hudson River Valley) was settled as a trading post by the Dutch West India Company.

1629–40: The Puritans migrated to New England.

1634: Lord Baltimore founded Maryland as a refuge for English Catholics.

1642: The outbreak of civil war in England brought a decrease in Puritan migration.

1648: The treaty ending the Thirty Years' War stipulated that only the Catholic, Lutheran, and Reformed religions would be tolerated in Germany henceforth. Religious intolerance motivated large numbers of Germans belonging to small sects, such as Baptist Brethren (Dunkers), to leave for America.

1649: Passage of Maryland Toleration Act opened the door to any professing trinitarian Christianity.

1654: North America's first Jewish immigrants fled Portuguese persecution in Brazil, arriving at New Amsterdam.

1660: Acting on mercantilist doctrine that the wealth of a country depends on the number of its inhabitants, Charles II officially discouraged emigration from England.

1670: English courtiers settled the Carolinas.

1681: Quakers founded Pennsylvania based on William Penn's "holy experiment" in universal philanthropy and brotherhood.

1683: The first German settlers (Mennonites) arrived in Pennsylvania.

1685: Huguenots fleeing religious intolerance in France and the Revocation of the Edict of Nantes by Louis XIV settled in South Carolina.

1697: The slave trade monopoly of the Royal African Company ended and the slave trade expanded rapidly, especially among New Englanders.

1707: A new era of Scottish migration began as a result of the Act of Union between England and Scotland. Scots settled in colonial seaports. Lowland artisans and laborers left Glasgow to become indentured servants in tobacco colonies and New York.

1709: In the wake of devastation caused by wars of Louis XIV, German Palatines settled in the Hudson Valley and Pennsylvania.

1717: The English Parliament legalized transportation to American colonies as punishment; contractors began regular shipments from jails, mostly to Virginia and Maryland.

1718: Discontent with the land system: a b s e n t e e landlords, high rents, and short leases in the homeland motivated large numbers of Scotch-Irish to emigrate. Most settled first in New England, then in Maryland and Pennsylvania.

1730: Germans and Scotch Irish from Pennsylvania colonized Virginia valley and the Carolina back country.

1732: James Oglethorpe settled Georgia as a buffer against Spanish and French attack, as a producer of raw silk, and as a haven for imprisoned debtors.

1740: The English Parliament enacted the Naturalization Act, which conferred British citizenship on alien colonial immigrants in an attempt to encourage Jewish immigration.

1745: Scottish rebels were transported to America after a Jacobite attempt to put Stuarts back on the throne failed.

1755: French Acadians were expelled from Nova Scotia on suspicion of disloyalty. The survivors settled in Louisiana.

1771–73: Severe crop failure and depression in the Ulster linen trade brought a new influx of Scotch-Irish to the American colonies.

1775: The outbreak of hostilities in American colonies caused the British government to suspend emigration.

1783: The revolutionary war ended with the Treaty of Paris. Immigration to America resumed, with especially large numbers of Scotch-Irish.

1789: The outbreak of the French Revolution prompted the emigration of aristocrats and royalist sympathizers.

1790: The first federal activity in an area previously under the control of the individual colonies:

An act of 26 March 1790 attempted to establish a uniform rule for naturalization by setting the residence requirement at two years. Children of naturalized citizens were considered to be citizens (1 Stat. 103).

1791: After a slave revolt in Santo Domingo, 10,000 to 20,000 French exiles took refuge in the United States, principally in towns on the Atlantic seaboard.

1793: As a result of the French Revolution, Girondists and Jacobins threatened by guillotine fled to the United States.

1795: Provisions of a naturalization act of 29 January 1795 included the following: free white aliens of good moral character; five-year residency with one year in state; declaration of intention to be filed after two years; petition to be filed three years after the declaration (1 Stat. 414).

1798: An unsuccessful Irish rebellion sent rebels to the United States. Distressed artisans, yeoman farmers, and agricultural laborers affected by bad harvests and low prices joined the rebels in emigrating.

U.S. Alien and Sedition Acts gave the president powers to seize and expel resident aliens suspected of engaging in subversive activities.

Naturalization requirements were changed to require fourteen years' residency; the declaration of intention was to be filed five years before citizenship (1 Stat. 566).

Aliens considered to be dangerous to the peace and safety of the United States were to be removed; passenger lists were to be given to the collector of customs (1 Stat. 570).

1802: Residency requirements of the 1795 act were reasserted; children of naturalized citizens were considered to be citizens (2 Stat. 153).

1803: War between England and France resumed. As a result, transatlantic trade was interrupted and emigration from continental Europe became practically impossible.

Irish emigration was curtailed by the British Passenger Act, which limited the numbers to be carried by emigrant ships.

1807: Congress prohibited the importing of black slaves into the country. Individual states previously prohibited importation of slaves: Delaware in 1776; Virginia, 1778; Maryland, 1783; South Carolina, 1787; North Carolina, 1794; Georgia, 1798. South Carolina reopened importation of slaves in 1803.

1812: The War of 1812 between Britain and the United States brought immigration to a halt.

1814: The War of 1812 ended with the Treaty of Ghent.

1815: The first great wave of immigration to the United States brought 5 million immigrants between 1815 and 1860.

1818: Liverpool became the most-used port of departure for Irish and British immigrants, as well as considerable numbers of Germans and other Europeans as the Black Ball Line of sailing packets began regular Liverpool-New York service.

1819: The first significant federal legislation relating to immigration: passenger lists to be given to the collector of customs; reporting of immigration to the United States on a regular basis; specific sustenance rules for passengers of ships leaving U.S. ports for Europe (3 Stat. 489).

1820: The U.S. population was at 9,638,453. One hundred and fifty-one thousand new immigrants arrived in 1820 alone.

The government of Prussia attempted to halt emigration by making it a crime to urge anyone to emigrate.

1824: Alien minors were naturalized upon reaching twenty-one years of age if they had lived in the United States for five years (4 Stat. 69).

1825: Great Britain officially recognized the view that England was overpopulated and repealed laws prohibiting emigration.

The first group of Norwegian immigrants arrives from their overpopulated homeland.

1830: Public land in Illinois was allotted by Congress to Polish revolutionary refugees.

1837: Financial panic. Nativists claimed that immigration lowered wage levels, contributed to the decline of the apprenticeship system, and generally depressed the condition of labor.

1840: The Cunard Line began passenger transportation between Europe and the United States, opening the steamship era.

1845: The Native American party, precursor of the nativist, anti-immigrant Know-Nothing party, was founded.

1846: Crop failures in Europe. Mortgage foreclosures sent tens of thousands of dispossessed to United States.

1846–47: Irish of all classes emigrated to the United States as a result of the potato famine.

1848: Failure of German revolution resulted in the emigration of political refugees to America.

1855: Castle Garden immigration receiving station opened in New York City to accommodate mass immigration.

Alien women married to U.S. citizens were considered to be citizens (10 Stat. 604).

1856: The Know-Nothing movement was defeated in the presidential election. An Albany convention to promote Irish rural colonization in the United States was strongly opposed by Eastern bishops and thus unsuccessful.

1860: New York became "the largest Irish city in the world." Of its 805,651 residents, 203,760 were Irish-born.

1861–65: The Civil War caused a significant drop in the number of foreigners entering the United States. Large numbers of immigrants serve on both sides during the Civil War.

1862: Aliens who received honorable discharges from the U.S. Army were not required to file declarations (12 Stat. 597).

The Homestead Act encouraged naturalization by granting citizens title to 160 acres, provided that the land was tilled for five years.

1864: Congress centralized control of immigration with a commissioner under the secretary of state. In an attempt to meet the labor crisis caused by the Civil War, Congress legalized the importation of contract laborers.

1875: The first direct federal regulation of immigration was established by prohibiting entry of prostitutes and convicts. Residency permits were required of Asians (18 Stat. 477).

1880: The U.S. population was 50,155,783. More than 5.2 million immigrants entered the country between 1880 and 1890.

1882: The Chinese exclusion law was established, curbing Chinese immigration. Further exclusions: persons convicted of political offenses, "lunatics," "idiots," and persons likely to become public charges. A head tax of fifty cents was placed on each immigrant.

A sharp rise in Jewish emigration to the United States was prompted by the outbreak of anti-Semitism in Russia.

1883: In an effort to alleviate a labor shortage caused by the freeing of slaves, the Southern Immigration Association was founded to promote immigration to the South.

1885: Contract laborers were denied admission to United States by the Foran Act. However, skilled laborers, artists, actors, lecturers, and domestic servants were not barred. Individuals in the United States were not to be prevented from assisting the immigration of relatives and personal friends.

1886: The Statue of Liberty was dedicated.

1888: The first act since 1798 providing for the expulsion of aliens became law.

1890: New York had the distinction of being home to as many Germans as Hamburg, Germany.

1891: The Bureau of Immigration was established under the Treasury Department to federally administer all immigration laws (except the Chinese Exclusion Act). Congress added health qualifications to immigration restrictions. Classes of persons denied the right to immigrate to the United States included the insane, paupers, persons with contagious diseases, persons convicted of felonies or misdemeanors of moral turpitude, and polygamists (26 Stat. 1084).

Pogroms in Russia caused large numbers of Jews to immigrate to the United States.

1892: Ellis Island replaced Castle Garden as the reception center for immigrants.

Immigration of Chinese to the United States was prohibited for ten years; Chinese illegally in the United States could be removed (27 Stat. 25).

1893: Chinese legally in the United States were required to apply to collectors of internal revenue for certificates of residence or be removed (28 Stat. 7).

Economic depression brought dramatic strength to the anti-Catholic American Protective Association.

1894: Congress created the Bureau of Immigration. The Immigration Restriction League was organized to lead the restrictionist movement for the next twenty-five years. The league emphasized the distinction between "old" (northern and western European) and "new" (southern and eastern European) immigrants.

Aliens who received honorable discharges from the U.S. Navy and U.S. Marine Corps were not required to file declarations (28 Stat. 124).

1894–96: To escape Moslem massacres, Armenian Christians began emigrating to the United States.

1897: President Cleveland vetoed literacy tests for immigrants.

1900: The U.S. Population at 75,994,575. More than 3,687,000 immigrants were admitted in the previous ten years.

1903: Extensive codification of existing immigration law. Added to the exclusion list were polygamists and political radicals (anarchists or persons believing in the overthrow by force or violence of the government of the United States or any government, or in the assassination of public officials—a result of President McKinley's assassination by an anarchist).

1905: As a protest against the influx of Asian laborers, the Japanese and Korean Exclusion League was formed by organized labor.

1906: The Bureau of Immigration and Naturalization was established. The purpose of the act of 29 June 1906 (32 Stat. 596) was to provide for a uniform rule for the naturalization of aliens throughout the United States. The law, effective 27 September 1906, was designed to provide "dignity, uniformity, and regularity" to the naturalization procedure. It established procedural safeguards and called for specific and uniform information regarding applicants and recipients of citizenship status. Rule Nine of the code required that all blank forms and records be obtained from and controlled by the Bureau of Immigration, "Those alone being official forms. No other forms shall be used." As a consequence of the act, the agency controlled the number of courts able to naturalize. Knowledge of English became a basic requirement for citizenship.

1907: An increased head tax on immigrants was enacted. People with physical or mental defects or tuberculosis and children unaccompanied by parents were added to the exclusion list. Japanese immigration was restricted.

1907–08: A Japanese government agreement to deny passports to laborers going directly from Japan to the United States failed to satisfy West Coast exclusionists.

1910: The Mexican Revolution sent thousands to the United States seeking employment.

1913: The Alien Land Law passed by California effectively barred Japanese, as "aliens ineligible for citizenship," from owning agricultural land in the state.

1914–18: World War I halted a period of mass migration to the United States.

1917: To the exclusion list were added illiterates, persons of "psychopathic inferiority," men and women entering for immoral purposes, alcoholics, stowaways, and vagrants.

The Jones Act made Puerto Ricans U.S. citizens and eligible for the draft.

1919: Anti-foreign prejudice was transferred from German Americans to alien revolutionaries and radicals in the Big Red Scare. Thousands of aliens were seized in the Palmer raids, and hundreds were deported.

1921: The first quantitative immigration law set temporary annual quotas according to nationality. The emergency immigration quotas heavily favored natives of northern and western Europe and all but closed the door to southern and eastern Europeans. An immediate drop in immigration followed.

1922: Alien wives of U.S. citizens were allowed to file for citizenship after one year of residency. The citizenship status of native-born American women was removed if they were married to aliens not eligible for citizenship (42 Stat. 1021).

1923: A strong anti-immigrant movement spearheaded by the Ku Klux Klan reached peak strength.

1924: The National Origins Act, the first permanent immigration quota law, established a discriminatory quota system, non-quota status, and a consular control system. The Border Patrol was established (49 Stat. 153).

1929: The National Origins Act came into effect. The stock market crash and economic crisis prompted demands for further immigration reductions. The Hoover administration ordered rigorous enforcement of a prohibition against the admission of persons liable to be public charges.

1930: The U.S. population was 123,203,000. Only 528,000 new immigrants arrived in the previous decade, the lowest number since the 1830s.

1933: As Hitler's anti-Semitic campaign began, Jewish refugees from Nazi Germany emigrated.

1934: Filipino immigration was restricted to an annual quota of fifty by the Philippine Independence Act.

1936: American women who had lost their citizenship because they married aliens were allowed to regain citizenship by taking oaths of allegiance to the United States (49 Stat. 1917).

1939: World War II began.

1940: The Alien Registration Act, also known as the Smith Act, called for registration and fingerprinting of all aliens. Approximately 5 million aliens were registered.

1941: Immigrant groups supported the united war effort as the United States entered World War II.

1942: Japanese-Americans were evacuated from their homes and moved to detention camps.

Through the Bracero Program, Mexican laborers were strongly encouraged to come to the United States to ease the shortage of farm workers brought on by World War II.

1943: Legislation provided for the importation of agricultural workers from North, South, and Central America—the basis of the "Bracero Program."

The Chinese exclusion laws were repealed.

1945: Thousands of Puerto Ricans emigrated to escape poverty. Many settled in New York.

1946: The War Brides Act facilitated the immigration of foreign-born wives, fiancé(e)s, husbands, and children of U.S. armed forces personnel.

1948: The Displaced Persons Act, the first U.S. policy for admitting persons fleeing persecution, allowed 400,000 refugees to enter the United States during a four-year period.

1950: Increased grounds for exclusion and deportation of subversives were enacted. All aliens were required to report their addresses annually.

1952: The Immigration and Naturalization Act brought into one comprehensive statute the multiple laws which governed immigration and naturalization to date: reaffirmed the national origins quota system; limited immigration from the Eastern Hemisphere while leaving the Western Hemisphere unrestricted; established preferences for skilled workers and relatives of U.S. citizens and permanent resident aliens; tightened security and screening standards and procedures; and lowered the age requirement for naturalization to eighteen years (66 Stat. 163).

The McCarren-Walter Immigration and Naturalization Act extended token immigration quotas to Asian countries.

1953–56: The Refugee Relief Act admitted more than 200,000 refugees beyond existing quotas.

Visas were granted to some 5,000 Hungarians after the 1956 revolt. President Eisenhower invited 30,000 more to come on a parole basis.

1954: Ellis Island closed, marking an end to mass immigration.

1957: Special legislation admitted Hungarian refugees.

1959: Castro's successful revolution in Cuba began the emigration of refugees.

1960: The United States paroled Cuban refugees.

1962: The United States granted special permission for the admission of refugees from Hong Kong.

1965: The National Origins Quota System was abolished, but the principle of numerical restriction by establishing 170,000 hemispheric and 20,000-per-country ceilings and a seven-category preference system (favoring close relatives of U.S. citizens and permanent resident aliens, those with needed occupational skills, and refugees) for the Eastern Hemisphere and a separate 120,000 ceiling for the Western Hemisphere was maintained (79 Stat. 911).

The Cuban refugee airlift program admitted Cubans to the United States under special quotas for the next eight years.

1970: The Immigration Act of 1965 was amended by President Nixon, further liberalizing admission to the United States.

1972: Congress passed the Ethnic Heritage Studies Bill, encouraging bilingual education and programs pertaining to ethnic culture.

1976: The 20,000-per-country immigration ceilings and the preference system for Western Hemisphere countries was applied, and separate hemispheric ceilings were maintained.

1978: The separate ceilings for Eastern and Western Hemisphere immigration were combined into one worldwide limit of 290,000.

1979: Congress appropriated more than $334 million for the rescue and resettlement of Vietnamese "boat people."

1980: The Refugee Act removed refugees as a preference category and established clear criteria and procedures for their admission, reducing the worldwide ceiling for immigrants from 290,000 to 270,000.

The so-called "Freedom Flotilla" of Cuban refugees came to the United States.

1986: Comprehensive immigration legislation legalized aliens who had resided in the United States in an unlawful status since 1 January 1982; established sanctions prohibiting employers from hiring, recruiting, or referring for a fee aliens known to be unauthorized to work in the United States; created a new classification of temporary agricultural worker and provided for the legalization of certain such workers; and established a visa waiver pilot program allowing the admission of certain non-immigrants without visas.

Separate legislation stipulated that aliens deriving their immigrant status based on a marriage of less than two years apply within ninety days after their second-year anniversary to remove conditional status.

1989: Adjustment from temporary to permanent status of certain non-immigrants who were employed in the United States as registered nurses for at least three years and met established certification standards.

1990: Comprehensive immigration legislation increased total immigration under an overall flexible cap of 675,000 immigrants beginning in fiscal year 1995, preceded by a 700,000 level during fiscal years 1992 through 1994; created separate admission categories for family-sponsored, employment-based, and diversity immigrants; revised all grounds for exclusion and deportation, significantly rewriting the political and ideological grounds and repealing some grounds for exclusion; authorized the attorney general to grant temporary protected status to undocumented alien nationals of designated countries subject to armed conflict or natural disasters, and designated such status for Salvadorans; revised and established new non-immigrant admission categories; revised and extended through fiscal year 1994 the Visa Waiver Program; revised naturalization authority and requirements; and revised enforcement activities.

Selected Addresses

Ethnic Societies, Resources, and Web sites

ACADIAN/CAJUN/CREOLE

Acadian Cultural Society Page de la Maison
P.O. Box 2304
Fitchburg, MA 01460-8804
E-mail: r-m-s-frazier@worldnet.att.net
URL: http://www.angelfire.com/ma/1755/index.html

Action Cadienne (Cajun Action)
P.O. Box 30104
Lafayette, LA 70593
URL: http://www.rbmulti.nb.ca/cadienne/cadienne.htm

Creole-American Genealogical Society, Inc.
P.O. Box 2666, Church Street Station
New York, NY 10008

Web sites:

Acadian Genealogy Homepage
http://www.freespace.net/~cajun/genealogy/

Genealogy of Acadia
http://www.cam.org/~beaur/gen/acadie-e.html

AFRICAN AMERICAN

African-American Cultural & Genealogical Society
314 North Main Street
P.O. Box 25251
Decatur, IL 62525
Tel: 217-429-7458
URL: http://www.decaturnet.org/afrigenes.html

African-American Genealogy Group (AAGG)
P.O. Box 1798
Philadelphia, PA 19105-1798
Tel: 215-572-6063
Fax: 215-885-7244
URL: http://www.libertynet.org/~gencap/aagg.html

Afro American Historical & Cultural Museum
7th and Arch Streets
Philadelphia, PA 19106
Tel: 215-574-0380
URL: http://www.fieldtrip.com/pa/55740380.htm

Afro-American Historical and Genealogical Society
P.O. Box 73086
Washington, DC 20056

Association for the Study of Afro-American Life and History
1407 14th Street, NW
Washington, DC 20005
Tel: 202-667-2822
Fax: 202-387-9802

Web sites:

Afrigeneas Homepage
http://www.msstate.edu/Archives/History/afrigen/index.html

Afrikaans-English Online Dictionary
http://dictionaries.travlang.org/AfrikaansEnglish/

Christine's Genealogy Website
http://ccharity.com/

ASIAN

Chinese Historical Society of America
650 Commercial Street
San Francisco, CA 94111
Tel: 415-391-1188

Filipino-American Historical Society
5462 S. Dorchester Avenue
Chicago, IL 60615-5309
Tel: 773-752-2156

Japanese American History Archives
1840 Sutter Street
San Francisco, CA 94115
Tel: 415-776-0661
URL: http://www.e-media.com/fillmore/museum/
jt/jaha/jaha.html

Morikami Museum and Japanese Gardens
4000 Morikami Park Rd.
Delray Beach, FL 33446
Tel: 407-495-0233

Pacific Asia Museum
46 North Los Robles Avenue
Pasadena, CA 91101
Tel: 818-449-2742

AUSTRALIAN

Australian Institute of Genealogical Studies
P.O. Box 339
Blackburn, Victoria, 3130
Australia
Tel: (613) 9887 3789
Fax: (613) 9887 9066
URL: http://www.cohsoft.com.au/afhc/aigs.html

Military Historical Society of Australia
P.O. Box 30
Garran, ACT 2605
Australia
E-mail: astaunto@pcug.org.au
URL: http://www.pcug.org.au/~astaunto/mhsa.htm

Web sites:

Australian Archives
http://www.aa.gov.au/

Australian Family History Compendium
http://www.cohsoft.com.au/afhc/

Genealogy in Australia
(Sponsored by the Canberra Dead Persons Society)
http://www.pcug.org.au/~mpahlow/welcome.html

BELGIAN/DUTCH

Belgian American Heritage Association (BAHA)
62073 Fruitdale Lane
LaGrande, OR 97850

Holland Library
Market Street
Alexandria Bay, NY 13607
Tel: 315-482-2241

Holland Society of New York
122 E. 58th Street
New York, NY 10022
Tel: 212-758-1875

Web sites:

Dutch-English Online Dictionary
http://dictionaries.travlang.org/DutchEnglish/

Genealogy in Belgium (Flanders)
http://win-www.uia.ac.be/u/pavp/index.html

Genealogy in Belgium (French)
http://www.cam.org/~beaur/gen/belgiq-f.html

Yvette's Dutch Genealogy Homepage
http://wwwedu.cs.utwente.nl/~hoitink/genealogy.html

CANADIAN

American-Canadian Genealogical Society (ACGS)
4 Elm Street
P.O. Box 6478
Manchester, NH 03108
E-mail: 102475.2260@compuserve.com
URL: http://ourworld.compuserve.com/homepages/
ACGS/homepage.htm

National Archives of Canada
Genealogy Reference Services
395 Wellington Street
Ottawa, Ontario KLA ON3
Tel: 613-996-7458
Fax: 613-996-6274
URL: http://www.archives.ca/

Web sites:

Canadian Genealogy Resources
http://www.iosphere.net/~jholwell/cangene/gene.html

Sources in Canada by National Archives of Canada,
Genealogical Reference Services
http://www.archives.ca/www/GenealogicalSources.html

EASTERN EUROPEAN

(See Also German)

American Hungarian Historical Society/Library
215 East 82nd Street
New York, NY 10028
Tel: 212-744-5298

Carpatho/Rusyn Society
125 Westland Drive
Pittsburgh, PA 15217
E-mail: ggressa@carpatho-rusyn.org
URL: http://www.carpatho-rusyn.org/

Croatian Ethnic Institute
4851 South Drexel Blvd.
Chicago, IL 60615
Tel: 773-373-2248

Croatian Heritage Museum & Library
34900 Lake Shore Blvd.
Willoughby, OH 44095-2043
Tel: 216-946-2044

Czech Heritage Preservation Society
P.O. Box 3
Tabor, SD 57063

Czechoslovak Genealogical Society Intl., Inc.
P.O. Box 16225
St. Paul, MN 55116-0225
E-mail: cgsi@aol.com
URL: http://members.aol.com/cgsi/index.html

Federation of East European Family History Societies
   (FEEFHS)
P.O. Box 510898
Salt Lake City, UT 94151-0898
E-mail: fcefhs@feefhs.org
URL: http://feefhs.org/masteri.html

Hungarian-American Friendship Society
2701 Corabel Lane #34
Sacramento, CA 95821-5233
Tel: 916-489-9599
E-mail: HAFS@dholmes.com
URL: http://www.dholmes.com/hafs.html

Hungarian Genealogical Society
124 Esther Street
Toledo, OH 43605-1435

Lithuanian American Genealogical Society
c/o Balzekas Museum of Lithuanian Culture
6500 South Pulaski Road
Chicago, IL 60629-5136
Tel: 773-582-6500

Moravian Historical Society
214 E. Center Street
Nazareth, PA 18064
Tel: 610-759-5070

Polish American Cultural Center
308 Walnut Street
Philadelphia, PA 19106
Tel: 215-922-1700

Polish American Museum
16 Bellview Avenue
Port Washington, NY 11050
Tel: 516-883-6542
URL: http://www.liglobal.com/t_i/attractions/
   museums/polish/

Polish Genealogical Society of America
Polish Museum of America
984 North Milwaukee Avenue
Chicago, IL 60622
Tel: 773-384-3352
URL: http://www.pgsa.org/

Polish Museum of America
984 North Milwaukee Avenue
Chicago, IL 60622-4101
Tel: 312-384-3352

Slovenian Genealogy Society
c/o Al Peterlin, Pres.
52 Old Farm Road
Harrisburg, PA 17011-2604
Tel: 717-731-8804
URL: http://feefhs.org/slovenia/frg-sgsi.html

Ukrainian Fraternal Association
440 Wyoming Avenue
Scranton, PA 18503
Tel: 717-342-0937

Ukrainian Museum/Archives
1202 Kenilworth Avenue
Cleveland, OH 44113-4417
Tel: 216-781-4329

Ukrainian National Museum
2453 West Chicago Avenue
Chicago, IL 60622-4633
Tel: 773-276-6565

Web sites:

Alex Glendinning's Hungarian Pages
http://user.itl.net/~glen/Hungarianintro.html

Eastern Slovakia, Slovak, and Carpatho-Rusyn Genealogy
    Resources
http://www.iarelative.com/slovakia.htm

Hungarian-English Online Dictionary
http://www.sztaki.hu/services/dictionary/index.html

Radio Prague History Online
http://www.radio.cz/history/

Slovakia Home Page
http://www.tuzvo.sk/homepage.html

FRENCH

(See also Acadian)

American-French Genealogical Society
(Library at the First Universalist Church
78 Earle Street
Woonsocket, RI 02895
P.O. Box 2113
Pawtucket, RI 02861
Tel/Fax: 401-765-6141
E-mail: afgs@ids.net
URL: http://users.ids.net/~afgs/afgshome.html

Web sites:

French-English Online Dictionary
http://dictionaries.travlang.com/FrenchEnglish/

GERMAN

American Historical Society of Germans from Russia
631 D Street
Lincoln, NE 68502-1199
Tel: 402-474-3363
Fax: 402-474-7229
E-mail: ahsgr@aol.com
URL: http://www.teleport.com/nonprofit/ahsgr/

Anglo-German Family History Society
14 River Reach
Teddington, Middlesex
England, UK TW11 9QL
URL: http://feefhs.org/uk/frgagfhs.html

Bukovina Society of the Americas/Museum
722 Washington
P.O. Box 81
Ellis, KS 67637
Tel: 913-625-9492
    913-726-4568
E-mail: owindholz@juno.com
URL: http://members.aol.com/LJensen/bukovina.html

Federation of East European Family History Societies
    (FEEFHS)
P.O. Box 510898
Salt Lake City, UT 94151-0898
E-mail: feefhs@feefhs.org
URL: http://feefhs.org/masteri.html

German-American Heritage Institute
7824 West Madison Street
Forest Park, IL 60130-1485
Tel: 708-366-0017

German-Bohemian Heritage Society
P.O. Box 822
New Ulm, MN 56073
E-mail: lalgbhs.@newulmtel.net
URL: http://www.qrz.com/gene/reg/SUD/
    sudet_GBHS.html

Germans from Russia Heritage Society
1008 East Central Avenue
Bismarck, ND 58501
Tel: 701-223-6167
E-mail: grhs@btigate.com
URL: http://www.teleport.com/nonprofit/grhs

Gluckstal Colonies Research Association
611 Esplanade
Redondo Beach, CA 90277-4130
Tel: 310-540-1872
E-mail: gcra31@aol.com
URL: http://www.dcn.davis.ca.us/feefhs/FRGGCRA/
    gcra.html

Palatines to America Society
Capital University, Box 101
Columbus, OH 43209-2394
E-mail: pal-am@juno.com
URL: http://genealogy.org/~palam/

Web sites:

Archives in Germany
http://www.bawue.de/~hanacek/info/earchive.htm

German and American Sources for German Emigration
 to America
by Michael P. Palmer
http://www.genealogy.com/gene/www/emig/emigrati.htm

German-English Online Dictionary
http://dictionaries.travlang.com/GermanEnglish/

German Genealogy Home Page
URL: http://www.genealogy.com/gene/

Internet Sources of German Genealogy
http://www.bawue.de/~hanacek/info/edatbase.htm

ODESSA...A German-Russian Genealogical Library
http://pixel.cs.vt.edu/library/odessa.html

Palatines to America: Immigrant Ancestor Register Index
http://genealogy.org/~palam/ia_index.htm

GREEK

Greek Family Heritage Committee
75-21 177th Street
Flushing, NY 11366
Tel: 718-591-9342

HISPANIC

American Portugese Genealogical & Historical Society
P.O. Box 644
Taunton, MA 02780-0644

Hispanic Genealogical Research Center-New Mexico
1331 Juan Tabo, NE
Suite P, No. 18
Albuquerque, NM 87112
Tel: 505-836-5438
E-mail: HGRC@HGRC-NM.ORG
URL: http://www.hgrc-nm.org/

Portugese Genealogical Society of Hawaii
810 North Vineyard Blvd., Room 11
Honolulu, HI 96817
Tel: 808-841-5044
E-mail: chism@hi.net
URL: http://www.lusaweb.com/pgsh.htm

Puerto Rican/Hispanic Genealogical Society
25 Ralph Avenue
Brentwood, NY 11717-2421
Tel: 516-834-2511
E-mail: prgen@aol.com
URL: http://www.linkdirect.com/hispsoc/

Society of Hispanic Historical and Ancestral Research
P.O. Box 490
Midway City, CA 92655-0490
E-mail: shharnet@webcom.com
URL: http://www.webcom.com/shharnet/

Web sites:

Basque Genealogy Homepage
http://www.concentric.net/~Fybarra/

Compuserve's Hispanic Genealogy
http://ourworld.compuserve.com/hompages/Alfred_Sosa/

Cuban Genealogy Resources
http://ourworld.compuserve.com/homepages/ee/

Hispanic Heraldry
http://www.ctv.es/artes/home.htm/home.html

Spanish-English Online Dictionary
http://dictionary.travlang.org/SpanishEnglish/

HUGUENOT

Huguenot Historical Society
P.O. Box 339
New Paltz, NY 12561
Tel: 914-255-1660
E-mail: Huguenothistoricalsociety@worldnet.att.net
URL: http://home.earthlink.net/~rctwig/hhs1.htm

Huguenot Society of America/Library
122 East 58th Street
New York, NY 10022
Tel: 212-755-0592

National Huguenot Society
9033 Lyndale Avenue, S. - Suite 18
Bloomington, MN 55420
Tel: 612-893-9747

Web sites:

Huguenots
http://www.geocities.com/SoHo/3809/Huguen.htm

HUNGARIAN

(See Eastern European)

IRISH

(See United Kingdom)

ITALIAN

Italian Cultural Center
1621 North 39th Avenue
Stone Park, IL 60165-1105
Tel: 630-345-3842

Italian Genealogical Group, Inc.
7 Grayon Drive
Dix Hills, NY 11746
Fax: 516-499-5524
E-mail: jdelalio@aol.com
URL: http://www.fgs.org/~fgs/soc0091.htm

Italian Genealogy Society of America
P.O. Box 8571
Cranston, RI 02920-8571

Italian Historical Society of America
111 Columbia Hts
Brooklyn, NY 11201
Tel: 718-852-2929

Web sites:

Italian Genealogy Homepage
http://www.italgen.com/

Italian Surname Database
http://www.italgen.com/surnames.htm

NATIVE AMERICAN

Anchorage Museum of History & Art
121 West 7th Avenue
P.O. Box 196650
Anchorage, AK 99519-6650
Tel: 907-343-4326
Fax: 907-343-6149
URL: http://www.ci.anchorage.ak.us/Services/
     Departments/Culture/Museum/index.html

Baranov Museum
Kodiak Historical Society
101 Marine Way
Kodiak, AK 99615
Tel: 907-486-5920
Fax: 907-486-3166

Bishop Museum and Library/Archives
1525 Bernice Street
P.O. Box 19000-A
Honolulu, HI 96817-0916
Tel: 808-848-4147/8
     808-848-4182/3
Fax: 808-841-8968
URL: http://www.bishop.hawaii.org/bishop/library/
     library.html
     http://www.bishop.hawaii.org/bishop/archives/
     arch.html

Bureau of Indian Affairs
U.S. Department of the Interior
Office of Public Affairs
1849 C Street, NW
Washington, DC 20240-0001
Tel: 202-208-3711
Fax: 202-501-1516
URL: http://www.doi.gov/bureau-indian-affairs.html
Genealogy Resources
URL: http://www.doi.gov/bia/ancestry/genealog.html

Dacotah Prairie Museum
21 S. Main
Aberdeen, SD 57401
Tel: 605-626-7117
Fax: 605-626-4010

Daughters of Hawaii
Queen Emma's Summer Palace
2913 Pali Highway
Honolulu, HI 96817
Tel: 808-595-6291
     808-595-3167
Fax: 808-595-4395

Mescalero Apache Cultural Center
P.O. Box 176
Mescalero, NM 88340
Tel: 505-671-4494

Native American Heritage Museum at Highland Mission
Route 1
P.O. Box 152C
Highland, KS 66035
Tel: 913-442-3304
URL: http://kuhttp.cc.ukans.edu/heritage/kshs/places/
     highland.htm

Pueblo Cultural Center
2401 12th Street, NW
Albuquerque, NM 87192
Tel: 505-843-7270
        800-766-4406
Fax: 505-842-6959
URL: http://hanksville.phast.umass.edu/defs/independent/PCC/PCC.html

Siouxland Heritage Museum
200 W. 6th Street
Sioux Falls, SD 57104-6001
Tel: 605-367-4210
Fax: 605-367-6004

Tanana-Yukon Historical Society
Wickersham House Museum
Alaskaland Park, Airport Way
P.O. Box 71336
Fairbanks, AK 99707
Tel: 907-474-4013
E-mail: tyhs@polarnet.com
URL: http://www2.polarnet.com/~tyhs/

Totem Heritage Center
601 Deermont Street
(Mailing Address: 629 Dock St.)
Ketchikan, AK 99901
Tel: 907-225-5900
Fax: 907-225-5602

Trading Post Historical Society/Museum
Trading Post, KS (mile post 96)
Route 2
P.O. Box 145A
Pleasanton, KS 66075
Tel: 913-352-6441

UCLA American Indian Studies Center
3220 Campbell Hall
Box 951548
Los Angeles, CA 90095-1548
Tel: 310-825-7315
Fax: 310-206-7060
E-mail: aisc@ucla.edu
URL: http://www.sscnet.ucla.edu/indian/CntrHome.html

Ute Mountain Ute Tribal Research Archives Library
Tribal Compound
Box CC
Towaoc, CO 81334
Tel: 303-565-3751 x257
Fax: 303-565-7412
URL: http://www.swcolo.org/Tourism/IndianCulture.html

Yupiit Piciryarait Cultural Center and Museum
420 Chief Eddie Hoffman State Highway
Mailing address:
AVCP, Inc.
P.O. Box 219
Bethel, AK 99559
Tel: 907-520-5312
Fax: 907-543-3596

Web sites:

Index of Native American Resources on the Internet
http://hanksville.phast.umass.edu/misc/NAresources.html

Native American Genealogy
http://members.aol.com/bbbenge/front.html

Native American Who's Hot
http://www.cris.com/~misterg/award/whoshot.shtml

NativeWeb
http://web.maxwell.syr.edu/nativeweb/index.html

POLISH

(See Eastern European)

POLYNESIAN

Polynesian Voyaging Society
1250 Lauhala Street, Apt. 314
Honolulu, HI 96813
Tel: 808-547-4172
E-mail: dennisk@hawaii.edu
URL: http://leahi.kcc.hawaii.edu/org/pvs/

RUSSIAN

American Historical Society of Germans from Russia
631 D Street
Lincoln, NE 68502-1199
Tel: 402-474-3363
Fax: 402-474-7229
E-mail: ahsgr@aol.com
URL: http://www.teleport.com/nonprofit/ahsgr/

Russian Baltic Information Center - BLITZ
907 Mission Avenue
San Rafael, CA 94901
Tel: 415-453-3579
Fax: 415-453-0343
E-mail: enute@igc.apc.org
URL: http://dcn.davis.ca.us/go/feefhs/blitz/frgblitz.html

Germans from Russia Heritage Society
1008 East Central Avenue
Bismarck, ND 58501
Tel: 701-223-6167
E-mail: grhs@btigate.com
URL: http://www.teleport.com/nonprofit/grhs

Web sites:

Russian Heraldry
http://sunsite.cs.msu.su/heraldry/

SCANDINAVIAN

American-Swedish Historical Museum
(in Franklin Delano Roosevelt Park)
1900 Patterson Avenue
Philadelphia, PA 19145
Tel: 215-389-1776
E-mail: ashm@libertynet.org
URL: http://www.libertynet.org/~ashm/

Concordia College
Carl B. Ylvisaker Library
Moorhead, MN 56562
Tel: 218-299-4239
E-mail: library@cord.edu
URL: http://home.cord.edu/dept/library/

Finnish-American Heritage Center
Suomi College
Hancock, MI 49930
Tel: 906-487-7367
Fax: 906-487-7383
URL: http://www.suomi.edu/Ink/FHC.html

Finnish-American Historical Archives
Suomi College
601 Quincy Street
Hancock, MI 49930
Tel: 906-487-7273

Finnish-American Historical Society, Minnesota
P.O. Box 34
Wolf Lake, MN 56593

Norwegian American Bygdelagenes Fellesraad
c/o Marilyn Somdahl, Pres.
10129 Goodrich Circle
Bloomington, MN 55437
Tel: 612-831-4409
E-mail: rsylte@ix.netcom.com
URL: http://www.lexiaintl.org/sylte/bygdelag.html

Norwegian-American Historical Association (NAHA)
1510 St. Olaf Avenue
Northfield, MN 55057
Fax: 507-646-3734
E-mail: naha@stolaf.edu
URL: http://www.stolaf.edu/stolaf/other/naha/naha.html

Norwegian Emigrant Museum
Akershagan
2312 Ottestad
Norway
Tel: +47 6257 85 77
Fax: +47 6257 84 59
E-mail: knut.djupedal@emigrant.museum.no
URL: http://www.hamarnett.no/emigrantmuseum/

Norwegian Emigration Center
Bergjelandsgt. 30
N-4012 Stavenger
Norway
Tel: +47 5150 1274
Fax: +47 5150 1290
E-mail: detnu@telepost.no
URL: http://home.sn.no/home/henningh/utvasent.htm

Scandinavian American Genealogical Society (SAGS)
P.O. Box 16069
St. Paul, MN 55116-0069
URL: http://www.mtn.org/mgs/branches/sags.html

Swedish-American Historical Society/Library
5125 North Spaulding Avenue
Chicago, IL 60625-4816
Tel: 773-583-2700 ext. 5267

Swedish-American Museum Center
5211 N. Clark Street
Chicago, IL 60640-2101
Tel: 773-728-8111

Swedish Colonial Society
c/o Wallace Richter, Registrar
336 South Devon Avenue
Wayne, PA 19087
Tel: 610-688-1766
URL: http://libertynet.org/~gencap/scs.html

Swenson Swedish Immigration Research Center
Augustana College
639 38th Street
Rock Island, IL 61201-2273
Tel: 309-794-7204
Fax: 309-794-7443
E-mail: swsa@augustana.edu
URL: http://www2.augustana.edu/admin/swenson/

Vesterheim Genealogical Center and Naeseth Library
415 W. Main Street
Madison, WI 53703-3116
Fax: 608-258-6842
E-mail: vesterheim@juno.com
URL: http://fjordinfo.vestdata.no/offentleg/sffarkiv/
sffutvgc.htm

Web sites:

Danish-English Online Dictionary
http://dictionaries.travlang.org/DanishEnglish/

Finnish-English Online Dictionary
http://dictionaries.travlang.org/FinnishEnglish/

Genealogy Finland
http://www.mediabase.fi/suku/genealog.htm

Norwegian Historical Data Centre
http://isv.uit.no/seksjon/rhd/

SCOTTISH

(See United Kingdom)

SOUTH AFRICAN

Albany Museum: Ancestry Research-Genealogy
Somerset Street
GRAHAMSTOWN, 6139
South Africa
Intl. Tel: +27 461 22312
Intl. Fax: +27 461 22398
E-mail: amwj@giraffe.ru.ac.za
URL: http://www.ru.ac.za/departments/am/geneal.html

Web sites:

Afrikaans-English Online Dictionary
http://dictionaries.travlang.org/AfrikaansEnglish/

SWISS

Swiss Society of Genealogy Studies
E-mail: nickj@3dplus.ch
URL: http://www.3dplus.ch/~nickj/Engl_SSEG.html

Web sites:

Swiss Genealogy
http://www.mindspring.com/~philipp/che.html

Swiss Genealogy on the Internet
http://www.kssg.ch/chgene/welcome-e.htm

UNITED KINGDOM / IRELAND / SCOTLAND

British Heritage Society
4177 Garrick Avenue
Warren, MI 48091
Tel: 810-757-4177
E-mail: Anton_The_Lord_Hartforth@msn.com

Clan MacDuff Society of America
Barabara Huff-Duff, Society Genealogist
237 Madeline Drive
Monrovia, CA 91016-2431
E-mail: huffduff@cco.caltech.edu
URL: http://www.crimson.com/scots_austin/macduff.htm

Irish-American Cultural Institute
683 Osceola Avenue
St. Paul, MN 55105

Irish-American Heritage Center Museum and Art Gallery
4626 North Knox Avenue
Chicago, IL 60630-4030
Tel: 773-282-7035

Irish American Heritage Museum
19 Clinton Avenue
Albany, NY 12207
Tel: 518-432-6598

The Irish Ancestral Research Association (TIARA)
Dept. W
P.O. Box 619
Sudbury, MA 01776
URL: http://world.std.com/~ahern/TIARA.html

Irish Family History Forum
P.O. Box 351
Rockville Center, NY 11571-0351
URL: http://www.fgs.org/~fgs/soc0090.htm

Irish Genealogical Society, Intl. (IGSI)
P.O. Box 13585
St. Paul, MN 55116-0585
E-mail: raymarsh@minn.net
URL: http://www.rootsweb.com/~irish/

Jersey Archives Service
The Weighbridge
St. Helier, Jersey
Channel Islands JE2 3NF
Tel: 01534-617441
Fax: 01534-66085
URL: http://www.jersey.gov.uk/heritage/archives/
    jasweb.html

National Library of Scotland
George IV Bridge
Edinburgh, EH1 1EW
Scotland
URL: http://www.nls.uk/

Office for National Statistics
1 Myddelton Street
London
EC1R 1UW
Tel: 0181 392 5300
Fax: 0181 392 5307

Public Record Office (PRO)
Ruskin Avenue
Kew
Surrey
TW9 4DU
Tel: 0181 392 5200
Fax: 0181 878 8905
E-mail: enquiry.pro.rsd.kew@gtnet.gov.uk
URL: http://www.open.gov.uk/pro/prohome.htm

Scotch-Irish Society of the U.S.A.
3 Parkway, 20th Floor
Philadelphia, PA 19102

Scottish Genealogy Society
15 Victoria Terrace
Edinburgh, EH1 2JL
Scotland
Tel: +44 0131 220 3677
E-mail: scotgensoc@sol.co.uk
URL: http://www.taynet.co.uk/users/scotgensoc/

Society of Genealogists
14 Charterhouse Buildings
Goswell Road
London EC1M 7BA
Tel: 0171-251-8799
URL: http://www.cs.ncl.ac.uk/genuki/SoG/

Web sites:

A Little Bit of Ireland
http://members.aol.com/LABATH/irish.htm

Channel Islands Genealogy
http://users.aol.com/johnf14246/ci.html

Electric Scotland; Scottish Clans
http://www.electricscotland.com/webclans/index.html

Genealogical Guide to Ireland
http://www.bess.tcd.ie/roots/prototype/genweb2.htm

GENUKI
http://cs6400.mcc.ac.uk/genuki/
or
http://midas.ac.uk/genuki/

Irish Emigrants
http://genealogy.org/~ajmorris/ireland/ireemg1.htm

Irish Family History Foundation
http://www.mayo-ireland.ie/ireland.htm

Irish Genealogy
http://genealogy.org/~ajmorris/ireland/ireland.htm

IRLGEN: Tracing Your Irish Ancestors
http://www.bess.tcd.ie/roots_ie.htm

National Archives of Ireland
http://www.kst.dit.ie/nat-arch/

Scotland Genealogy: Tracing Your Scottish Ancestry
http://www.geo.edu.ac.uk/home/Scotland/genealogy.html

Scottish Reference Information (Database)
http://www.ktb.net/~dwills/13300-scottishreference.htm

Federal Government Agencies

FEDERAL GOVERNMENT AGENCIES

Bureau of Indian Affairs
U.S. Department of the Interior
Office of Public Affairs
1849 C Street, NW
Washington, DC 20240-0001
Tel: 202-208-3711
Fax: 202-501-1516
URL: http://www.doi.gov/bureau-indian-affairs.html
Genealogy Resources
URL: http://www.doi.gov/bia/ancestry/genealog.html

Bureau of Land Management (Headquarters)
1849 C Street
Washington, DC 20240
URL: http://www.blm.gov/

Dept. of Veterans Affairs
810 Vermont Avenue, NW
Washington, DC 20420
Tel: 202-233-4000
    800-827-1000
URL: http://www.va.gov/foia/index.htm

Office of Information and Privacy
SAIS-IDP-F/P, Suite 201
1725 Jefferson Davis Highway
Arlington, VA 22202-4102
Tel: 703-607-3377
URL: http://www.usdoj.gov/oip/oip.html

Government Printing Office (GPO)
Washington, DC 20401
Tel: 888-293-6498
    202-512-1530
Fax: 202-512-1262
E-mail: gpoaccess@gpo.gov
URL: http://www.access.gpo.gov/
GPO Access Databases
URL: http://www.access.gpo.gov/su_docs/aces/
    aaces003.html

Immigration and Naturalization Service (INS)
425 I Street, NW
Room 5304
Washington, DC 20536
Tel: 800-755-0777
    800-870-3676 (To request forms)
http://www.ins.usdoj.gov/
Forms Download
http://www.ins.usdoj.gov/forms/index.html
Request Forms by Mail
http://www.ins.usdoj.gov/exec/forms/formsbymail.asp

INS Regional Offices

Alaska
620 East 10th Avenue
Anchorage, AK 99501-7581

Arizona
2035 N. Central Avenue
Phoenix, AZ 85004

California
865 Fulton Mall
Fresno, CA 93721-2816

California
Chet Holifield Federal Building
24000 Avila Road
P.O. Box 30080
Laguna Niguel, CA 92607-0080

California
300 North Los Angeles Street
Los Angeles, CA 90012

California
711 J Street
Sacramento, CA 95814

California
880 Front Street
San Diego, CA 92188

California
630 Sansome Street
San Francisco, CA 94111-2280

California
280 South First Street, Room 1150
San Jose, CA 95113

Colorado
Albrook Center
4730 Paris Street
Denver, CO 80239-2804

Connecticut
Ribicoff Federal Building
450 Main Street
Hartford, CT 06103-3060

Florida
400 West Bay Street, Room G-18
P.O. Box 35029
Jacksonville, FL 32202

Florida
7880 Biscayne Blvd.
Miami, FL 33138

Florida
5509 W. Gray Street, Suite 113
Tampa, FL 33609

Georgia
77 Forsyth Street, SW
Room 284
Atlanta, GA 30303

Guam
801 Pacific News Building
238 O'Hara Street
Agana, Guam 96910

Hawaii
595 Ala Moana Blvd.
Honolulu, HI 96813

Illinois
10 West Jackson Blvd., 2nd Floor
Chicago, IL 60604
Indiana
Gateway Plaza
950 North Meridian, Suite 400
Indianapolis, IN 46204

Kentucky
Gene Snyder Courthouse
West 6th and Broadway, Room 601
Louisville, KY 40202

Louisiana
Postal Service Building
701 Loyola Avenue, Room T-8005
New Orleans, LA 70113

Maine
739 Warren Avenue
Portland, ME 04103

Maryland
Equitable Bank Center
100 South Charles Street, 12th Floor Tower
Baltimore, MD 21201

Massachusetts
JFK Federal Building
Government Center
Boston, MA 02203

Michigan
Federal Building
333 Mt. Elliott Street
Detroit, MI 48207-4381

Minnesota
2901 Metro Drive, Suite 100
Bloomington, MN 55425

Minnesota
Bishop Henry Whipple Federal Building
One Federal Drive
Fort Snelling, MN 55111-4007

Missouri
9747 North Conant Avenue
Kansas City, MO 64153

Missouri
Robert A. Young Federal Building
1222 Spruce Street, Room 1100
St. Louis, MO 63101-2815

Montana
2800 Skyway Drive
Helena, MT 59601

Nebraska
3736 South 132nd Street
Omaha, NE 68144

Nebraska
Northern Service Center
850 S. Street
Lincoln, NE 68508

Nevada
300 Las Vegas Blvd., Room 1430
Las Vegas, NV 89101

Nevada
3373 Pepper Lane
Las Vegas, NV 89120

Nevada
712 Mill Street
Reno, NV 89502

New Jersey
Federal Building
970 Broad Street
Newark, NJ 07102

New Mexico
517 Gold Avenue, SW
Room 1010
P.O. Box 567
Albuquerque, NM 87103

New York
James T. Foley Federal Courthouse
445 Broadway, Room 220
Albany, NY 12207

New York
130 Delaware Avenue
Buffalo, NY 14202

New York
26 Federal Plaza
New York, NY 10278

North Carolina
6 Woodlawn Green, Room 138
Charlotte, NC 28217

Ohio
J.W. Peck Federal Building
550 Main Street, Room 8525
Cincinnati, OH 45202

Ohio
Anthony Celebreeze
Federal Building
1240 East 9th Street, Room 1917
Cleveland, OH 44199

Oklahoma
149 Highline Blvd., Suite 300
Oklahoma City, OK 73108

Oregon
Federal Office Building
511 NW Broadway
Portland, OR 97209

Pennsylvania
1600 Callowhill Street
Philadelphia, PA 19130

Pennsylvania
Federal Building, Room 2130
1000 Liberty Avenue
Pittsburgh, PA 15222

Puerto Rico
P.O. Box 365068
San Juan, PR 00936

Rhode Island
Federal Building
203 John O. Pastore
Providence, RI 02903

Tennessee
245 Wagner Place, Suite 250
Memphis, TN 38103-3815

Texas
7701 North Stemmons Freeway
Dallas, TX 75247-9998

Texas
8101 North Stemmons Freeway
Dallas, TX 75247

Texas
700 E. San Antonio Street
P.O. Box 9398
El Paso, TX 79984

Texas
1545 Hawkins Blvd., Suite 170
El Paso, TX 79925

Texas
P.O. Box 152122
Irving, TX 75105-0212

Texas
2102 Teege Road
Harlingen, TX 78550

Texas
509 North Belt
Houston, TX 77060

Texas
8940 Fourwinds Drive
San Antonio, TX 78239

Utah
5272 South College Drive
Salt Lake City, UT 84123

Vermont
Eastern Service Center
75 Lower Welden Street
St. Albans, VT 05479-0001

Vermont
70 Kimball Avenue
South Burlington, VT 05403-6813

Virginia
Norfolk Federal Building
Norfolk, VA 23510

Virginia
4420 North Fairfax Drive
Arlington, VA 22203

Washington
815 Airport Way, South
Seattle, WA 98134

Washington
691 U.S. Courthouse Building
Spokane, WA 99201

Wisconsin
517 E. Wisconsin Avenue
Milwaukee, WI 53202

Passport Office
Dept. of State
1111 19th Street, NW
Suite 200
Washington, DC 20522
Tel: 202-955-0291

Social Security Administration
Office of Disclosure Policy
3-A-6 Operations Building
6401 Security Boulevard
Baltimore, MD 21235
http://www.ssa.gov/

U.S. Census Bureau
1201 E. Tenth Street
P.O. Box 1545
Jeffersonville, IN 47131
http://www.census.gov/
Census records after 1920

U.S. Geological Survey
Tel: 800-USA-MAPS
Fax on Demand: 703-648-4888
URL: http://www.usgs.gov/

USGS REGIONAL LIBRARIES

U.S. Geological Survey Library
950 National Center
12201 Sunrise Valley
Reston, VA 20192
Tel: 703-648-4302 (Reference)
        703-648-6080 (History Project)
Fax: 703-648-6373
TDD: 703-648-4105
E-mail: library@usgs.gov
URL: http://library.usgs.gov/reslib.html

U.S. Geological Survey Library
345 Middlefield Road, MS 955
Menlo Park, CA 94025-3591
Tel: 415-329-5009
Fax: 415-329-5132
TDD: 415-329-5094
E-mail: men_lib@usgs.gov
URL: http://library.usgs.gov/menlib.html

U.S. Geological Survey Library
2255 N. Gemini Drive
Flagstaff, AZ 86001
Tel: 520-556-7272
Fax: 520-556-7156
E-mail: flag_lib@usgs.gov
URL: http://library.usgs.gov/flaglib.html

U.S. Geological Survey Library
Denver Federal Center, Building 20
Box 25046, MS 914
Denver, CO 80225-0046
Tel: 303-236-1010
Fax: 303-236-0015

TDD: 303-236-0998
E-mail: dcn_lib@usgs.gov
URL: http://library.usgs.gov/denlib.html

USGS Mapping Information: Geographic Names Information System
Online Data Base Query Form
URL: http://mapping.usgs.gov/www/gnis/gnisform.html

U.S. Patent and Trademark Office Library
Crystal Park 3, Suite 481
Washington, DC 20231
Tel: 703-308-5558
Fax: 703-306-2654
URL; http://www.uspto.gov/web/offices/ac/ido/cpti/
        ptdlhm3.htm
Searchable Patent Database 1976–1997
URL: http://patents.uspto.gov/patbib_index.html

NATIONAL ARCHIVES AND RECORDS ADMINISTRATION

URL: http://www.nara.gov/

National Archives and Records Administration (NARA)
Archives I
8th & Pennsylvania Avenues
Washington, DC 20408
Tel: 202-501-5410 (Genealogical Staff)
        202-501-5400 (Record Availability)
Fax: 301-713-6905 (Fax-on-Demand Information)
E-mail: inquire@arch1.nara.gov
URL: http://www.nara.gov/nara/dc/Archives1_info.html

National Archives and Records Administration (NARA)
Archives II
8601 Adelphi Road
College Park, MD 20740
Tel: 202-501-5400 (Record Availability)
        301-713-6800 (General Reference)
        301-713-7040 (Cartographic Reference)
Fax: 301-713-6905 (Fax-on-Demand Information)
E-mail: inquire@arch2.nara.gov
URL: http://www.nara.gov/nara/dc/Archives1_info.html

NATIONAL RECORDS CENTERS

National Personnel Records Centers, NARA
http://www.nara.gov/nara/frc/nprc.html

Civilian Records Facility
111 Winnebago Street
St. Louis, MO 63118-4199
Tel: 314-425-5761

Fax: 314-425-5719
E-mail: center@cpr.nara.gov
URL: http://www.nara.gov/nara/frc/cpr.html

Military Records Facility
9700 Page Avenue
St. Louis, MO 63132-5100
Recorded Information Lines
  314-538-4243 Air Force
  314-538-4261 Army
  314-538-4141 Navy/Marine/Coast Guard
Fax: 314-538-4175
E-mail: center@stlouis.nara.gov
URL: http://www.nara.gov/nara/frc/mpr.html

Pittsfield Federal Records Center, NARA
100 Dan Fox Drive
Pittsfield, MA 01201-8230
Tel: 413-445-6885
Fax: 413-445-7305
E-mail: center@pittsfield.nara.gov
URL: http://www.nara.gov/nara/frc/1ncloc.html

Washington National Records Center, NARA
Shipping Address:
4205 Suitland Road
Suitland, MD 20746-2042
Mailing Address:
4205 Suitland Road
Washington, DC 20409-0002
Tel: 301-457-7000
Fax: 301-457-7117
E-mail: center@suitland.nara.gov
URL: http://www.nara.gov/nara/frc/ncwbloc.html

REGIONAL ARCHIVES

NARA Pacific Alaska Region (Anchorage)
654 West Third Avenue
Anchorage, AK 99501-2145
Tel: 907-271-2443
Fax: 907-271-2442
E-mail: archives@alaska.nara.gov
URL: http://www.nara.gov/nara/regional/11nsgil.html
(Alaska)

NARA Central Plains Region
2312 East Bannister Road
Kansas City, MO 64131-3011
Tel: 816-926-6272
Fax: 816-926-6982
E-mail: archives@kansascity.nara.gov
URL: http://www.nara.gov/nara/regional/06nsgil.html
(Iowa, Kansas, Minnesota, Missouri, Nebraska, North
    Dakota, and South Dakota)

NARA Great Lakes Region
7358 South Pulaski Road
Chicago, IL 60629-5898
Tel: 773-581-7816
Fax: 312-353-1294
E-mail: archives@chicago.nara.gov
URL: http://www.nara.gov/nara/regional/05nsgil.htm
(Illinois, Indiana, Michigan, Minnesota, Ohio, and Wisconsin)

NARA Mid-Atlantic Region (Center City Philadelphia)
900 Market Street
Philadelphia, PA 19107-4292
Tel: 215-597-3000
Fax: 215-597-2303
E-mail: archives@philarch.nara.gov
URL: http://www.nara.gov/nara/regional/03nsgil.html
(Delaware, Maryland, Pennsylvania, Virginia, and West Virginia)

NARA Northeast Region (Boston)
380 Trapelo Road
Waltham, MA 02154-6399
Tel: 781-647-8100
Fax: 781-647-8460
E-mail: archives@waltham.nara.gov
URL: http://www.nara.gov/nara/regional/01nsbgil.html
(Connecticut, Maine, Massachusetts, New Hampshire,
    Rhode Island, and Vermont)

NARA Northeast Region (New York City)
201 Varick Street
New York, NY 10014-4811
Tel: 212-337-1300
Fax: 212-337-1306
E-mail: archives@newyork.nara.gov
URL: http://www.nara.gov/nara/regional/02nsgil.html
(New Jersey, New York, Puerto Rico, and U.S. Virgin Islands)

NARA Pacific Alaska Region (Seattle)
6125 Sand Point Way, NE
Seattle, WA 98115-7999
Tel: 206-526-6507
Fax: 206-526-4344
E-mail: archives@seattle.nara.gov
URL: http://www.nara.gov/nara/regional/10nsgil.html
(Idaho, Oregon, and Washington)

NARA Pacific Region (San Francisco)
1000 Commodore Drive
San Bruno, CA 94066
Tel: 650-876-9009
Fax: 650-876-9233
E-mail: archives@sanbruno.nara.gov
URL: http://www.nara.gov/nara/regional/09nssgil.html
(Northern California, Hawaii, Nevada (except Clark
    County), Guam, American Samoa, and the Trust
    Territory of the Pacific Islands)

NARA Pacific Region (Laguna Niguel)
24000 Avila Rd., First Floor—East Entrance
P.O. Box 6719
Laguna Niguel, CA 92607-6719
Tel: 949-360-2641
Fax: 949-360-2624
E-mail: archives@laguna.nara.gov
URL: http://www.nara.gov/nara/regional/09nslgil.html
(Arizona, Southern California, and Clark County, NV)

NARA Rocky Mountain Region
Denver Federal Center, Building 48
P.O. Box 25307
Denver, CO 80225-0307
Tel: 303-236-0817
Fax: 303-236-9354
E-mail: archives@denver.nara.gov
URL: http://www.nara.gov/nara/regional/08nsgil.html
(Colorado, Montana, New Mexico, North Dakota, South
     Dakota, Utah, and Wyoming)

NARA Southeast Region
1557 St. Joseph Avenue
East Point, GA 30344-2593
Tel: 404-763-7477
Fax: 404-763-7033
E-mail: archives@atlanta.nara.gov
URL: http://www.nara.gov/nara/regional/04nsgil.html
(Alabama, Florida, Georgia, Kentucky, Mississippi, North
     Carlina, South Carolina, and Tennessee)

NARA Southwest Region
501 W. Felix Street, Building 1
P.O. Box 6216
Fort Worth, TX 76115-0216
Tel: 817-334-5525
Fax: 817-334-5621
E-mail: archives@ftworth.nara.gov
URL: http://www.nara.gov/nara/regional/07nsgil.html
(Arkansas, Oklahoma, Louisiana, and Texas)

HELPFUL NARA WEB SITES

American Indians
http://www.nara.gov/publications/microfilm/
     amerindians/indians.html

Black Studies
http://www.nara.gov/publications/microfilm/
     blackstudies/blackstd.html

Census Records
http://www.nara.gov/publications/microfilm/census.html

Federal Court Records—A Select Catalog of NARA
     Microfilm Publ.
http://www.nara.gov/publications/microfilm/
     courts/fedcourt.html

Genealogical and Biographical Research
http://www.nara.gov/publications/microfilm/
     biographical/genbio.html

Genealogical Searchable Database-NAIL
http://www.nara.gov/nara/nail/nailgen.html

Genealogy Page
http://www.nara.gov/genealogy/genindex.html

Immigrant and Passenger Arrivals
http://www.nara.gov/publications/microfilm/immigrant/
     immpass.html

Microfilm Resources for Research
http://www.nara.gov/publications/microfilm/
     comprehensive/compcat.html

Military Service Records
http://www.nara.gov/publications/microfilm/military/
     service.html

Naturalization Records
http://www.nara.gov/genealogy/natural.html

Post Office Records
http://www.nara.gov/genealogy/postal.html

HELPFUL WEB SITES

Ancestry.com
http://www.ancestry.com/

The Attic-Genealogy Resources
http://www.geocities.com/TheTropics/1127/attic.html

Barrel of Genealogical Links
http://cpcug.org/user/jlacombe/mark.html

Cemetery Internment Lists on the Internet
http://users.deltanet.com/~steven/cemetery.html

Charlotte's Web Genealogical Gleanings
http://www.charweb.org/gen/gleanings/

Charts for Reference in Genealogy Research
http://members.tripod.com/~Silvie/charts.html

Christine's Genealogy Website
http://ccharity.com/

Cyndi's List of Genealogical Sites
http://www.CyndisList.com

Directory of Underground Railroad Operators
http://www.ugrr.org//ur-names.html

Emigration/Ships Lists and Resources
http://www.geocities.com/Heartland/5978/Emigration

Genealogical Resources on the Internet
http://www.tc.umn.edu/~pmg/genealogy.html

Genealogical Websites of Societies and CIGs
http://genealogy.org/PAF/www/gwsc/

Genealogy
http://pibweb.it.nwu.edu/~pib/genealo.htm

Genealogy Home Page
http://genhomepage.com/

Genealogy Online
http://genealogy.emcee.com/

Genealogy's Most Wanted
http://www.citynet.net/mostwanted/

Geneanet (Surname Database)
http://www.geneanet.org/

Helms Genealogy Toolbox
http://genealogy.tbox.com/

IMC's Genealogical Listings
http://www.memphismemphis.com/genealogy/states/
        main.htm

Land Records
http://www.ultranet.com/~deeds/

Lineages, Inc.
http://www.lineagesnet.com/

Mailing Lists, from Genealogy Resources on the Internet
http://users.aol.com/johnf14246/gen_mail.html

MapQuest
http://www.mapquest.com/

Maritime History on the Internet
http://ils.unc.edu/maritime/home.html

Maritime History Virtual Archives
http://pc-78-129.udac.se:8001/WWW/Nautica/
        Nautica.html

Olive Tree
http://www.rootsweb.com/~ote/

Online Genealogical Databases
http://www.gentree.com/

Oregon-California Trails Association
http://calcite.rocky.edu/octa/octahome.htm

Political Graveyard
http://www.potifos.com/tpg/index.html

Railroad Historical
http://www.rrhistorical.com/index.html

Rand Genealogical Group
http://www.rand.org/personal/Genea

Rootsweb
http://www.rootsweb.com/

Roots-L Resources (State by state listings for resources)
http://www.rootsweb.com/roots-l/usa.html

Travlang's Translating Dictionaries
http://dictionaries.travlang.com/

U.S. GenWeb Project
http://www.usgenweb.org/

DIRECTORIES AND SEARCH ENGINES

Alta Vista
http://altavista.digital.com/

Big Yellow Directory
http://s11.bigyellow.com/t_how_to_advertise/
        t_whybigyellow.html

DejaNews
http://www.dejanews.com/

Excite
http://www.excite.com/

Lycos
http://www.lycos.com

MetaCrawler (Search Engine)
http://www.metacrawler.com/

NAIS Private Investigator's Link List (Lots of directories,
        search engines, and other goodies)
http://www.pimall.com/nais/links.html

Switchboard (Directory)
http://www.switchboard.com/

WebCrawler
http://webcrawler.com

Yahoo
http://www.yahoo.com/

Zip+4 Code Lookup from the US Postal Service
http://www.usps.gov/ncsc/lookups/lookup_zip+4.html

555-1212's Fast Area Code Lookup
http://www.555-1212.com/aclookup.html

APPENDIX C

U.S. Department of Justice
Immigration and Naturalization Service

OMB No. 1115-0087
Freedom of Information/Privacy Act Request

START HERE - Please Type or Print and read instructions on the reverse before completing this form.

1. Type of Request: (check appropriate box)
- ☐ a. Freedom of Information Act (FOIA) *(complete all items except 6)*
- ☐ b. Privacy Act (PA) *(item 6 must be completed in addition to all other applicable items)*
- ☐ c. Amendment *(PA only)*

2. List below, the name and telephone number of the person to whom the information should be released. By my signature, I consent to the following *(check applicable boxes)*:
- ☐ a. Pay all costs incurred for search, duplication, and review of materials up to $25.00, when applicable. *(see reverse)*
- ☐ b. Allow the person named below to see my record or a portion of my record *(specify)*_____
     (Consent is required for records for United States Citizens (USC) and Lawful Permanent Residents)
- ☐ c. Proof of death is attached for deceased subject *(obituary or death certificate)*

Please type or print all information, except where signature is requested:

Name of person authorized to see record:	Signature of person giving consent:
Name of requester:	Daytime phone number: ( )
Address *(street number and name)*:	Apt. No.:
City:	State:	Zip Code:

3. Action Requested *(check one)*:
- ☐ a. Copy
- ☐ b. In-person Review

4. Information needed to search for record(s):
Specific information, document(s), or record(s) desired *(identify by name, date, subject matter, and location of information)*:
_____
_____
_____

Purpose *(optional; you are not required to state the purpose for your request, however, doing so may assist the INS in locating the records needed to respond to your request.)*:
_____

5. Data NEEDED on SUBJECT of Record *(if data marked with an asterisk (*) is not provided records may not be located)*:

*Family Name:	Given Name:		Middle Initial:
*Other names used, if any:	*Name at time of entry into the US:		I-94 Admissions #:
*Alien Registration #:	*Petition #:	*Country of birth:	*Date of birth or Age:
Names of other family members that may appear on requested record(s) *(i.e. spouse, daughter, son)*:			Passport #:
Country of origin:	Port-of-Entry into the US:		Date of entry:
Manner of entry *(air, sea, land)*:	Mode of travel *(name of carrier)*:		SSAN:
*Name on Naturalization Certification:		Certificate #:	Naturalization date:
Address at time of Naturalization:		Court and location:	

6. Verification of subject's identity *(see reverse for explanation)* *(check one box)*:
- ☐ a. In-person, with ID
- ☐ b. Notarized Affidavit of identity
- ☐ c. Other *(specify)*:

Signature of Requester:	Date:
	Telephone #: ( )

Form G-639 (03-21-94) No prior versions may be used   *(See Reverse)*

This form may be photocopied and submitted to the Immigration and Naturalization Services.
(Continued on the following page.)

NOTARY (normally needed from individuals who are the subject of the record sought *(see below)* or a sworn declaration under penalty of perjury.

subscribed and sworn to before me this_____day of _____,19_____.

Signature of Notary_____ My Commission Expires_____

OR

If a declaration is provided in lieu of a notarized signature, it must state, at a minimum, the following: (Include Notary Seal or Stamp in this space)

If executed outside the United States: "I declare (certify, verify, or state) under penalty of perjury under the laws of the United States of America that the foregoing is true and correct.

Signature:_____ "

If executed within the United States, its territories, possessions, or commonwealths: "I declare (certify, verify, or state) under penalty of perjury that the foregoing is true and correct.

Signature:_____ "

INSTRUCTIONS

PLEASE READ ALL INSTRUCTIONS CAREFULLY BEFORE COMPLETING THIS FORM.
Applicants making false statements are subject to criminal penalties [Pub. L. 93--579.88 stat. (5 U.S.C. 552a (i)(3)].

Do Not Use This Form for the Following Reasons:
(1) Determine status of pending applications - call nearest INS office. (2) Consular notification of visa petition approval - use Form I-824. (3) Return of Original documents - Use Form G-884. (4) For records of naturalization prior to Sept. 27, 1906, - write to the clerk of court where naturalization occurred. (5) INS arrivals prior to 1891, except for arrivals at the port of NY, which began as of June 16, 1897, - write to the National Archives.

How to Submit a Request.
Person requesting a search for access to INS records under the Freedom of Information or Privacy Acts may submit the completed application to the INS office nearest the applicant's place of residence. Requests may be submitted in person or by mail. If an application is mailed, the envelope should be clearly marked *"Freedom of Information"* or *"Privacy Act Information Request."*

Information Needed to Search for Records.
Please Note: Failure to provide complete and specific information as requested in item 5, may result in a delay in processing or inability to locate the records or information requested.

Verification of Identity in Person.
Requesters appearing in person for access to their records may identify themselves by showing a document bearing a photograph *(such as an Alien Registration Card, Form I-551, Citizen Identification Card, Naturalization Certificate, or passport) or two items which bear their name and address (such as driver's license and voter's registration).*

Verification of Identity by Mail.
Requesters wanting access to their records shall identify themselves by name, current address, date and place of birth, and alien or employee identification number. A notarized example of their signatures or sworn declaration under penalty of perjury must also be provided (this form or a DOJ Form 361, Certification of Identity, may be used for this purpose).

Verification of Identity of Guardians.
Parents or legal guardians must establish their own identity as parents or legal guardians and the identity of the child or other person being represented.

Authorization or Consent.
Other parties requesting nonpublic information about an individual usually must have the consent of that individual on Form G-639 or by an authorizing letter, together with appropriate verification of identity of the record subject. Notarized or sworn declaration is required from a record subject who is a lawful permanent resident or US Citizen, and for access to certain Legalization files.

Fees.
Except for commercial requesters, the first 100 pages of reproduction and two hours of search time will be furnished without charge. For requests processed under the Privacy Act, there may be a fee of $.10 per page for photocopy duplication. For requests processed under the Freedom of Information Act, there may be a fee for quarter hours of time spent for searches and for review of records. Search fees are at the following rates; $2.25 clerical; $4.50 professional/computer operator; and $7.50 managerial. Other costs for searches and duplication will be charged at the actual direct cost. Fees will only be charged if the aggregate amount of fees for searches, copy and/or review is more than $8.00. If the total anticipated fees amount to more than $250.00, or the same requester has failed to pay fees in the past, an advance deposit may be requested. Fee waivers or reductions may be requested for a request that clearly will benefit the public and is not primarily in the personal or commercial interest of the requester. Such requests should include a justification.

Manner of Submission of Fees When Required.
Do not send cash. Fees must be submitted in the exact amount. When requested to do so, submit a check or a United States Postal money order (or, if application is submitted from outside the United States, remittance may be made by bank international money order or foreign draft drawn on a financial institution in the United States) made payable, in United States currency, to the "Immigration and Naturalization Service". An applicant residing in the US Virgin Islands shall make his/her remittance payable to "Commissioner of Finance of the Virgin Islands," and, if residing in Guam, to "Treasurer, Guam".

A charge of $5.00 will be imposed if a check in payment of a fee is not honored by the bank on which it is drawn. Every remittance will be accepted subject to collection.

Privacy Act Statement.
Authority to collect this information is contained in Title 5 U.S.C. 552 and 552a. The purpose of the collection is to enable INS to locate applicable records and to respond to requests made under the Freedom of Information and Privacy Acts.

Routine Uses.
Information will be used to comply with requests for information under 5 U.S.C. 552 and 552a; information provided to other agencies may be for referrals, consultations, and/or to answer subsequent inquiries concerning specific requests.

Effect of Not Providing Requested Information.
Furnishing the information requested on this form is voluntary. However, failure to furnish the information may result in the inability of INS to comply with a request when compliance will violate other policies or laws.

General Information.
The Freedom of Information Act (5 U.S.C. 552) allows requesters to have access to Federal agency records, except those which have been exempted by the Act.

The Privacy Act 1974. (5 U.S.C. 552a), with certain exceptions, permits individuals (US citizens or permanent resident aliens) to gain access to information pertaining to themselves in Federal agency records, to have a copy made of all or any part thereof, to correct or amend such records, and to permit individuals to make requests concerning what records, pertaining to themselves, are collected, maintained, used or disseminated. The Act also prohibits disclosure of individuals' records without their written consent, except under certain circumstances.

Public Report Burden for this collection is estimated to average 15 minutes per response, including the time for reviewing the instructions, searching existing data sources, gathering and maintaining the data needed, and completing and reviewing the collection of information. Send comments regarding this burden estimate or any other aspect of this collection, including suggestions for reducing this burden , to: US Department of Justice, Immigration and Naturalization Service, Policy Directives and Instructions Branch, Washington, DC 20536; and to the Office of Management and Budget, Paperwork Reduction Project: OMB No. 1115-0087, Washington, DC 20503.

*U.S.GPO:1996-509-749/70060

Index

P

About the Author

Loretto Kathryn Dennis Szucs—"Lou"—holds a B.A. degree in history from Saint Joseph's College in Indiana and has been involved in genealogical research, teaching, lecturing, and publishing for more than twenty-five years. Previously employed as an archives specialist for the National Archives, she is currently vice-president of publishing for Ancestry Incorporated. She has served on the Illinois State Archives Advisory Board and on the governing boards of the Chicago Genealogical Society, the South Suburban Genealogical and Historical Society (Illinois), and the Illinois State Genealogical Society. Lou was the founding secretary for the Federation of Genealogical Societies and has held various positions in that organization, including editor of the FGS *Forum*. She is currently a member of the History Advisory Committee of The Statue of Liberty-Ellis Island Foundation.

Lou is the author of several publications, including *Chicago and Cook County Sources: A Genealogical and Historical Guide*. With Sandra Luebking, she co-authored *The Archives: A Guide to the National Archives Field Branches*. She and Sandra are also co-editors of *The Source: A Guidebook of American Genealogy* (rev. ed.). Honors Lou has received include a 1984 citation from the Archivist of the United States for her work to establish the volunteer program at the National Archives' Chicago Regional Archives Branch; a 1987 National Genealogical Society Award of Merit for *Chicago and Cook County Sources*; the 1990 David S. Vogels, Jr., Award for outstanding contributions to the Federation of Genealogical Societies; the 1991 Award for Excellence in Genealogical Methods and Sources from the National Genealogical Society; and a 1992 Special Award from the Illinois Genealogical Society. In 1995 she became a fellow of the Utah Genealogical Association.